Producing Web Hits

Producing Web Hits

David Elderbrock, Jonathan Ezor,
Laura Dalton, and Jed Weissberg

Created by James Nadler

IDG BOOKS WORLDWIDE, INC.
AN INTERNATIONAL DATA GROUP COMPANY

Foster City, CA ★ Chicago, IL ★ Indianapolis, IN ★ Southlake, TX

PRODUCING WEB HITS

Published by
IDG Books Worldwide, Inc.
An International Data Group Company
919 E. Hillsdale Blvd.
Suite 400
Foster City, CA 94404
http://www.idgbooks.com (IDG Books Worldwide Web site)

Copyright © 1997 IDG Books Worldwide, Inc. All rights reserved. No part of this book, including interior design, cover design, and icons, may be reproduced or transmitted in any form, by any means (electronic, photocopying, recording, or otherwise) without the prior written permission of the publisher.

Library of Congress Catalog Card No.: 96-79762

ISBN: 1-7645-3034-8

Printed in the United States of America

10 9 8 7 6 5 4 3 2 1

1E/QX/QT/ZX/FC

Distributed in the United States by IDG Books Worldwide, Inc.

Distributed by Macmillan Canada for Canada; by Transworld Publishers Limited in the United Kingdom and Europe; by WoodsLane Pty. Ltd. for Australia; by WoodsLane Enterprises Ltd. for New Zealand; by Longman Singapore Publishers Ltd. for Singapore, Malaysia, Thailand, and Indonesia; by Simron Pty. Ltd. for South Africa; by Toppan Company Ltd. for Japan; by Distribuidora Cuspide for Argentina; by Livraria Cultura for Brazil; by Ediciencia S.A. for Ecuador; by Addison-Wesley Publishing Company for Korea; by Ediciones ZETA S.C.R. Ltda. for Peru; by WS Computer Publishing Company, Inc., for the Philippines; by Unalis Corporation for Taiwan; by Contemporanea de Ediciones for Venezuela. Authorized Sales Agent: Anthony Rudkin Associates for the Middle East and North Africa.

For general information on IDG Books Worldwide's books in the U.S., please call our Consumer Customer Service department at 800-762-2974.

For reseller information, including discounts and premium sales, please call our Reseller Customer Service department at 800-434-3422.

For information on where to purchase IDG Books Worldwide's books outside the U.S., please contact our International Sales department at 415-655-3023 or fax 415-655-3299.

For information on foreign language translations, please contact our Foreign & Subsidiary Rights department at 415-655-3021 or fax 415-655-3281.

For sales inquiries and special prices for bulk quantities, please contact our Sales department at 415-655-3200 or write to the address above.

For information on using IDG Books Worldwide's books in the classroom or for ordering examination copies, please contact our Educational Sales department at 800-434-2086 or fax 817-251-8174.

For press review copies, author interviews, or other publicity information, please contact our Public Relations department at 415-655-3000 or fax 415-655-3299.

For authorization to photocopy items for corporate, personal, or educational use, please contact Copyright Clearance Center, 222 Rosewood Drive, Danvers, MA 01923, or fax 508-750-4470.

> **LIMIT OF LIABILITY/DISCLAIMER OF WARRANTY**: AUTHOR AND PUBLISHER HAVE USED THEIR BEST EFFORTS IN PREPARING THIS BOOK. IDG BOOKS WORLDWIDE, INC., AND AUTHOR MAKE NO REPRESENTATIONS OR WARRANTIES WITH RESPECT TO THE ACCURACY OR COMPLETENESS OF THE CONTENTS OF THIS BOOK AND SPECIFICALLY DISCLAIM ANY IMPLIED WARRANTIES OF MERCHANTABILITY OR FITNESS FOR A PARTICULAR PURPOSE. THERE ARE NO WARRANTIES WHICH EXTEND BEYOND THE DESCRIPTIONS CONTAINED IN THIS PARAGRAPH. NO WARRANTY MAY BE CREATED OR EXTENDED BY SALES REPRESENTATIVES OR WRITTEN SALES MATERIALS. THE ACCURACY AND COMPLETENESS OF THE INFORMATION PROVIDED HEREIN AND THE OPINIONS STATED HEREIN ARE NOT GUARANTEED OR WARRANTED TO PRODUCE ANY PARTICULAR RESULTS, AND THE ADVICE AND STRATEGIES CONTAINED HEREIN MAY NOT BE SUITABLE FOR EVERY INDIVIDUAL. NEITHER IDG BOOKS WORLDWIDE, INC., NOR AUTHOR SHALL BE LIABLE FOR ANY LOSS OF PROFIT OR ANY OTHER COMMERCIAL DAMAGES, INCLUDING BUT NOT LIMITED TO SPECIAL, INCIDENTAL, CONSEQUENTIAL, OR OTHER DAMAGES.

Trademarks: All brand names and product names used in this book are trade names, service marks, trademarks, or registered trademarks of their respective owners. IDG Books Worldwide is not associated with any product or vendor mentioned in this book. For Web site credits, see the list at the back of the book.

 is a trademark under exclusive license to IDG Books Worldwide, Inc., from International Data Group, Inc.

ABOUT IDG BOOKS WORLDWIDE

Welcome to the world of IDG Books Worldwide.

IDG Books Worldwide, Inc., is a subsidiary of International Data Group, the world's largest publisher of computer-related information and the leading global provider of information services on information technology. IDG was founded more than 25 years ago and now employs more than 8,500 people worldwide. IDG publishes more than 275 computer publications in over 75 countries (see listing below). More than 60 million people read one or more IDG publications each month.

Launched in 1990, IDG Books Worldwide is today the #1 publisher of best-selling computer books in the United States. We are proud to have received eight awards from the Computer Press Association in recognition of editorial excellence and three from *Computer Currents'* First Annual Readers' Choice Awards. Our best-selling ...For Dummies® series has more than 30 million copies in print with translations in 30 languages. IDG Books Worldwide, through a joint venture with IDG's Hi-Tech Beijing, became the first U.S. publisher to publish a computer book in the People's Republic of China. In record time, IDG Books Worldwide has become the first choice for millions of readers around the world who want to learn how to better manage their businesses.

Our mission is simple: Every one of our books is designed to bring extra value and skill-building instructions to the reader. Our books are written by experts who understand and care about our readers. The knowledge base of our editorial staff comes from years of experience in publishing, education, and journalism — experience we use to produce books for the '90s. In short, we care about books, so we attract the best people. We devote special attention to details such as audience, interior design, use of icons, and illustrations. And because we use an efficient process of authoring, editing, and desktop publishing our books electronically, we can spend more time ensuring superior content and spend less time on the technicalities of making books.

You can count on our commitment to deliver high-quality books at competitive prices on topics you want to read about. At IDG Books Worldwide, we continue in the IDG tradition of delivering quality for more than 25 years. You'll find no better book on a subject than one from IDG Books Worldwide.

John Kilcullen
CEO
IDG Books Worldwide, Inc.

Eighth Annual Computer Press Awards ≥1992

Ninth Annual Computer Press Awards ≥1993

Tenth Annual Computer Press Awards ≥1994

Eleventh Annual Computer Press Awards ≥1995

IDG Books Worldwide, Inc., is a subsidiary of International Data Group, the world's largest publisher of computer-related information and the leading global provider of information services on information technology. International Data Group publishes over 275 computer publications in over 75 countries. Sixty million people read one or more International Data Group publications each month. International Data Group's publications include: **ARGENTINA:** Buyer's Guide, Computerworld Argentina, PC World Argentina; **AUSTRALIA:** Australian Macworld, Australian PC World, Australian Reseller News, Computerworld, IT Casebook, Network World, Publish, Webmaster; **AUSTRIA:** Computerwelt Osterreich, Networks Austria, PC Tip Austria; **BANGLADESH:** PC World Bangladesh; **BELARUS:** PC World Belarus; **BELGIUM:** Data News; **BRAZIL:** Annuario de Informática, Computerworld, Connections, Macworld, PC Player, PC World, Publish, Reseller News, Supergamepower; **BULGARIA:** Computerworld Bulgaria, Network World Bulgaria, PC & MacWorld Bulgaria; **CANADA:** CIO Canada, Client/Server World, ComputerWorld Canada, InfoWorld Canada, NetworkWorld Canada, WebWorld; **CHILE:** Computerworld Chile, PC World Chile; **COLOMBIA:** Computerworld Colombia, PC World Colombia; **COSTA RICA:** PC World Centro America; **THE CZECH AND SLOVAK REPUBLICS:** Computerworld Czechoslovakia, Macworld Czech Republic, PC World Czechoslovakia; **DENMARK:** Communications World Danmark, Computerworld Danmark, Macworld Danmark, PC World Danmark, Techworld Denmark; **DOMINICAN REPUBLIC:** PC World Republica Dominicana; **ECUADOR:** PC World Ecuador; **EGYPT:** Computerworld Middle East; PC World Middle East; **EL SALVADOR:** PC World Centro America; **FINLAND:** MikroPC, Tietoverkko, Tietoviikko; **FRANCE:** Distributique, Hebdo, Info PC, Le Monde Informatique, Macworld, Reseaux & Telecoms, WebMaster France; **GERMANY:** Computer Partner, Computerwoche, Computerwoche Extra, Computerwoche FOCUS, Global Online, Macwelt, PC Welt; **GREECE:** Amiga Computing, GamePro Greece, Multimedia World; **GUATEMALA:** PC World Centro America; **HONDURAS:** PC World Centro America; **HONG KONG:** Computerworld Hong Kong, PC World Hong Kong, Publish in Asia; **HUNGARY:** ABCD CD-ROM, Computerworld Szamitastechnika, Internetto online Magazine, PC World Hungary, PC-X Magazin Hungary; **ICELAND:** Tolvuheimur PC World Island; **INDIA:** Information Communications World, Information Systems Computerworld, PC World India, Publish in Asia; **INDONESIA:** InfoKomputer PC World, Komputek Computerworld, Publish in Asia; **IRELAND:** ComputerScope, PC Live!; **ISRAEL:** Macworld Israel, People & Computers/Computerworld; **ITALY:** Computerworld Italia, Macworld Italia, Networking Italia, PC World Italia; **JAPAN:** DTP World, Macworld Japan, Nikkei Personal Computing, OS/2 World Japan, SunWorld Japan, Windows NT World, Windows World Japan; **KENYA:** PC World East African; **KOREA:** Hi-Tech Information, Macworld Korea, PC World Korea; **MACEDONIA:** PC World Macedonia; **MALAYSIA:** Computerworld Malaysia, PC World Malaysia, Publish in Asia; **MALTA:** PC World Malta; **MEXICO:** Computerworld Mexico, PC World Mexico; **MYANMAR:** PC World Myanmar; **NETHERLANDS:** Computer! Totaal, LAN Internetworking Magazine, LAN World Buyers Guide, Macworld Netherlands, Net, WebWereld; **NEW ZEALAND:** Absolute Beginners Guide and Plain & Simple Series, Computer Buyer, Computer Industry Directory, Computerworld New Zealand, MTB, Network World, PC World New Zealand; **NICARAGUA:** PC World Centro America; **NORWAY:** Computerworld Norge, CW Rapport, Datamagasinet, Financial Rapport, Kursguide Norge, Macworld Norge, Multimediaworld Norge, PC World Ekspress Norge, PC World Nettverk, PC World Norge, PC World ProduktGuide Norge; **PAKISTAN:** Computerworld Pakistan; **PANAMA:** PC World Panama; **PEOPLE'S REPUBLIC OF CHINA:** China Computer Users, China Computerworld, China InfoWorld, China Telecom World Weekly, Computer & Communication, Electronic Design China, Electronics Today, Electronics Weekly, Game Software, PC World China, Popular Computer Week, Software Weekly, Software World, Telecom World; **PERU:** Computerworld Peru, PC World Profesional Peru, PC World SoHo Peru; **PHILIPPINES:** Click!, Computerworld Philippines, PC World Philippines, Publish in Asia; **POLAND:** Computerworld Poland, Computerworld Special Report Poland, Cyber, Macworld Poland, Networld Poland, PC World Komputer; **PORTUGAL:** Cerebro/PC World, Computerworld/Correio Informático, Dealer World Portugal, Mac*In/PC*In Portugal, Multimedia World; **PUERTO RICO:** PC World Puerto Rico; **ROMANIA:** Computerworld Romania, PC World Romania, Telecom Romania; **RUSSIA:** Computerworld Russia, Mir PK, Publish, Seti; **SINGAPORE:** Computerworld Singapore, PC World Singapore, Publish in Asia; **SLOVENIA:** Monitor; **SOUTH AFRICA:** Computing SA, Network World SA, Software World SA; **SPAIN:** Communicaciones World España, Computerworld España, Dealer World España, Macworld España, PC World España; **SRI LANKA:** Infolink PC World; **SWEDEN:** CAP&Design, Computer Sweden, Corporate Computing Sweden, Internetworld Sweden, it.branschen, Macworld Sweden, MaxiData Sweden, MikroDatorn, Natverk & Kommunikation, PC World Sweden, PCaktiv, Windows World Sweden; **SWITZERLAND:** Computerworld Schweiz, Macworld Schweiz, PCtip; **TAIWAN:** Computerworld Taiwan, Macworld Taiwan, NEW ViSiON/Publish, PC World Taiwan, Windows World Taiwan; **THAILAND:** Publish in Asia, Thai Computerworld; **TURKEY:** Computerworld Turkiye, Macworld Turkiye, Network World Turkiye, PC World Turkiye; **UKRAINE:** Computerworld Kiev, Multimedia World Ukraine, PC World Ukraine; **UNITED KINGDOM:** Acorn User UK, Amiga Action UK, Amiga Computing UK, Apple Talk UK, Computing, Macworld, Parents and Computers UK, PC Advisor, PC Home, PSX Pro, The WEB, UNITED STATES: Cable in the Classroom, CIO Magazine, Computerworld, DOS World, Federal Computer Week, GamePro Magazine, InfoWorld, I-Way, Macworld, Network World, PC Games, PC World, Publish, Video Event, THE WEB Magazine, and WebMaster, online webzines: JavaWorld, NetscapeWorld, and SunWorld Online; **URUGUAY:** InfoWorld Uruguay; **VENEZUELA:** Computerworld Venezuela, PC World Venezuela; and **VIETNAM:** PC World Vietnam.

Credits

Acquisitions Editor
Michael Roney

Development Editor
Michael Koch

Technical Editors
Paul and Mary Summitt

Copy Editors
Hilary Powers
Larisa North
Carolyn Welch

Project Coordinator
Ben Schroeter

Book Designer
Kurt Krames

Graphics and Production Specialists
Tom Debolski
Renée Dunn
Andreas F. Schueller

Quality Control Specialist
Mick Arellano

Proofreader
Mary C. Oby

Indexer
Rebecca Plunkett

About the Authors

Laura Dalton is editor of *Digitrends* magazine, a quarterly publication covering Internet advertising and marketing issues and applications. She is based in Southern California and can be reached at lddalton@aol.com.

David Elderbrock has been involved in the design and development of web sites since 1993, when he worked as Humanities Coordinator for the Instructional Technology Program at the University of California at Berkeley. Since then, he has contributed to a wide range of commercial web site projects, with clients including Pacific Bell, Apple Computer, Barclays Global Investors, and Citibank CA/NV. His expertise runs from site architecture and design to database design and programming. Mr. Elderbrock graduated from U.C. Berkeley in 1995, with a Ph.D. in English literature.

Jonathan Ezor is an attorney in New York City, practicing new media and computer law with a focus on advertising and marketing issues. His work includes advising clients on the establishment and maintenance of Internet resources, the creation of strategic relationships in the new media field, multimedia, and online promotion and marketing, and software and hardware licensing. Mr. Ezor received his B.A. degree from Brandeis University and his J.D. degree from Yale Law School, where he served as a Senior Editor on the Yale Law Journal. Mr. Ezor can be reached at jezor@panix.com.

James Nadler is a New York City-based author, computer consultant, and partner in Novent, a small professional organization offering new technology solutions to the local business community, with a focus on the investment banking field. Before entering the microcomputer field, James worked for six years as a business affairs manager and producer in the entertainment industry. He began his career with five years in a family-owned sportswear firm, managing a fully integrated vertical business with responsibility for manufacture, distribution, and retailing. His most recent books include, *How To Keep Your Novell Network Alive* (co-authored with Don Guarnieri) and

NetWare Answers, Certified Support. Mr. Nadler holds a Bachelor of Arts Degree in Philosophy from Reed College.

Jed Weissberg creates original online entertainment. He is a graduate of the Interactive Telecommunications program at New York University. This book could not have been accomplished without the help of his wife, Jamie Heller.

For Sylvie, David, and Thomas

Foreword

It would be hard to overstate the degree to which the World Wide Web will revolutionize business, art, entertainment, education, and society itself. Today we can just catch glimpses of it, from Web sites that offer literally hundreds of thousands of books or CDs for immediate delivery, to large enterprises like FedEx or Cisco, saving themselves hundreds of millions of dollars each year just by using the Web, rather than the phone, to handle routine customer service issues.

Fundamentally, what is happening is that businesses are returning to an era of personalized service, with questions quickly and effortlessly answered and individual customers' wants and preferences conveniently remembered — except this time it is the computer that is doing the remembering, rather than the proprietor or craftsman himself. And the computer's memory is perfect.

Everyone is getting on the Web, it seems, from the community hospital to global pharmaceutical companies, from the local grade school to the graduate studies program in Cambridge. Six-year-olds play at Lego.com or look up the latest Disney movie; ten-year-olds do their research on the Vikings, or on Admiral Byrd, or on women in ancient Greece; grandparents send electronic greeting cards to their far-flung families; and business executives dig up the scoop on their prospective customers or competitors.

But it is not a slam dunk. Creating the right kind of Web site is 10 percent software and programming and 90 percent knowing your objectives and executing from a well-considered plan. It can be a complicated and sometimes costly task. Is the site designed to attract visitors with entertainment and to pay for itself with advertising? Or is it for current customers to look up account information? Or was it designed to provide access to a database of art work, or monographs, or medical research studies? Or does it facilitate visitors getting together to exchange ideas, creating an electronic community of people with certain interests in common?

Whatever you do with your Web site, don't expect it to stand alone as a separate, isolated part of your business. It just doesn't work that way.

The World Wide Web represents an order-of-magnitude increase in the cost efficiency of interacting — with customers or prospective customers, family members, associates, and strangers. It will bring businesses closer to their customers, yes. But it will also bring us all closer to one another.

Don't wait any longer. It's time to learn how to use the Web now, and this book is the best place to start.

Don Peppers and Martha Rogers, Ph.D.
Co-authors of *Enterprise One to One:Tools for Competing in the Interactive Age*, and *The One to One Future: Building Relationships One Customer at a Time*

Preface

Something really big is happening out there on the millions of miles of cable called the Internet, but like Mr. Jones in Bob Dylan's *Ballad of the Thin Man*, many of us are unsure about what it is. It's practically impossible to pick up a newspaper these days without reading something about the Internet or the Web, and yet at every level of contact where viewers and information providers interface with this new medium, the same cyber-existential question surfaces: what am I doing here? With all of its promise for creating a true global village, the beef still seems to be missing. At the viewer level the symptoms of this dilemma are epitomized by thousands of hours spent surfing from lists of places to go, to other places with lists of places to go in a seemingly endless loop. At the information provider level, the Web is crowded with corporate signposts for companies who — judging by the content that many of them offer— feel that their absence in cyberspace is so conspicuous that they will broadcast practically anything to justify their presence. If you are on the provider side, there's a good likelihood that you are faced with some element or offshoot of this situation. Hopefully, you've come here to get some answers.

This book provides a context in which to evaluate, plan, and execute a presence on the Web. It's designed to answer big picture issues about operations and marketing, and to provide a framework for figuring out why one is or should be on the Web, how to get there, and what to do about bringing something interesting to the party once you arrive. This is a challenging series of issues to address in a world that changes faster than one can document it, but hopefully the mainstream elements of cyberspace are actually moving at a speed that some of us can hope to keep up with. As Dave Barry points out poignantly in his new book *Lost in Cyberspace*, "…the Internet does not operate at the speed of light; it operates at the speed of the Department of Motor Vehicles…" Anyone who has waited through a few cups of coffee for a graphically loaded homepage to appear can testify to that.

In developing this context the book presents original structures for analyzing certain aspects of a Web presence. Chapter 4, Creating a Web Identity, for example, groups site themes into two types: research and entertainment. They are designed to help develop a vocabulary and scale for evaluating what you and the people whose sites you're checking out are doing out there. The book also explains the standard vocabulary of the medium by defining common marketing terms such as hits, visits, click-through rate or impressions, or large technical issues such as bandwidth. The idea here is to make you a little more comfortable in discussing these issues with other members of the Web community such as designers, service providers, and programmers.

WHO SHOULD READ THIS BOOK

This book is not for technical people! This is a manager's handbook for the design, implementation, and administration of commercial Web sites.

HOW THIS BOOK IS ORGANIZED

This book is designed for random access. The chapters, while related, are about more or less self-contained subjects that touch on different aspects of building and maintaining a Web presence. The idea is, since you may have entered this process at any of the points mentioned above (start-up, half-built/half-baked, needs renovation or requires maintenance), you should be able to go to a section that you find relevant without wading through the whole thing. On the other hand, if you're looking for a primer and general background, you can read the book sequentially and hopefully walk away fluent enough to go into that next meeting armed with enough information to hold you own.

* **Chapter 1**, Hit Factory: Making a Splash on the Web, describes how you can take advantage of the Internet as a new marketing and advertising vehicle. The material ranges from planning a marketing strategy on the Web to measurement and tracking methods for user

demographics, standards for ad banner sizes and ad pricing rates, and electronic commerce issues.

- **Chapter 2**, Clarifying Your Mission, helps you identify and articulate the mission and purpose of a Web site project. It presents a model for Web project missions, and then maps the model and its components to examples of successful Web sites.

- **Chapter 3**, Building the Organization, focuses on the particular challenges that Web development poses for project leaders. General guidelines and common strategies are identified through three fictional projects, which discuss the solution to these problems in small, medium, and large organizations.

- **Chapter 4**, Creating a Web Identity, helps you develop and maintain a thematic and audio-visual identity for a Web site. This is about as technical as the book gets with site- and page-design issues (which is not very technical), but the chapter should provide you with enough vocabulary and conceptual information to talk with a few designers and sound like you have some background.

- **Chapter 5**, Registering and Staking Out Cyberturf, helps prospective developers sort through the issues related to establishing a physical Web site, including options for hosting services, assessing infrastructure needs, and advice on choosing and obtaining an appropriate domain name. This is about as technical as the book gets on the operational side (again, not too technical), but it should give you the juice to speak with potential service providers and see if they've got what you need. With competitive prices falling for hosting facilities, it's easy to get burned these days.

- **Chapter 6**, Acquiring Irresistible Content, discusses where to get it, how to develop it, and when to license it, and offers some good guidelines for protecting it once you've got it. Content is arguably the single most important element in creating a site to which visitors will want to return. After the flash and the games, it's the true beef on the cable. By comparison, how many TC reruns can you watch before you become bored? Without a long-range plan for content development and update, there is virtually no chance for success on the Web.

- **Chapter 7**, Getting Seen, is about drawing an audience to your site. It provides techniques and tips for how to get them there and keep them coming back through both online and offline promotions. Implementing a well-rounded marketing strategy is a key element in building a successful site.
- **Chapter 8**, Making Use of the Medium, is about leveraging all of the unique Web advantages for building an electronic franchise and measuring its success. There's never been a richer opportunity to communicate with your audience one-to-one.
- **The Appendixes** are filled with product listings, technology views, as well as tips and hints to make you more fluent in the next meeting, and advice for building a production site.

CHECK OUT THE BOOK'S WEB SITE AND WEB REFERENCES

The book contains over 300 exemplary site references that demonstrate excellence in design, identity, mission, content, application, marketing references, promotion, service, and practically every other facet of site development and maintenance you can think of. *Check them out*! Collectively they embody some of the best of the Web. They are also all conveniently organized and linked at the HitFactory pages on IDG's Web site at `http://www.idgbooks.com`. Explore! That's what the new medium is all about. A picture is worth a thousand words, and seeing these sites in action is the most powerful demonstration and substantiation of the analysis they get in this book.

ABOUT RECOMMENDATIONS

There are no rules other than physical laws out on the Web. The concepts introduced in this book are not recommendations for Web behavior, structure, or design. Remember, the book is trying to guide you, not scold or admonish you.

Acknowledgments

This was a difficult book to produce and one that owes a debt of gratitude to many players. Janet Carlson for stepping in and up to the line with help in a critical chapter in the eleventh hour. Jamie Heller, managing editor of TheStreet.com for editing portions of this book. Don Guarnieri for help with the Appendixes and all around technical support. Debra Venzke for securing the permissions for our screen shots. Mike Roney for seeing the need for the book in the first place, and for riding the wave through to the end in helping to make a quality product. Especially to Michael Koch, my development editor at IDG, for putting up with the ridiculous and the sublime, tantrums and freakouts, never dropping the ball, and providing excellent guidance and advice in structuring and editing. Most of all to my four writers, Jed, David, Laura, and Jonathan for an outstanding job of shedding light on the murky waters of the Web.

Contents at a Glance

Chapter 1 **HIT FACTORY: MAKING A SPLASH ON THE WEB** 1

Chapter 2 **CLARIFYING YOUR MISSION** 65

Chapter 3 **BUILDING THE ORGANIZATION** 113

Chapter 4 **CREATING A WEB IDENTITY** 145

Chapter 5 **REGISTERING AND STAKING OUT CYBERTURF** 203

Chapter 6 **ACQUIRING IRRESISTIBLE CONTENT** 243

Chapter 7 **GETTING SEEN** 281

Chapter 8 **MAKING USE OF THE MEDIUM** 317

Appendix A **KILLER APPS** 343

Appendix B **FILE FORMAT AND TYPES** 389

Appendix C **SCREEN RESOLUTIONS** 395

Appendix D **WEB DEVELOPER'S WORK STATION** 397

Appendix E **RECOMMENDED WEB SITES** 401

Contents

Foreword   xi

Preface   xiii

Acknowledgments   xvii

Introduction   xxxi

Chapter 1   HIT FACTORY: MAKING A SPLASH ON THE WEB   1

Planning a Marketing Strategy   2

Gauging the Web Advertisement Industry   9
- Promotional sites   11
- Content sites   13
- Transactional sites   15
- Measuring success   17
- Auditing   22
- Standardizing advertising models   23
- Building an advertising program   27
- Deciding on a pricing mode   131

Targeting Your Audience   38
- Who's online?   40
- What are people doing online?   43
- Targeting advertisers   44
- What works?   51

Understanding Electronic Commerce   52
- What sells?   52
- Electronic payment systems   54
- Online customer service   55

　　　　Web commerce servers   56
　　　　A case in point: Virtual Vineyards   57
　　Words to the wise   59
　　Summary   62

Chapter 2   CLARIFYING YOUR MISSION   65

　　The Mission Proposition   66
　　　　Defining the product   67
　　　　Defining your audience   71
　　　　Defining your business objective   72
　　Mission Implementations   76
　　　　Corporate identity   76
　　　　Product and event promotion   82
　　　　Publishing (news and magazines)   87
　　　　Reference and information   91
　　　　Customer service and support   93
　　　　Reservations, ticketing, and sales   98
　　　　Community   101
　　　　Entertainment   104
　　　　Event programming and live broadcast   108
　　Summary   111

Chapter 3   BUILDING THE ORGANIZATION   113

　　Introducing the Case Studies   114
　　　　A small marketing and PR site   114
　　　　A medium-sized community information service   116
　　　　A large corporate communications site   116
　　Selecting Personnel   117
　　　　Identifying job functions   118
　　　　Organizing the teams   120

Contractors versus employees 122
Working with agencies 123
Personnel for a small project 124
Personnel for a medium-sized project 125
Personnel for a large project 126

Estimating a Budget 126
Development costs 127
Budget for a small project 128
Budgeting for a medium-sized project 129
Budgeting for a large project 130

Establishing a Time Line 131
Web development tasks 132
Keeping a project on track 134
Updating the site 135

Testing 137
Testing for a small project 141
Testing for a medium-sized project 142
Testing for a large project 142

Summary 143

Chapter 4 CREATING A WEB IDENTITY 145

Establishing Some Guidelines 147

Preparing a Presentation Strategy 151
Research design strategies 152
Entertainment design strategies 157
www.lifescene.com — a case study in trapping a surfer 161

Leveraging Design Elements 166
Graphic design 166
User interface 178
Interactivity 191

Summary 201

Chapter 5   **REGISTERING AND STAKING OUT CYBERTURF   203**

   Establishing Criteria for Your Location   205
      Assessing bandwidth and
       communication lines   207
      Gauging horsepower   212
      Server-side programming resources   213
      E-mail   214
      Disk space and transfer allowances   215
      Unscheduled downtime   215
      Technical support   216
      Server usage logs   216
      Content updates   217
      Firewalls and security   218
      Future growth potential   222
      Customer recommendations   222

   Looking at the Alternatives   224
      AOL PrimeHost   225
      BBN Planet   226
      BEST Internet Communications   227
      DigiWeb   228
      EarthLink   228
      Echo   229
      Netcom   229
      Web Condo   230
      In-house server options   232

   Assessing Infrastructure Needs   235

   Securing a Domain Name   237
      How to obtain a name   237
      Domain names and trademarks   238
      Completing the InterNIC registration   239

   Summary   240

Chapter 6   ACQUIRING IRRESISTIBLE CONTENT   243

Viewing Content in Three Dimensions   246

Looking for Sources   247
- Original content   248
- Licensing content   256
- Public domain content   259
- Links and user input   264

Pondering Legal Issues   266
- Copyright and trademark issues   267
- Look for the union label   269
- The content of the content   271
- Development and hosting contracts   272
- Strategies for using content legally   276
- The law protects you too!   279

Summary   280

Chapter 7   GETTING SEEN   281

Providing Compelling Content   282

E-Mail   286
- Using e-mail to reach the media   287
- Using e-mail to reach everyone else   288
- Reminder services   292
- Instant notification services   294
- Newsletters   295
- games and contests   296

Hyperlinks   299

Search Engines   300
- Registering with a search engine   301
- One-stop services   304

Internet Directories   305

Newsgroups   307
   Netiquette   309
   Posting to a newsgroup   310
Cross-Marketing with the Giants   311
Offline Promotions   312
Summary   315

Chapter 8   MAKING USE OF THE MEDIUM   317

Tools and Tips for Analyzing Your Site   318
   Server logs   320
   Viewership packages   323
   Independent services   324

Leveraging Your Database   325

Support and Information Services   327
   FAQ lists   327
   Mailing lists   329
   New information alerts   330

Interactive Features   332
   Conferences   332
   Chat   335
   Games   337

Product Management and Customer Service   338

Summary   340

Appendix A   KILLER APPS   343

HTML Editors   345
   HTML tag editors   346
   WYSIWYG editors   348

Multimedia Software   352
   Images   353
   Animation   357

Sound editors 358
  Java applet designers 360

Webcasting Software 363
  BackWeb 363
  Castanet 364
  PointCast 364

Servers 365
  Server programming methods 365
  Server software and databases 367
  Database server tools 369
  Security tools 372

Add-on Technologies 374
  Enliven 375
  FutureSplash 375
  RealAudio 376
  Shockwave 377
  StreamWorks 377

Session Analyzers 378
  Bolero 378
  Hit List Pro 378
  InContext WebAnalyzer 379
  net.Sweep/net.analysis Pro/
    net.analysis Desktop 379
  WebTrends 380

Utilities 380
  Adobe File Utilities 381
  CrossEye 381
  CuteFTP 381
  Fetch 382
  WebWhacker 382
  WS_FTP 383

Shareware Sites 383

New File Formats 384
- Cascading Style Sheet Specification 384
- Envoy 384
- PDF 385

Future Technologies 385
- ActiveX OLE2 385
- ADSL 386
- Cable Modems 386
- JavaScript 386
- OpenDoc and Cyberdog 387
- QuickTime 387
- TCI@Home 387
- VRML 388
- WebTV 388

Appendix B **FILE FORMATS AND TYPES** 389

- HTML 390
- GIF and JPEG 390
- QuickTime 391
- Shockwave 392
- Acrobat 392
- AU, AIFF, and RealAudio 393
- JAVA 393
- ActiveX 394

Appendix C **SCREEN RESOLUTION** 395

Appendix D **WEB DEVELOPER'S WORKSTATION** 397

- Computer and Peripherals 398
- System Software 398
- Acquisition and Manipulation 399

Web Development 399
Web Browsers 400

Appendix E **RECOMMENDED WEB SITES 401**

Glossary 413

Index 421

Web Site Credits 430

Introduction

> *"This life is a test. It is only a test. If it had been an actual life, you would have received further instructions on where to go and what to do."*
>
> —Unknown

This is a manager's handbook for the design, implementation, and administration of commercial Web sites. The issues discussed span the gamut from technical to administrative and marketing issues that may face a manager or make-shift manager who is faced with the dilemma of overseeing a Web site. The ideas, suggestions, trends, and resources described here are relevant whether you have a staff of only one (yourself), or have dominion over substantial corporate resources. In either scenario, and in all of those in between, there is now a community of professionals who have been thrown with both feet into the cyberspace pool and handed the responsibility for overseeing a commercial presence on the Web without the necessary background and information.

During the first PC invasion (1982-1986) while microcomputers made their way onto the corporate desktops of the world, personal ignorance and lack of skills had a chance of staying in the closet. If you didn't know how to create a financial model on a spreadsheet or publish a hot-looking document on a word processor, you could get away with it. Even if someone else did it for you, the final output of the medium was a paper document that you could talk around in familiar terms and evaluate with recognizable measurement standards. Even during the second wave in networking (1986-1992), this situation changed very little as PCs within individual companies became able to communicate with each other. During the current wave, the Global-Electronic Village (1992-present), as the manager of a Web presence, the party is over: suddenly a potential audience of 20,000,000 is looking at your work, and there are no clear guidelines for success or failure.

The dialogue concerning the cyber-void goes up and down, from you to those you report to and from you to those who report to you (in-house or freelance), and some of the questions that make up the conversation sound like....

* Why can't I measure the success of my sight?
* What do you mean we can't have animations?
* It will cost HOW MUCH!!!???
* How can we make our site more interesting?
* How come we're doing this anyway?

In New York these days there are more Web designers than personal trainers (two favorite occupations of the late nineties). People in every imaginable field from neurosurgery to mountain-climbing are hanging out their shingle on the Web. Everyone enters the fray from a different doorway. Some need to build a sight from the ground up, starting in the planning stages. Others may walk into a half-built, half-baked scenario where certain factors such as designer or ISP have already been decided upon, but there's still need for design input and content development. Still others may have inherited an unsuccessful site in need of renovation or a successful one that requires superior maintenance. Whatever your situation, there's a good likelihood that programming, telecommunications, graphic design, media research, or content development may not be your chosen field of work, even though you now find yourself responsible for some or all of these issues for your company's Web presence. Until the Web takes on an official status on the order of television or print media, it will remain a black sheep in the company. The number of uninitiated professionals who have been saddled with the task of overseeing a Web presence in addition to their normal business responsibilities is simply astonishing. The myriad of marketing and administrative issues that one needs to face in this task is large. Unfortunately, this is not a test, but you do have some time to make the real thing work.

chapter 1

Hit Factory: Making a Splash on the Web

EVEN IF YOU'RE NOT OLD ENOUGH to remember the Burma-Shave road signs that delighted motorists with strings of roadside jingles back in the 1930s and 1940s, you may have heard of them. Today the Burma-Shave signs are part of an advertising legend—but what happened to them, and to Burma Shave? When television arrived in the 1950s, Burma Shave did not adopt it as an advertising medium, preferring to stick with tried-and-true methods. As a result, the product eventually lost market share to newer brands that were quick to seize television as a marketing tool. While other factors may have contributed to Burma Shave's demise, it is difficult to imagine that ignoring a new advertising and marketing medium was not a strong contributor. Television, of course, has arguably been the most impressive marketing medium in history. Will the Web affect marketing as dramatically? Only look at the relative incubation periods for these two broadcast media—the time it took for each to take root and begin to affect consumer behavior—and you'll see it's impossible for any serious advertiser to ignore the Web. TV took 30 to 40 years to reach more than 100 million households; the Web reached 20 percent of that market in less than 2 years after it went commercial.

Back in the early days of the Web—circa 1994—a common business adage ran something like "If you build it, they will come." The accepted illusion was that if one slapped together a Web site, millions of people would visit it, buy the products offered there, and cough up tons of cash. Those days never really existed, and as larger companies and more sophisticated technologies enter the medium, the possibilities of haphazard success grow ever slimmer. While a new user goes online for the first time every 1.6 seconds, new sites appear almost as fast, all competing for each user's attention. In addition, electronic purchasing has not yet reached a comfort level where consumers regard this form of shopping as commonplace. Advertisers and marketers are to some extent caught in a nether world: They feel compelled to establish a presence on the Web but know they have no possibility of immediate fulfillment—a form of commercial sexual torture through the expansion of modern media.

This chapter examines the various ways you can take advantage of the Internet as a new marketing and advertising vehicle. The first part discusses the issues you should consider when planning a marketing strategy on the Web. The second part outlines the Web advertising industry, measurement and tracking methods for compiling user demographics, and standards for ad banner sizes and ad pricing rates. The last part of the chapter gives an overview of electronic commerce to provide a better understanding of where online retailing is headed.

Planning a Marketing Strategy

When planning a marketing strategy on the Web, you should consider the following background issues that run through marketing in any medium:

* Skills and opportunities
* Audiences
* Cautions

chapter 1 HIT FACTORY

The term *marketing* covers a truly diverse range of activities and sciences. It is a difficult business area to describe at best, even for everyday products such as cereal and automobiles and for conventional channels such as supermarkets and television. When people say that they are *in marketing*, a listener can rarely guess at their job description: the speaker could function as a graphic designer, researcher, telephone solicitor, manager, or strategic planner—among literally dozens of other possible positions. There are, however, some traditional ways to segment the term and develop a framework for understanding and analyzing the new medium—the Web—in terms of its predecessors. Consider the following breakdown for the field:

- **Research.** Almost all good product design is rooted in market research. Sure, the Wright Brothers probably didn't run any *focus groups* or perform extensive *gap analysis* on whether folks thought flying was a good idea and how much they would pay for it, but almost all contemporary product specification and development comes from market segmentation and a combination of consumer and technical research.

- **Distribution.** How a product arrives at market, its availability, and the associated costs dramatically affect the success or failure of the effort. A sales force can only operate if the company can deliver product. Establishing the channels and methods of distribution is a pure marketing function.

- **Communications.** Letting the target consumer know *where, when, for how much, why,* and even the sheer *what* of a product is probably the foremost image that one has of marketing activities. Advertising, public relations, point of purchase displays, and so on are the glitzier and more commonly thought of areas of this discipline—properly called marketing communications—but they are only a part of the pie.

Two of these issues—research and communications—migrate almost perfectly to the Web. The possibilities for both quantitative and qualitative research have never been so profound. Simple subscribership demographics are available from server logs, not to mention more sophisticated tracking programs. Thanks to the interactive nature of the new medium, in-depth and even live interviews are also available. As to communications, there has never

3

been a less expensive or more expansive means of getting more information to more people in the history of mass media. Distribution methods are also affected, but in more subtle ways. Communications and research, after all, are pure information, so they travel effortlessly over the Web. Most products and services, by contrast, involve physical things and actions that the Web can only describe, not deliver. We return to aspects of research and communications later in this chapter, but consider the following new opportunities as only a few of the ways in which cyberspace extends the marketing arena.

* **Interactivity.** For the first time in history, remote communication is two-way, increasing the possibilities for navigation and information exchange exponentially. Even simple hyperlinks can infuse an average Web site with more information than most other forms of media simply because of the scope of material to which the user can chain and self-direct.
* **24 × 7 × 365 availability.** The Web is the marketplace that never sleeps. As long as the server is up 24 hours a day, 7 days a week, year-round, the doors are always open and the help is never tired or bored.
* **Global reach.** The Web makes online businesses accessible from anywhere in the world by anyone with a computer, a modem, and a phone line. Most forms of modern media—magazines, journals, TV, and radio—base their advertising rates on the number of people they reach. The costs can range from $50 a week for a small classified ad in a local paper that goes to a few thousand households to millions of dollars for a 30-second spot during the Super Bowl, which may reach half the households in America. Most ISPs now provide space for a home page for less than $20 a month—and the Web's entire international population of 20+ million users can see it.
* **Real-time information.** All other forms of mass media have a publication date or scheduled airtime for the distribution of new information. The Web is truly *virtual* in this respect, and even small but useful changes in company offerings can go online as they occur.

Clearly each of these new opportunities can expand the fields of research and communications in dramatic new ways. Remember watching TV quiz shows as a kid, and wishing you had the time and money to go to Hollywood

chapter 1 HIT FACTORY

so you could have a chance at the prizes? Now consider a multiuser game played globally around the clock in a giant cybermall and sponsored by a consortium of packaged goods manufacturers who offer their own products as prizes, but whose actual agenda is market research. The game never stops and you needn't leave your desk to play or to win. Win, lose, or wait for your turn, you can always go shopping. If this sort of customer-lure sounds both devious and intriguing, it is, and it's probably only the tip of the iceberg that will float into the electronic marketplace in the next few years.

Theoretically, a Web site could function like a giant superstore where everyone in the world can conveniently go shopping. In the physical world, such a store would be an impossibility (that's why retail chains exist), but on the Web a virtual superstore makes perfect sense. Ordering a product through the Web is a relatively straightforward endeavor, but what about filling the order? Product delivery should operate no differently than it does in the case of mail-order or telephone sales. Once the order comes in, a distribution center processes it and ships the product to the customer. Electronic commerce may streamline the order-taking process, but the rear-end distribution machine is not affected: cybertoasters don't toast English muffins very well. There are, however, two ways in which the Web can influence the distribution sector of marketing: data and metadata information.

> **In the physical world, a giant superstore where everyone in the world can conveniently go shopping would be an impossibility (that's why retail chains exist), but on the Web a virtual superstore makes perfect sense.**

If the product is *data*, the delivery can be instantaneous. One of the most attractive uses of online services is research. In most cases, access to such data is automated through database queries and therefore becomes both faster and more accurate. The amount of time, trouble, and expense associated with other forms of archival research is staggering by comparison. (Remember waiting in line at the library for the magazine clerk to see if the two periodicals you just spent an hour looking for on the microfiche reader are checked out or not?) Telephone calls are all local. Travel is eliminated. Downloads are virtually instantaneous.

Metadata, or information about distribution, also becomes much easier for the consumer to access, and this is both convenient for the user and effective for the vendor. For example, Domino's Pizza sells delivery, but they also sell a hard product (pizza), so their Web site (http://www.dominos.com) uses a map system to show hungry users how to get to Domino's locations, as shown in Figure 1-1.

Figure 1-1a

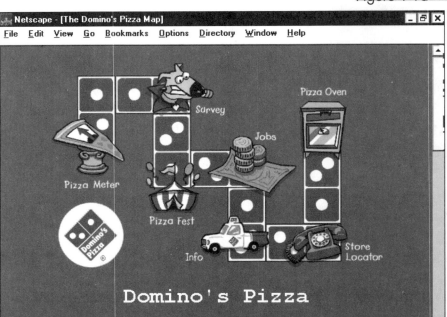

At the Domino's Pizza Web site ...

Like Domino's, Federal Express sells delivery. The Federal Express Web site (http://www.fedex.com) in Figure 1-2 features extensive tools for customers to track their own shipments.

Figure 1-1b

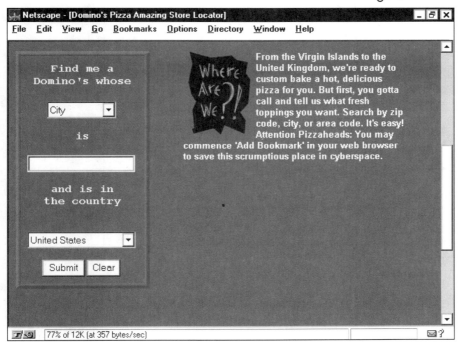

... you can look up a Domino's outlet near you.

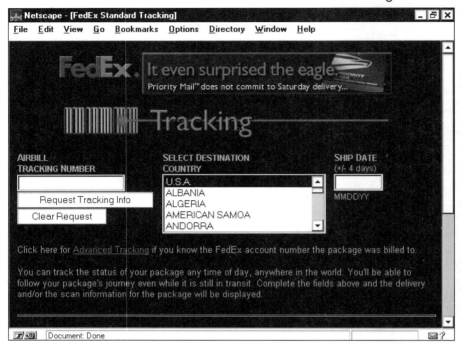

Figure 1-2

The Federal Express online tracking form for same-day pickup

These are just a few examples of how products can be disseminated effectively through the Web.

chapter **1** HIT FACTORY

Gauging the Web Advertisement Industry

Compared to the more than half-million nationally advertised U.S. brands, the Web advertiser market is still tiny—but it's growing fast. According to Jupiter Communications (http://www.jup.com), there were 270 Web advertisers who spent between $5,000 and $500,000 in the fourth quarter of 1995. In 1996, the company tracked more than 500 Web advertisers who spent in excess of $500,000 apiece placing ads online. Advertisers are clearly strengthening their online involvement, with an overwhelming majority of advertisers interviewed by a Cambridge, Massachusetts-based technology research group Forrester Research (http://www.forrester.com), saying they are now committed to online advertising, rather than simply experimenting with it. Although no more than a fraction of the ad expenditures of other media, Web advertising continues to grow. "It's expanding fast," according to Peter Storck, a senior analyst at New York-based Jupiter and editor of Jupiter's AdSpend, a report that tracks Internet advertising. "Revenues for advertising are on track to reach Jupiter's projection of $5 billion a year by [the year] 2000." Jupiter's reports show online revenue growing by more than 80 percent per quarter.

Why sell advertising on the Web? People usually sell Web advertising to recoup some of the expense of going online—and, of course, to earn a profit. The cost of establishing and maintaining a Web site is increasing with each new technology introduced. For example, the cost to use Seattle-based Progressive Networks' RealAudio Server (http://www.realaudio.com) to deliver live, on-demand streaming audio costs upwards of $10,000—a major impact on any Web marketer's budget. Some sites are offsetting this kind of cost by selling sponsorships to online audio programming, inserting commercial messages within online audio programming, as well as through additional ad banner sales. For an example of this approach see the National Public Radio site (http://www.npr.org), shown in Figure 1-3.

Figure 1-3

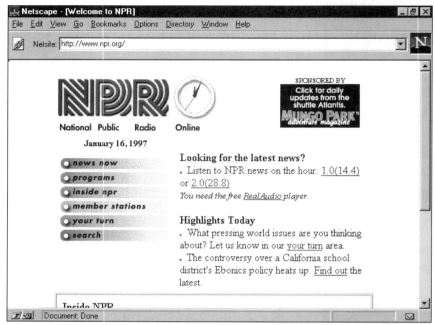

National Public Radio inserts commercial
messages within online audio programming.

The costs to establish and maintain different types of Web sites varies. In "What Web Sites Cost," Forrester Research points out that Web site development and maintenance costs are continuing to skyrocket, and marketers and content providers are feeling increasing pressure to show some kind of return on their Internet investment.

For many businesses, the decision to sell advertising space is not only a matter of economics, it is also part of the nature of the site and the purpose for which it was built. Forrester Research classifies Web sites into three distinct categories, each with its own associated costs. At the bottom tier of the classification are promotional sites, followed by content sites, and transactional sites. The classification of a site (and the purpose for which it was built) often dictates whether it carries advertising.

PROMOTIONAL SITES

The promotional site is typically a brand-building site established by a marketer to create awareness, stimulate demand, and foster good will among customers for its products. This mainly marketing-driven type of site costs the least, averaging $300,000 to launch and maintain for one year. Examples of promotional sites include those established by Coca-Cola (http://www.cocacola.com), Toyota (http://www.toyota.com), and Levi Strauss (http://www.levi.com)—the latter shown in Figure 1-4.

Figure 1-4

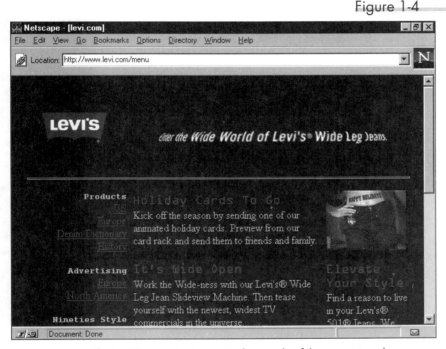

The Levi Strauss site is a typical example of the promotional genre.

Of course, these sites represent the marketing muscle of some of America's largest companies, which can afford to spend the kind of money cited in Forrester's study. A Web site doesn't have to cost even half that much, but Webmasters, creative agencies, and service bureaus will charge what the market will bear, and with the current rush of marketers going online, Web-related services get more costly and businesses pay more.

You can establish your own site offering information about your company's products and services for far less money—usually well under $10,000—if you go with the bare necessities and avoid *eye candy* like rotating Java applets and animated images, and stay away from sound files. By forgoing some of the extras, you might garner additional kudos from visitors who can get the information they need without waiting a long time for your page to download.

For example, 1-800-MATTRESS (shown in Figure 1-5), a New York-based company that has built a reputation for itself as a no-nonsense direct marketer of mattresses, opened a no-nonsense Web site this year (http://www.sleep.com). There are no wiggling, jiggling, or dancing box springs or mattresses, no large graphic files to download. Instead, the marketer offers pricing and shipping information in an easy-to-find manner. Although 1-800-MATTRESS isn't selling online, it does offer users a coupon they can print out for $45 off any mattress and box spring set, or $25 off any mattress. And, of course, the company's name and phone number appear prominently on every page of the site.

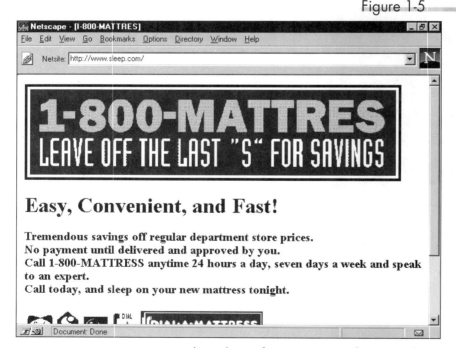

Figure 1-5

The Web site of 1-800-MATRESS focuses on the bare necessities of the company's business.

CONTENT SITES

The content type of site offers users compelling entertainment or information. Sometimes these sites carry material from traditional media, such as television shows, magazines, or newspapers. Time Warner's Pathfinder site (http://www.pathfinder.com), for example, features content from its stable of magazines including *Life, Time, People, Sports Illustrated,* and *Entertainment Weekly,* although it also offers additional content to the online community. Some content sites are pure Web-only products. Examples of this variety are digital magazines or *digizines* such as Addicted to Noise (http://www.addict.com), which offers music industry news, and Expedia (http://www.expedia.msn.com), an online travel magazine from Microsoft.

Still others, such as MSNBC (http://www.msnbc.com) the joint-venture news service from Microsoft and NBC, shown in Figure 1-6, and CNN Interactive (http://www.cnn.com), use the Web to augment and update content limited by the constraints of other media, such as television, which often force information providers to reduce an information-packed 30-minute interview to a 30-second sound bite. The cost for this kind of site is much higher, of course, averaging $1.3 million a year to establish and maintain, according to Forrester.

Figure 1-6

MSNBC uses the Web to add depth to issues that other broadcast media allot insufficient time.

Most content providers try to offset these costs by selling advertising, while others—such as The Wall Street Journal Interactive (http://www.wsj.com) and ESPN SportZone (http://www.espnet.sportszone.com) (shown in Figure 1-7)—charge users subscription fees to access some or all areas of the site. Many subscription sites also sell online ads. ESPN offers access to its entire site for $39.95 annually, while The Wall Street Journal Interactive charges users $49 annually—subscribers to the print edition can access the site for $29 annually. Most, if not all, of the successful online content providers are hoping to make a profit from advertising, although few have succeeded with this model as yet.

chapter 1 HIT FACTORY

Figure 1-7

ESPN SportZone charges subscription fees to access some areas of the site. It also sells online ads.

TRANSACTIONAL SITES

Transactional sites sell goods, offer customer service, or conduct financial transactions. These sites connect directly to databases that manage content and deliver updated information on the fly for each user. This is the most expensive kind of site, costing upwards of $3.4 million to establish and maintain for a year. Examples of transactional sites include the Internet Shopping Network site (http://www.internet.net), the Security First Network Bank site (http://www.sfnb.com/), and the Federal Express site (http://www.fedex.com) shown in Figure 1-8. As more technologies are introduced offering higher levels of personalization and interaction with online users, costs will continue to increase. These technology-related costs could rise anywhere from 52 percent to 320 percent before the year 2000, Forrester said.

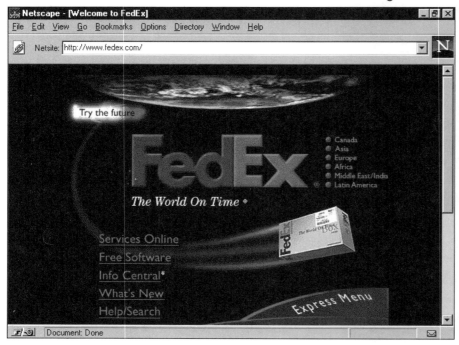

Federal Express has a high-end transactional site.

To stay ahead of their competitors in an increasingly competitive online information marketplace, operators of sites such as Yahoo!, Netscape, Time Warner's Pathfinder, and Lycos are employing *smart agent* software to personalize content and advertisements based on the user's preferences and previous choices. Smart agents, also called intelligent agents, gather information the user is interested in and present it to the user on a periodic basis predefined by the user. By offering a customized experience and making it as effortless as possible, these information providers are hoping to win users' repeat traffic.

Future cost increases will also come from higher levels of traffic anticipated as more users go online, and users' expectations of what the Web experience should be increase. In addition to adding the latest technologies, online content providers will also need to install additional equipment and network connections to serve the growing online community. The market for Internet advertising will increase as content providers increasingly look to sponsors to help offset the cost of maintaining their presence on the Web.

However, marketers' interest in driving a majority of revenue through the electronic commerce model must wait because consumers are still wary of using the Internet to make purchases and transactions online, and technology is still being developed that will lay their security and privacy concerns to rest. For now, advertising is the primary source of revenue for consumer-oriented Web sites. According to CyberAtlas (http://www.cyberatlas.com), a San Francisco-based group that offers research and analysis on Web measurement and marketing, 63 percent of Internet and online users favor advertising as a way to reduce the cost of Internet services.

If you are going to sell advertising on your Web site to offset your own site expenditures, or plan to launch an advertising campaign on the Web for branding purposes, you will need to understand the nature of the Web advertising business, from its unique audience measurement techniques to new standards being issued by advertising groups and others who are already working to drive the Internet forward as a mass marketing delivery system.

MEASURING SUCCESS

As an advertising vehicle, the Internet is still in its infancy. Most people in the industry tend to agree that Web advertising began in October 1994, when *Wired* magazine launched HotWired (http://www.hotwired.com), a cool Web site for the digital elite. The company sold a 12-week sponsorship at $30,000, and set a new industry off to its less-than-humble beginnings. In the rocky two years that have followed, the industry has grappled with such challenging issues as measurement and tracking methods, and establishing standards for ad banner sizes and ad pricing rates.

Advertising is a major source of revenue for online content providers, so measuring the exposure to online advertising is critical—as is measuring the demographics of the people who see the ads. Different methods are currently in use for measuring Internet traffic, but none of them has yet been accepted as standard. Several third-party companies are working to help online content providers discern the numbers, while traditional media auditors BPA International and the Audit Bureau of Circulations (ABC) have entered the Internet business to verify the figures and help advertisers in their media buying decisions.

Measurement terms

While people in the Internet industry have yet to agree on the most effective way to measure online activity, those involved tend to agree at least on the following terms for online traffic:

- **Hit.** Every time a Web server sends a file to a browser, the server log file records it as a *hit*. Hits appear for every element on a requested page, including graphics and text. So if a user views one page with four graphic elements, that's five hits—four for the graphic elements and one for the page itself. In other words, don't be too impressed when you hear about the high number of hits a site receives, because the numbers are probably wildly inflated due to users accessing multiple files on a single Web page.

- **Valid hit.** *Valid hits* are hits that deliver page information to a user. They provide somewhat more refined information than plain hits, as they exclude hits such as redirects, error messages, and computer-generated hits (where a computer is programmed to access a particular file over and over to inflate the number of hits a site receives).

- **Unique users.** The *unique user* count is the number of different users who access a site within a given time period. Webmasters usually rely on some form of user registration or other identification system to track unique users.

- **Visits.** A *visit* is a sequence of requests made by a single user at one site. If a user doesn't request additional information on a site for a period of time, this is called the *time-out* period. Following a time-out period, the next request made by the user is considered a new visit. A 30-minute interval is commonly used to measure time-out periods.

- **Impressions** (a.k.a. *ad views*). When a user actually views an ad banner—or there's reasonable certainty that the user has done so—it counts as a *Web impression*, with one impression equal to one user. The term is thus akin to *net impressions* in traditional media, which refers to the unduplicated number of people or households exposed to the message. Impressions are difficult to measure within the

Internet environment due to caching (the storage of frequently accessed Web pages for faster loading). Web publishers have no way of determining whether their pages (and the accompanying banner ads) are being accessed by users as cached pages or in real time.
* **Click-through.** This term refers to the number of times users click on an ad banner and are taken to the advertiser's site.

Measurement guidelines

Last fall, the Coalition for Advertising Supported Information and Entertainment (CASIE), a joint committee of the American Association of Advertising Agencies and the Association of National Advertisers, proposed guidelines for measurement standards. The verdict is still out on whether these guidelines will be adopted as a set standard. Most online publishers, however, follow their basic principles, including:

* Audience measurers should employ the best existing media research practices.
* Objective third parties should do the measuring and auditing.
* Measurers should fully disclose methods and data to research subscribers.
* Measurement should be comparable across online vehicles (for example, from Web site to Web site).
* Measurers should be innovative in method and practice.
* Consumer privacy should be maintained.
* Measurement methods should be as nonintrusive to consumers as possible.
* Measurements should be reported within the context of a total medium measurement.
* Measurement standards should be set by broad representation of the advertising industry, including advertisers, agencies, researchers, and industry groups.

Measurement companies

To help with accountability of the new medium, a variety of third-party Web tracking services have developed measurement systems. Even though the following services may differ in the ways they measure online activity, they are building the kind of credibility that advertisers and content providers can use with confidence.

Internet Profiles Corporation (I/PRO)

San Francisco-based I/PRO (http://www.ipro.com) has been in the online measurement game longer than the other players, and its software is among the most commonly used by Web sites to count traffic. I/PRO clients include Yahoo!, Playboy, Chrysler, and CBS. I/PRO's products include I/COUNT to analyze visits or pageviews and I/CODE to collect user information through a registration process. Another product, I/AUDIT, provides third-party auditing of ad banners. I/PRO is also working with another San Francisco Web measurer, Andromedia (http://www.andromedia.com), to find ways to get users to provide more data about themselves.

> **Advertising is a major source of revenue for online content providers, so measuring the exposure to online advertising is critical—as is measuring the demographics of the people who see the ads.**

NetCount

Another big player in the measurement arena is NetCount (http://www.netcount.com), a Web-tracking tool created by the Los Angeles-based creative agency Digital Planet, and now the foundation of a separate company. NetCount has a strategic relationship with Price Waterhouse, and markets its products under the NetCount/Price Waterhouse brand name. Clients include such entertainment heavyweights as MGM/UA and MCA, ad agency Young & Rubicam, and Nissan USA. The company's products include HeadCount to track Web usage and demographic profiles of users, and AdCount to track banner exposures and click-throughs by hour and day.

NetGravity

Yet another recognized player in the third-party measurement game is NetGravity (http://www.netgravity.com), which markets AdServer software, an online ad management system that helps publishers keep track of ad schedules and rotations on their Web sites. Technology in the software also allows the Web server to match the types of ads it displays to each visitor based on his or her specific interests as entered in a consumer profile. NetGravity's system has been in use by Yahoo!, CNET, Netscape, and Pathfinder to manage their advertising inventories and serve ads to their visitors. NetGravity has aligned with I/PRO; the two companies found that their services complemented each other. NetGravity published a set of application programming interfaces (APIs) that enables I/PRO product users to validate the data generated by the AdServer in a simple and timely fashion.

Intersé

A fourth contender in the Web measurement group, with a fast-rising profile, is Intersé (http://www.interse.com), which offers Web measurement software called Market Focus, a Windows-based tool that uses statistical modeling to measure and analyze site traffic. The software enables marketers to extract any type of information in any level of detail from their Web site. Market Focus meets the measurement and auditing standards set by both of the major online auditors, ABC's Audit Bureau of Verification Services and BPA International.

Other contenders

Besides these companies, a host of less visible companies are developing programs and software to measure and track online users and advertisements. Among them:

* **Arbitron New Media** (http://www.arbitron.com/newmedia.html) —in conjunction with Next Century Media—offers the CyberMeasurement Index (CMI), a product that aggregates Web site data across the industry. (Next Century Media is also developing a *Cyberspace Index* database of traffic reports supplied by Web sites participating in its program to generate comparative reports.)

- **Accrue Software** (http://www.accrue.com) has developed Accrue Insight, a Web-tracking program that measures hits, visits, and users, how long it takes a page to download, and whether a user downloads an entire page.
- **ASI Market Research** (http://www.asiresearch.com)—in a venture with A.C. Nielsen—has launched NET*VIEWS 96, a product that helps marketers measure the Web's efficacy as a marketing vehicle for packaged goods. (Glendale, California-based ASI Market Research was recently acquired by Audience Research and Development of Dallas.)
- **The Delahaye Group** (http://www.delahaye.com) offers NetBench, a service that compares the value of marketing dollars spent on the Web with other forms of media. (This product was created in conjunction with Internet Media Services of Palo Alto.)
- **Group Cortex** (http://www.cortex.net) markets the SiteTrack Tracking System, an add-on to the Netscape server that allows it to track users as they move through a Web site.
- **Streams Online Media Development** (http://streams.com) markets Lilypad, a product that traces the path a Web user takes to a certain site, helping advertisers learn how people find the site.

AUDITING

Given the complexity of Web measurement and the different methods employed to track and monitor audiences, third-party auditors are providing advertisers the kind of verification they need, enabling media planners and buyers to compare Web site traffic and usage delivered. The two primary auditors come from the traditional media side, and are recognized names among advertisers and media planners: as noted earlier, they are the Audit Bureau of Circulations (ABC) and BPA International.

ABVS Interactive (http://www.accessabc.com), the ABC interactive auditing unit, was created in 1995 in response to demand from the online advertising community and ABC members to provide independent third-party audits and industry-developed standards for Web site and other online advertising. ABVS currently conducts audits for the following online publishers: Car and Driver, Classifieds2000, Cool Site of the Day, Datamation, Disney Online, Elle, Epicurious Food, Epicurious Travel, FoxWorld, George, GameFan Online, HealthGate, Lycos, Nando.net, National Geographic, Premiere, SonicNet, Swoon, Texas Monthly, Video Games Online, and Worth Online. In addition, ABVS is creating a customized audit for PointCast Network's SmartAd Broadcast System. ABC is working with fellow audit bureaus in Denmark, Germany, Sweden, Spain, Switzerland, and the United Kingdom to implement global standards for auditing Web site activity.

Third-party auditors are providing advertisers the kind of verification they need, enabling media planners and buyers to compare Web site traffic and usage delivered.

BPA International (`http://www.bpai.com`), based in New York, only recently completed its first audit report—in March 1996. BPA uses a system from NetCount to track *page requests* to verify the number of pages of any size users have seen. BPA is auditing Web sites for Cowles Business Media, The Economist Group, Mecklermedia, Ziff-Davis Publishing's ZD Net, and nine of IDG's online publications.

STANDARDIZING ADVERTISING MODELS

Apart from measurements, marketers also grapple with another issue—the standardization of Internet ad banners. On just about any Web site you visit, you'll see a variety of sizes of ad banner, from 375 pixels wide by 48 pixels high on some pages to 468 pixels wide by 60 pixels high on others. There are as many variations to these sizes as there are Web pages.

A *pixel* is a measurement term used by graphic designers. As defined by the *Oxford Dictionary,* a pixel is "any of the minute areas of uniform illumination of which an image on a display screen is composed." The term is an abbreviation of the words "picture element." What you really need to know is that there are 72 pixels per inch. In the reference in the previous paragraph, we could say that the banners range in size from 5.2 inches wide by 1.5 inches high on some sites to 6.5 inches wide by 1.2 inches high on others.

To help make buying and placing Web ads easier and eliminate the time and expense necessary to recreate the same ad to fit different Web sites' specifications, ad industry group CASIE and the Internet Advertising Bureau (IAB), a new group representing sellers of online ad space, issued a landmark set of guidelines in December 1996 for creating Web advertising.

The IAB and CASIE identified the sizes in Table 1-1 as the most commonly accepted banner sizes. Examples can be seen in Figure 1-9.

Table 1-1 Common Ad Banner Sizes

SIZE (PIXELS)	SIZE (INCHES)	TYPE
468 × 60	6.50 × .83	Full banner
392 × 72	5.44 × 1.00	Full banner with vertical navigation bar
234 × 60	3.25 × .83	Half banner
125 × 125	1.74 × 1.74	Square banner
120 × 90	1.67 × 1.25	Button #1
120 × 60	1.67 × .83	Button #2
88 × 31	1.22 × .43	Micro button
120 × 240	1.67 × 3.33	Vertical banner

Source: Internet Advertising Bureau & CASIE, 1996

Use of these sizes as a model is strictly voluntary. However, since the members of CASIE and IAB represent some of the nation's biggest agencies and advertisers as well as the Web's largest publishers, the proposed model will in all likelihood become the accepted standard for online banner ads. Also, although they've gone to all the trouble of classifying banner sizes and establishing these proposed standards, the IAB and CASIE both recognize and intend that their member companies and the advertising community as a whole are free to experiment with, use, adopt, and propose other sizes and types of banners.

chapter **1** HIT FACTORY

Figure 1-19

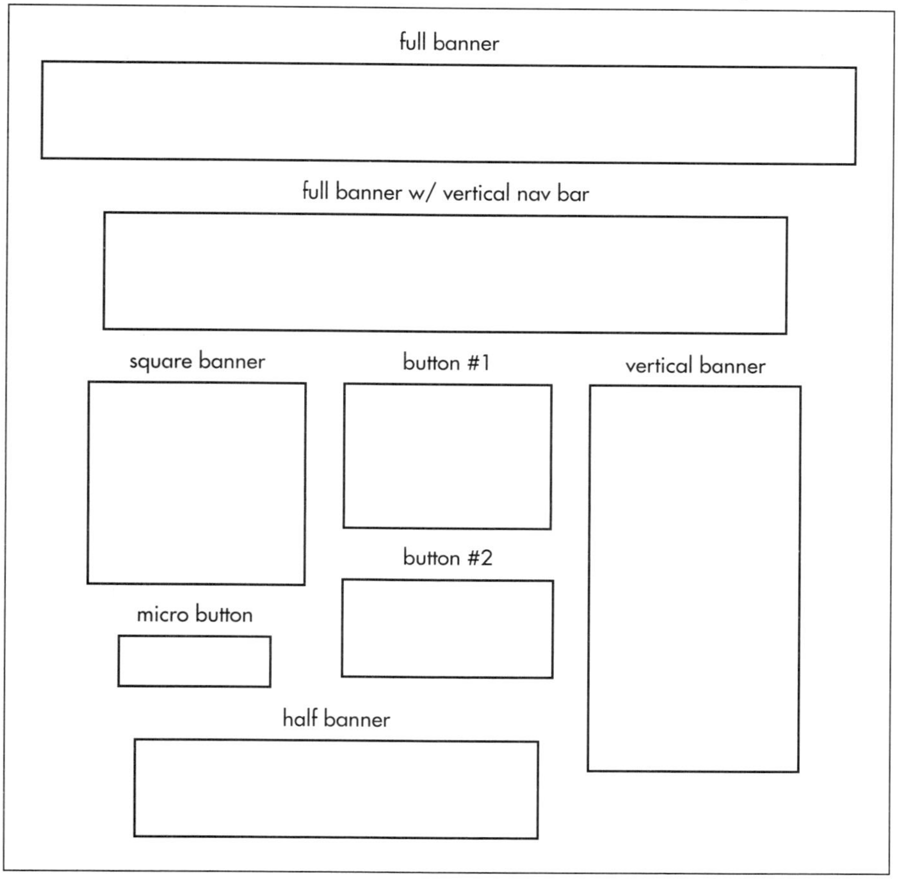

```
full banner
[                                    ]

full banner w/ vertical nav bar
[                                    ]

square banner    button #1       vertical banner
[          ]    [         ]      [            ]
                                 [            ]
                 button #2       [            ]
 micro button   [         ]      [            ]
[      ]                         [            ]
                                 [            ]
       half banner
      [              ]
```

Examples of various ad banner sizes

In fact, the IAB and CASIE are encouraging the continued exploration of other, more creative, advertising models. These models include:

* **Bridge pages.** A bridge or interstitial page is a promotional page accessed via an ad banner or button that leads to the sponsor's own Web site.
* **Push advertising.** A push advertisement is *forced* onto users' desktops via offline delivery methods including products from PointCast, Marimba, and BackWeb. These products are free-to-user, advertiser-supported news delivery vehicles that automatically cull

Web news sites for information based on the user's preferences and then download that material to a specially formatted screensaver on the desktop.

* **Microsites.** Microsites are multipage areas created within a Web site where all or a portion of the content is sponsored by a marketer. By sponsoring content within a site, marketers boost their companies' credibility with the online audience as valued sources of information rather than just advertisers. Microsites are also commonly used by content providers to run a contest or promotion for a sponsor but without redirecting users away from the site. ICon New Media Productions, a New York-based creative firm, has applied for a trademark on the term microsite. The company, which operates the online publications Word (http://www.word.com) and Charged (http://www.charged.com), has developed microsites for such sponsors as Altoids, Saab, and Signet Books.

* **Web advertorials.** Web advertorials are sponsor-supported areas within Web sites that give marketers a greater online presence through content sponsorship. For example, Kraft Foods has signed a major sponsorship deal for an integrated content area featuring more than 600 original recipes on the Hearst HomeArts site (http:www.homearts.com). This kind of content makes perfect sense on a site where users are looking for new recipe ideas.

* **Content integration.** Also known as *environmental advertising*, content integration weaves the sponsor's product into the story line of an online serial or game. This type of ad model typically requires the user to interact with the product, making it a meaningful experience and therefore making it more likely that the user will respond to the ad message. Digital Planet, a Los Angeles-based Web production company, sold Intel the concept of content integration into its online game, Madeleine's Mind. Showing computers with the "Intel Inside" logo was a natural, according to Thomas Lakeman, senior vice president of Creative Affairs at Digital Planet, since the game is all about using the mind, and the PC is a tool that assists and benefits the mind. Since most of the game's primary users are twenty-somethings with a cynical view of advertising, Intel felt it was important for the ads to be as unobtrusive as possible.

While experimentation is encouraged on the Internet and is often expected in this new medium, you still need to establish methods for ad placement on your site that give advertisers the kind of traffic and exposure they want.

BUILDING AN ADVERTISING PROGRAM

When you begin selling advertising on your site, you'll want to consider developing various programs that advertisers can buy into, giving them a flexible range of pricing options. For example, Netscape offers advertisers several different advertising programs ranging from its Platinum Program, which rotates its advertisers' banners on five popular content areas within the Netscape site, to a Silver Program with ad rotation on five somewhat less high-traffic areas. Advertisers pay $20,400 per month on the Platinum Program for 1 million monthly impressions, and $17,000 on the Silver Program for 750,000 monthly impressions.

Other commonly sold *avails* (commercial positions available for purchase by an advertiser) include run of site (that is, the placement of ad banners anywhere on the site as opposed to placement in certain predefined areas), general rotation of a banner randomly within the entire site, fixed banner ads on a single page or area, and keyword or phrase sales—a popular method in search engines and directories. With a little software customization, advertisers can better target their message to individuals based on the user's demographics, psychographic profile, domain type, and location. For example, New York-based Internet media rep firm DoubleClick lets advertisers who buy into its network of Web sites target their ads to users arriving from specific domains, such as aol.com or any .edu host computer. Similar types of ad management systems are being offered by NetGravity (http://www.netgravity.com), Accipiter (http://www.accipiter.com) and Focalink Communications (http://www.focalink.com).

As with traditional media, there are many things to consider with Internet advertising, whether you're embarking on your first online ad campaign or selling banner space on your own site. Most of what you've already read in this book can help you in your efforts, but you may decide to let a professional agency take over your Internet advertising needs so you can focus on what you do best—run your business.

Consider working with an agency

An agency can take over the promotional aspects of your site for you. Agency personnel can help evaluate the best placement of your ads in the digital and traditional media, evaluate the frequency of the advertisements (that is, the number of times people or homes are exposed to an advertising message), and then execute the buy. Similarly, they can also help you target sponsors, determine where within your own site you can place ads, and develop sponsor campaigns.

If you already work with an agency, check with your rep first to see if the agency works in the interactive environment. Besides yourself, who best understands your product and the message you want to convey to your target audience? If your agency doesn't work in interactive environments—or if you've never worked with an agency at all and need to locate one—you can turn to a number of sources to get agency leads.

A good starting point is with advertising industry trade magazines such as *Advertising Age* (http://adage.com) and *Adweek* (http://www.adweek.com), both of which have added an interactive category to their weekly coverage of industry happenings. These publications offer objective coverage of the industry and analysis of which agencies are setting benchmarks for interactive marketing performance.

There are also a number of Web sites offering content relevant to Internet advertising and marketing. Several good ones include the Advertising Resource Guide (http://www.ipac.net/irgad/irgadhome.html), the Internet Advertising Resource Guide (http://www.voyager.net/adv/internet-advertising-guide.html), and Advertising World (http://www.utexas.edu/coc/adv/world/). Other places to look for ad agencies are with trade groups and associations. These include the Advertising Research Federation, American Advertising Federation, American Association of

Advertising Agencies (4 A's), Association of National Advertisers, CASIE, and the Interactive Services Association.

Evaluating an agency's expertise

Advertising agencies range in size from gigantic multinational corporations to the small new media development shops that seem to spring up almost daily. The expertise of traditional agencies lies in promoting and creating awareness for the brand, but they don't always understand the possibilities of interactive digital communications. Newer interactive agencies dedicated to the medium, by contrast, have a firm grasp of the sophisticated database marketing tools upon which one-to-one relationships with consumers are built.

> **When you are evaluating candidates to administer your next interactive marketing campaign or client promotions on your site, the considerations and criteria listed here will help you compare agencies and the types of services they can provide.**

As it has become clearer that *interactivity* is a necessity in an integrated marketing campaign, traditional agencies have started dabbling in new media. Larger firms including Grey Advertising, Saatchi & Saatchi, Leo Burnett, and Young & Rubicam have opened up in-house divisions dedicated to interactive experimentation. Others, such as True North Communications, have purchased smaller interactive agencies in an effort to gain immediate expertise in the medium.

When you are evaluating candidates to administer your next interactive marketing campaign or client promotions on your site, the considerations and criteria listed here will help you compare agencies and the types of services they can provide. Remember to apply these in light of the prospective agency's experience with new media, not just traditional marketing channels.

- ★ **Experience.** Is it an established agency? Can it provide profiles of account team members, including experience in interactivity, promotion, marketing, technology, and your industry? Can it provide a client roster (including the tenure of the clients or statements from clients)? Can it provide case studies and success stories, including client objectives and results? How many interactive campaigns has it worked on? Is the agency financially stable?

- **Project plan development.** Can the agency provide a detailed campaign strategy? What kind of research will it conduct prior to campaign development? Can it give you a manageable time line as well as program performance milestones and measurements?
- **Creativity.** What are the agency's capabilities in terms of copywriting, scripting, graphic design, and concept development? Are you pleased with work they've done for other clients?
- **Account management.** What kind of end-to-end supervision does the agency offer? Is anyone at the agency dedicated to your account (and is that necessary)?
- **Program management.** What steps does the agency go through in terms of implementation, testing, monitoring, and reporting?
- **Reporting.** What kind of reports can the agency provide? Are they standard or customizable? What kind of flexibility in reporting does the agency have? Does it offer the frequency in reporting you need? Is the data accurate?
- **Ancillary services.** Does the agency have media buying and databasing capabilities?
- **In-house versus outsourced.** Are services like media buying, production, strategy development, creative execution, and reporting handled in-house, or are they farmed out to others?
- **Fee structure.** Are all fees outlined from the get-go, including creative development, program management, retainers, markups on outsourced services, and customized or standard reports?
- **Procedures, workflow, quality control.** What systems are in place at the agency for contract administration, client approval, testing, estimates and billing, exclusivity, reports, and security of client information?

While you may be at the mercy of the agency to take whatever answers they provide at face value, the best way to verify information is to ask for multiple references and then check all of them. Don't stop at one or two. Most agencies are more than willing to provide references to satisfied clients, but are they willing to part with the name of a not-so-happy client? You want multiple answers from multiple sources so you can get a cross-sample of responses. Find out from the references what their experience was with the agency in question. How did the agency perform? Was the agency easy to work with? Did the agency meet the client's goals on time and in the prescribed manner? You may find after your fact-checking that the agency in question is not right for you, thereby saving a lot of unnecessary hassles and headaches—or that the agency is a perfect fit and can help you meet your Internet marketing objectives.

> **Those who act on the message by clicking on the banner are more valuable to the marketer than those who simply see the ad banner but don't immediately act upon it—interaction is better than branding.**

Already in this chapter we've seen that much of the Web advertising industry has yet to be standardized—from audience measurement and auditing practices to advertising models. Establishing set criteria for each of these issues is critical in nurturing the growth of the Internet as a valid advertising vehicle so sponsors can compare their ad buys from Web site to Web site on a consistent basis.

DECIDING ON A PRICING MODEL

While no standards exist for Web advertising pricing, almost all online advertising models have been built on the print and television advertising frameworks that media planners are already familiar with. The most common pricing scheme currently used is the Cost-Per-Thousand-Impressions (CPM) model. Because CPM is difficult to quantify, some Internet publishers are instead using a Click-Through model, giving their advertisers increased accountability.

 CPM refers to the cost per thousand people (or homes) delivered by a medium or media schedule. The term comes from the traditional advertising world, where it originally referred to "cost per million." In the 1980s, when the three major television networks began experiencing fragmented audiences for the first time due to the advent of cable television, media pricing was restructured to reflect thousands rather than millions of viewers. CPM has thus become a standard term to refer to thousands of people. Coincidentally, the term *impression* is used in the advertising world to refer to the people (or homes) that the message was delivered to.

The CPM model

The CPM model is similar to models used to sell advertising in other media such as TV, radio, and print. Media planners and buyers have used it in the past and are generally comfortable with it. The CPM model assumes marketers will place their ad on the site due to the sheer number of people who will see the advertiser's message. Heavily trafficked sites are more likely to take advantage of this plan due to the number of *eyeballs* they attract. It's a mass audience approach employed by popular television shows such as *Home Improvement* and *Monday Night Football,* which can command higher advertising prices due to the vast numbers of people who tune in. The CPM rate reflects the cost per thousand impressions—for example, a Web site that charges $15,000 per banner and guarantees 600,000 impressions has a CPM rate of $25 ($15,000 divided by 600).

Rates vary from site to site. Many Web sites publish their media kits online, and you can spend time researching various rates to get an idea of what Internet publishers are charging. The Netscape site (http://home.netscape.com) shown in Figure 1-10, one of the most heavily-trafficked sites on the Web, charges $20,400 per month for 1,000 impressions ($20.40 CPM). IGuide (http://www.iguide.com), News Corporation's Web site for *TV Guide, X-Files,* and other entertainment properties, charges a monthly rate of $12,500 for 1,000 impressions ($25 CMP). The Wall Street Journal Interactive Edition (http://www.wsj.com), charges upwards of $80 CPM, while advertisers on Playboy's site (http://www.playboy.com) may pay as little as $3 CPM. Table 1-2 summarizes various representative ad rates, including cost-per-thousand-impressions (CPM) and cost-per-impression rates (CPI).

Figure 1-10

Netscape's rate card is based on $20.40 CPM.

Table 1-2 Representative Ad Rates and CPMs

SITE	RATE	IMPRESSIONS	CPM	CPI
CNET	$15,000/month	200,000	$75	$0.07
HotWired	$15,000/month	100,000	$150	$0.15
S.J. Mercury	$200/day	3,000	$67	$0.07
WhoWhere (regular program)	$2,500/month	100,000	$25	$0.03
Yahoo!	$7,500/month	250,000	$30	$0.03

Source: 1996 CyberAtlas

The Click-Through model

The Click-Through model works like direct marketing, where the advertiser pays only for those people who actually click on the ad to investigate further. This rate plan assumes that the message only has value to those who act on it, as opposed to all who see it. In other words, those who act on the message by clicking on the banner are more valuable to the marketer than those who simply see the ad banner but don't immediately act upon it—interaction is better than branding.

Procter and Gamble (P&G), for example, makers of such brand-name goods as Sunny Delight, Crisco, and Max Factor Cosmetics—and one of the nation's biggest spenders on all forms of advertising—favors the click-through approach. In 1996 the company instructed its agency, Grey Advertising (New York), not to place P&G banner ads on any Web site that charged per impression (the CPM model). Instead, the company said it would pay only for those users who clicked on its ads and that it would not recognize Internet users who had simply *seen* its ad. This was seen as a heavy-handed media tactic, because it makes the Web publisher dependent upon the quality and effectiveness of the advertising. Online content providers said P&G would be getting something for nothing, that is, exposure of its brand name to all who see its banner ads, whether or not those visitors clicked over to P&G's Web site. The company was advertising on search engines Excite, Yahoo!, and WebCrawler, but only Yahoo! scrapped its CPM pricing scheme to keep P&G's money. The others insisted on using the CPM model, thereby eliminating themselves from P&G's media purchase. Figure 1-11 shows P&G's main site.

The number of people who click on an ad banner is usually not proportionate to overall site traffic, but depends primarily on the ad banner's creative execution—both the design of the ad and the advertising message work equally to compel the user to take the extra step and click on the ad. In addition to creative execution, other variables influencing whether a viewer responds to an ad banner include the perceived value of the offer, the content environment the ad appears in, the frequency of the ad, and the willingness or reluctance of the user to interact with the ad.

Internet researcher CyberAtlas reports that Webmasters who have analyzed their *clickstreams* report ad-click rates ranging from 0.36 percent to 2.8 percent for general interest sites to 30 percent for highly targeted sites.

CyberAtlas's parent company, I/PRO, found that the average click-through rate is 2.6 percent based on a survey it conducted of approximately 184 million ad views. Additionally, CyberAtlas reports that sites have charged advertisers anywhere from 31 cents to $1.36 per ad click, although it didn't give an average price.

Figure 1-11

P&G has led the push toward a click-through model for advertising fees.

A case in point: Toyota

To drive awareness for the release of its 1997 Camry, Toyota Motor Sales USA ran a promotion on search engine Yahoo!, a detail of which appears in Figure 1-12. SOFTBANK Interactive Marketing (SIM), the El Segundo, California-based Internet media rep firm for Yahoo!, recommended its client's site for two reasons: first, the site has mass appeal — SIM guaranteed Toyota would get at least 14 million impressions during the course of the two-week promotion, which ran from September 23 to October 6, 1996, and second, Yahoo! was able to lock in specific dates corresponding with the national Camry campaign in more traditional media—radio, TV, newspaper, and magazine advertising.

Figure 1-12

Toyota's Camry promotion was an extraordinary success.

According to Jonathan Anastas, interactive marketing manager at Toyota's ad agency, Saatchi & Saatchi Pacific, the agency had previously avoided search engine-based promotions because of his client's requirements to qualify specific types of customers. He eventually recommended Yahoo! because of the sheer volume of traffic on that site. "The launch of the Camry is so big and is such a high-volume vehicle that we thought that a high profile was necessary. There may be a lower percentage of qualified traffic, but ultimately, it will be more cost-efficient for Toyota," Anastas said. The promotion was simple yet highly effective. Users who clicked to the Yahoo! home page immediately saw the Toyota banner at the top of the page. The text adjacent to the illustration read: "Want To Win A New Camry? Click Here."

Viewers who clicked on the banner ad went to a *bridge page* for the 1997 Toyota Camry Better-Than-Ever Sweepstakes, where they filled out a short online form asking for limited demographic information in return for entry in the sweepstakes. From here, sweepstakes entrants could return to the Yahoo! or Toyota home page or progress through a series of qualifier Web pages, each asking for additional demographic information, such as the kind of car they currently own and their annual household income, in return for an MCI calling card worth 60 minutes of free long distance time. The proviso: a visit to a local Toyota dealership to activate the card and take a test drive — a clever way for Toyota to increase foot traffic into its showrooms!

The campaign exceeded Toyota's expectations, according to June Okamoto, Toyota's interactive marketing manager. The company averaged more than 1.5 million impressions each day, and more than 16 million during the course of the promotion — exceeding by more than 2 million impressions the campaign's original expectations. The *rate of conversion* was approximately 2 percent to 3 percent for people clicking into the promotion from Yahoo!.

"The promotion was an effective way for potential customers to learn more not just about the 1997 Camry, but everything they ever wanted to know about Toyota's products and services," Okamoto said. Although Toyota doesn't yet know how many sales resulted from the promotion, the initial results were encouraging. Okamoto said Toyota plans to launch additional interactive marketing campaigns in 1997. "We know that the Internet is here to stay and we will continue to use it as another effective medium to increase car sales."

Several variables worked together to make Toyota's promotion on Yahoo! succeed: the prominent placement of the banner at the top of the page where most visitors to Yahoo! would see it, the call to action in the ad's text, and the perceived value of the calling card.

Targeting Your Audience

The type of advertiser your site attracts will depend on the type of people visiting your site. Although the Internet is still populated mainly by a relatively narrow demographic group, the number of people online has been increasing, as has the diversity of the people going online. In 1993, the Internet was still basically a resource and communications tool used by academics and government employees. Since that time, more than 35 million Americans have gone online, according to CyberAtlas. This number has doubled in just the past year alone, and as household PC penetration, as well as the integration of browser software into many desktop applications, increases, the number of people online will skyrocket.

Another factor influencing the number of people going online is the amount of compelling information available on the Internet. In 1993, there were approximately 6,000 domain names registered with InterNIC (`http://www.internic.net`), the group that tracks Internet domain name registration (for more details in InterNIC, see Chapter 5, Registering and Staking Out Cyberturf). By the end of 1996, the number of domain names was nearing the 500,000 mark. At its current pace, the Web is adding about 50,000 new sites per month.

Getting a handle on the audience—exactly who are those 20+ million people on the Web — is a slippery business.

While market research firms can provide demographics on the existing population, it's not always clear whether your audience is among them. If you have an existing business and are planning to migrate or augment your operation to the Web, it is probably worth your while to conduct a little market research of your own. This is most easily (and inexpensively) accomplished with a survey. Incentives for participation can help foster response. Following are some basic questions that the survey might include:

1. Do you own a computer? If not, do you plan on purchasing one within the next six months?
2. Do you use a computer at work? How much time do you spend on the computer at work? What are your primary activities?
3. Do you use a computer at home? How much time do you spend on the computer at home? What are your primary activities?
4. Are you a member of any online services such as America Online or CompuServe? How much time do you spend using the service? For what reason?
5. Do you have an account on the Internet? How much time do you spend on the Internet? What are your primary activities?
6. Do you use electronic mail? If so, what are your primary purposes?
7. What information about [**our company**] would you like to see accessible through the Internet?
8. Have you ever made purchases through the Internet? If so, how often?
9. Would you do business on the Internet with [**our company**]?
10. What aspects of your business relationship would most benefit you through online access?
    * Product information
    * Sales orders and order tracking
    * Customer service
    * Support
    * Other (please specify)

Sooner or later some aspect of online convenience will almost certainly have appeal to your client base. Learning about your clients' needs is better done early in the evolution of the medium than late: remember Burma Shave!

WHO'S ONLINE?

The typical Internet user in the past has mirrored the typical computer user: male, college educated, middle to high income. Of the U.S. online population, approximately 65 percent is male. The percentage of women online, while only at 35 percent now, is growing, according to a recent research conducted by FIND/SVP, a New York-based research and consulting firm. Minorities are also getting online in large numbers: a 1996 Yaneklovich Survey found that blacks made up 15 percent of the cyber-population, nearly doubling the previous year's figure. The average age of online users is 36.

Seventy percent of people on the Internet live in *married/couple* households; 67 percent are college graduates. Mixed use of the Internet, for both personal and business, is common, with 60 percent of adult users saying they use it for both. The average income of Internet users is $62,000, with 31 percent earning more than $75,000 annually; 40 percent earning between $40,000 and $74,900; and 29 percent in the under $40,000 bracket. These figures are also shown in Figure 1-13.

chapter 1 HIT FACTORY

Figure 1-13

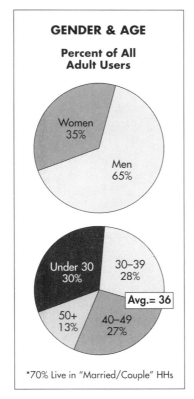

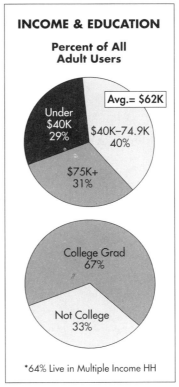

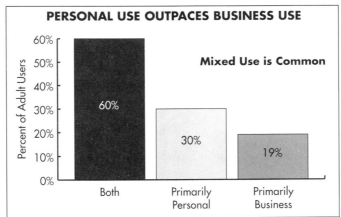

Income breakdown of online users

41

How do online users find out about Web sites? Here are some things to remember when planning your publicity campaign. The majority of online users (68 percent) told FIND/SVP they learn about Web sites through magazine and newspaper articles; 63 percent learn about sites through word of mouth; 51 percent find sites because the URL was printed on an advertisement; and 32 percent said they learn about new sites through books (see Figure 1-14). Note: These figures refer to the popularity of methods employed to find out about Web sites, based on a checklist presented to people filling out the FIND/SVP survey.

Figure 1-14

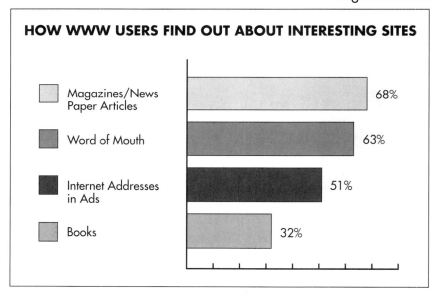

How do users find out about Web sites?

Of the information researchers have catalogued on Internet users, A.C. Nielsen found these interesting statistics in its 1996 Netviews survey of 16,200 households. Online consumers spend 40 percent more on disposable diapers, 25 percent more on breakfast foods, and 23 percent more on yogurt than offline consumers. Online consumers also spend more money on office supplies, electronics, health foods, and toys. As you can probably guess, they are also quite fond of home-delivered goods, having outspent their offline counterparts by 46 percent.

WHAT ARE PEOPLE DOING ONLINE?

As far as visiting sites, Web use is selective for most visitors. Seventy-seven percent of respondents in FIND/SVP's study said they have visited fewer than 100 sites in-depth (see Figure 1-15); of these, the average number of sites visited regularly is a measly 11. The typical user has registered with seven Internet sites; 52 percent said they have registered with at least one site. Only 7 percent said they were not willing to register at all. Online users are beginning to see the Internet as more than just an entertainment vehicle; nearly half of those online have retrieved product information, and 20 percent said they have made a purchase online. Of these, 65 percent put credit card information online. Another 59 percent said they were interested in making purchases via the Internet over the next 12 months.

Figure 1-15

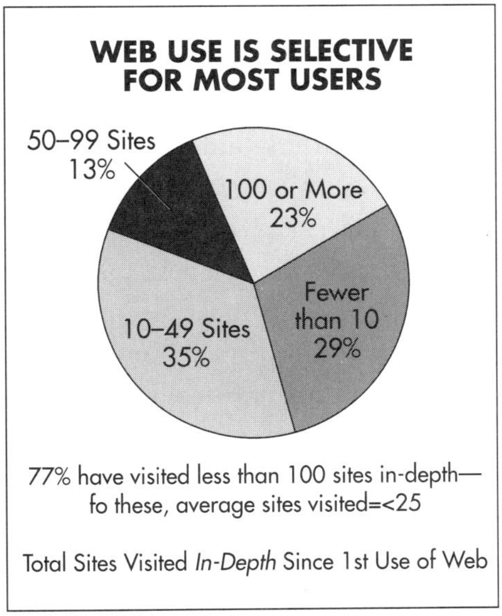

WEB USE IS SELECTIVE FOR MOST USERS

- 50–99 Sites 13%
- 100 or More 23%
- 10–49 Sites 35%
- Fewer than 10 29%

77% have visited less than 100 sites in-depth—
to these, average sites visited=<25

Total Sites Visited *In-Depth* Since 1st Use of Web

Online usage breakdown

If so many people are going on the Internet as a source for communication, entertainment, and information, what aren't they doing? Most respondents told FIND/SVP they've cut out a portion of their prime-time television viewing to log on, while others have reduced the time they spend reading books and magazines. It's no wonder advertisers are turning to the Net, trying to recapture some of the audience they're losing from the more traditional media sources.

TARGETING ADVERTISERS

Because the Web reaches a worldwide population, even the most narrowly targeted site can attract a large audience. There are sites for gaming enthusiasts, sports fans, working parents, housewives, music aficionados, researchers, local community activists, you name it. Sites with very clear audiences are valuable to advertisers. How do you determine which advertisers will want to target your audience? One way is to research Web sites with content similar to your own and learn what types of marketers advertise there. You can use a variety of sources to find out which Web sites accept advertising. These include AdSpend, a subscription service from Jupiter Communications (http://www.jup.com) that tracks Web advertising revenue based on both online advertisers and publishing sites, and the Interactive Advertising Sourcebook, a directory from Standard Rate and Data Services (http://www.srds.com), a publisher who has been compiling media directories for over 75 years. These sources separate their listings into categories, so finding Web sites similar to your own is much easier.

Jupiter's AdSpend tracks advertising on over 100 Web sites, which the research firm estimates collect 93 percent of all Web ad revenue. The highest-spending category of Internet advertiser is Web-related products and services (39 percent), followed by computer-related goods (24 percent), consumer goods (8 percent), telecommunications products (8 percent), cars and automotive accessories (5 percent), financial services, insurance, and real estate (4 percent), and publishing and media (4 percent). The two final categories, other services and all other, both came in at 4 percent (see Figure 1-16).

Figure 1-16

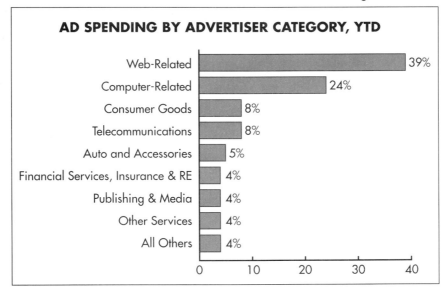

Categories of Internet advertisers

At the time of this writing, the top 20 online advertisers according to AdSpend (shown in Table 1-3) represent only a handful of marketer categories, including search engines and other online services (Lycos, Yahoo!, Sportsline USA), computer hardware and software and related products (Netscape, Microsoft, Oracle), telecommunications (AT&T, Nynex, Sprint), and automobiles (Toyota, Ford).

Table 1-3 Top 20 Internet Advertisers

RANK	ADVERTISER	MONTHLY SPENDING	YTD SPENDING	YTD RANK
1	Microsoft	$1,033.8	$4,660.7	1
2	Netscape	680.0	3,439.7	2
3	IBM	556.0	3,122.8	3
4	InfoSeek	537.4	2,826.8	5
5	Excite	527.4	2,821.8	6
6	AT&T	505.6	2,912.8	4
7	Nynex	472.3	2,344.8	8
8	McKinley Group	469.1	2,392.7	7
9	Lycos	431.0	2,151.4	10
10	Yahoo!	416.7	2,173.3	9
11	Sportsline USA	233.1	1,196.6	14
12	MSNBC	185.6	299.4	63
13	Toyota Motor Sales USA	182.6	1,247.3	13
14	Amazon.com	173.9	657.1	26
15	Travelocity	172.2	747.1	23
16	Individual Inc.	170.7	1,160.1	15
17	Oracle	166.3	553.5	31
18	Ford	166.2	505.7	36
19	Digital Equipment	165.0	1,571.0	12
20	Sprint	154.9	923.7	17

Source: Jupiter Communications, 1996

In its monthly tracking of Web advertiser revenue, AdSpend shows that certain categories of Web sites—a small percentage of all types of Web sites—garner the bulk of online ad dollars. In general, Web-related sites (those sites offering information, products, and services relevant to the World Wide Web) pick up 53 percent of all online ad revenue, while 16 percent and 15 percent goes to computer and publications Web sites, respectively. Four percent of online ad revenue each went to general interest sites, publishing sites, and sports and outdoor-oriented sites, while only 2 percent went to listings sites and 1 percent to entertainment sites. A final 1 percent was doled out to "other" sites (see Figure 1-17).

Figure 1-17

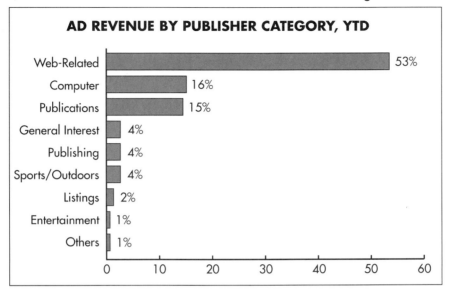

The flow of advertising dollars

The top 20 online publishers getting all of this dough can be divided into a handful of categories: search engines, content sites from traditional media, computer-related products, and sports. These appear in Table 1-4.

In addition to visiting the major online players and any Web sites with content or purpose similar to your own, be sure to visit some other heavily trafficked sites. Two excellent sources to use to find out which sites are the current online favorites are PC-Meter, from Port Washington, New York-based NPD Group (http://www.npd.com), and Web21 (http://www.web21.com/).

PC-Meter provides a cross-sample of U.S. households owning PCs running the Windows operating system. It monitors activity by user, across browser types, across online services, and page-by-page Web surfing. PC-Meter is unlike other methods of tracking Web usage because it is a controlled group. The people in the group have software installed on their PCs to record what pages are being displayed on the user's screen, whether stored locally on the user's PC, a service proxy server, or a commercial online service.

Table 1-4 Top 20 Publishers

RANK	PUBLISHER	MONTHLY REVENUE	YTD REVENUE	YTD RANK
1.	Netscape	$2,795.6	$15,017.8	1
2.	Yahoo!	1,712.2	9,051.8	2
3.	InfoSeek	1,529.7	8,766.1	3
4.	Excite	1,105.0	5,741.0	5
5.	Lycos	1,080.0	6,213.2	4
6.	WebCrawler	958.0	4,058.0	8
7.	CNET	879.8	4,862.3	6
8.	ZD Net	677.6	4,514.3	7
9.	Magellan Internet Directory	591.5	2,214.0	13
10.	CMP TechWeb	526.7	2,894.7	12
11.	Pathfinder	508.6	2,927.8	11
12.	Wall St. Journal Interactive	484.0	1,641.7	17
13.	ESPN SportsZone	460.0	3,605.0	9
14.	Individual NewsPage	446.0	3007.1	10
15.	CNN Interactive	380.0	2,200.0	14
16.	USA Today	362.3	1,710.2	16
17.	Jumbo!	228.0	1,041.8	19
18.	HotWired	225.0	1,916.3	15
19.	Playboy	175.3	1,009.9	21
20.	Hearst HomeArts	157.0	609.0	26

Source: Jupiter Communications, 1996

Web21 is another service that measures popular Web sites. Based in Palo Alto, California, Web21 conducts weekly rankings of Web sites based on data obtained from server file logs, traffic samples at key points on the Internet, and interviews with Webmasters. Founded in May 1995, Web21 was the first online service to rank the top 100 Web sites by the number of hits and links to each site. (Web21 excludes X-rated sites from its listings.) Web21 lists sites that belong to a single source, for example, the sites hosted by StarWave include ESPN SportsZone, Mr. Showbiz, and the NBA Web site, which rank at number 2 in the most recent poll. A comparison of the findings from both of these sources appears in Table 1-5.

chapter **1** HIT FACTORY

Table 1-5 Top 50 Consumer Web Sites

RANK	PC-METER	WEB21
1	Netscape	Yahoo!, Yahooligans!, Yahoo! Sports, My Yahoo!
2	America Online	ESPN SportsZone, Mr. Showbiz, NBA Web site
3	Yahoo!	America Online, WebCrawler
4	WebCrawler	Pathfinder, Warner Bros., HBO, DC Comics, CNN
5	Excite	ZD NET
6	Infoseek	HappyPuppy
7	Lycos	Excite, Magellan, City.Net
8	Prodigy	Internet Movie Database, the UK Edition
9	Alta Vista	Alta Vista
10	GNN	Sun Microsystems' Java site
11	Microsoft	RealAudio, TimeCast
12	MSN (Microsoft Network)	USA Today
13	GeoCities	Lycos, Point
14	CompuServe	Sony, Sony Music, Sony Interactive Entertainment, Sony Computer Entertainment
15	Magellan	Apple Computer
16	Netcom	SportsLine
17	Earthlink	Silicon Graphics, Reality Studios
18	CRIS	HP Computers
19	Angelfire	cInet, Search.com, News.com
20	Shareware.com	The World Wide Web Organization
21	University of Illinois, Urbana	United Media
22	ZD Net	WebChat Broadcasting System
23	M.I.T.	Windows95.com's Software Repository
24	AT&T Toll-Free Directory	Imagine Publishing's TheNet, Ultra Game Players, PCGamer, MacAddict, Next Generation, BootNet
25	MSNBC	WhoWhere?
26	Pathfinder	Disney
27	NBC	IBM
28	WebCom	Intel
29	AT&T	Games Domain
30	CNET	NFL Online

continued

49

Table 1-5 (Continued)

RANK	PC-METER	WEB21
31	CNN	The China Times Online
32	Switchboard.com	Macromedia Multimedia
33	RealAudio	Jumbo
34	Playboy	Adobe
35	PrimeNet	Shareware.com
36	Tripod	Neosoft, Inc.
37	Best	Star Trek: First Contact
38	University of Michigan	The Center for Disease Control
39	Sprynet	CricInfo, Cricket Home Page
40	Carnegie Mellon University	The City of Los Angeles
41	Mindspring	HotWired, HotBot
42	IOS	Web Personals
43	IBM	MTV
44	Search.com	Hong Kong Star
45	Xmission	Intellicast Weather
46	Teleport	Gamelan Java Repository
47	NOAA (U.S. Dept. of Commerce, National Oceanic and Atmospheric Admin.)	Hollywood Online
48	International Olympic Committee	FreeBSD Inc.
49	Disney	Cisco Systems
50	University of North Carolina, USA Today (tie)	AsiaOne Online Commerce Center

Source: September 1996 PC-Meter   Source: December 1996 Web21

WHAT WORKS?

After visiting various sites, you'll see that they vary greatly in their advertising presentation. You'll find ad banners both at the top and the bottom of pages. Eye-tracking research conducted by Perception Research Services (Fort Lee, New Jersey) shows that elements on the top half of Web pages are nearly twice as likely to be seen and considered than those on the bottom half of the screen.

In determining how to create advertising possibilities, consider why a user is at your site. If users typically come looking for specific information and don't plan to linger, they are far more likely to notice and act upon an ad at the top of the page — either while they are obtaining the information they were originally looking for, or while they are waiting for the information or graphics to download. However, in those instances where users will have to read a lengthy document, you might want to place an additional ad banner at the bottom of the page, where they will see it when they finish reading. Wherever you place ads on your site, if the message has relevance, the user will be more inclined to pay attention to it and recall it later. A recent online poll conducted via New York ad agency BBDO's TechSetter Hotline asked users: "How much attention do you pay to advertising on the Internet?" Fifty-one percent said some; 19 percent said a lot; 25 percent said not much; and 5 percent said none.

Advertising on the Web is clearly gaining ground as content providers experiment with the new medium and marketers commit to it as part of their media plans. Marketers are proceeding cautiously when it comes to advertising on the Internet, but once the confusion and uncertainty over standardized models clears up, the Web will reach its full potential as a viable communication medium.

The Internet also holds promise as a medium for commercial enterprise, from conducting banking and stock transactions to purchasing items online via cash or credit card. Online merchants have had to navigate the shoals of a narrowly defined and skeptical buyer population as well as the limitations of currently available technologies.

Understanding Electronic Commerce

While some computer-savvy professionals regularly buy goods over the Internet, most consumers are still reluctant to give out their credit card numbers online, where they assume would-be hackers are lurking to steal their personal information at the click of a mouse. A survey conducted in November 1996 by Visa International found that only 4 percent of adult credit card holders have ever purchased anything via the Internet.

In spite of consumer reluctance to make purchases online, a recent report from Forrester Research cites three-quarters of the Fortune 1,000's leading-edge Web developers expecting to deliver online transactions via the Internet in 1997. This represents a doubling of companies' efforts to do business over the Internet, as businesses expand their use of the Web beyond *brochure-ware* to a transactional Web where customers place orders online. Factors driving businesses toward electronic commerce (e-commerce) include the number of U.S. households going online, the number of businesses connecting to the Internet, and the availability of e-commerce technology solutions for secure transactions.

WHAT SELLS?

Some are finding that Internet retailing is already a very lucrative business. In fact, the market for consumer online retail sales should reach $7 billion in the year 2000, according to Forrester Research. The key is building trust with consumers through branding and security assurances. Another key is offering the kind of products that will sell online. These typically include things that consumers research prior to making their purchase, such as vacation and travel packages as well as computer hardware and software, books, records, and games.

It is harder to sell things that usually require try-ons or tactile stimulation to make the sale, and things people buy mainly on impulse. Many savvy retailers like Express (http://www.express.style.com; site shown in Figure 1-18) offer online coupons to pull consumers into the store where the product can make a broader sensory appeal. Others offer discounts on their online goods to encourage online spending.

chapter **1** HIT FACTORY

Figure 1-18

The Express site offers online coupons to pull consumers into the store.

Internet-based stock-trading is quite successful among a certain group of people. Charles Schwab's *Web Trading* program, launched in March 1996, has grown to more than 100,000 users, according to Chief Information Officer Dawn Lepore, and that's without advertising the service. People in the program trade stocks, treasury bonds, mutual funds, options, and the like. Forrester Research predicts that revenue from Internet financial services will grow from $240 million in 1996 to over $22 billion in 2000 due to the rise in PC banking and mutual fund transactions online. At Wells Fargo, approximately 110,000 customers are using the Internet to do their day-to-day banking. The financial institution is working on security and encryption methods with standards organizations and on its own, in an effort to get additional consumers to do their banking online due to the cost advantages of conducting transactions online.

ELECTRONIC PAYMENT SYSTEMS

In late 1995, Visa and MasterCard International agreed to codevelop SET, an open, interoperable standard for secure electronic transactions on the Internet. This agreement, in conjunction with the rise of other electronic payment systems, will help fuel e-commerce revenues. Microsoft and Netscape Communications both support the SET standard on their browsers. In addition to its work with MasterCard, Visa is pursuing more than a dozen electronic commerce ventures around the world and plans to launch an Internet-based secure commerce program in 1997.

MasterCard is testing a secure digital wallet developed by IBM that should be available toward the end of 1997. The digital wallet is a password-protected program that holds a consumer's encrypted credit card information in one place (the "wallet"), and is part of IBM's CommercePOINT family of electronic commerce solutions. It will be offered with Netscape Navigator and will incorporate the Visa and MasterCard SET protocol, allowing consumers and merchants to conduct bankcard transactions in cyberspace as securely as they do in retail stores. Other secure electronic payment systems currently available for wary online shoppers include the CyberCash Wallet and the CheckFree Digital Wallet.

> **The Internet is a buyer-driven, not a sales-driven, medium.... To deal with customers on the Internet effectively, you'll need to handle customer service issues online and understand the unique characteristics of the online shopping experience.**

The CyberCash Wallet from Reston, Virginia-based CyberCash (http://www.cybercash.com) is a secure password-protected digital wallet that encrypts credit card information as well as the details of any online purchase. The wallet works with virtually any online browser, and is automatically called up when a user clicks on a designated button in the merchant's order page. When a user makes a purchase, the transaction is sent to the merchant, who adds additional transactional information and sends the information along to CyberCash. CyberCash then reformats it and sends it to the bank. After the bank approves the purchase, the transaction is sent to the CyberCash server for secure encryption and back to the merchant, who then sends the consumer an electronic receipt and fills the order. From the user's standpoint, this entire process is virtually seamless and takes just a moment to complete.

In addition to CyberCash, the company also offers CyberCoin, a micropayment service that enables cash transactions over the Internet. CyberCoin was created to handle smaller online purchases that cost between 25 cents and $10, like software downloads or access to certain information areas of a Web site. Like the CyberCash Wallet, CyberCoin secures a consumer's financial information using encryption technology. It is FDIC-insured and, like an ATM card, debits the user's checking account when a purchase is made.

The CheckFree Digital Wallet from Columbus-based Checkfree Corporation (http://www.checkfree.com) enables consumers to securely hold financial information for up to 11 checking accounts from multiple banks. It is compatible with CyberCash, and can be used at any participating CyberCash merchant as well as participating CheckFree merchants and banks. Consumers can use CheckFree to make a single online purchase, and can also schedule CheckFree to make regular payments to creditors. Like CyberCoin, the CheckFree system debits a user's checking account and sends an electronic credit to the payee. Partners in the product include AT&T, Tribune, payroll services giant ADP, and a host of banks that have agreed to validate Checkfree's product.

ONLINE CUSTOMER SERVICE

The Internet is a buyer-driven, not a sales-driven, medium. The customer seeks you out and makes contact with you, thereby turning the traditional selling process upside down. To deal with customers on the Internet effectively, you'll need to handle customer service issues online and understand the unique characteristics of the online shopping experience. While many of your customers will be happy contacting you via e-mail, you should also supply an 800 number for those who want more immediate service. Be sure to make the number easy to find on your Web site—it's all too easy for a potential customer to get frustrated and click away to another merchant's site.

When dealing with customers who do communicate with you via e-mail, remember that netiquette requires a response to e-mail within 24 to 48 hours. Indeed, due to the inherent immediacy of the medium, most users are not willing to tolerate anything short of one-day turnaround. In a call center environment, you wouldn't expect your customers to wait on hold for 20 minutes (especially while they're racking up online connection fees). Additionally, the online world is a more casual environment. People type e-mail in lowercase, often abbreviating or sometimes omitting standard punctuation. While this is not an excuse for you to conduct sloppy customer service, you should communicate with your customers in the same open, friendly spirit they communicate with you.

In a study conducted this year by Matrixx Marketing, the Ogden, Utah-based call center service bureau surveyed companies to gauge their customer service effectiveness. The company e-mailed a simple question to 100 randomly selected Fortune 500 companies and tracked the response time and quality of their answers. The company also noted the method of customer contact each company provided on its Web page, including e-mail, postal service, or telephone.

The findings were quite surprising. Only 25 percent of the companies responded to the question within two weeks, and only 17 percent of those responded via e-mail, which was the medium that their customers chose to communicate with them. That kind of treatment is almost like telling your customers you have an 800 number and not answering the phone, or asking them to leave a message but then never returning their calls.

WEB COMMERCE SERVERS

To conduct transactions on the Internet and make your site ready for online retailing, you will need to install a Web commerce server. Commerce-based Web server software (as opposed to publishing-based Web server software) supports the Secure Sockets Layer (SSL) and the S-HTTP Secure Hypertext Transfer Protocol (S-HTTP), which form the basis of encryption between Web browsers and Web servers, allowing for security in handling sensitive information on the Internet. (For more details on security issues, see Chapter 5, Registering and Staking Out Cyberturf.) The three top-selling

Web server software products for Internet transactions are Microsoft's Internet Information Server, Netscape's Commerce Server, and O'Reilly & Associates Web Site Professional. All three offer secure transaction processing, and all run on the Windows NT operating system, a platform commonly used to host Web sites.

A CASE IN POINT: VIRTUAL VINEYARDS

In January 1995, the Internet welcomed a direct marketer who pioneered what a successful e-commerce site could do—Virtual Vinyards (http://www.virtualvin.com). The site was founded by two friends, Peter Granoff and Robert Olson. Granoff, a wine connoisseur, had long been distressed by the trend in the wine-making industry to reduce wine-making from a fine craft to a numerical scoring system. The trend, he believed, was especially harmful to those who made wine as an art. Olson's background was in computers, and he'd spent several years studying the potential of interactive marketing. The World Wide Web looked like the perfect platform to put his ideas in practice, but he lacked a product to sell. As the two discussed their theories over a bottle of wine, an idea was born—why not sell bottled wines from northern California to consumers worldwide via the World Wide Web?

How often had someone they known been perplexed over the appropriate type of wine to purchase for various occasions? Salesclerks offered little or no help; the buying environment was often intimidating. By selling wine over the Web, one could offer buyers in-depth information about products and the people who made them in a nonthreatening environment and in a friendly fashion, allowing consumers to shop and learn about wine at their own pace.

San Francisco-based Virtual Vinyards (shown in Figure 1-19) launched its Web site offering fine wines from California shipped directly to the consumer, anywhere, worldwide. Based on customer requests, the site added specialty foods from the state to its portfolio in the fall. The customers who make their purchases through the online retailer have been identified as technologically affluent, busy people who are repeat buyers. Customers can research products themselves through an online directory, or they can get suggestions and advice from Peter Granoff personally. Although the folks at Virtual Vinyards won't reveal their sales figures, Marketing Manager Cyndy

Ainsworth said the site receives several thousand visitors daily. During the holiday season, the traffic rises tremendously, she said.

Figure 1-19

Virtual Vineyards is a true cybersuccess story.

Virtual Vinyards' two most effective methods of advertising are public relations and word of mouth. The online retailer uses an outside public relations agency in the Bay Area that has been successful in getting wide press coverage in both traditional print and online publications. There have also been interviews with Mr. Olson and Mr. Granoff in the audio and video media, Ainsworth said, adding, "When we're featured somewhere, we see a bump in traffic, so we know that's one way people find out about us."

Those who shop at Virtual Vinyards tell their friends about their online experiences. "We often call people who have shopped our store and talk to them about how they liked the service and how they found out about us," Ainsworth said. "Many times they say they heard about us through a friend."

chapter **1** HIT FACTORY

When Virtual Vinyards spends money on advertising, it's usually in precisely targeted areas. The company has purchased the keyword *wine* on the Excite and InfoSeek search engines, so people who are looking for information related to wine will see a banner ad from Virtual Vinyards. In addition, the company has a link on America Online that also pulls traffic from AOL's 6 million subscribers.

Outside the Internet environment, the company has placed a limited amount of print ads in food sections of newspapers when a feature on wine is running. The company is looking more closely at increasing its expenditure on print advertisements to target people who already have access to the Internet or those who are interested in it. Other advertising methods have included a direct mail campaign offering users free biscotti for coming to the site and registering, and a free six-bar sampler of Belgian chocolate with any $25 purchase. Ainsworth said the jury is still out on this advertising method, but the company can track the registrations to find out exactly who responded to their offer. Another traffic-driving campaign was a CD-ROM created in conjunction with Condé Nast's Epicurious food site (http://www.epicurious.com). The CD-ROM contains a direct Internet connection that links users to a jointly developed Virtual Vinyards/Epicurious Web site, so people coming online from the CD-ROM will know where to locate the retailer.

In addition to increasing its print advertising expenditures in 1997, Virtual Vinyards is also considering expanding into other lifestyle products, although Ainsworth would not say what types of products that represents. Regardless of their plans, it's almost certain that Olson and Granoff are toasting the success of their online operations over a fine bottle of California wine.

Words to the wise

It's easy to get caught up in the bells and whistles of new technology and forget the primary objective in setting up a Web site. Regardless of mission, your objective is not very different from the guidelines that a business of any size has followed for centuries: (1) get the potential customer in, (2) get the potential customer involved, and (3) make the prospect a repeat customer. Similarly, there are some age-old guidelines for business courtesy that can be effectively applied to online offerings:

* Design an intuitive Web site — one that's easy for a first-time customer to use.
* Use English or some other well-known language.
* Be proactive in offering support.
* Be sure that your server offers round-the-clock service.
* Respect the users' privacy.
* Be alert to security issues.
* Understand the difference between marketing your site and marketing your products.

Design an intuitive Web site. Not everyone has a super-fast modem and the latest Java-enabled browser. In the 1950s the number of color versus black-and-white TVs never stopped anyone from seeing *I Love Lucy*. Unfortunately, many of today's Web sites are a challenge for even the fastest and most advanced computer systems to download and run. Making a site easy to load and navigate should come before making it glitzy. If you use *image maps*, also provide text-based links. Avoid obscure icons: even if everyone in your department knows what they are, outside users might not. Make the pages short and quick to load, with standard HTML that most browsers can deal with.

Try accessing your Web site from a computer with a slow connection — a 14.4 modem, for instance. This may give you some insight into what your users experience when they access your site. If loading the site seems frustrating, it's time to make some technical changes.

Use English or some other well-known language. Think about how your copy is going to be read online. Being in cyberspace doesn't suspend grammar, and if you're trying to reach those older adults all the surveys say are flocking to the Web, remember that they may not appreciate too much liberalness with contemporary jargon—technical or social. If your copy is hard to read, users are going to move on. Use short paragraphs and short words; they're easier to read onscreen than long ones. Use bulleted lists wherever possible.

Be proactive in offering support. Too many Web sites follow the *set 'em and forget 'em* model for interactivity. Once users are online, so the belief goes, the work is done, and the site has no further responsibility for keeping users involved. This is particularly evident in the infrequency with which some sites change their content. As more people get on the Web, though, it's crucial that Web sites be proactive and up to date. Respond to e-mail promptly, whether it's from people looking for more information on your business, customers offering compliments or complaints, or students looking to do reports on your company. Community relations are important, and on the Web *community* can be anywhere on the globe. Act on the suggestions, comments, and criticisms you receive on your Web site. If they're complaints, don't take them personally, but rather see what's going wrong (or what's going right) and do something about it.

Be sure that your server offers round-the-clock service. As a global medium, the Web doesn't end its business hours at 5 p.m. in your time zone. Indeed, Web sites generate a surprising amount of activity during off hours.

Respect the users' privacy. It wasn't that long ago that business transactions of any kind on the Internet were sneered at. In fact, they were largely forbidden before the Internet went commercial in the early 1990s. Even today, in the Net's more business-friendly climate, the wrong business strategies can get you into trouble, and one of the ways this can happen fastest is if you violate a user's privacy.

For example, when users volunteer information for a survey, you have a special responsibility to keep that material confidential. Don't sell or give this information to others, and don't mail, fax, or e-mail users future notices from your company unless they have agreed to receive such information. Survey pages should expressly mention that any information provided by the visitor will be held in the strictest confidence. Give users the option of refusing future notices and updates.

Be alert to security issues. This has become a major concern on the Web. Simply put, servers, companies, and customers are all vulnerable to security breaches if careful technical and legal steps are not taken to guard against them. Your server should have robust firewall software (for more details on security issues see Chapter 5, Building the Organization, and Appendix A, Killer Apps), and your system for distributing and maintaining passwords should be as foolproof as possible. Investigate methods of secure credit card transactions as they become available. Alert your attorney to the possibility of someone establishing a bogus site using your corporate image —as a joke, a scam, an act of sabotage, or simple harassment. There's little that can be done to preempt such an action. Legal alternatives will become clearer as the judicial system gains experience with cyberspace law.

Understand the difference between marketing your site and marketing your products. Too many marketing efforts smell of confusion about what their mission is: to market the site or the product. While this problem usually arises due to lack of forethought about the appropriate mission, both efforts need attention and often require different strategies. Huge hitcount or click-through rates are not goals in themselves, and in spite of the astonishing growth of the Web, it has nowhere near the importance or impact of other major media. Significant growth in the viewership of a site simply cannot be achieved without the use of traditional media. However, significant support for overall marketing and sales efforts can be achieved on the Web. Don't lose sight of the message of the medium. The audience is there to be led, but if you lead them astray you can use the medium to lose them as well.

Summary

In its short existence, the Web has come a long way toward becoming a mass vehicle for communications efforts. Savvy marketers are using it to expand their brand messages, interact with consumers, and conduct transactions in real time. By embracing the Web as a marketing vehicle, you can reap the benefits of the Web's practically limitless ability to communicate with your customers. If Burma Shave had embraced television—and, ultimately, the Internet—as an advertising medium, it surely would have placed billboards on the information superhighway along with those road signs along the asphalt highways. The possibilities for the emergence and acceptance of new products and services face us with unprecedented opportunity: reaching global markets at small town marketing rates. Arguably, there are lower barriers to entry now than at any other time since media became the predominant financial element in bringing a new product or service to market. There are simply too many possibilities to imagine as this technology evolves into the next millennium.

chapter 2

CLARIFYING YOUR MISSION

IN THE RUSH to retain a competitive advantage in the global marketplace of the twenty-first century—or just to get *something* online—designers often lose track of a site's underlying mission. In the early days of commercial Web development, a company planning a site might have been able to get away with a less-than-thorough analysis of the business case behind their plan. Simply having a Web site was rare enough that it made a valuable statement—on the order of displaying commissioned artwork in the reception area of the company headquarters. As Web sites have proliferated, however, and users have become more sophisticated, sites are increasingly judged in terms of the coherence and quality of their offerings, not simply for the fact of their existence. As a result, in spite of the drudgery involved, it is as vital to formulate a clear expression of a Web project's mission as it is for any new business undertaking. Having a clearly articulated mission statement affords a Web project several advantages:

- It enables the project mission to be integrated with the existing company mission.
- It provides for alignment of team members around a common, agreed-upon vision.
- It ensures that business principles rather than technology for its own sake will drive the site design.
- It provides benchmarks by which to measure the success or failure of the site.

This chapter aims to reinforce the importance of clearly identifying and articulating the mission and purpose of a Web site project *before* diving into detailed design specifications. The first section of the chapter, "The Mission Proposition," identifies the principal components of an appropriate mission statement and briefly describes the main varieties of each component. The second section, "Mission Implementations," maps the model and its components to examples of several successful Web sites.

The Mission Proposition

A comprehensive mission statement identifies

- The product to be developed
- The target audience
- The business objectives for delivering this product

Figure 2-1 lists major categories for each of these components, and the following sections describe each in more detail. Keep in mind that the categories are descriptive rather than prescriptive. Many Web site projects incorporate some of the characteristics of several different missions; others defy simple categorization.

chapter **2** CLARIFYING YOUR MISSION

Figure 2-1

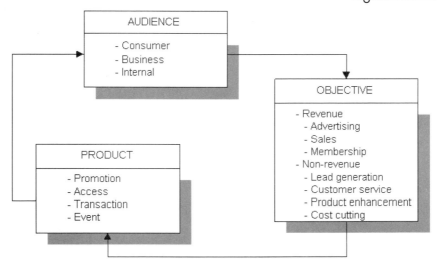

The three dimensions of a Web site mission

DEFINING THE PRODUCT

Web sites typically offer a combination of *goods* and *services*. Goods means any content, information, or commodity that might be stored by the site and delivered electronically. Services means the methods by which the goods are delivered. Web site goods are related to a company's standard products in one of the following ways:

* **Conventional**. Existing products that use the Web merely as a delivery channel—electronic catalogs, software distributed online, or corporate statements that are also distributed in print format.

* **Extended**. Enhanced or adapted products that take into account the Web as a medium in which to develop goods—a database of company information, a tracking service, or an online customer service center.

* **Original**. New goods that create an original business enterprise with the Web as part of its foundation—a new electronic publication or a game.

67

Most business sites fall into the first or second categories. They do not have the resources to launch an entirely new enterprise in what is still a volatile, entrepreneurial climate. Nor are they in a position to use the Web as a replacement for other practices, such as 800 number services or direct mail campaigns. Instead, most companies in these first two categories use the Web as another channel of distribution or communication to

- Articulate corporate identity
- Identify prospective customers
- Promote products and services
- Provide customer support for products
- Archive and provide access to company information resources
- Sell products

While these communications may be initially more complicated to manage than their offline counterparts, they offer a safe way for companies to evolve their Internet strategy as they wait to see how their customers react to these new channels.

The third category of Web site products involves enterprises designed from the ground up as stand-alone Web ventures. While you may not be planning to launch such a venture, it is worth considering this type of enterprise, since any corporate Web site might include elements of it in its design. For example, you may not be planning to build the next great online magazine, but your company may decide to publish a magazine-style online periodical. Similarly, you may not want to have a site devoted to entertainment or to fostering community, but there may be good reason to include these as one aspect of your site's mission statement. Companies in this category use the Web as Internet-based services with the goal to

- Foster community
- Publish news and magazine content
- Provide directory, reference, and research services
- Entertain
- Broadcast event-based content

There are four distinct orientations toward the delivery of content: promotions, access, transactions, and events. These elements may exist separately or in combination on a given site. Identifying them is important, in part because it indicates the central functions of the site, and also because each service has particular back-end needs, in terms of the technology and management required to maintain it.

Promotions

Promotional sites are in the business of generating sales, either directly or indirectly. Some of the more common direct promotional methods include contests, giveaways, special discounts, and coupons. Indirectly, promotions tend to foster a sense of community so that the product or sponsoring company figures as an important part of the consumer's experience. Indirect promotion also helps to establish brand awareness—people enjoy the fun and games at the Disney site, for example, and their interest in the company's new movie productions grows at the same time.

Promotional sites are frequently time sensitive. A good deal of work is required to put them up in a timely fashion and to take them down or reorganize them when they have served their promotional purpose. Disney (`http://www.disney.com`) launched an extensive Web promotion for its movie *Toy Story*. Once the movie was released, aspects of the *Toy Story* site were integrated into the Disney site as a whole and became more of a supplement to the movie than an introduction to it. Other examples of time-sensitive Web sites include Apple Computer's Webcast promotion of the 1997 MacWorld show in San Francisco and the Mediadome broadcast of the San Francisco New Year's Eve celebration.

Access

Sites that provide access to text-based or multimedia content constitute a large percentage of existing Web applications. Some, such as Microsoft's Slate (`http:www.slate.com`), follow a standard publishing model where content is submitted to an editorial staff on a regular basis. Others — such as discussion forums like AOL's Motley Fool — rely more heavily on content from users.

There are two principal means of providing user access to content: browsing and searching. Browsing involves creating lists of content and allowing users to navigate through the lists to find what they want. Searching consists of free text or field-oriented (database) searching. In either case the user generates and directly inputs a request, and the system matches and delivers replies.

Some sites focus on the information itself as a product, serving as electronic magazines. Examples of this type of information access include Starwave's Mr. Showbiz (`http://www.mrshowbiz.com`) and CNN Interactive's news and information site (`http://www.cnn.com`). Although these sites incorporate a search engine, their content is designed to be explored one page at a time, much as one might flip through a print magazine. Other information-access sites focus on more sophisticated means of locating and delivering information, such as directory or reference services. These sites tend to require more technical development to be successful, and are usually database driven. Examples of this kind include Travelocity (`http://www.travelocity.com`), a travel information and reservations system, and MapQuest (`http://www.mapquest.com`), which provides access to an extensive collection of geographical maps.

Transactions

A transaction is an exchange of goods for consideration conducted between a user and the site. Transaction-based sites are among the most expensive to develop, involving both sophisticated means of recording and tracking transactions and methods for ensuring their security. Many transaction sites already exist on the Web, embracing a wide range of products from books and electronic equipment to equities, mutual funds, insurance policies, and employee health benefits. Online banking services have appeared that offer deposit and withdrawal, check writing, and loan applications.

Events

Web sites that provide event-driven services are a relatively new but burgeoning online offering, thanks primarily to a host of rapidly improving technologies that allow for the real-time delivery of audio and video content. As a result, sites that feature event programming are beginning to spring up. Some of these sites resemble traditional radio and television broadcasting more than they resemble traditional Web publishing.

Like TV and radio, Webcasting can be a production-heavy enterprise, requiring a staff with both technical and creative skill sets as well as equipment for capturing live events or recording material for future broadcast. In addition to state-of-the-art *Webcasts*, there are other high-end event services like interactive soap operas and network-based gaming environments. Other event offerings such as online chats and groupware environments require some initial set-up and ongoing moderation, but carry less overhead requirements than the high-end stuff.

DEFINING YOUR AUDIENCE

Daytime soap operas are for homebodies and the staffs that support them. Drivetime radio is for business commuters. Cartoons are for kids (usually). To whom are you talking? Audience is a critical component in the mission of any media venture, and should be a consideration in the very core of design. The clarification of this element can also be critical if you plan to support your site with advertising revenues, and need to document demographics on your visitors to potential sponsors. Web audiences can be broken down into three types:

* Consumers
* Internal staff
* Business-to-Business

Consumers. This is the most general audience group. They may go to a site for a specific reason, out of general curiosity, or because they were enticed there by an ad banner. Consumer-oriented sites are likely to offer a high degree of eye candy, fun and games, and other techniques to draw visitors into exploring the site further. Just because people are casual visitors, however, doesn't mean they are without expectations. If they are at your site to make a purchase of some kind, they are likely to want results, and they will judge the quality of the service provided—not the quality of the special effects. Sites designed for consumers need to be easy to use, because in many cases the visitor is not an experienced computer user and requires more hand-holding than other audience sectors.

Internal staff. About the time that companies began to wonder whether their Web sites were really providing any value to the world at large, a new phenomenon dubbed *intranets* hit the Internet community. An intranet is simply an internal corporate network that makes use of Internet technologies to provide the same sorts of communication and information delivery services within an organization that the Internet offers the world at large. The intranet concept has caught on rapidly because the technology *works;* managers unhappy with homegrown internal business networks are eager to switch their existing corporate infrastructure over. The virtue of the Web as an information delivery mechanism is that it is relatively easy and cost-effective to use.

> **The virtue of the Web as an information delivery mechanism is that it is relatively easy and cost-effective to use.**

The upshot of this movement is a new class of audience consisting of a company's employees. In general they want access to employee information and the ability to conduct company business efficiently more than they want entertainment. On the other hand, promotion has internal value as any human resources specialist will tell you, and an intranet site needs to communicate in ways that more resemble the promotional character of many consumer-oriented Web sites.

Business-to-business. Recently, a new kind of network has begun to attract attention. Called an *extranet*, this variation on the Internet theme involves an Internet-based network to serve a company's business partners. An extranet is typically secured behind a firewall much like an intranet except that it extends beyond the company's physical boundaries. The focus of a business-to-business network is on establishing easy and effective means of communicating and transacting business activities. Currently the number of sites devoted to business-to-business activity is still relatively small, but look for this class of networks to develop rapidly in the near future.

DEFINING YOUR BUSINESS OBJECTIVE

In the midst of competitive pressure to create a Web site presence and technological pressure to make use of all the latest advances, it is surprisingly easy to lose sight of a simple but critical question: Why does the company want a Web site? An astounding number of very impressive sites have been developed without a clear sense of why, from the owner's standpoint, they were built. Efforts such as these sometimes result in excellent sources of information, but are doomed to disappear if they lack a means of justifying their existence and supporting themselves. Business objectives come in two flavors: direct revenue and indirect revenue.

Direct revenue

Sites that generate revenue, although growing in number, remain something of the Holy Grail of Web development. Everyone wants a profitable site, everyone knows of the handful of successes, and everyone believes that the Internet is rife with profit-making opportunities. However, still precious few organizations are actually making money from their Web sites. Currently there are four models for generating income from a Web site:

- Advertising
- Sales
- Membership and subscriptions
- Technology licensing

Of these four, advertising has picked up steam the most quickly. At this time, almost every major revenue-generating site includes some measure of advertising as a way of paying the bills. Many more sites have begun to offer online sales, typically using some form of security to protect themselves and their customers, but there is not yet a strong confidence level among consumers about online shopping. Membership models are the most difficult to make work, in part because of the Internet's tradition of free information. Most publishing enterprises have found it easier to charge advertisers than to exact a fee from users. However, the number of successful subscription-based services is steadily increasing, a sign perhaps of the increasing value of the information available as well as of changing Internet mores.

The licensing of Web technology has only emerged recently as a revenue-generating source, and although it is only applicable in a small percentage of cases, it is nonetheless worth mentioning. One way that services relying on proprietary Web technologies can make money is to charge a fee to allow other companies to provide access to their service. MapQuest, for example, offers customized access to their map generation services for a small fee. One of the virtues of the distributed nature of the Internet is that it makes it easy for technology owners to distribute their services through other entities without relinquishing control of the technology itself.

Indirect revenue

A Web site mission premised on generating revenue is still something of an uncertain venture, and the vast majority of Web site owners continue to operate with other objectives in mind. However, although trying to collect revenue from a Web site involves taking a risk, you can at least tell whether the site works or not by the amount of money it generates. If you're not trying to collect revenue, you face the challenge of measuring the site's success. With any of the non-revenue-generating rationales, make sure you set up some quantitative models to determine whether your site is actually achieving its stated objectives. Here are some of the reasons to set up a site without direct revenue:

* Lead generation and prospecting
* Sales and marketing support
* Brand awareness
* Product supplementation
* Cost Reduction

Lead generation and prospecting. This is the Web equivalent of direct marketing. The standard approach is to offer something to users — such as free software, magazine subscriptions, sweepstakes entry, or access to information — in exchange for filling out a registration form that the site sponsor can add to its database of contacts. A more sophisticated approach invites visitors to complete a personal profile that can be used to customize future information delivery to the needs and interests of each member of the audience. It can likewise be used to narrow-cast marketing communications to a more targeted audience. This strategy is often used in combination with direct revenue-generating objectives, especially when advertising revenue is involved.

Sales and marketing support. In some cases the Web also serves as a tool for a remote sales force. Sales information, demos, and presentations may be placed online for sales personnel or qualified prospects. As an alternative, companies may create Web-based presentations and then have their sales team run them locally on laptop computers. These are both ways of bolstering the Web's inherent problem—it's a pull communication venue; that is, people can't see what it has to offer unless they do something to go and look. So a snazzy presentation and a sales force to talk about it are great ways to draw visitors to your site.

Brand awareness. TV advertisements don't simply focus on the merits of the product being advertised. A great deal of energy goes into displaying products in contexts that tend to associate them with particular lifestyles or values. A Web site can provide an interactive version of brand awareness. You can establish product associations by sponsoring a particular kind of content, service, or event: *fostering community*. The Levi-Strauss Web site, described later in the chapter, provides an excellent example of this technique.

Product supplementation. Some industries, notably the computer game industry and the banking and investment industries, are beginning to use the Web to extend their products and services. These extensions are usually couched as additional services to the customer—for example, buy the CD-ROM product and you also get free access to an associated customer Web site that may provide extended content, functionality, updates, and so on. Place investments with a brokerage firm that has online services, and you can use the service to track your investments or conduct transactions. The virtue of a model that integrates online and offline services in this way is that the fee for the standard service can be adjusted slightly to absorb some of the costs of the Web site, without making the company levy an additional charge solely for the online component.

Cost reduction. This rationale is used in two circumstances: when customer-related services are moved to the Internet (perhaps as a way of replacing more expensive operator services), and when the Internet as a communication channel is seen as a means of improving corporate productivity. This has been one of the chief rallying cries of intranet development.

The mission elements discussed in this section are broad guidelines to consider in developing the mission for your site. They are not hard-edged, but rather often overlap and blend. Nonetheless, they provide a framework from which to analyze and construct the rationale for what you want to broadcast. The following section provides some specific examples.

Mission Implementations

This section provides a discussion of successful Web sites organized according to mission goals. Each is analyzed in terms of the three-dimensional mission model described earlier in this chapter. A list of all sites discussed appears in Table 2-1.

Table 2-1   List of Web Sites Reviewed

NAME	GOAL	URL
Levi-Strauss	Corporate identity	http://www.levi.com
Honda	Corporate identity	http://www.honda.com
Disney	Promotion	http://www.disney.com
MacWorld Expo	Promotion	http://live.apple.com/macworld
CNN Interactive	Publishing	http://www.cnn.com
Mr. Showbiz	Publishing	http://www.mrshowbiz.com
MapQuest	Information access	http://www.mapquest.com
Hewlett-Packard	Customer service	http://www.hp.com
Quicken Financial Network	Customer service	http://www.qfn.com
Travelocity	Sales	http://www.travelocity.com
Amazon Books	Sales	http://www.amazon.com
Electric Minds	Community	http://www.minds.com
Women's Wire	Community	http://www.womenswire.com
Riddler	Entertainment	http://www.riddler.com
Total Entertainment Network	Entertainment	http://www.ten.net
TheSpot	Events	http://www.thespot.com
Mediadome	Events	http://www.mediadome.com

CORPORATE IDENTITY

A Web site designed for corporate identity has as its principal objective to broadcast and reinforce its company's name, branding, and core messages. Some of the strategies usually employed to these ends include publishing the company mission statement, providing a description of the corporate history and background, offering biographies of principals and employees and photos of the company's physical plant, and reprinting company press releases or other PR materials. These direct methods are more or less a requisite part of any corporate identity Web site. They suffer from two shortcomings, however. In the first place, they tend to be dull; it is challenging to make this type of material interesting reading for a general audience. In the second place, direct methods of communicating identity messages suffer a credibility problem; as with individuals, what a company says about itself is often suspect. People tend to regard what others say about themselves as interesting, but not as the only or even the best way to come to know that person. One often learns more about a person's identity by observing and experiencing him or her in action. In analogous ways, the most successful corporate identity sites have devised ways of *showing* rather than *telling* their identity. Demonstrating a company identity on a Web site is a subtle art that should involve providing information, entertainment, or services that associate the company and its name with a certain style or ethos. Such methods of establishing corporate identity tend to focus more strongly on cementing the emotional bond between customer and company.

Levi-Strauss

URL	http://www.levi.com
Product	Promotion
Audience	Consumers, particularly Generation X types
Objective	Nonrevenue, brand awareness

The Levi's Web site epitomizes the best of the indirect methods of communicating corporate identity. There is very little standard direct corporate identity content, and nothing on the site that reads like dry corporate background copy. Yet the site is saturated with identity messages, communicated through a variety of visually compelling and entertaining content and activities. Its primary audience is a hip, twenty-something crowd, though some of the content targets a more mature though still with-it viewer. The product being sold on the Web site is not so much jeans as such (no online sales catalog here) as it is the identification of Levi's with a particular attitude and way of life.

As you can see in Figure 2-2, the Levi-Strauss home page resembles an online magazine more than it does a corporate home page. Prominently absent are the large graphics and navigation buttons that have become conventional for corporate home pages. This is not because Levi-Strauss wants to save money on graphic design: the site is full of sophisticated graphics and fashion photography. The downplaying of interface elements such as banners and buttons allows the site to focus more on images that establish brand identity, product identity, and customer identity. On the home page, the most prominent image is the Levi's logo, its red and white accentuated by a black background and echoed in the colors of the text. All the other graphics on the page are product shots. On subsequent pages, the one consistent navigational element is another logo image, which takes one back to the home page.

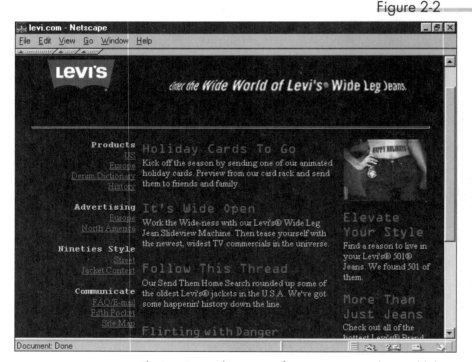

Figure 2-2

The Levi-Strauss home page focuses on images that establish brand identity, product identity, and customer identity.

The home page has a multicolumn text layout with a prominent headline inviting visitors to explore various site features. To the left, in smaller type and much less prominent, is a more conventional index, with familiar categories such as "Products," "Advertising," and "Communicate." The index provides some orientation for those who are accustomed to structured Web sites, but the overall effect of the home page copy is to invite the user to explore the site. One only realizes later that these invitations really lead to the same content accessible via the more conventional navigation index.

The guts of the site consists of fashion-magazine style articles and activities: every feature of the site is geared to be fun and entertaining, and to inculcate basic identity messages: "Levi's is concerned with quality," "Levi's is in tune with today's youth," "Levi's is cool, artsy, and technically hip." The messages are communicated through magazine-style articles (which seem to have volume and issue numbers, although without a table of contents or list of available issues), multimedia elements, contests, and games. For example, the site reported the results of a search the company had sponsored to find the oldest Levi's jackets in the United States. The search unearthed an unworn jacket dating from around 1910, and culminated in an invitation to viewers to send in narratives detailing where they imagined they and their jackets would be in another 86 years.

Another section called *Street* contains reports from trend-spotting journalists around the globe—in San Francisco, New York, Tokyo, and Sydney—who had interviewed kids in each of these locations. In *Flirting with Danger*, visitors are invited to immerse themselves in an interactive story, presented in a variety of formats, based on a current Levi's fantasy advertisement involving a rich swimsuit-clad young woman lounging by her pool near a handsome denim-clad hired hand. In short, almost everything about the Levi-Strauss Web site is compelling and enticing, with enough tone to be cool without becoming overly saccharine.

Honda

URL	http://www.honda.com
Product	Promotion
Audience	Upscale consumers
Objective	Nonrevenue, brand awareness, lead generation

The automobile industry provides a good test case for the challenges involved in turning a physical sales area into a virtual one. Practically every major car manufacturer has made an initial attempt to provide Web surfers with an interactive equivalent to visiting a showroom. A survey of the technologies deployed in the process would constitute a catalog of the principal interactive technologies: Shockwave, QuickTime VR, VRML, GIF animations, and Java have all been implemented with varying degrees of success.

The recently revamped Honda site represents a successful implementation of a corporate identity showcase that combines superlative design with useful and unobtrusive technology and realistic objectives. As a showcase, it is more directly focused on the company's physical product than is the Levi-Strauss site. Interestingly, the style of the site departs rather dramatically from the typical Honda identity messages, which tend to be hip in feeling. On the Web site, the company has decided to emphasize elegance and simplicity through draftsman-style graphics and rich colors. Perhaps the site designers took a look at Web demographics and decided to target a wealthier potential owner seeking a more opulent car than the one featured in other Honda advertising. In addition to fostering brand awareness (the Honda logo calls attention to itself in the upper left-hand corner of every page by doing a little morph), this site appears aimed at lead generation. It invites readers to request a brochure after it presents any vehicle to the viewer.

The site has a background section on Honda; another section for Honda owners that provides customer support information; a promotional section titled Drive One Home that provides links to dealers, announcements of special offers, financing information, and a request for brochures; and a Model Lineup section that showcases the cars themselves.

In contrast to several other automotive sites, the Honda site has chosen to take the high ground, emphasizing elegance of design over aggressive sales messages. The home page features an artistic, designer-colored background rendering of the Honda logo and name, a simple welcome message, and links to the other sections of the site. No flashing graphics, no sales talk — it is more like entering an art museum than a car dealership. The page designers here seem to assume that visitors come to make introductions and gather preliminary information in preparation for buying a car rather than be talked into buying one. This site does not pose as a substitute for the real-world experience of car buying; it simply enables potential buyers to make initial inquiries. Having a realistic objective is part of why this site succeeds. Ensuring that all avenues of the site drive toward that objective is another part.

Within the Model Lineup section of the site, users are offered a list of car models to select from. Selecting a model takes one to an introductory screen containing a handsome image of the selected model, with caption text and a pop-down menu of information options. The Honda site has not attempted, as some other automobile sites have, to create a virtual or metaphoric version of a physical showroom. The designers have opted instead for a simpler and in some ways more straightforward approach. The jury is still out on to what extent three-dimensional virtual reality simulations provide a satisfying version of real experience. However, it is fair to say that the Honda site manages to provide a satisfying experience. For each car model, one can see an overview of available models, look at photos (and in some cases QuickTime VR), obtain customized specifications, and view the various car color options using a tool called Color Your Car, shown in Figure 2-3. The pop-down menu is nicely implemented using Javascript so that a selection automatically loads without the user having to click on a "Submit" button.

The specifications page and the Color Your Car feature also make very effective use of technology. Rather than provide a standard HTML version of the printed specification sheet, the Honda site draws the specification data from a database using CGI programming. As a result, users can select the specification options they wish to see and build a custom spec sheet. Color Your Car is the slickest feature, using Javascript to paint a photo of the selected car automatically whenever the user moves the cursor over a color palette option.

The final option on the menu in the Model Lineup section is a link to a form requesting a brochure. This is very much a soft sell, and if anything the site might do more to encourage this next step from users. There is also some sense of redundancy in this outcome. A brochure would likely provide little more information than the user has already obtained from the site itself. For this reason, it would be nice to see an option to locate a dealer from within this section, since presumably the desired outcome is that having gathered information, the customer is now ready to go look at a real Honda. Services and offers designed to propel the user out of his or her computer chair and into the nearest Honda dealer would be appropriate here as well.

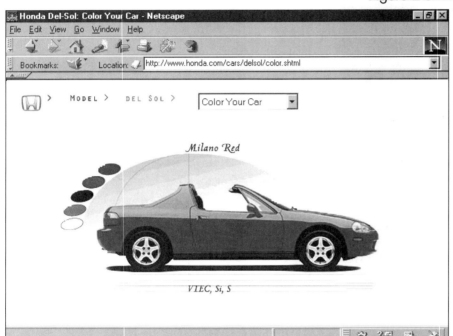

Figure 2-3

Honda's Color Your Car page lets visitors view car color options.

PRODUCT AND EVENT PROMOTION

The main objective of a promotional site is to encourage the sale of a company's products or services. This can include announcements of special offers or discounts (sometimes available only to site visitors), sweepstakes-style contests, free sample giveaways, or demonstration versions of products. Since a promotional campaign relies on the ability to attract participants, many promotion-oriented sites extend their reach with Web advertising on other selected Web sites and with offline marketing support.

Disney

URL	http://www.disney.com
Product	Promotion
Audience	Consumers, children and parents
Objective	Brand awareness, revenue

The Disney site is an extravaganza of self-promotion for the vast Disney empire. The site is chock-full of games, contests, and content—all directed at promoting the sale of Disney products, which can be ordered online. The content consists of a wide variety of information on Disney books, videos, movies, music, software, television specials, and vacation theme parks. In addition to standard product offerings and online sales, the site features promotional information for each of Disney's recently released feature movies, including background stories describing how the movies were made and games involving movie characters. The principal audience is probably kids, but (like all Disney productions) the Web site also appeals to parents. In contrast to many so-called *kids-only* sites, the general look and feel of the Disney site is more grown-up; it is mainly the activities that are intended for kids. The content is driven both by the enticements that promote the products and by the activities themselves, which develop name recognition and affinity with the various Disney figures as well as encouraging the purchase of the many interactive spin-off products.

For each of its feature movies, Disney has mounted an online prerelease promotion. One of the most successful of these was for *Toy Story;* the site offered information related to the movie as well as a variety of fun and games involving the movie characters. One path to success in any promotional campaign is to make participants feel that they have been winners (while at the same time providing a clear benefit to the promoting company). This benefit might be in the form of a potential sale, or the collection of market data from the participants.

Disney's *Toy Story* Adventure Game

In the case of Disney's *Toy Story* adventure contest, there was a weekly giveaway that involved several return visits on the part of the contestants. The adventure furthered audience recognition of *Toy Story* characters and *Toy Story* products, while also encouraging users to fill out registration information. The *Toy Story* adventure was more complex than most contests, since it was multipart. Each week there was a new adventure, involving the successful completion of a series of puzzles spread out over several days. The game interface, illustrated in Figure 2-4, was elaborately designed and visually appealing, although possibly a little overwhelming to the casual participant, particularly if that participant happened to be a child.

The *Toy Story* campaign has since been replaced by other promotions, highlighted in the home page banner graphic. A good deal of *Toy Story* content remains, now relegated to the video section of the Web site. Although much of the content and some of the activities have remained the same, the contest is gone and the focus has shifted to encouraging the sale of the *Toy Story* video and other paraphernalia.

Apple's MacWorld Expo Webcast

URL	http://live.apple.com/macworld
Product	Event/Promotion
Audience	Consumers, consummate Macintosh fans
Objective	Nonrevenue, product supplementation

MacWorld Expo took place in San Francisco in January 1997; the Apple Webcast site, shown in Figure 2-5, ran a week-long promotion of the show. The promotions featured live video and audio broadcasts of keynotes and other addresses, live chats, spy-cam shots from the floor of the hall, navigable VRML maps of the exhibit hall, as well as special sales on Macintosh hardware and software, news reports, contests, polls, and other just-for-fun stuff. To a certain extent the Webcast supported the expo itself, although encouraging attendance was not its primary objective. The main objective was to extend the promotional character of the expo to the Web, reaching all those who could not attend. The target audience was both would-be attendees and attendees themselves (it would make an interesting study to find out what percentage of visitors to the site were there in lieu of attending and what percentage went to the site *because* they had attended the expo). And if you had attended the event, you would have discovered that the expo was in fact promoting the Web site, with rows of dedicated computers logged onto the site and inviting attendees to come and surf.

To participate in all the activities available on the Web site, users needed an arsenal of helper applications: QuickTime TV and VDOLive for streaming video; QuickTime VR and RealAudio for audio broadcasts; and Global Chat for chat sessions. The site featured a whole section on getting and configuring the necessary tools, including a special application that, when downloaded and run, could check one's system (Macs only, of course!), identify the missing applications, and point out where to get them. Another convenient feature was a configurable schedule of live events that allowed users to set the times to their local time zone so they would be sure not to miss any important broadcasts. While waiting for that broadcast, users could check out other expo-related activities, including plenty of hot news items and press releases as well as a Just For Fun section including an Apple Trivia game, contests, daily polls, the lowdown on the expo party scene, and T-shirt giveaways.

Figure 2-5

The Apple Webcast of MacWorld San Francisco, January 1997, ran a week-long promotion of the show.

The Apple Webcast of MacWorld Expo was an event in itself designed to promote new Macintosh technologies and products as well as the show. At the time of this writing it remained to be seen how, if at all, Apple would attempt to reuse the site after the expo itself had concluded. Certainly there is opportunity to archive the audio and video materials collected during the show. There is also the possibility of using the site to continue to promote the companies, products, and technological innovations highlighted by the show.

PUBLISHING (NEWS AND MAGAZINES)

The publishing industry has rushed to embrace the Internet, in spite of an ostensible dearth of revenue models to support online publishing. In most cases, with some notable exceptions, the most successful online publishing ventures have had roots in print or broadcast publishing, with an established base of advertisers willing to follow the publishers to the Internet. All the major players appear to be still testing the waters, both in terms of the product they offer and their objective. The majority rely on advertising to underwrite the effort. Only a handful have ventured to charge a subscription price. Some offer a selection (or occasionally even the entirety) of their print magazine. Others have evolved compatible but new content to put on the Web site. Still others have created whole new e-zine ventures.

CNN Interactive

URL	http://www.cnn.com
Product	Access to news and information
Audience	Consumers who like to keep up with current news
Objective	Revenue from advertising

The Cable News Network Interactive Web site, updated 24 hours a day, 7 days a week, is an example of a well-designed news and information Web site. The home page, shown in Figure 2-6—though crowded with top news stories, a scrolling headline banner, and dozens of links to the many sections of the site—is both attractive and easy to use. Stories offer a short synopsis and accompanying photo with a link to the full story. The text of news items frequently includes links to background or related information, including previous articles from CNN archives as well as from other Web sites. These online stories thus have consistently deeper and broader coverage than a conventional newspaper article or TV news spot.

In fact, the Web site provides the equivalent of several newspapers in one. Organized in fairly traditional newspaper sections such as World, Sports, Travel, and Style, the CNN Web site also contains a news digest that repeats some of the top stories from each section in a condensed format. There is also a search feature that allows users to comb through the CNN news archives, and a Video Vault that provides access to CNN video clips. In this way the Web site accommodates both users seeking a quick update on current news stories and those who want more detail.

CNN also participates in the development of two separate news ventures. CNNfn (http://www.cnnfn.com), the financial network, provides financial news, market information and analyses, and other features for the business and investment community. AllPolitics (http://www.allpolitics.com), a site developed in partnership with *Time* magazine, contains in-depth coverage of political news and issues.

Figure 2-6

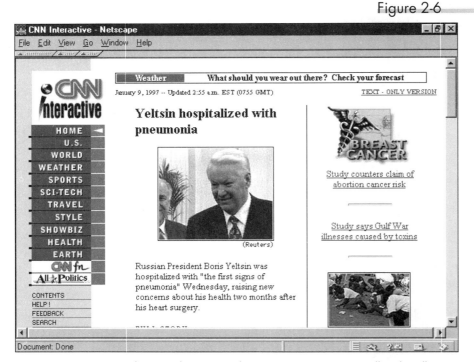

The CNN home page has top news stories, a scrolling headline banner, and dozens of links to the many sections of the site.

CNN Interactive represents one of the best current examples of news and information Web sites on the Internet. A fairly early entrant in the online news market, it retains a relatively conventional news format. There is little opportunity besides a standard feedback form and comment page for readers to influence the content of the site. It would be useful, for example, if one could create a profile that would build a custom newspaper composed of the news categories one was most interested in. Other news sites also offer an e-mail-based delivery option that allows readers to have top news stories delivered directly to them. Providing news updates by e-mail is not only a convenience to readers, it also provides a means of encouraging readers to return to the site for complete stories. Surprisingly, CNN has also not instituted any live broadcast news coverage using one of the emerging Internet broadcast technologies. This would seem to be another natural extension for the site. On the other hand, the relative lack of interactive elements on the CNN site is a sign that the CNN objective is to deliver news stories in an attractive format without frills.

Mr. Showbiz

URL	http://www.mrshowbiz.com
Product	Entertainment industry news and reviews
Audience	Consumers
Objective	Revenue from advertising

The Mr. Showbiz site is an online entertainment industry publication, developed and maintained by Starwave, which is responsible for several top Web sites including ESPN SportZone, Family Planet, Castle Infinity (a games site), and Ticketmaster Online. Mr. Showbiz has highly targeted content, in this case news and gossip from the always entertaining world of entertainment. The site has several characteristics that add up to success: an attractive, easy-to-use design, an eclectic feature set using a variety of technologies, and lots of fresh content. In contrast to the CNN site, this publication contains many interactive features and involves its audience to a much larger extent.

Figure 2-7

The Mr. Showbiz home page reflects the de facto
standard du jour for online publishing ventures.

As seen in Figure 2-7, the Mr. Showbiz interface shows what online publishing ventures can do to make themselves useful and attractive: at the top, graphical buttons linking to major content areas, a left-hand sidebar with a complete table of contents in small type, a center area with headlines, thumbnail photos, and links to feature stories. There is also an inset panel called The Water Cooler Poll, devoted to continually changing reader polls, a nice touch that provides user interaction with the site from the very first page.

There is ample variety of content here: news flashes, feature articles, reviews of movies, TV shows, music and video, ratings, interviews, star bios, an Ask Mr. Showbiz column, and a great deal more — including a vocabulary-builder dictionary, just to prove that entertainment can also be educational. In addition to the updated content, there is also a searchable archive of information, a chat section, and lots of fun and games.

The site maintains a reasonable balance between things to read and things to do. It also does an effective job of cross-linking its content. For example, the movie review section offers full-length reviews supported with links to background information on the stars contained in the biographies section. Accompanying the reviews are opportunities to enter the weekly "Pick 'Em" contest, which invites readers to select which movies will have the best box office returns or to respond to the reviews. Other activities include a Plastic Surgery Lab, where viewers can construct a home-grown movie star from a selection of star facial parts, a haiku section with user-submitted samples of varying quality, as well as the aforementioned reader polls. The result is a site that delivers more than entertainment news. Mr. Showbiz gives its readers lots of opportunities to contribute to the content of the site.

REFERENCE AND INFORMATION

Reference and information Web sites often rely on fairly robust technology, and almost all make use of some kind of database for information storage and retrieval. Because they are so technology driven, these sites are frequently separate Web ventures rather than offshoots of existing companies. However, many companies are beginning to provide access to portions of their corporate knowledge bases, merging conventional information access with client or customer service.

MapQuest

URL	http://www.mapquest.com
Product	Access, map-based information
Audience	Consumers, general audience, travelers
Objective	Advertising and licensing revenue

MapQuest, developed by GeoSystems Global, calls itself an "interactive atlas." MapQuest derives its data from two principal sources: GeoSystems U.S. Digital Map Database, which contains over 675,000 miles of roads as well as information about transportation classes, political boundaries, population centers, parks, and bodies of water, and the U.S. Census Bureau's 1994 TIGER files, a digital representation of the U.S. street network. The audience is highly generic — anyone who needs to find a location or obtain directions might profitably make use of this site. In keeping with the breadth of the potential audience, MapQuest has a relatively plain, easy-to-learn interface, the initial screen of which appears in Figure 2-8. The Interactive Atlas interface consists of a row of tabs. These provide access to the two principal ways to search the map database as well as several features for customizing and saving the results. One can either *find* locations by typing the name or address of a business establishment to be located into a standard form, or *view* locations via a series of maps that zoom in to a location down to street level. The maps can display points of interest from dining, lodging, and shopping facilities to health care, banks, and civic offices. In addition, users can add their own custom points of interest to a given map and then save the map on the MapQuest site for future retrieval. To perform these functions, users need only complete a simple registration form, providing name and e-mail address.

Figure 2-8

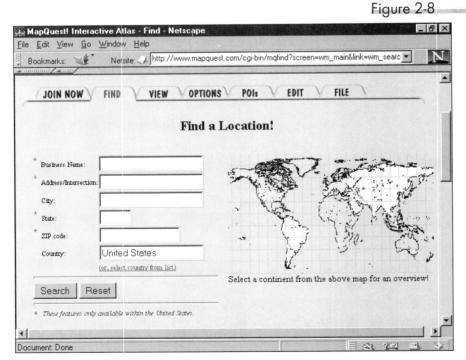

MapQuest provides an interactive database of maps and business location services.

In addition to the Interactive Atlas, MapQuest has another service called TripQuest, which can provide door-to-door directions between locations in major metropolitan areas and city-to-city directions between other locations. Users enter the beginning and ending locations, and the search engine returns both written directions and maps with the locations starred. Both TripQuest and the Interactive Atlas are available in original format as well as Java and Microsoft ActiveX applications.

The MapQuest site is a well-executed example of direct user access to a highly useful company asset. As an application, its focus is consistent and its interface is clear and intuitive. GeoSystems' basic revenue model appears to be free membership combined with on-site advertising, although at the moment advertising appears to be sparse. It is likely that the more targeted TripQuest service will more readily attract advertisers, since it is easier to predict the demographics of its users.

In addition to soliciting advertisers, the company has developed a tiered set of paid services offering to augment its free membership model. These allow customers to create customized interfaces to portions of the MapQuest data from their own sites. So, for example, if a company wanted to provide potential customers with a map to its nearest outlet or to all its offices around the globe, it could create a map and point visitors to it while the map itself would stay on the MapQuest site. These value-added services may also provide a source of revenue for the site.

CUSTOMER SERVICE AND SUPPORT

The ability to provide customers with service and support without forcing them to endure lengthy holds on the telephone has been a driving force behind building customer-support Web sites for many companies, although few start with full-blown online service centers. Most begin by making support documentation available. This content is fairly easy to convert and provides at least a first line of support for many customers seeking help. From there, companies can evolve increasingly targeted services. In some cases, as in the Quicken Financial Network, sponsored by Intuit and described later in this chapter, the service section of the Web site can take on a life of its own.

Hewlett-Packard Electronic Support Center

URL	http://www.hp.com
Product	Access
Audience	Customers
Objective	Indirect revenue, cost reduction

Hewlett-Packard maintains an extensive corporate Web site that offers standard product information, selected vertical market information, feature articles promoting Hewlett-Packard technology, and also sponsors an electronic business magazine, E Business. One component of this large site is Hewlett-Packard's Electronic Support Center. The Support Center, shown in Figure 2-9, is representative of many well-developed online support systems in the computer industry. Its main goals are to provide access to technical information and updates and software patches for HP customers, both consumer and corporate.

The center has two main sections—Software, Drivers, and Support, which provides open access to updates and technical information on the HP consumer and small business products; and UNIX/MPE Software Support, which provides support for HP high-end products to companies who have a paid service and support contract with HP. There are also separate sections for Americas/Asia support and Europe, the Middle East, and Africa.

It is an impressive customer service offering, in keeping with a global company. However, all this makes for a somewhat overwhelming organization, which is only partially allayed by the existence of a support search engine. The site houses a vast array of support documentation for each of Hewlett-Packard's products. Take for example the links to the HP Deskjet printer. There are ten links to the various Deskjet printer series, and each of these leads to a comparable quantity of model numbers for each series. There are nearly thirty support documents listed for each of these models, although many of the documents are listed under several models. This mass of material probably includes answers to a large number of the support problems encountered by consumer and business users of HP products, and if it were possible to locate pertinent information quickly, this site would be extensively helpful and save waiting on hold for an answer to a simple question. The sheer volume of information to scroll through is somewhat daunting, however, and it might be that a more service-oriented interface would make the information more palatable.

In addition, the overall tone of the site appears aimed more at Hewlett-Packard's corporate clients than its consumer base. A consumer looking for help with a product purchased for home use could find the sheer quantity of information and the relatively objective presentation of content daunting. Overall, the HP Support Center successfully implements an online model for extending service to customers. It does, however, point up some of the challenges — of design and project coordination — that face companies with very large and complex knowledge bases to publish and with several distinct user groups who may be located around the globe.

Figure 2-9

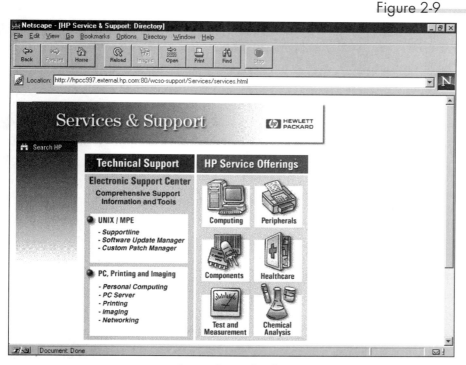

The Hewlett-Packard Support Center is representative
of many well-developed online support systems.

Quicken Financial Network

URL	http://www.qfn.com
Product	Access to financial news, information; investment transactions
Audience	Intuit customers, investment-conscious consumers
Objective	Revenue from advertising

The Quicken Financial Network (QFN), sponsored by Intuit, the makers of the Quicken line of accounting and tax preparation software, brings financial information, products, and services to personal investors. Originally part of the Intuit Web site, this service has evolved into its own entity through a combination of development efforts and strategic alliances. It is an excellent example of those services on the Web that collect together in one convenient location information distributed elsewhere. The site's mission, according to its own statement, is "to help people make better financial decisions." Its founders "envision that QFN will become the most trusted financial services marketplace for Web users." The site offers an extension to the financial tools that Intuit sells, making it at once a promotional instrument for consumers who do not own the Quicken product and effectively a customer service for those who do. To make all this possible, the site includes advertising from Intuit as well as other related products. The service to consumers is free of charge — targeting, of course, the increasing number of do-it-yourself investors.

In keeping with a site whose goal is to provide a service, the QFN home page has an efficient, professional look. Navigation is clear and unobtrusive. Advertisement banners are labeled as such — part of Intuit's desire to indicate that the financial services are not influenced by advertisers. Currently, the main areas of the site include Retirement, Investments, Tax Center, News, Library, Banking, and Insurance.

The Retirement section contains links to retirement planning information and features a Java applet to help investors analyze their retirement needs and develop an appropriate savings plan. The Tax Center, besides including several plugs for the Quicken tax preparation software, contains information on tax law changes, a calendar of important tax deadlines, and advice on how to save money on your taxes. The Insurance section links to Quicken's InsureMarket site, which provides access to insurance policy information and allows users to purchase policies online. The Banking section describes Intuit's online banking products, lists the company's many financial partners, and provides a financial marketplace for partner banks offering online services.

The Investments section connects to the NETworth site, developed and maintained by Galt Technologies (`http://networth.galt.com`). NETworth contains a vast assortment of investment-related documents, data collections, and market tracking and analysis tools. Highlights of the site include the Mutual Fund Market Manager, an Equities Center, Graphing, and the ability to create a Personal Portfolio. All features are free, although access to some requires registration.

The News and Library sections of QFN consist of links to services provided by other entities. The News section provides access to business and financial news headlines, summaries and articles from Individual's NewsPage service (`www.newspage.com`). Users of QFN can also create customized newspapers for free by indicating their news interest and preferences from among the news items available to Quicken users. Full subscriptions to NewsPage are also available. The Library section links to Infonautics' Electric Library, an online reference and information site (`www.elibrary.com`). QFN users can search for information in the Financial Electric Library. In addition, this section features a financial question of the day, as well as an archive of past questions, and the opportunity for users to suggest new questions. Full subscriptions to the Electric Library are available for $9.95 per month and provide unlimited personal access to Electric Library — no additional fees or charges for searches, document retrievals, or connection time.

Though it continues to evolve, the QFN site is already very successful. Its interface shows the designers had the needs of its users in mind. All the content and features are accessible with one click from the home page, and users can, in a single glance at the home page, take in what's new on the site. There are many useful tools available to users. Not as many, perhaps, as some more commercial investment services, but it is important to recall that this service is not Intuit's core business. The site demonstrates the company's commitment to investors and its expertise — in the name of selling more Intuit software. In this regard, it is not exactly competing with a Web-based enterprise devoted to providing investment service, or even with an investment company that is offering such a service. QFN combines elements of information access and customer service with product and company promotion.

RESERVATIONS, TICKETING, AND SALES

One of the main objects of online sales is to make the selection and purchase of products easy. This is not always a simple task, in part because of the impersonal nature of the online experience. For this reason, Web sites are still usually better at providing presales information than they are at actually consummating a sale. To consumers, the online shopping experience has the advantage of producing less pressure to buy (no aggressive salespeople). This advantage does decrease the incentive to buy, of course. It can also make it more difficult for the user to arrive at the psychological level of comfort needed to stop looking and make a purchase — a mental state that informed salespeople can help build.

Travelocity

URL	http://www.travelocity.com
Product	Access to travel information, transactions
Audience	Vacation-minded consumers
Objective	Revenue from advertisers, sponsors

Travelocity, a service of SABRE Interactive and Worldwide Systems Corporation, is a one-stop guide to travel information and reservations. The site relies on advertising and sponsors for its revenue, and a good portion of the interface is given over to ad banners and announcements of special discounts and travel-related promotions. Access to all parts of the site is free, although some sections require a minimal registration. The audience is primarily consumers — individuals and families planning to travel or take a vacation.

The site consists of four major areas: Travel Reservations, Destinations and Interests, Points of View, and Travel Merchandise. The main attraction of the site is its airline, car rental, and hotel reservation system. Users can check flight timetables, fares, and availability. One of the highlights of the reservation section is the 3 Best Itineraries feature. Based on user criteria, this search engine will return the three flights that best match the requirements. This section also includes a Fly AAway Vacation section with package vacation deals sponsored by American Airlines. The emphasis on finding discounts and bargains is one sign of the site's focus on consumer rather than business travelers.

In addition to the reservation system, Travelocity also maintains a wealth of other vacation and travel information. In Destinations and Interests one will find guides for Places to Go and Things to Do around the world. The wealth of information is supported with a wide array of multimedia elements, including maps, photos, and audio and video clips. There are listings on over 9,500 restaurants, 1,400 museums, 11,000 bed and breakfasts, 3,000 theater, dance, and music performances, and 30,000 hotels, not to mention condominiums, golf courses, exhibits, shows, and festivals. This makes it a good information resource as well as a transaction system.

For those who prefer information from experienced individuals, Points of View contains chats and forums for swapping ideas and experiences with fellow travelers or for chatting with scheduled travel experts. This section also has feature articles and a monthly spotlight destination, as well as contests and games with prizes. Travel Merchandise is an online shopping mall for travelers, with an index of merchants, product directory, and mall specials. It features a shopping basket and secure server for collecting items and making purchases.

Travelocity is an ambitious, well-thought-out, and successful undertaking. It is not particularly flashy, but it has a clean, inviting look. It provides a good example of a site that has built revenue-generating opportunities around a core of consumer transaction and information services for a well-defined audience. Combining elements of publishing, information access, and transactional services, Travelocity is likely to serve as a model for similar Web enterprises in other vertical markets.

Amazon.com

URL	http://www.amazon.com
Product	Transaction
Audience	Consumers, book lovers
Objective	Revenue from advertising

Amazon.com—by its own designation "Earth's biggest bookstore"—has done an excellent job of capitalizing on the advantages of online sales and has also made an effort to surmount some of the potential drawbacks. Book lovers who know what they are looking for can use the site's search engine to locate books by author, title, or subject. For those needing guidance, there are browsable lists of Editor's Favorites, Best Sellers, Award Winners, and books reviewed by a variety of sources, such as *The New York Review of Books*, National Public Radio, HotWired, and even a list of customer reviews. The site also provides other means of encouraging book sales: featured books with review articles, chats with prominent authors, and daily updates marking the birthdays and deaths of noted writers. One nice touch is the presence of recommended book summaries at the top and bottom of selected pages. These include a thumbnail image, a short synopsis, and a link to additional recommended titles, all providing a gentle encouragement to readers fishing for a good book to buy. In all these ways, Amazon.com has positioned itself as the place to look for a book when you don't know what you are looking for, to some extent overcoming the challenge of trying to derive sales from a Web site.

Amazon.com's purchasing technology is representative of what has become something of the standard for Web site ordering systems. Users browse through catalog entries, adding items they would like to buy to an electronic *shopping cart*, which stores titles and calculates the charges. Once customers are ready to make their purchases, the site switches them to a secure server that encrypts all information. For those who do not yet trust even this method of sending credit card information, there is the option to fill out the form and then call in the credit card number. There is also a help line number to call if problems arise. All these features add to the overhead of the process for both Amazon.com and the user, but they are still pretty much necessary for any online shopping venture.

In addition to bringing effective technology to bear on online sales, Amazon.com has also implemented some strategies for encouraging customer participation on the site. Anyone using the site can submit recommendations on any book in the catalog—and join a monthly contest for the best review submitted by a customer. In addition, the site solicits authors and publishers to add their comments to books. These techniques all help foster the sense of a book-reading community that helps personalize the faceless online sales process even as it encourages more book buying. To this end, Amazon.com has also instituted an associate program, where people can sell books from the Amazon.com catalog from their own Web sites and receive a modest referral fee for their trouble.

COMMUNITY

The notion that the Internet could bring together "virtual communities" of people with similar interests is an idea that predates the commercial explosion of the Web. Commercial entities have been quick to seize on the concept, however, and apply it to groups of people with similar demographics and similar potential interests in targeted products. This is not to imply that any rhetoric about fostering community in the commercial world is entirely bogus — it is just the case that online community development and product marketing often prove to enjoy a nicely symbiotic relationship. The sites discussed in this section have as their primary motive the advancement of communication among their constituencies. But even these communities can look like attractive locations for advertisers to put up a banner.

Electric Minds

URL	http://www.minds.com
Product	Access
Audience	Literate, urbane folks interested in online community
Objective	Revenue from advertising

Electric Minds is in essence a metacommunity, a community-oriented site focused on the topic of online communication, published by the guru of virtual communities, Howard Rheingold. As one might expect, this is not a site that simply gives lip service to the notion of virtual communities. Community building is a clear part of its design and functionality. In some ways this site resembles an online publication. There are feature commentaries by a number of writers who more or less regularly report in from around the globe. It may be more accurate to say, though, that the product this site seeks to deliver is access to communication rather than information. The site demonstrates its focus on communication and community building in several ways. One subtle but pervasive angle is the emphasis on individuals in all the content on the site. The evidence of this begins on the home page, shown in Figure 2-10, which prominently features a photo of Howard himself, the virtual emcee, waving at the viewer. In all other sections, too, there are photos of contributing writers, establishing a sense of the writer's physical presence in the emptiness of cyberspace. In similar fashion, the section entitled World Wide Jam is an attempt to bring the global village together metaphorically in one virtual space. This goal is emblemized as well in the site's navigation graphic, a swirling rainbow of color that draws together the navigation buttons like satellites in a colorful cosmos.

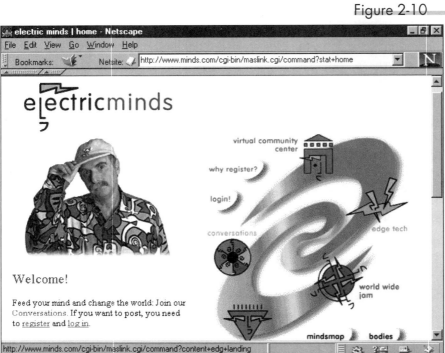

Figure 2-10

Electric Minds, presided over by Harold Rheingold, is a community of people fostering virtual communities.

Another sign of the emphasis on conversation over information is the fact that every article has a sidebar at the top level with an excerpt from and link to a related conversation. The design, in other words, invites readers to move beyond reading and enter into ongoing dialogs that surround the texts. It would be nice to see the extent to which conversation spawns articles as well as the reverse. This site demonstrates a clear and successfully implemented mission.

Women's Wire

URL	http://www.womenswire.com
Product	Information access, community fostering
Audience	Consumers, upwardly mobile professional women
Objective	Revenue from advertising

Women's Wire began as a bulletin board service before the explosion in commercial online services began. In its Web incarnation, the site has taken on more the guise of a publishing effort, even as it retains its original commitment to fostering communication among women. The Web site's stated goal is to "provide a great place for women from around the world to connect with one another." There are book reviews, interviews, soap opera updates, feature articles, and horoscopes, all targeted to a global audience of women, with an emphasis on the upwardly mobile professional woman.

Although its ostensible mission is focused on bringing women together, the site is built on a publishing model. Features appear in regular weekly issues. Main areas of each issue include News, Style, Work, Body, Buzz (entertainment industry info), Cash (financial news and information), Web, and Go Shop (links to selected online shopping). The News section gets daily updates. Other sections get weekly updates on a revolving basis, so that on any given day at least one section contains new material. Content comes in light doses, and although the articles range from serious to whimsical, the general tone of the site is upbeat and positive.

On the surface, Women's Wire appears to do a better job of bringing its readership entertaining, informative, sometimes provocative content than it does in fostering a sense of connection and community. In part this may be simply a matter of positioning. The site does afford ample opportunities for users to respond to articles, to submit their own op-ed pieces, or to pose questions to the editors of the various content areas. In addition, it has recently opened a live chat area, with a variety of ways to connect to it. All of this simmers beneath the surface, however, rather than appearing front and center in the organization of the site. To the casual observer, the site looks like a well-maintained publishing venture.

If the connections among women are easily missed on Women's Wire, the advertising is not. Women's Wire, shown in Figure 2-11, has numerous small ad banners displayed prominently at the top and in the margins of all of their Web pages, a clear sign that fostering a community in cyberspace also has substantial commercial potential.

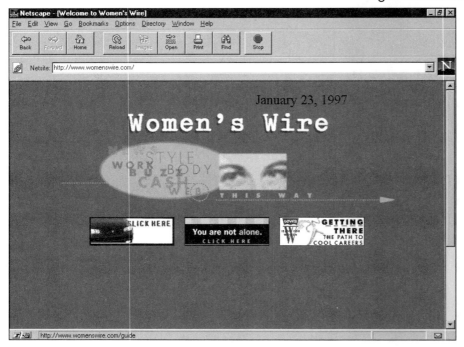

Women's Wire targets upwardly mobile professional women with book reviews, interviews, soap opera updates, feature articles, and horoscopes.

ENTERTAINMENT

The potential opportunities for the entertainment industry on the Internet are immense. Currently, however, development efforts are somewhat limited by network bandwidth constraints—but this has not stopped enterprising companies from beginning to explore the possibilities for playing games in a network environment. The two examples of entertainment sites described in this section present very different approaches to delivering this product— and very different models for profiting from the effort.

Riddler

URL	http://www.riddler.com
Product	Events, games for prizes
Audience	Consumers, game players
Objective	Revenue from advertising

Riddler is a games site that features online trivia, puzzles, and word games. Riddler operates on a registration system, but unlike most of the gaming environments, it does not charge a fee for playing. Instead, it relies on advertising for its revenue. In exchange it imposes on users a fairly rigorous registration form — and it won't accept incomplete answers to any of the questions. Riddler is part of the Softbank-backed Commonwealth Network, an association of Web site owners and developers who collect royalty fees in exchange for posting advertisement banners on their Web pages. Riddler also engages in some fairly aggressive advertising practices. Users who click to enter a game wind up looking at the game sponsor's complete home page in a frame window. Access to the game itself is at the bottom of this page.

Riddler has an elaborate system for encouraging game playing and collecting prizes. Members receive a stash of *Riddlets*, the basic currency that allows entrance into games. Game winners receive a certain number of promotional *CAPS*, which can be cashed in for prizes when enough have been collected, or exchanged for additional Riddlets.

Riddler, shown in Figure 2-12, has a rich, colorful, and inviting look. There are a variety of games to choose from, including no-pressure games that are easy and just for fun like Mental Floss trivia, Klondike solitaire, and Incognito word search. For members, there are several additional games that offer prizes, including King of the Hill, a multiperson, Java-based trivia game; Checkered Flag, a multiperson crossword puzzle; Bloodhound, a game that sends players out on the Web searching for CAPS; and !AHA!, a palindrome puzzler game built using Microsoft's ActiveX. Because it features mostly brain games, Riddler would appear to target a slightly older audience than the standard gaming environment aims to reach. This is also consistent with Riddler's sweepstakes-like approach to encourage visitors to keep playing, a motivation that is usually associated with an older crowd.

Figure 2-12

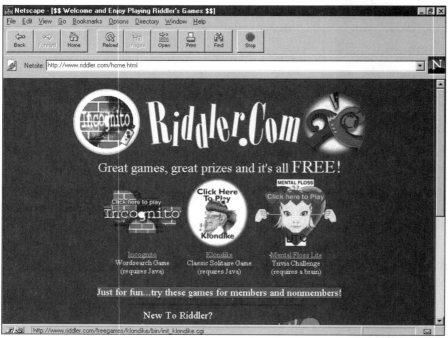

The Riddler site has a rich, colorful, and inviting look.

TEN (Total Entertainment Network)

URL	http://www.ten.net
Product	Events, network games
Audience	Consumers, gamers
Objective	Revenue from membership, connect charges

Some entertainment-oriented sites, like Riddler, provide fun and games as a way to entice people into an environment where they can be barraged with advertising messages. The Total Entertainment Network (TEN), on the other hand, treats games as serious business. Its objective is to take existing commercial electronic games and adapt them to a multiplayer, network-based environment. At present it has an impressive list of games available, including Duke Nukem 3D, Command and Conquer, Dark Sun, Quake, Diablo, and Nascar Racing Online, with an even longer list of games promised for the near future.

chapter **2** CLARIFYING YOUR MISSION

The main thing that makes TEN stand out among Web gaming environments is the fact that it charges a membership fee, a clear sign that it is attracting serious game players. You don't just happen to drop in on TEN. It requires its own software, which is best obtained the old-fashioned way, by ordering the free CD-ROM. The software can also be downloaded, but it is time-consuming, particularly if one needs to download the games (all of which exist in shareware as well as commercial versions) as well as the TEN software. TEN offers two different membership rates — a minimal fee for casual gamers that also accrues hourly charges for game-playing time, and a somewhat higher flat-rate membership for people who plan to play a lot of games.

Figure 2-13

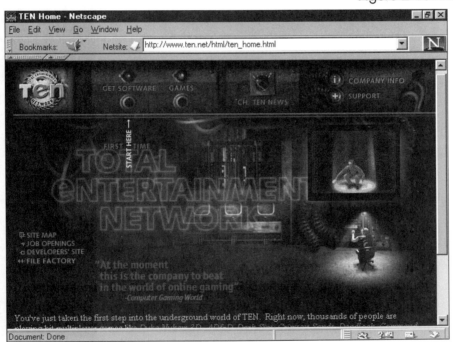

TEN's Web site objective is to take electronic games and adapt them to a multiplayer, network-based environment.

Although the TEN Web site is not really as important as the gaming environment itself, the company has taken steps on the Web site to serve the community of gamers. There are discussion forums, plenty of information on

107

the latest games, online help and hints, and ongoing tournaments and contests. The Channel TEN news page provides the latest updates on all the goings on at TEN. With its ultra-cool underground world interface (shown in Figure 2-13), its long list of games, and its support for the gamer community, TEN looks to be a winner in the multiplayer gaming arena.

EVENT PROGRAMMING AND LIVE BROADCAST

It is said that revolutionary technologies invariably begin by attempting to replicate the older technologies they are destined to replace before they move on to develop their own approach. The Web, by contrast, seems to have gravitated increasingly toward older modes of broadcast communication the longer it has been in existence. There has been a recent explosion in the number of sites offering scheduled live programming. Most of these offer entertainment, with sports and music broadcasts probably topping the list. Some others have taken a more social, interactive approach to the concept of Web events, acknowledging that one of the attractions of the Web in contrast to TV is its two-way nature. The examples described in this section serve as evidence of both these trends.

TheSpot

URL	http://www.thespot.com
Product	Event—an online, interactive soap
Audience	Consumers, twenty-somethings
Objective	Advertising revenue

TheSpot, which premiered on June 7, 1995, was a relatively early entry in the increasingly crowded field of online soaps, a variety of event-driven programming that in addition to providing intimate glimpses into the lives of a cast of characters also allows visitors to interact with the cast in various ways. Produced by American Cybercast, it follows the lives of a cast of five twenty-something L.A. folk — Jeff, Carrie, Michelle, Lon, and Jordan — and their *cyberian husky*, Spotnik. TheSpot is supported by advertising revenue. It clearly targets an audience of teens and twenty-somethings who identify to some degree with the cast of the show.

The plot of this online soap opera is carried along in several ways. Every day there are journal entries from one or more or the characters who form the heart of TheSpot. Each entry has links to the series of journal entries written by that character. There are also links to the journals of the other characters. To truly follow the story line, one must read all the journal entries and then piece together the plot, much like watching a TV soap, except that a fair degree of active effort is required of the viewer (reader). Previous writings are accessible in Still Fresh, in case one needs to catch up quickly with the action. SpotGate, narrated by Spotnik, provides a weekly synopsis of the plot for those short on time. In the Viewing Room there are photo albums and audio and video galleries that depict some of the notable activities of the cast members — the Pool Party, the Shop-O-Rama, the Spot house fire, the trip to Las Vegas, and so on.

There are plenty of opportunities for viewers to chime in — as well as assurances from the production staff that e-mail can make a difference in the story lines. Visitors can reach all the principal communication features from the Voices section. The Spotboard is a forum for users to post threaded messages to the cast and to one another. It is even linked to a page where users can add their own bios and pictures to a list of Spot Fans. Alternately, one can e-mail a cast member privately. There is an IRC link for live chatting. A recent addition, the Spot Palace, is a graphical chat environment built with the Time Warner Palace software. Other features include a subscriber-based e-mail newsletter, a search engine, a behind-the-scenes section that provides insights into how TheSpot is produced, and, for nostalgic Spot old-timers, a link to a previous incarnation of TheSpot, called Spot Classic.

TheSpot started as a hobby, then grew into a business venture. It still carries some of the low-budget, shoot-from-the-hip feel that undoubtedly accounts for its charm and gives it a following that a more heavily produced undertaking might lack. It manages to have both a cool L.A. feel and a low-key Internet attitude. Quite likely it is the combination of chic attitude and interactive content that has made TheSpot an ongoing success.

Mediadome

URL	http://www.mediadome.com
Product	Events, referred to as "Webisodes"
Audience	Consumers
Objective	Revenue, ostensibly from advertising

Mediadome, shown in figure 2-14 is the latest of several ventures produced by CNET in conjunction with Intel. The goal of Mediadome is to deliver state-of-the-art entertainment experiences that promote anything from "music artists to comic book heroes." It features events — which it terms *Webisodes* — that incorporate interactive elements and rely principally on RealAudio technology for streaming audio broadcasts and Stream Works for video.

Mediadome's inaugural Webisode was SFNYE, a San Francisco New Year's Eve party that featured a variety of musical acts including Chris Issaks and Lyle Lovett. Another attraction featured promotion for the movie *Turbulence*, including interactive games as well as video from the film's trailer. In addition to providing live broadcasts, the site also maintains an archive of past performances. It also enables visitors to register to receive the Dispatch, Mediadome's free weekly e-mail newsletter with information on upcoming events.

Mediadome is a free service to users, and it appears to be built on an advertising and sponsorship revenue model. The registration form for the Dispatch includes several optional demographic questions, which an accompanying policy note indicates are requested in order to help Mediadome understand its users' demographic profile and thereby presumably attract appropriate advertisers. Its target audience is the young, technologically savvy, early-adopter crowd. Live event broadcasting is still not yet ready for prime time; sound and video quality are still fairly primitive, and it remains unclear how event-driven ventures like Mediadome will fare. In the long run, however, it appears quite clear that Internet broadcasting will continue to grow in popularity as the technology matures.

Figure 2-14

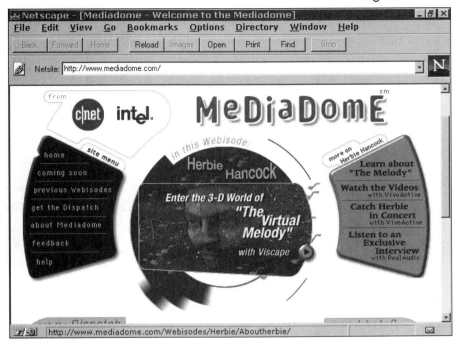

The goal of mediadome is to deliver state-of-the-art entertainment experiences.

Summary

The Web sites examined here represent a broad range of content, styles, and technological sophistication. They share one important characteristic, however, that helps to define their success—they all have a design that reflects a well-defined, easy to grasp, Net-appropriate mission. Each has a straightforward purpose, a clearly identifiable target audience, and a set of consistent objectives. Of course, a carefully crafted mission is no guarantee of a successful implementation, but experience suggests that without one, the odds of success are greatly reduced.

By way of capturing and restating the main themes of this chapter, here is a checklist of questions to help project managers hone their Web site mission statements:

- Is the site mission consistent with the company's overall mission?
- Is it achievable (logistically, financially, technically)?
- Does it benefit its audience?
- Does it benefit the company?
- Are the desired outcomes measurable?

It's a good idea to cycle through the process of answering these questions over and over, even after your site is up and running. The material on a site can evolve quickly, and the original mission may either change or get lost in the course of development.

chapter 3

BUILDING THE ORGANIZATION

JUST HOW BIG is the Web picture? This is a tough question to answer. The potential scope of the medium is larger and deeper than anything ever used to communicate information, but its importance, impact, and structure are constantly changing. If you speak with the Web's most zealous and devoted supporters, they'll tell you it's time to drop practically everything else you're doing and pour everything you've got into an online effort. On the other hand, many management consulting and advertising types display a more cautious wait-and-see approach. Whatever ground you take in this dialogue, a project by any other name is still a project, and traditional means of management still apply. From an operational point of view, this entails creating a budget, determining requirements, establishing a time line, and working through quality assurance issues.

This chapter focuses on the particular challenges these issues pose for Web development project leaders. The basics should be familiar to any manager, and certainly to anyone who has participated in software development, but it's useful to take another look in the context of the Web. The chapter follows three fictional projects through each issue to give you a close-up look at the challenges in the order they're likely to arise and to see some ways Web developers can deal with them. Though invented, the cases are woven from strands of real experience (with just a touch of whimsy) so as to be at once plausible, instructive, and entertaining. Your particular project may not correspond exactly to any one of these cases, but you can use them as benchmarks to help forecast the kinds of challenges you are likely to encounter, and as models of how to meet those challenges.

Introducing the Case Studies

The three cases are distinguished principally by their size: small, medium, and large. They vary as well in the type of project involved, from marketing and PR to community information services and enterprise applications. To make it easier to keep track, the complexity of each project is roughly proportionate to the size of the company involved, so that the larger companies have the larger projects and the more ambitious and complex objectives. In real life, you could build each type of project at any size level. This section lays the groundwork for each case study; later sections will revisit them and discuss the choices the various Web site developers make in the course of the project.

A SMALL MARKETING AND PR SITE

Canby, Marcus, and Wells is a small legal firm specializing in copyright law. The firm consists of three partners, four part-time legal consultants, and three full-time office staff. Although none of the partners has much direct

chapter 3 BUILDING THE ORGANIZATION

experience with the Internet, they agree on the need to develop a Web site for several reasons. Many of their clients have expressed an interest in communicating via e-mail, and several have recently expressed mild dismay that the firm is not yet on the Web. The partners' sense of being slightly behind the curve was reinforced when two of the firm's biggest competitors put up Web sites. In addition, the firm deals in copyright issues, and the partners have recognized the business opportunities involving online copyright and intellectual property issues. A Web site, they realize, would help demonstrate that the firm understands this new information medium. These business justifications make them ready to listen when one of the staff members, who had taken a class in HTML, puts together a simple demonstration of what the company's Web site might look like. In fact, the presentation strikes a chord with two of the legal professionals. One would like the opportunity to create a set of personal Web pages devoted to the topic of his hobby—home microbrewing. The other, equally taken with the Web's self-publishing capabilities, has offered to translate her studies of online copyright issues into a monthly column for the Web site.

Setting up a corporate Web site is like opening a new channel of communication with the world.

In committing themselves to the Web site, the partners share several underlying assumptions. Although they see a clear value to the Web site, they do not believe that Web development is one of the firm's in-house competencies. They are happy to have a staff member who can assist in day-to-day maintenance, but they foresee outsourcing all the initial development work. They do not anticipate any real revenue from their Web site. They envision it as simply an extension of the existing means by which the firm promotes its services. The firm does not have a large advertising budget to begin with, and this will consume only a portion of it, so they need an economical solution. They also agree, however—especially after reviewing their competitors' Web sites—that it is very important to have a well-designed site that communicates appropriate messages, both verbally and visually, about the firm. (Eventually, even the microbrewing partner agrees that the Canby, Marcus, and Wells site doesn't have room for beer—but at least he can use the background info when he develops his own private site.)

A MEDIUM-SIZED COMMUNITY INFORMATION SERVICE

The executive manager of pop music radio station KRNY has devised a plan for expanding the station's current Web site. Six months ago the company put up a Web site with information about the station's DJs, along with program schedules, links to recording artists, and advertising for existing radio sponsors willing to pay a little extra. Now, what the exec would like to do is create a local pop music resource—an online magazine targeted to listeners. This *digizine* will include monthly feature articles, a calendar of local music events updated daily, a weekly poll of listener music preferences, artist promotions, and a forum where listeners can discuss music-related questions. The exec wants this to be a cool, state-of-the-art resource. It will have Java and—as one of its central features—a VRML-based virtual listening studio, a 3D space where users can wander around and select audio and video clips to preview. If the station can provide a great service to its listeners, he reasons, it will attract more ad revenue to the site. He also envisions adding an online store if the digizine can generate sufficient interest.

To get this project going, the exec turns to the marketing director, who created the initial Web site. When she started the Web project six months ago, the marketing director knew relatively little about the Web. Since then she has learned a good deal, but this project poses a number of new challenges, primarily in the need for more frequent updating of content and in the technical challenges associated with the VRML and multimedia aspects of the project.

A LARGE CORPORATE COMMUNICATIONS SITE

No Strings Attached, a Silicon Valley company making a pocket-size wireless personal communication device, plans to implement a multifaceted corporate Web site that will focus on two key components: employee services and customer service. Two years ago, this company was a start-up with seven employees and a shoestring budget. Now it employs over 200 people and has $10 million in venture capital backing. The new Web site is to be a company showpiece as well as a cost-savings operation. The company employs a large number of technically oriented people, who will be attracted to a system that is leading the way in providing employee services over the Internet. The first application for the site is directed at employees: an online help-line that features a complete Java-based employee benefit enrollment system.

On the customer service side, one corporate goal is to improve customer service response time and customer satisfaction while at the same time trimming the costs associated with providing customer service. In addition to providing a repository of online information resources, an online customer service center can feature a customer service *wizard* that will provide answers to many of the questions most frequently asked of customer service personnel. The center will also enable real-time communication between customers and customer service staff and provide a problem resolution tracking mechanism, enabling customers to trace how their questions are being addressed.

> **The more critical the site is to your mission, the more it needs conceptual experts, such as systems designers, business strategists, and marketing experts to ensure that the product meets more exacting standards.**

This project involves the development of a good deal of proprietary programming. The company envisions that this code, which will first be made freely available to all employees and customers on the Internet, will at a later date be bundled into their hardware and sold as a service, both to individuals who buy the product and to other companies who could then use the product to develop similar online services.

The project leader also faces a significant challenge in terms of ensuring a sufficient level of security for the transfer of confidential information. The development will require coordination among a number of internal departments as well as with external developers.

Selecting Personnel

Three or four years ago, there were no commercial Internet jobs. The only Internet experts were academic researchers at a handful of large universities. Since that time, the industry has exploded, proliferating new job titles almost as rapidly as new Web sites. Designers, marketing experts, programmers, database administrators, and consultants of every ilk have migrated from related fields—among them advertising, multimedia, networking, information systems, and programming. The fact that the industry is still in its infancy, even measured in Internet years, has not prevented anyone from becoming an expert overnight.

This wealth of options is both a blessing and a curse for anyone seeking to put together a team to design, build, and maintain a Web site. How does one decide which job functions are essential and which are superfluous? Is it better to hire employees, contractors, a development company, or an advertising agency? How does one coordinate all the various specialties involved? These are some of the questions addressed in this section.

IDENTIFYING JOB FUNCTIONS

For a short window of time a couple years ago, calling someone a Webmaster conferred an almost mystical status. The Webmaster (a term intended to encompass both the male and female genders) was the cyber-age equivalent of the Renaissance man. Webmasters could do it all—from UNIX system administration and C programming to graphic design and 3D modeling, with a bit of Internet salesmanship thrown in on the side.

These days, as the size, scope, and sheer number of Internet projects has expanded, the Webmaster has been replaced by an army of specialists. This change was probably inevitable—there are not enough true Webmasters to go around, and even when one turns up, few enterprises are willing to entrust the success of an entire project to a single individual.

If the reality of the jack-of-all-cybertrades Webmaster has diminished, however, the name remains in circulation. One sees it on almost every Web site, as the person to whom one should send comments and feedback. Many companies have taken to calling anyone involved with a Web development project a Webmaster, whether a manager, a system administrator, programmer, or designer. Perhaps as a result of its devaluation, the term has lost much of its original cachet. At this point, you are probably better off identifying the job positions you need to fill with more precise designations. Table 3-1 should give you ample options to choose from.

chapter 3 BUILDING THE ORGANIZATION

Table 3-1 Typical Web Project Job Functions

TYPE	JOB TITLE	DESCRIPTION
Management	Project manager	Oversees and coordinates project
	Technical director	Coordinates site programming
	Art or Creative director	Directs interface, graphic design, look and feel
	Content manager	Coordinates the creation and workflow for all content
Development	Systems engineer	Designs the system infrastructure
	Information architect	Designs the structure and layout of information on the site
	Interface designer	Designs the site navigation
	HTML programmer	Writes HTML code to build the site
	Graphic designer	Designs site graphics
	CGI programmer	Writes custom programming for site functionality
	Database developer	Builds database applications
	Content converter	Transfers content to usable Web formats
Content Provision	Copywriter	Writes text for Web pages
	Illustrator	Designs illustrative graphics for Web pages (as distinguished from graphics which are part of the site itself)
	Multimedia developer	Develops digital video, audio, animation, 3D models
Review	Editorial reviewer	Proofreads copy on site
	User reviewer	Provides informal target user response to site
	Sign-off reviewer	Authorizes site content
Testing	Quality assurance specialist	Tests for correct functionality
	Compatibility tester	Tests site with various browsers for appropriate operation under all conditions
	Usability tester	Tests to see that site is "user friendly"
Maintenance	System administrator	Maintains network and hardware infrastructure
	Webmaster	Maintains Web server and site
Marketing	Marketing director	Identifies Web revenue opportunities
	Ad sales representative	Sells Web ad banner space
	Market analyst	Forecasts market trends, conducts research

How many of these job functions you need—and how many people you need for the ones that can take more than one set of hands—depends on your project objectives and your budget. A small Web project might require only a graphic designer and a programmer. The more critical the site is to your mission, the more it needs conceptual experts, such as systems designers, business strategists, marketing experts, and so on to ensure that the product meets more exacting standards. Similarly, the more content and functionality involved, the more technical experts you will need to include. For some representative examples, see the discussion of personnel issues for the three case studies later in this section.

ORGANIZING THE TEAMS

No matter how many people are involved in a project, it is important to establish an organizational model that facilitates communication among team members and increases the efficiency of the project operation. An organizational model helps constrain the participation of team members to the aspects of the project for which they have direct responsibility. Without an organizational structure, a project is more likely to get bogged down in rehashing issues and is also more likely to waste time in unnecessary meetings. In contrast to the standard top-down corporate organizational model, a Web development project team is perhaps best organized in terms of a series of concentric circles. How close to the center each person is depends on the degree of his or her contact and participation in the project (see Figure 3-1).

At the core of the circle are the managers and directors who are responsible for getting decisions made and getting the work done. The project manager oversees the project as a whole to coordinate the work and ensure that all participants understand and complete their assigned tasks. One manager may be sufficient for most small to medium-sized projects. In larger projects it is appropriate to designate managers for each of the components of the project, such as content creation, graphic design, programming, or testing.

chapter 3   BUILDING THE ORGANIZATION

Figure 3-1

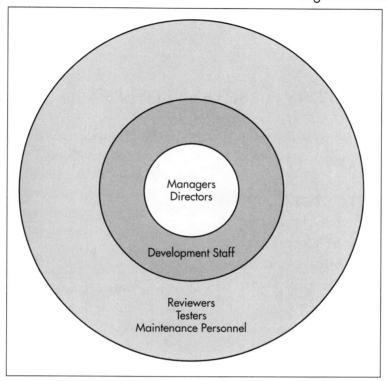

An organizational model helps constrain the participation of team members to the aspects of the project for which they have direct responsibility.

The development staff is one level removed from the core team. This group consists of two distinct types of contributors: concept-level developers who define the product—the architects, in essence—and production-level developers who do the actual building. At the next level are the content providers, who are principally responsible for generating and handing off materials to the production staff for incorporation into the Web site. Their main role is to review and sign off on content. In cases where content already exists and only needs adaptation for a Web site, the content owner is typically an in-house employee. If the Web site needs newly created content, this group consists of two entities: content producers and content owners. In practice, content producers are typically also part of the Web site production staff, not only because there is an economic savings but also because it is a good idea to have content generated by developers who understand the medium for which they are developing. In the outer circle of the organization are reviewers, testers, and maintenance personnel.

CONTRACTORS VERSUS EMPLOYEES

In addition to determining which job functions are needed for a project, the project manager must make a decision about how to fulfill those functions, either by enlisting or hiring employees or by bringing in temporary contractors to do the work. From a management standpoint, there are some strong incentives for using internal resources. It is easier to oversee employees directly, which in turn makes it easier to coordinate the work among team members. There is also a fairly strong economic incentive to stay in-house, since employee wages are typically less than contractor fees, assuming that there is enough work to keep the employee 100 percent productive.

> **Good contractors with a long list of clients bring a level and variety of experience to a project that would be difficult for an ad hoc in-house team to match.**

However, most companies today do not have sufficient expertise in-house to put together a complete Web development team, nor do they have sufficient ongoing demand to justify hiring a full-time staff for this purpose. Good contractors with a long list of clients bring a level and variety of experience to a project that would be difficult for an ad hoc in-house team to match. Contractors also tend to be more accustomed to the vagaries of project work—long hours, intense time pressures, and last-minute crises. Projects conducted in-house at a normal business-as-usual pace invariably take longer than projects built around teams of dedicated contractors. In addition, a good contractor is used to self-management, so the job may actually require less oversight on the project manager's part. A successful contractor will have a lot of contacts in the industry, which means he or she may be able to help you locate other talent for your team. Even if you hire contractors for the bulk of the development work on the project, however, you need to keep a core team of managers and reviewers in-house. Frequently, a company begins a project with only one or two internal resources involved and then gradually evolves a staff to operate the site.

WORKING WITH AGENCIES

In the past year or two, many advertising and PR firms have added the Web to the list of media in which they work. These entities have a strong background in corporate communications and can provide a host of valuable services to a company looking to develop and launch a Web presence. Agencies of this sort charge premium prices for their services. Are they worth the price? The answer, of course, depends on the nature of the project and the quality of the agency. If your project is primarily an exercise in corporate communications or you are attempting to coordinate a Web-based promotional campaign with other media, an ad agency may be exactly the right approach. If you are considering hiring an agency or any other development company, here are some guidelines that will help ensure that you get your money's worth:

- **Make sure deliverables and time lines are clearly defined.** Most good contractors will do this, as much for their own benefit as for yours. See that a plan for contingencies is explicitly addressed. Some companies are more open than others to changes you may want to make down the road.
- **Screen the development team.** Even if an agency or development company has a corps of production workers, they may not specify in their proposal who will be doing the work. If they don't, you should find out who will be on the project and meet them prior to any agreement. Most larger entities rely on outsourced talent, which can vary widely in quality. A good agency should do its best to match your needs to its pool of talent, but you don't need to accept their judgment without question.
- **Make sure that the number of personnel budgeted by the agency is commensurate with the needs of the project.** There are two reasons why an agency might include more people than necessary to complete a project: a legitimate effort to finish the project more

rapidly, or an illegitimate effort to pad the price for unwary clients. To tell the difference, check that the total number of man-hours to be expended is in line with the scope of the project.

* **Evaluate the agency's ability to develop the Web site separately from their ability to provide expertise on how it should be developed.** Many agencies offer excellent development services, but others may still be operating with design assumptions more appropriate for print or multimedia than for the Web. You may find it more useful to hire the agency to consult on the content and design and hire another team to provide the actual development services. Be prepared for the possibility that the agency may have more expertise in design than in technology issues.

PERSONNEL FOR A SMALL PROJECT

One of the partners in the Canby, Marcus, and Wells law firm volunteers to head up the project with the help of the administrative assistant who started things by learning some HTML. They set up a small business account with a local ISP and register a domain name. The ISP offers Web development services, but the project manager decides to hire a separate development team recommended by another law firm. The development team consists of an account manager to handle the business relations, a lead creative designer to define the site interface, an HTML programmer, and a production graphics designer. The project manager also contracts separately with a writer who has experience writing legal review articles to assist in the creation of content for the site.

> **Evaluate the agency's ability to develop the Web site separately from their ability to provide expertise on how it should be developed.**

In the interest of keeping the ongoing budget down, Canby, Marcus, and Wells opts to have in-house staff perform monthly content updates. Professional staff writes and reviews proposed text, then hands it off to the administrative assistant who turns it into HTML and uploads it to the site. The administrative assistant performs all the other updating tasks as well, including checking to make sure links to external resources are still valid, archiving out-of-date content, and filtering e-mail comments from visitors to the site. Since she still has all her old duties—a full-time job on their own—the administrative assistant is heavily overworked. It soon becomes evident that the partnership needs another solution.

They consider hiring the teenaged son of one of the partners to do the updates. Although this would keep them within their budget, the partners are not certain they will get the level of professional service they need. In the end, they find another Web site development company that offers maintenance contracts and specializes in legal profession sites. They are forced to move the domain name to a new location and host it with the development company, but each month they simply send any new content to the maintenance company for updating. At $500 a month, maintenance now costs more than initially budgeted, but as part of the arrangement, they gain links into a community of legal professionals and traffic to their site increases. They further justify the arrangement by noting that it is cheaper than hiring a part-time staff person, and it frees them up to concentrate on their legal business.

PERSONNEL FOR A MEDIUM-SIZED PROJECT

Because she knows she will have fairly heavy need for ongoing content development, the KRNY radio station project manager assembles a team of three contractors—a graphic artist, a programmer, and a content manager—to assist with the production work during and after development. Content for the site comes from the radio station's own staff of music researchers.

In addition to the basic corps of developers, the manager also hires three outside companies. She hires a design firm with extensive VRML experience to build the virtual sound studio and a technical group with Java experience to build the Java applets. She also elects to hire a local advertising agency to develop a marketing strategy and to participate in the initial definition of the site, to improve its chances of generating the revenue the station needs to realize from it. The agency provides design and technical leads to help define the initial project specifications. The production work is then handed off to the VRML and Java teams and to the radio station's own team of developers. The internal developers are also charged with testing all aspects of the project.

PERSONNEL FOR A LARGE PROJECT

The first group hired for the No Strings Attached project is a technical consulting group with expertise in Wide Area Networking and enterprise security. This group helps define the technical specifications for the infrastructure necessary to deliver the human resources (HR) and customer service applications over the Internet. The internal information services (IS) department did insist that it could provide the same service at a much reduced cost, but the project manager rejected their proposal. Instead, she invites selected IS representatives to participate in the selection of a group to do the work, since the IS department will be responsible for maintaining the system once it is in place.

The project manager sets out to find a single development company capable of building the two principal applications, one for the human resources department and the other for customer service. Instead, she happens upon another Silicon Valley start-up that has already built an HR package for handling employee benefits over the Internet. Rather than build a proprietary product from scratch, she decides to license this product and to strike a partnership agreement with its developers for any remarketing of the product the company may do. This still leaves the customer service application, and for that the manager hires a technical group that has developed other projects involving intelligent agents like the tech support wizard application.

Internally, the manager forms teams within HR and customer services to assemble the knowledge bases that will become part of their respective applications and to participate in the review of the products as they are implemented. In addition, she hires an outside testing group to conduct usability and quality assurance testing for the products.

Estimating a Budget

Chapter 5, Registering and Staking Out Cyberturf, examines the range of costs for hosting and maintaining a Web site. This section is primarily concerned with the costs of planning, developing, and updating a site. Table 3-2 lists some representative examples of line items in a Web project budget.

Table 3-2 Sample Budget Items

Planning
- Business and marketing strategy
- Technical design analysis
- Technical writing

Development and Update
- Graphic design
- Systems design
- Interface design
- Content development
- Content licensing
- Copywriting
- Project management
- Web development
- Programming
- Testing

Hosting and Maintenance
- Web site hosting
- Domain name service
- Site updates

DEVELOPMENT COSTS

How much one pays for any of the services listed in Table 3-2 can vary widely. Currently one can hire HTML programmers for between $30 and $75 an hour, graphic designers between $50 and $100 an hour (although many charge by the project rather than by the hour), and programmers and database developers from between $75 and $150 an hour, depending on the particular kind of programming required. This translates into a rough average of about $150 to $250 of production work per page on an average Web site. These and other production activities have the virtue of being fairly measurable. There are other aspects of a Web development project that are more difficult to estimate in advance, such as marketing and advertising campaigns, Internet business strategy consulting, and licensing fees. Table 3-3 estimates costs of Web site development based on the relative size of the site.

Table 3-3 Estimated Budgets for Web Site Development

PROJECT SIZE	HTML PAGES	TOTAL FILE SIZE	ESTIMATED BUDGET RANGE
Small Business Web Site	10 – 20	1 – 2MB	$10,000 – $30,000
Medium to Small Corporate Site	20 – 50	2 – 5MB	$30,000 – $80,000
Medium to Large Corporate Site	50 – 200	5 – 15MB	$80,000 – $150,000
Large Corporate Site	200 +	15MB +	$150,000 – $500,000

These estimates provide some general guidelines for project managers, either when locating funds for a project or when evaluating a proposal from a development company.

BUDGET FOR A SMALL PROJECT

Budgeting for the Canby, Marcus, and Wells project is relatively straightforward, as shown in Table 3-4. The partners initially budgeted $10,000 for development, but ended up spending a little more to get a graphic design team they were comfortable with and a copywriter with whom they had worked before. Their one unpleasant surprise came when they realized that they could not support the amount of work required to keep the site updated internally as they had initially envisioned. They considered abandoning their plans for monthly updates and just leaving the site as it was, but on reflection chose instead to extend their budget and to hire a maintenance company that could provide the services they needed. This arrangement costs the firm $9,000 a year. This is far less than they were already paying for other advertising campaigns, and if the Web site brings them even one or two new clients a year, it will effectively pay for itself. They plan to review the project with the maintenance company at the end of the year and then make a decision about how to proceed in the upcoming year.

Table 3-4 A Small Project Budget

BUDGET CATEGORY	DETAILS	ONE-TIME	MONTHLY	YEARLY	TOTALS
Planning					$0
Development					$12,000
	Project Management	$3,000			
	Interface Design	$3,000			
	Graphic Design	$2,000			
	HTML Programming	$2,000			
	Copywriting	$2,000			
Testing					$0
Operations					$9,000
	Hosting		$150	$1,800	
	Site Updates		$350	$4,200	
	Content Updates		$250	$3,000	
Actual Totals		**$12,000**	**$750**	**$9,000**	**$21,000**
Projected Totals		$10,000	$350	$5,000	$15,000

BUDGETING FOR A MEDIUM-SIZED PROJECT

Radio KRNY calls its site a community information service, but from a budgeting standpoint the project is a vehicle for self-advertising that also has the potential to produce an advertising revenue stream. Management has given the project 18 months to break even. In the interim, funds will come out of the station's advertising budget. Overall, the radio station manager does a fairly accurate job of predicting costs, but two items go over budget. The first is the amount required in licensing fees for the audio clips in the virtual sound studio. The second overage is the development of the studio itself. For various reasons—partly because it is relatively new technology, partly because the design for this section changed repeatedly, partly because possible problems were not identified until late in the process (see the "Testing" section in this chapter for more details)—the VRML project required an additional outlay of funds. Table 3-5 contains KRNY's budget breakdown.

Table 3-5 Medium-Sized Project Budget

BUDGET CATEGORY	DETAILS	ONE-TIME	MONTHLY	YEARLY	TOTALS
Planning					$30,000
	Marketing Agency	$30,000			
Development					$90,000
	VRML Development	$50,000			
	Java Development	$40,000			
Testing					$0
Operations					$88,000
	HTML Programming		$2,500	$30,000	
	Graphic Design		$2,000	$24,000	
	Content Management		$1,500	$18,000	
	Licensing Fees for	$10,000			
	Audio Hosting		$500	$6,000	
Actual Totals		**$130,000**	**$6,500**	**$78,000**	**$208,000**
Projected Totals		$110,000	$6,500	$78,000	$188,000

BUDGETING FOR A LARGE PROJECT

Surprisingly enough, initial projections for the cost of the No Strings Attached Web project actually exceeded the actual cost, as you can see in Table 3-6. This is primarily because projections were made on the assumption that they would have to build both of the two main applications—HR and customer service—from scratch. Instead, they licensed an HR benefits enrollment package from another Silicon Valley company. This initial savings will be offset in future years by lower income generated by any resale of the product. Rather than owning all the profits, they will have to settle for a commission.

Table 3-6 Large Project Budget

BUDGET CATEGORY	DETAILS	ONE-TIME	MONTHLY	YEARLY	TOTALS
Planning					$30,000
	Infrastructure and Firewall	$30,000			
Development					$186,000
	Interface and Graphic Design	$30,000			
	Customer Service Application Development	$120,000			
	Software Licensing Fees for HR Application		$3,000	$36,000	
Testing		$30,000			$30,000
Operations					$111,000
	HR Benefits Enrollment Management (Paid by HR)		$1,250	$15,000	
	Customer Service Content Management (Paid by CS)		$3,000	$36,000	
	Hosting (Paid into IS budget)		$5,000	$60,000	
Actual Totals		**$210,000**	**$12,250**	**$147,000**	**$357,000**
Projected Totals		$250,000	$10,000	$120,000	$370,000

Establishing a Time Line

Depending on the size of the project, it can take anywhere from six weeks to six months to plan and implement a Web site. The chart in Table 3-7 indicates some approximate time lines based on project size. In general, developers try to keep the project duration under three or four months. Given the rapid rate of change on the Internet, a project that takes much longer than this to develop may find itself lagging behind current Internet technology even before it hits the Web. This is another consideration to keep in mind when calculating how many people you need for a project.

Table 3-7 Estimated Time Lines for Web Site Development

PROJECT	ESTIMATED TIME REQUIRED
Small Business Web Site	6 – 10 weeks
Medium to Small Corporate Site	8 – 12 weeks
Medium to Large Corporate Site	12 – 20 weeks
Large Corporate Site	16 – 24 weeks

WEB DEVELOPMENT TASKS

Most development projects divide themselves into three distinct phases: planning, development, and operation (see Table 3-8 for a breakdown of tasks within each phase). Testing may be considered a fourth phase, although for the purpose of this list it has been subsumed under development because testing can occur at repeated intervals within the development stage. Of the entire time allotted to the project, roughly 20 percent to 40 percent will be spent planning, 40 percent to 60 percent developing, and 10 percent to 20 percent testing. How much time ongoing operations will require depends entirely on how much of the site you plan to update and how often. We return to the topic of updating a site later in this section.

Table 3-8 A Sample Web Project Task List

Planning Phase
    Define project goals and requirements
    Identify personnel needs
    Identify hosting and maintenance needs
    Develop request for proposals (RFP)
    Solicit proposals
    Select developer

continued

Table 3-8 *(Continued)*

    Select hosting service
    Develop maintenance schedule

Development and Testing Phase
    Define initial functional specifications
    Identify, buy, and install any required application software
    Define site architecture (structure)
    Identify site content elements
    Define site look and feel (site design)
    Sign off on interface elements (site design, structure)
    Implement site interface
    Obtain preliminary site content
    Conduct preliminary site review
    Conduct browser testing of preliminary site
    Conduct user testing of preliminary site
    Edit finalized content
    Sign off on site contents
    Develop post-development operational procedures
    Sign off on list of changes to site
    Conduct final site review
    Conduct quality assurance (QA) testing
    Sign off on corrections list
    Implement and review final corrections
    Open live site
    Publish project design and technical specifications

Maintenance and Operations Phase
    Obtain periodic usage reports
    Perform periodic site backups
    Update and archive periodic content
    Conduct review of site goals

KEEPING A PROJECT ON TRACK

Web site development project delays typically result from one or more of three causes:

* **Programming snafus**—always a danger when custom code is involved
* **Delays getting site content**—usually a problem when the individuals producing the content have other company business to attend to
* **Interminable requests for changes**—always a problem when people can keep changing their minds about the site design, its content, its functionality, even its scope and purpose

Of these three, the last is the easiest to prevent with good management. A Web development project involves technology that makes it relatively easy to implement changes, even late in the process. This makes it tempting to postpone final decisions about key elements of the project—which, in turn, poses the danger (even in small projects) that repeated revisions may pull the project off schedule. For this reason, the project manager must establish and actively manage reviews and sign-offs. If you are hiring a development company, the degree to which it promises project staff will conduct formal reviews is one indicator of the company's level of professionalism (but keep in mind that a high level of professionalism is not always an accurate indicator of a company's ability to deliver an outstanding product). Elements of the project that lend themselves to review and sign-off include:

* Project functional specification document
* Site architecture (structure)
* Interface design elements (graphics)
* Content elements (text, multimedia)
* Site functionality (programming)
* The completed site

If the project is simple, it might proceed through this list in a linear fashion. More complex development projects involving many interdependencies may involve cycles of this process for each major component. Larger, more complex sites will most likely be put into production in phases. Each phase hopefully will be a functioning subset of the entire site. In all cases, though, the goal is to organize development around key decision points, so that everyone can progress to the next stage with solid footing underneath.

UPDATING THE SITE

The Web demands regular, frequent updates. A Web site that remains static or that gets updated only once a quarter is unlikely to succeed. To some extent, evidence of recent changes is a mark of credibility in an environment where so many Web sites are put up and then abandoned. Users need to know that someone at the other end is actually paying attention to the site and keeping it up to date. More important, though, updating a site is the best way to generate repeat traffic, and getting visitors to return is both a challenging and an essential task. A successful plan needs to provide for site content that lends itself to change and for staff to monitor and implement those changes. What to update and how often to update depends entirely on the size and nature of the site as well as on the availability of personnel to perform updates. Consider the following variety:

> **A Web site that remains static or that gets updated only once a quarter is unlikely to succeed.**

- **Time-sensitive information** such as press releases, product release information, employment opportunities, or a calendar of events
- **Journalistic content** such as newsletters, editorials, or bulletins
- **Time-limited events** such as promotions, sales, contests, or polls
- **User-contributed content** such as forums, comments, contests, or poll responses
- **Visual makeovers** to refresh the look, much as new packaging updates a product

Brainstorming for fresh content is usually less of a problem than finding people to contribute more or less regularly to updates. Ideally, a project should include a number of contributors providing new content on a scheduled basis. If circumstances permit, consider giving these contributors special recognition on the site—after all, the Web is about self-publishing, and the more contributors feel this, the more incentive they will have to produce. The same is true for user-solicited content—any forum for communication will generate fresh content, although user content may require some editorial control to keep it useful to the site's target audience.

If establishing a team of content contributors is not feasible, another alternative is to give one person the responsibility of collecting content from various content owners. Often content suitable for a Web site is originally generated for other purposes, and all that you need is to have someone keep tabs on who has new content and to make sure the content makes its way to the Web site. Figures 3-2, 3-3, and 3-4 present typical time lines for updating small, medium-sized, and large projects, respectively.

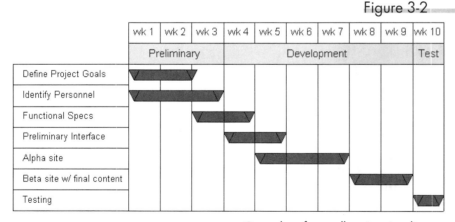

Figure 3-2

Gantt chart for small project time line

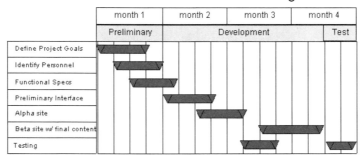

Figure 3-3

Gantt chart for medium-sized project time line

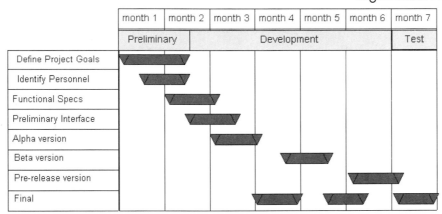

Figure 3-4

Gantt chart for large project time line

Testing

Testing, like ongoing maintenance, is sorely underappreciated and overlooked. This is partly because basic Web development seems so easy and partly because most Web projects are done on a short time line. Proper testing, however, more than repays the time and trouble involved—both in site redesign and in responding to customer complaints. At a minimum, a good testing timetable should include some provision for:

- Content editing and proofing
- Quality assurance and bug testing
- Browser compatibility testing
- Usability testing

How much testing to do and how formally to do it depends on the size and complexity of the project. A small project might make provision for showing the interface to selected users and reporting their responses. Either the developers or the client are likely to take care of quality assurance and browser compatibility testing toward the end of the project. A larger project, by contrast, is likely to involve a series of incremental testing sessions at the end of each development cycle. At each stage, developers will revisit all aspects of testing, but the tests will only evaluate new work. After any necessary revisions are made, that aspect of development will be frozen for the duration of the project.

Both user testing and quality assurance testing are standard practices in the software development industry, and a full treatment of them is beyond the scope of this book. For the average Web site project, these issues are often handled more in the fashion of a design project, with repeated rounds of development and presentation for client approval. QA testing tends to be more ad hoc.

Testing for browser capability, on the other hand, is absolutely necessary because of the way the Web browser market has developed. Initially, HTML was envisioned as an open, cross-platform standard to which all Web browsers would comply. Commercial interest in the Web, combined with competition among Web browser developers for market advantage, has resulted in increasingly wide divergence among features supported by various browsers. Make sure your Web site supports the appropriate range of browsers. (At least prepare for Microsoft Internet Explorer, Netscape Navigator, and the AOL browser.) Web sites often look different depending on which browser is in use. Check out your Web site with different browsers to make sure you convey the same image, message, and services with all of them. Where a year or more ago the commercial online service providers all had their own proprietary browsers, today they're partnering with either Netscape or Microsoft and using their respective browsers to take advantage not only of the advanced capabilities these browsers offer, but also to capture new users by going with a more open architecture and letting users pick which browser they prefer.

In the initial planning stages of a Web project, consider who the target users will be and what browsers they are likely to use before you define site functionality or design—there's no point in building something your audience can't see. As of this writing, the main browser war continues to be between Netscape Navigator and Microsoft Explorer. These two browsers account for more than 90 percent of the browser market, and this number continues to rise. For those who need to be confident that they support all possible users, it might be necessary to restrict development to the old HTML 2.0 standard, which at this point is fairly universally supported. A project that restricts its support to the Microsoft and Netscape browsers can make use of all the features of the current HTML 3.2 standard. Unfortunately, this is not the end of the story. In the first place, each of the main browsers supports an attractive superset of enhanced features that do not necessarily work with the other. With the recent addition of scripting abilities like Netscape's Javascript and Microsoft's ActiveX, the scene has become even more complicated. Both browsers also have the ability to work with a wide range of plug-ins that provide support for a dizzying array of content formats. This, too, adds to the number of choices to be made about what kinds of content to use and what assumptions to make about what users will be able to access.

Moreover, despite the frantic pace with which new versions of browsers are being released, many users continue to rely on previous versions that do not support all the features of the latest versions. In addition, browser development has not proceeded at an equal pace for all computer platforms. You may find that a particular enhanced feature works fine on one platform but poorly on another platform—or even worse, that it sends any computer based on that platform into a tailspin.

In cases where a desired design feature conflicts with the need to support a certain class of user, there are three ways to proceed:

> **Given the rapid rate of change on the Internet, a project that takes much longer than this to develop may find itself lagging behind current Internet technology even before it hits the Web.**

* Develop the feature and advise users of the need for particular browsers.
* Develop multiple versions of the site to accommodate different users.
* Abandon the feature in the interest of a lowest-common-denominator interface.

Whatever your choice, the need to check browser compatibility will complicate the testing process. Ideally, of course, the tester would have a lab equipped with every combination of computer platform and browser. At the very least, you should make sure that all functionality is checked with the most recent versions of Netscape Navigator and Microsoft Explorer on both Macintosh and Windows platforms. A better plan would also check for compatibility with the previous release versions of both applications, and would check the various flavors of Windows in active use (Windows 95, NT, and 3.x). Even before you begin, check out some of the Web sites devoted to the issue of browser compatibility shown in Table 3-9. Knowing up front which browsers support which features will save a good deal of pain later in the project.

Table 3-9   Web Sites with Information on Browser Compatibility

NAME	URL	COMMENTS
BrowserCaps	http://www.pragmaticainc.com/bc	A database of information on browser HTML support. Data come from an online survey people complete by using their browsers.
BrowserWatch	http://browserwatch.iworld.com	A compendium of browser-related information, maintained by Mecklermedia's *iWorld* magazine.
ThreeToad WWW Browser Comparison	http://www.threetoad.com/main/Browser.html	A set of snapshots showing how given HTML pages look in various browsers.

Apart from browser compatibility, you should also consider the following to make sure that your Web site is ready for business and accessible to all who venture by:

- **Assume the customer has a slow modem.** Use a slow modem to check how well the site performs, including graphics load times and the appearance of fancy apps. None of your online toys will do you any good if users find it too frustrating to stay around and watch things take shape on the screen!
- **Make sure all your internal links work and that you have the equipment necessary to handle the type of traffic you hope to receive.** There's nothing worse than going to a site and not gaining access because the server is too busy, except perhaps gaining access and then learning that the area of the site you wanted to go to is still *under construction*.

Eliminate glitches that can turn visitors away. Once you've worked all the bugs out of your site, you're ready to go into production.

TESTING FOR A SMALL PROJECT

The Web development company implementing the Canby, Marcus, and Wells Web site schedules one week at the end of the development period for testing. Given that the project involves very little programming, and that graphic design and copy have been reviewed and proofed at earlier stages of the process, one week seems ample. However, they run into a snag when the senior partner (who has paid little attention to the project until the last week) decides to check the site from home using his America Online account. He discovers that one section of the site, which contains three pages from the firm's four-color brochure, looks like a disaster. The firm had requested that these pages look as much like the print version as possible, including two-column layouts, embedded graphics, and a particular font, and the Web development company dutifully complied. Now the partner finds out the hard way that AOL's browser chokes on the HTML codes required to get the fancy formatting. To get around the problem, the developers create a plain vanilla version of the brochure—one that looks the same on all browsers—to appear as the initial view of the material, with a link to the original version for those with more sophisticated browsers.

TESTING FOR A MEDIUM-SIZED PROJECT

The radio station builds in two rounds of testing: a week of initial user testing at the end of the first development cycle, and two weeks of user and quality assurance testing before the final release. The testing is mostly aimed at the custom Java and VRML applications. Initial testing focuses mainly on the virtual sound studio. On the basis of this, the developers discover that many users can't view VRML environments, and if they can, they rarely understand how to navigate in these worlds. Worse, even those who did know how to get around found the environment provided a slow and frustrating way to preview music clips. Consequently, the station management decides to scale down the VRML project. They retain the VRML studio space as an alternate means of navigating the site, but provide a simpler two-dimensional control panel using HTML and Java for selecting music.

TESTING FOR A LARGE PROJECT

No Strings Attached, perhaps because it is accustomed to testing new computer industry products, reserves a full month for testing before final release of the product—as well as time at the end of each of three development cycles. The project manager hires a software development testing firm, which promises to conduct user response surveys, controlled user testing, and rigorous quality assurance.

The fact that No Strings Attached has purchased a license to a Java-based HR product gives the developers a leg up for their testing. Once the product is installed, they use it to test both customer responses to the concept of providing online services and also as an additional test of the infrastructure and firewall. As they had suspected, they discover that the employees, who are for the most part quite technically oriented, are very enthusiastic about the idea of online access to benefits enrollment and information. However, they also discover some unanticipated difficulties transferring data via the Web and across the firewall to the existing employee database systems. This sets back the development schedule a couple of weeks, but they make up some of that time during the final month of testing, which goes much more smoothly.

Release of the entire project is only one week behind the projected date, a highly commendable outcome for a multifaceted six-month project.

Summary

Most of the topics discussed in this chapter are familiar to those with project management experience, even if they have never tackled a Web project before. That's because most general management skills and techniques apply to Web development. This chapter has presented some of the particular challenges that Web development projects present for selecting personnel, creating a budget, building a time line, and conducting testing.

Many Web projects are born of *Web fever*, the cyber-age equivalent of the gold rush mentality that deludes many companies into believing that they must have a Web site immediately or lose out to their competitors. Such projects typically focus on the Web site as an end product that will be shipped out to customers. In point of fact, setting up a corporate Web site is more akin to opening a new channel of communication with the world. How successful the site becomes depends largely on the ongoing communication that takes place through the channel.

Finding ways to use the channel is a new operational task that may produce changes in how a company itself operates. Such shifts can be stressful and exhilarating, but failure to anticipate them is likely to result in a project that grossly underestimates the time and resources required to keep the Web site alive and well after it is launched.

chapter 4

Creating a Web Identity

I<small>N COINING THE TERM</small> *information superhighway,* Al Gore may have branded the Web with an identity from which it will take years to recover. Probably his intention was to refer to the Internet as a whole, but it is the Web that most common citizens experience and associate with the term, and in many ways Gore's choice of words was unfortunate. A public identity is a collection of images and associations that people can relate to, a point of view and presentation of information that fits with the general feelings, perceptions, and needs of a certain audience. The concept is not difficult to grasp when applied to a TV show, a magazine, a line of clothing, or a company—lots of people, for example, identify with *Seinfeld, Cosmopolitan,* the Gap, or Marlboro Country, Phillip Morris' famous cigarette campaign that captured exactly the sense of where an audience of many millions wanted to go, and even convinced them to start smoking to get there. Terrific concept, terrible cause, but a striking example of how a powerful identity can affect the public. But how does this concept translate to the World Wide Web?

The Web provides a fascinating vehicle for implementing a public identity in new ways because it is live, interactive, and global in reach. Consequently, the presentation strategies and design elements that go into building an identity on the Web are found neither in conventional media such as TV and magazines nor in familiar venues such as stores, libraries, or movie theaters. In addition, both the tools that designers have at their disposal in creating Web sites and the online mission models that companies have developed in their rush to understand and exploit the new medium have led to something of an *identity crisis*. From e-zines to cyberchannels, billion-dollar enterprises such as Ziff-Davis and Microsoft are reaching to create new idioms for this elusive medium. The situation is as exciting as it is confusing, and is no doubt inevitable at a monumental coincidence like the concurrent birth of new technologies and a new medium. The image, however, is more like a scene out of Bob Dylan's *Highway 61* than Al Gore's much-cited information superhighway. Given the presentation and access to new experiences on the Web, that's not such a bad analogy. With so much going on, keeping an eye on the conventional reasons for building a public identity is even more important in cyberspace than on Route 66 or Highway 61. The rationale for presence and the parameters of the environment are simply not that clear, and the onus rests on the developer or manager to provide support for the site's existence.

This chapter is about helping you develop an identity for your Web site prior to and during its launch, and maintaining that identity throughout the site's life cycle. The chapter discusses the development of an online identity in terms of *presentation strategies* and *design elements*. Presentation strategies are big-picture issues that anticipate the users' experience and expectations at both the site and page levels—for example, are people here for fun or business? Design elements are more granular components, from the style of typography employed on the site to its level of interactivity. They help support a strategy and overall mission.

The Web provides a fascinating vehicle for implementing a public identity in new ways because it is live, interactive, and global in reach.

Establishing Some Guidelines

However, before getting down to the nitty-gritty of building an identity for your site, consider the following guidelines for the process:

- **Be flexible.** Your Web identity does not have to match your corporate identity.
- **Be consistent.** The identity of your site should be consistent and apparent throughout all its pages and activities.
- **Be clear.** Your mission and the impressions that you want users to gain from your site should be clear as development continues after the launch.

Although your corporate identity can help you define your Web identity, keep in mind that the two are not necessarily the same. If you are trying to target a specific set of customers or promote a specific product through the Web, your broad corporate identity may not be precisely the one you want to convey at your site. Take, for example, a retail bank that hopes to attract tech-savvy baby-boomer customers with a Web-based home-banking program. Its traditional traits of stability, security, and even stodginess are probably not the qualities that the bank's new marketing manager wants to highlight on its Web site. Instead, efficiency and convenience could be the characteristics to promote. Consider San Francisco's Bank of America site (`http://www.bankamerica.com`). The site creates an aura of fun and self-sufficiency. Figure 4-1 shows off the innovative Build Your Own Bank feature at the site, as well as the use of loosely placed cubes as navigational icons. These elements contrast dramatically with the timeworn banking notion of impenetrable brick and mortar.

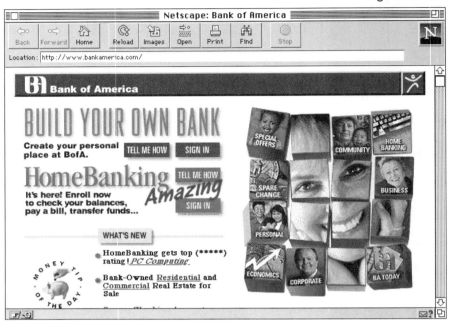

Figure 4-1

The Bank of America site sheds the brick-and-mortar banking image in favor of an image of efficiency and convenience.

Security First Network Bank (http://www.sfnb.com), by contrast, the Web's first Internet-only bank, is as virtual as it gets, but you'd never know it from its Web site. As you can see in Figure 4-2, the bank's home page depicts a dull, conservative, prototypical bank lobby, security guard and all. Why no fun or gimmicks here? The company lacks a brick-and-mortar counterpart on the scale of a Bank of America, and management probably felt the need to relay a sense of security at the site. Strictly virtual, but wholly dependable. Corporate identity can guide Web identity, but ultimately the latter must be consistent with a specific mission on the Web.

Figure 4-2

No fun or gimmicks here—Security First Network Bank hides its virtual identity behind the image of a prototypical bank lobby, complete with security guard (center right).

As you consider how visitors to your site will perceive its identity, keep in mind that each user designs an individual experience when interacting with a site. The site's identity should be consistent and apparent regardless of where visitors come from, and no matter what they do after they arrive. The Disney site (http://www.disney.com), for example, shown in Figure 4-3, has the same slick, clean corporate look—complete with Mickey Mouse ears—on every page.

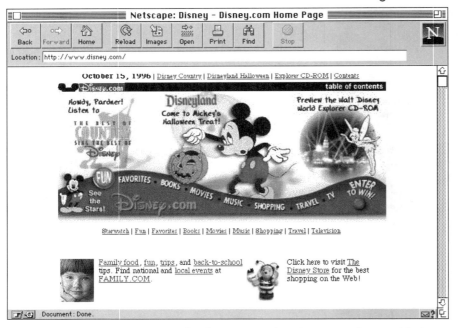

Note the ubiquitous Mickey Mouse ears that provide the user with a visual thread throughout the Disney site.

Finally, remember that maintaining a Web identity is an ongoing process. As you enhance your site with new content, icons, forums, programs, and so on, always ask yourself whether these additions complement and support your site's identity. Take Bills Khaki's Web site (`http://www.iliad.com/bkhaki`), a Pennsylvania retail clothing store. It has a list of favorite sites featuring one entry: A tour guide to New England with hyperlinks to other sites in that region. Why New England? Why not some local center of commerce, and why give the shopper a chance to get out of the store so easily? This feature of the site simply does not help drive its identity. Be clear about your mission and the impressions that you want users to have about your site. Commerce-related sites, for example, should offer content that attracts visitors and motivates sales. If you're targeting a high-tech audience, be sure to keep adding the latest features supported by Netscape Navigator and

Microsoft Explorer, as well as Java applications, multimedia plug-ins, and real audio features.

 Remember, whenever you create a link to another site, you risk losing the user to the new location. Always ask yourself "What do I gain from this link?"—and try to provide a clear route back before allowing your visitors to escape.

Preparing a Presentation Strategy

Web site design offers two basic presentation strategies: *research* and *entertainment*. A site that embodies research design strategies reacts to queries from visitors and returns archival information; users arrive at such a site with specific tasks and goals in mind. Web search engines such as InfoSeek, AltaVista, and Yahoo! are good examples of research sites. A site that incorporates entertainment design strategies, by contrast, provides the user with its own editorial judgment, point of view, or original content; output is spontaneous and proactive—that is, planned in advance and leaving the user little to do but read and enjoy. It would be a mistake, however, to think of these two strategies as polar extremes. Many successful sites (and pages) embody characteristics of both research and entertainment design strategies. If you think at the outset of the design process about where on this spectrum your site and pages fall, it will help you implement their identity. Table 4-1 lays out the fundamental distinctions between these two site strategies.

Table 4-1   Site Strategies

STRATEGY	CHARACTER	CONTENT
Research	reactive	archival
Entertainment	proactive	original

RESEARCH DESIGN STRATEGIES

The prototypical research site serves as a library. A user goes there to find a specific fact or tool. As with a library, the user evaluates the experience at the site based on whether the information is reliable, current, and easy to gather. For example, a visitor might want to see the latest quotes for all the stocks in a portfolio, or retrieve copies of this year's federal income tax forms. In these two instances, success means entering ticker symbols and getting back prices, or locating the 569 federal tax forms and downloading or printing the ones you want.

If you've decided on a mission for your site, the odds are that you've already selected a major content area: weather, travel information, product listings, and so on. If yours is predominantly a research site, you must next consider certain issues surrounding the creation, access, and presentation of archival data, including

- **Data processing.** Secure a source for data, a method for updating your database, and an update schedule.
- **Security.** Decide on a security model and permissions for use of the content, if necessary. (For more information on these issues, see Chapter 6, Acquiring Irresistible Content.)
- **Comprehensiveness.** Consider how much scope to offer. In the case of a weather site, for example, should the data be local, regional, or national? Should the site include forecasts, maps, weather history, or all three?
- **Accessibility.** How simple or complex will the search criteria and access process be for visitors to the site? At a travel site, for example, can people request information by city, or just by country? Will queries concerning lodgings and restaurants be available by budget group, ambiance, guide rating, or all three?

As the range of choices that you offer your users grows more elaborate, the programming and design solutions for their visual presentation become more complicated—which equates to more cost for you and slower online

chapter **4** CREATING A WEB IDENTITY

response time for the user. Ultimately, the depth, richness, and complexity of your content as well as your decisions concerning access methodology will have an enormous impact on the identity of your site.

Two of the most popular search engines, Yahoo! (`http://www.yahoo.com`) and AltaVista (`http://www.altavista.digital.com`), are research sites. Both use distinctive but equally successful identities in creating a site that helps Web surfers find resources. Check out Figure 4-4 to see how Yahoo! styles itself as user-friendly and helpful. It takes surfers where they want to be with a sense of fun, excitement, and even rebellion that contrasts favorably with the dull notion of searching through hundreds of thousands of sites and page references. Consider the outrageous name: Yahoo! Note the icons along the banner: New, Cool, Random, and Daily Picks. Homing in on the lifestyle of its users, Yahoo! is trying to create a culture around a mere search engine by catering to the quirky needs of a cyberhappy but not necessarily cybersavvy user group.

Figure 4-4

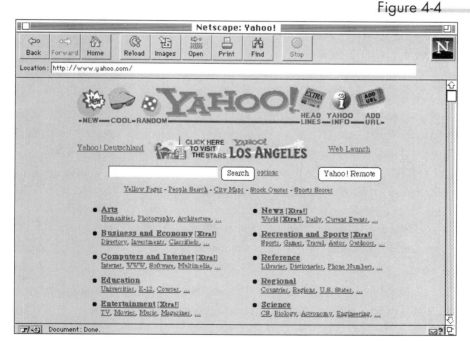

The Yahoo! site caters to the quirky needs of a cyberhappy user group.

Technical Design Choices

From a technical point of view, there are two main ways to assemble information for presentation on the Web: *hardcoding*, which is simple and static, and *dynamic page creation*. Each one affects the way users can search your site, as well as your site's complexity and output—and thus its identity. Hardcoding is nothing more than creating a series of hot links that call up static HTML pages. Page content changes only if someone literally handkeys it in HTML. Although hardcoding is time-consuming, in the short run it is effective and economical if the information at your site changes infrequently and is limited in scope. As of this writing, most research sites on the Web are hardcoded, as are the majority of corporate sites, because they have no need for elaborate data manipulation capabilities.

If the content at your site changes often, or if users need to perform complex searches, hardcoding is not for you. Imagine precoding an individual Web page for each of the stocks of the thousands of publicly traded companies every time the price of a stock changes! In a case like this, use dynamic page creation. Dynamic pages are generated spontaneously—on the fly—based both on changes in a database and in response to individualized user inputs. For example, when a visitor requests a list of prices for common stocks, the resulting page will be a unique combination of the user's choice of stocks and their prices at the time of the query. If the user were to pose the same query five minutes later, it would produce a page with different results to reflect any price changes in the interval.

 Yahoo! also has full stock market quote facilities, including a way to create your own private portfolio using a browser feature called a *cookie*. A cookie is a file with specific information that the Web site places on a visitor's computer in the Netscape folder—in this case, a list of stock symbols. Each time the user goes to the site, the cookie can refresh the marked information—in this case, the portfolio.

The underlying technology at Yahoo! also affects the way users relate to the site. It's based on a qualified list of Uniform Resource Locators (URLs), or Web addresses, submitted by site owners for listing in various categories. This makes the results of a query crisp, short, and snappy—just what

Yahoo!'s audience is looking for—but not as thorough as other methods. Also, Yahoo! takes users to a home page, which is not necessarily the page containing the specific information the user wants.

AltaVista, on the other hand, speaks to the user who values comprehensiveness over guidance and ease. AltaVista means *high view*. As you can see in Figure 4-5, there are no zany antics at this site; instead, its supporting graphic is a broad vista: mountains, valleys, peaks. Sponsored by Digital Equipment Corporation, AltaVista's selling point is number-crunching power: its ability to deliver the fastest, largest, and most complete set of matches to a user's search criteria. AltaVista's home page boasts its range of access and sophisticated technologies, something you won't find on Yahoo! because its technology is more limited. Technically, AltaVista is a spider: it searches the pages of Web sites, adds them to its database, and then presents a list of pages, not sites. AltaVista does not offer categories the way Yahoo! does, but can be much more effective in leading a surfer to a page containing specific information.

Figure 4-5

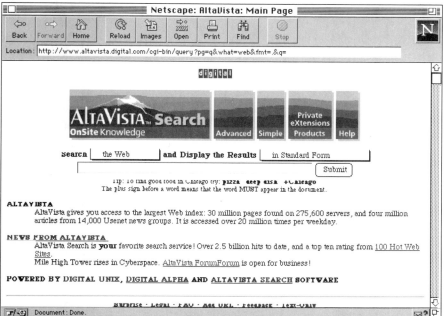

The AltaVista site speaks to users who value comprehensiveness over guidance and ease.

Search Options

Some commercial search engines create a text index of all the words on a site. Research sites such as AltaVista, Excite, Inktomi, and Lycos have no hardcoded information except their search forms; a component of the engine formats the results of each search into a new HTML page. The *text DataBlade* portion of the Illustra database from Informix is an example of a text search engine you can use to do indexing for your own site.

Databases, on the other hand, cannot be searched by a text DataBlade since no pages exist prior to the query. However, it is possible to detail and customize queries against a database. The search engine processes user input against records in the database and lists the results in a dynamically created Web page. Queries can include ranges and Boolean operators such as logical *And*s and *Or*s. Of course, more choice begets more complication and expense. The amount of system design and programming necessary to respond to the query "List all Italian restaurants" increases dramatically with the query "List all Italian and Chinese restaurants in San Francisco with an average price of $50 to $100 per person." An example of this type of query can be found at Urban Access (http://www.urbanaccess.com), a database of restaurants and places to go in New York City. Databases can also perform calculations and include them in the results of a query. For example, a stock portfolio program not only searches for stock price, it also multiplies that price by a number of shares to produce a portfolio value. (For more information on databases, see Appendix A, Killer Apps.)

These issues and how you resolve them ultimately influence your site's identity. For example, you have to determine the look, feel, and content both of pages that solicit user input and of pages that display results. You must also decide on the back-end technology that will drive your system: text DataBlade, SQL database, and so on. To ensure a consistent and clear identity on your site, it is therefore critical to keep open the lines of communication between programmers and graphic designers throughout the launch and the lifetime of your Web site.

Besides the clear difference in graphic design between these two sites, their identities play out strongly through their user interface. At Yahoo!, content has been arranged in numerous recognizable categories, subcategories, and sub-subcategories. Sometimes the breakdown is so helpful that you can find a site without ever inputting a search term. While Yahoo!'s home page is dense with text—Countries, Regions, U.S. States, and so on—it's laid out in a clear and functional manner. At AltaVista, by contrast, it's all search terms. Visitors can define the level of detail they want retrieved for each match, but not much more than that. The search engine simply lists matches in order of highest confidence, and response is rarely less than 50,000 matches. In short, both sites do a terrific job of promoting their identities.

 Making difficult issues seem simple to handle with database programs can win a lot of praise: success translates into easy input and display of information. However, if the system doesn't work as expected, you can take a lot of heat. If you're wary of the time and money involved with database programs, look around to see if other sites are doing what you are setting out to do. You may be able to establish a link that will enable users to take advantage of another site's capabilities. For example, the *New York Times'* site links to `http://www.quote.com` to provide its users with stock quotes.

ENTERTAINMENT DESIGN STRATEGIES

Entertainment sites typically offer amusement, editorial comment, advertising, and news. Some of the most popular examples are the so-called *e-zines*, electronic magazines such as Suck (`http://www.suck.com`) and Word (`http://www.word.com`)—the latter shown in Figure 4-6. These magazines are only available on the Web, and users visit them for their original editorial content, insight, and attitude. Visitors may be familiar with the magazine's style, but have no idea what articles, advertisements, stories, or games they are going to find when they log on. Users judge the site as they would a newspaper or TV show.

Figure 4-6

The Word site is one example of an entertainment site.

Movie sites have been a popular way for film producers and distributors to hype a new movie. For example, at the Web site for the Disney movie *Toy Story* (http://www.toystory.com), the visitor can see more on the rivalry between Woody and Buzz by viewing a computer animation film (a mother download, by the way!), play games, take a quiz, or download clips of the film. It's entertainment—pure and simple.

There are some important site design issues specific to entertainment strategies:

* **Direction.** Make sure that the user knows what is new (what you want to emphasize), and how to get to that information quickly. Since new visitors don't know exactly what an entertainment site has to offer and have no explicit expectations, you need to help them discover and focus on the most intriguing areas.

chapter **4** CREATING A WEB IDENTITY

* **Visual Appeal.** The graphic design elements of entertainment sites are critical because the experience (as opposed to the results) is an important part of the attraction.
* **Archiving.** Decide what will happen to the *old* content, once you replace it with new material. Will it go into a user-accessible archive, or will it simply disappear?

CNET (http://www.cnet.com), shown in Figure 4-7, is an e-zine about the computer and communications industries, and an excellent example of a proactive site with a well-defined identity and lots of promotional support in multiple media: print, broadcast, and online. There are also satellite search-engine sites (http://www.search.com and http://www.shareware.com). A CNET television show on the Sci-Fi cable station works in conjunction with the Web site, and there's a weekly e-mail bulletin for registered members (registration is free), so it's really wired on the entertainment side.

Figure 4-7

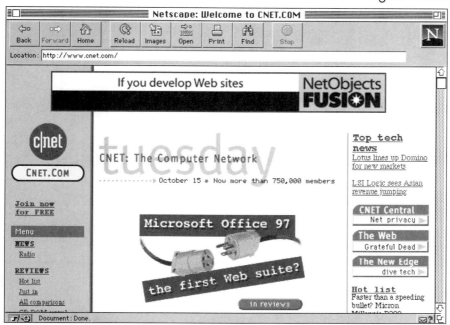

The CNET site is an excellent example of a proactive Web site with a well-defined identity and lots of promotional support in multiple media.

By highlighting what's new, CNET helps users, especially veteran users, decide where to go. The color scheme is the same throughout the site, and it brings a sense of consistency to an otherwise hectic environment. CNET's user interface makes navigation manageable. Check out the control bar (index) on the left-hand side of the screen. It appears in the same place on every page at the site and it takes visitors everywhere they want to go. CNET has many features designed to make user input part of its identity, in particular an entire page devoted to *community*. There are daily polls that enable users to participate and hear from each other, and bulletin board topics are strongly promoted. The weekly e-mail bulletin helps make visitors feel part of the endeavor.

The nature of your mission and content may well dictate the dominant presentation strategy that you take in developing a site, and of course many sites use a combination of strategies to succeed: research-oriented sites need not be without some fun to make the research process more enjoyable, and entertainment-oriented sites are not necessarily devoid of useful and practical information. Table 4-2 summarizes some of the considerations for building both research and entertainment sites.

Table 4-2 Strategy Checklist

ENTERTAINMENT	RESEARCH
How are you coordinating the production of textual content and graphic design?	What types of information will users want to access?
How often do you need to update your content?	What search criteria will you offer to users?
What is the best method of access: hardcoding or a database?	What is the best method of access: hardcoding or a database?
How are you alerting your users to new content?	How will users input the criteria on the screen?
Is there a way for your users to locate old content?	How will you display search results?

There is, however, a great deal of vagueness on the Web concerning mission and identity. To avoid getting lost in the fog, you need to focus on specific goals in developing an online presence. The example in the following section demonstrates an excellent and well-thought-out blending of both strategies.

WWW.LIFESCENE.COM—A CASE STUDY IN TRAPPING A SURFER

BroadVision, a California-based developer of tools for electronic commerce on the Web, developed the excellent model described in this section to demonstrate how to use the interplay of reactive and proactive strategies to produce a compelling environment. BroadVision's LifeScene is a hypothetical Web site launched by Quastar, an imaginary international corporation specializing in consumer electronics. The site is dedicated to providing individuals with a compelling cyberdestination that combines lifestyle-oriented editorial content with promotional programs and shopping services for brands offered by Quastar and affiliated companies. Consider the following scenario for catching a typical Web surfer and making him a regular visitor.

The bait

Mike discovers LifeScene while surfing the Web one January afternoon. The site presents him with a logon screen that invites him to enter a LifeScene user name if he has one. Mike has never been to LifeScene before, so he clicks on the *Enter* button without specifying a user name. LifeScene welcomes him and offers him a 10% discount coupon for products in the LifeScene store, BuyScene, if he registers. Mike decides to register and fills out a simple form with basic profile information:

Name: Mike
Zip code: 94070
Sex: Male
Age: 30-35

Education: College

Marital status: Married

Number of children: 2

Age range of children: Under 10

Income range: (Omitted)

Modem speed: 28.8

Interests: Sports, Family, Health, Photography

Mike selects a privacy profile option for all the elements in his profile to prevent his information from being used outside the site. LifeScene verifies that Mike's registration is not a duplicate, enters his profile information into its visitor database, and then presents Mike with a personalized home page. If Mike had elected not to register, LifeScene would have allowed him to enter as a guest and built him a generic home page.

The hook

Mike's personalized home page has icons pointing to SportsScene, HealthScene, and FamilyScene, which relate to his profiled areas of interests. The SportsScene icon links him to a page containing results and commentary on his local professional sports teams, a listing of local and national sports telecasts, and a bulletin board with a discussion on last night's games. The HealthScene icon leads to a directory of local health clubs, an article titled "How to Avoid Sports Injuries," and Common Children's Ailments, a discussion group for users of the site with comments and advice about the topic. An advertisement displayed prominently at the top of the page shows a picture of a Ford minivan driving down a snow-covered country road. If Mike clicks on the picture he sees the address of the local Ford showroom, and gets access to consumer reports on the van. He also has the opportunity to get a free Ford sweatshirt by entering his current car model and its date of manufacture, printing out a coupon, and taking it to the local dealer in the next month.

Mike also notices that he has two icons called Profile and Electronic Wallet. He clicks on Profile, and the result is a page containing the information he gave the site about himself. The page gives Mike the option to update, delete, or extend the profile with information and preferences such as his address and credit card number for purchases. A privacy option for each profile entry is always available. Mike clicks on the Electronic Wallet, and sees that it contains the 10% discount coupon for the BuyScene store, just as the registration screen promised. In addition, he has received various coupons targeted to his interests, including a $10-off coupon for a children's electronic game called *Look and Spell* and a two-for-the-price-of-one offer on camera film.

Always interested in exploring family-related topics, Mike decides to go into the FamilyScene area and chooses an article on "How to Take Pictures of Children," which is consistent with his interest in photography. An ad for Quastar's Compact Video Camera appears offering a winter season special of 20% off at the BuyScene store. Mike browses a few articles on photography highlighted by the FamilyScene library and associated bulletin boards offering articles and tips such as "What Light Is Best" and "How to Get Your Kids to Cooperate for the Camera." In a bulletin board associated with camera models, Mike reads multiple reviews for Quastar's Point-and-Shoot Camera from customers who had purchased it at the BuyScene store. Based on some outstanding comments from like-minded customers who provide excellent insight into the strengths and weaknesses of the product, Mike decides to buy one, too.

BroadVision's hypothetical www.lifescene.com demonstrates how to use the interplay of reactive and proactive strategies to produce a compelling environment.

No sting, just a win for everyone

Mike clicks on the BuyScene icon and is greeted by a Personal Sales Assistant (PSA). The PSA notices that Mike has a two-for-the-price-of-one coupon on film, and gives him the option to obtain information about the film or to simply leave it in his Electronic Shopping Cart. Mike decides to buy the camera first, and quickly finds the exact model he is looking for by searching a Virtual Product Catalog by manufacturer and price range. He reviews the features he wants and previews a zoom lens by viewing what the picture looks like of some kids playing in the snow at both 80mm and 110mm zoom. Satisfied, he tells the PSA he wants to buy it. The PSA places the camera in his Electronic Shopping Cart, then asks Mike if he would like a carrying case for the camera or an extended warranty option. Mike decides to take both and the PSA adds them to the shopping cart.

Mike is satisfied with the items he has found, so he asks the PSA to make the purchase. The PSA calculates and displays the total price, including state and local sales tax and shipping at a two-day rush option Mike selects from a menu of shipping options. The PSA also detects that Mike has a 10% discount coupon and asks if he wants to use it now or save it for another visit. Mike elects to use it now. The PSA then prompts Mike for his credit card information and address, assuring him of the security of the transaction. Mike enters the information and it is processed. The PSA gives Mike the option to store his address and credit card information in his profile to speed up transactions at a later date, and Mike agrees. The PSA confirms his payment and shows Mike a copy of the receipt that will go into his Electronic Wallet. The receipt shows what was bought, when, and for what amount, including a confirmation number to use with the BuyScene's Customer Service Department. The 10% discount coupon disappears from Mike's wallet, but shows up on the receipt. Mike is happy with his purchase and logs off after bookmarking LifeScene, ready for his return next time he logs on.

Case study summary

LifeScene works because it understands its mission—to create a quality professional lifestyle experience that incorporates and promotes the purchase of tools that support the extension of that experience into one's day-to-day offline environment—and it creates an environment that fulfills the mission with an identity that Mike can relate to: it provides value and convenience that sets a new agenda for electronic commerce by blending research and entertainment strategies to engage the visitor. Table 4-3 illustrates how parts of LifeScene's sales mission map to identity components that deliver the right result at the site.

Table 4-3 Fulfilling the Mission

MISSION TACTIC	SOLUTION
Attract and retain visitors.	LifeScene provides personalized content, related community bulletin boards, targeted ads, and merchandise recommendation. A sense of community combined with targeted, compelling, Java-enhanced animation draws Mike into the site.
Engage visitors in personalized dialogue.	LifeScene asks the user for preferences and presents content tailored to those preferences. Mike gets the opportunity to add to his profile and give feedback on what he sees and does. He adds his credit card information profile and helps Ford identify the age and make of his current car. This information helps LifeScene better understand and cater to his needs.
Motivate visitors.	LifeScene offers incentives based on Mike's personal profile (interests in family, health, and photography) and his interests and behavior as a visitor (interest in camera and observation of purchase). This triggered the giving of a range of incentives from a generic coupon for 10% off at the entire site to a coupon for film targeted to Mike's profile.
Fulfill transactions.	LifeScene processes the order and authorizes and handles secure payment. Mike's Personal Sales Assistant efficiently handled all the steps needed for a successful transaction, including the pricing, the tax, what coupons to use, and the back office integration for closing the sale.

Other sites are breaking ground in creating original identities as well. Bristol Meyers, for example, has created an extraordinary site aimed at women's wellness called http://www.womenslink.com. The PointCast Network (available at http://www.pointcast.com), while not a site, is software that broadcasts breaking news in a unique and intriguing way by delivering a personalized set of information and advertising according to a viewer's interests. Part of what is so exciting (and confusing) about cyberspace is that new idioms for the Web presence are appearing all of the time. With a comprehensive outlook for evaluating sites based on mission, content, and identity, it becomes easier to separate quality material and efforts from the chaff.

Leveraging Design Elements

There is so much fluff in discussions of the Web that it is difficult to identify tangible and succinct factors in the success or failure of a site. Even the concept of presentation strategies can be elusive, given that the two aspects—research and entertainment—often combine in a successful site. Design elements, by contrast, are more granular components, from the typographical style to the level of interactivity. Used in conventional media and software to support a strategy and overall mission, they are less elusive, and therefore easier to critique. Comments such as "That font is too frivolous" or "There is no tension in this layout" hint at design issues that clearly affect a site's sense of identity.

> **Graphic design is as important to a Web site as clothes are to a person. It may not be the only thing that defines your Web identity, but it certainly makes a significant impression.**

These issues are just as relevant on the Web as they are in other media, and add to the manager's vocabulary in describing and evaluating a design effort. This section focuses on three important design elements:

* Graphic design
* User interface
* Interactivity

While the choices in these areas can differ depending on whether a site employs research or entertainment strategies, these elements have a dramatic impact on the user's experience regardless of design strategy.

GRAPHIC DESIGN

Graphic design is as important to a Web site as clothes are to a person. It may not be the only thing that defines your Web identity, but it certainly makes a significant impression. In this discussion, graphic design refers to:

- Typography
- Images
- Color
- Layout

These choices enable you to determine the character, look, and feel of words and icons. Is the font serious or fun? Are the pictures staid or whimsical? Are the colors bright or understated? All these elements contribute to a site's overall look, message, and attraction. If you are already familiar with the basic graphic design process involved in desktop publishing, there are some special cautions to consider along the way to designing a good Web interface. The Web's graphic design options are more limited than those print media offer. In page layout, for example, the full panoply of paragraph alignment options available in desktop publishing doesn't carry over onto the Web. Also, as every Web surfer knows, images—from a logo to a cartoon—take longer to download than text, often a lot longer. However, if you understand your resources, there are plenty of tools around to make your graphic design effective. (See Appendix A, Killer Apps, for a detailed description of tools.)

Typography

Typography has a dramatic effect in practically every major modern medium from newspapers to television to individual correspondence. Designers specializing in corporate identity pay particular attention to typographical detail in creating a logotype for their clients. Consider some of the more ubiquitous innovations over the past ten years from companies such as IBM and AT&T. Modern word processing and desktop publishing programs brought a new level of typographical control to the everyday consumer. In HTML there are basic tags for type manipulation supported by most browsers. Your font options include

- Bold
- Italic
- Underline
- Blinking

- Emphasized
- Text color
- Heading levels (six)

Don't be tempted to make all text the same color. Variations help the users determine what's clickable, and enable them to keep track of where they've already been. However, don't choose different colors for things that are essentially the same.

Designers can decide on different colors for when text is readable (default, black), clickable (default, blue), and clickable/visited (default, red). There is also a tag to identify the font in a document—<FONT FACE=>—and now both Microsoft Internet Explorer and Netscape Navigator support this tag. Netscape Navigator supports specific font size tags that make a font larger or smaller (relatively) from 1 to 7, similar to WordPerfect's font manipulation commands. Each tag uses the base font as a starting point and grows from the baseline. The Web designer can change any of these with tags; users, however, can override designer choices about text, colors, and fonts by changing certain preferences in their browser.

Most users either don't know how or don't bother to change font style and size in their browser. The *proportional* default on most browsers is Times 12 point, and the fixed is Courier 12. Most site designers use proportional type most of the time, assuming Times 12 will appear; they save fixed for text that they want to stand apart. However, in HTML, the site designer and the user share control over how text appears on the screen. The designer has control over things like color, underlining, bold, and italics (the latest browsers can throw this into question), but the user can choose the style of the proportional font from any font on the browser's font menu. The user also chooses the baseline size, and all text is produced in proportion to that size. For example, if a user chooses Helvetica 16 as the baseline, text will be Helvetica, and some function of 16—either 16 (1 × 16), or 8 (0.5 × 16), and so on. The designer can maintain more control using *fixed* fonts, although this option offers the user a smaller font menu. As for size, there's no proportionality: the size is whatever the user chooses.

If you want complete control of type, say for a logo, then you must forgo HTML altogether and create an image file for the text—the user can't interfere with that. All those fancy shazam-style fonts that paper the Web are actually images (and that's why they require so much download time). Whether you use an image file or HTML to provide text depends on how much control you want over its appearance.

A good example of effective use of HTML fonts can be seen at the site of New York University's Interactive Telecommunications Program (http://www.itp.tsoa.nyu.edu), shown in Figure 4-8. The big ITP in the middle is an image file, but the rest of the words are HTML text. The designers used proportional fonts for most of the text, but switched to fixed fonts for information that they wanted to emphasize, such as the date. Try experimenting with various fonts in your browser to see the effects on the type at the site.

Figure 4-8

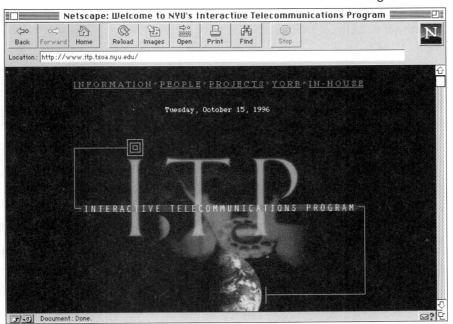

The ITP site contains fixed (date) and proportional fonts (control bar).

When evaluating a page, you should view it on both a Macintosh computer and a Windows PC. The point size specifications have different effects on each platform. Many designers actually do their work on a Mac, but most users view the screens with a PC. By looking at the site on both platforms, you can help make sure that the design doesn't change too drastically from one to the other. Typically, Windows type appears larger than Macintosh type.

Images

Images are a huge and ubiquitous element in Web design. Even if you want to avoid long downloads and are not out to create a high-end visual site, there are important ways to use images to enhance your project. In general, simple images use GIF format—8-bit images suited for line art graphics, and typically used in buttons, toolbars, and logos. A GIF file can have a limited palette (up to 256 colors) making the file small enough to be used as a navigation aid without slowing the user down too much. JPEG files, by contrast, are 24-bit and can have a palette of millions of colors. These are great for photographic images.

 The Macintosh and the PC Windows versions of Navigator and Internet Explorer have palettes that only share 216 of the 256 colors. You can get the 216-color palette for Adobe Photoshop from Adobe at `http://www.adobe.com/newsfeatures/palette/#palettesanddithering`. Use it to ensure that the image looks the same on a Windows or Macintosh computer.

The most basic use of images is as a background for a page. Clever use of the background image tag in HTML can make a page appear extremely sophisticated. Background images tile according to their size until they fill a page—that is, an image is as big as the screen will appear once; an image 40 pixels square will repeat as many times as the screen is wide and high.

Another basic use of images is as navigational helpers. Use a small graphic to highlight features of your site, such as new information, a help center, or a special department. A good example of this technique is the Web site at Brill Information Services (`http://www.brill.com`). While mutual

chapter **4** CREATING A WEB IDENTITY

funds information may seem like a dull topic, this site spices up its page with a tiny dancing tomato dude talking about what's new. (There's no sample here because the printed page can't give you an animated image, but the site is worth checking out.)

 The animated tomato at the Brill site makes use of a format known as multiframe *GIF89a*. Something like this is easy to create but takes more download time than a still. A good program for creating GIF89a images is GifBuilder for the Mac, available on shareware sites (such as `http://www.shareware.com`). PC equivalents are Egor and the GIF Construction Set for Windows.

Some sites get cluttered with *eye candy*: graphics that do little for the user either aesthetically or functionally. For example, the IRS Web site (`http://www.irs.ustreas.gov`) shown in Figure 4-9, displays enormous pictures that add little to the Web experience except download time.

Figure 4-9

Loaded and cluttered: The IRS site.

171

Other sites hit it just right. Check out HotWired (`http://www.hotwired.com`), shown in Figure 4-10, the e-zine created by the publishers of *Wired* magazine. The colors here are bright and intense. The drawings help users navigate. Although simple, they have a futuristic style consistent with the identity of the site.

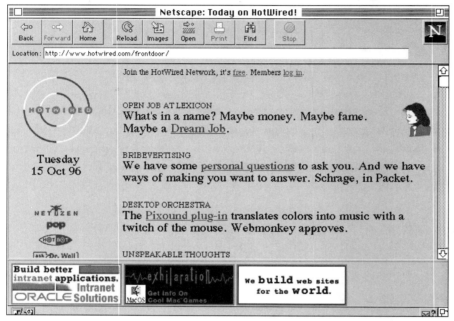

Figure 4-10

Simple but futuristic: Cyberstyled graphic images at the HotWired site

Using the same tools, an insurance company has created a completely different visual identity. No three-dimensional swirling magenta icons for the Atlantic Benefit Group site (`http://www.cross.net/abg`), shown in Figure 4-11. Rather, a clean, quiet, simple design with seashell images and light blues gives an appropriate sense of serenity and security. Remember, images are information, not just accents or diversions. Always use them thoughtfully to support the mission and identity of a site.

Figure 4-11

Serene and thoughtful: The Atlantic Benefit Group site

Working with layout

The positioning and alignment of text and images on a page, also known as layout, contributes strongly to the feel of a site, as well as to its ease of use. As noted earlier, layout options on the Web are more limited than in desktop publishing. HTML gives the designer relatively few reference points for placing text and objects. For example, without defining a table of frames, one cannot easily justify text and images except in relation to the left, right, or center of a page. There is no *ruler* or *indent* option in HTML, except the <BLOCKQUOTE> tag, which functions much like the Tab key in word processors. Using <BLOCKQUOTE>, you can indent some or all of your text. Using more than one <BLOCKQUOTE> tag increases the size of the indent. While HTML options are beginning to expand, the current options for layout are most easily broken into three classes:

* **Frames.** Artificial subwindows created within the main browser window.
* **Tables.** Grids created within a browser window through HTML tags.
* **Alignment.** Positioning of objects with respect to a page, table, or frame.

Frames

Frames permit designers to segment the screen into separate windows. With support from the latest browsers, Netscape 3.0 and Microsoft Explorer 3.0, frames have become popular lately. Aesthetically, they help keep a site looking sleek and organized. Functionally, they enable users to change content on one section of a site (within a frame), while maintaining content in other frames. One of the most common uses of frames is for navigation. For example, an index appears in a frame at the left on the site of investment advisor Compass Funds (http://www.compassfunds.com) shown in Figure 4-12. As the user clicks on sections, the content changes in the right frame. This is done by having the link on the navigation frame be targeted at the output frame, allowing the user to jump from one part of the site to another without having to scroll down and look for navigation tools, or constantly hit the *Back* button on the browser. Frames are another example of something that looks clear when you see it, but are an ugly experience to build with HTML. There are several WYSIWYG (What-You-See-Is-What-You-Get) HTML editors that can make frame design easier. (For more details on HTML editors, see Appendix A.)

Figure 4-12

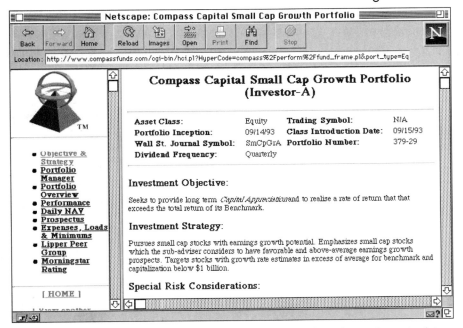

The Compass Funds site with its Index frame (left) and Main frame (right)

Tables

You can define tables with any number of rows and columns much as you can on a word processor. While the options are not as precise or extensive as those found in page layout programs for printed matter, the formatting tools can create a pleasing Web page layout when used in the right combinations.

Tables can be used on the Web in the same way as they are in desktop publishing or word processing: to organize text and graphics in a defined format. However, in HTML a table doesn't always look like a rigid grid with lines and borders used to display columnar data. For example, on the home page of the Weather Channel (http://www.weather.com), shown in Figure 4-13, the layout depends on a table, but an outside user would never know it. Tables divide a Web page into a grid. You can use each cell in the grid to place and align text and images—a much richer set of options than straightforward page alignment. When creating a table, the designer can control the amount of space around each cell, make the borders of the table invisible, and merge cells vertically or horizontally. The Weather Channel image makes extensive use of hidden borders and merged cells to cause images and text on the page to appear as if they were not dependent on a grid. Tables are perhaps the ugliest type of HTML tag combination you will ever see. This is a place where a WYSIWYG HTML editor is most useful.

Figure 4-13

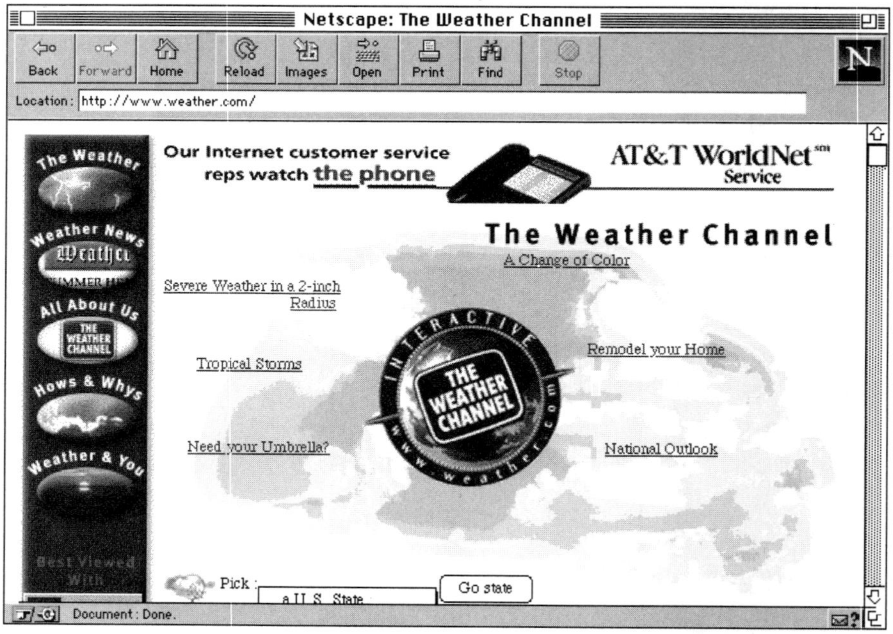

At the Weather Channel site, a table keeps the busy home page organized.

Alignment

Alignments are limited, but can still produce satisfying results if used in conjunction with frames and tables. The basic paragraph tags are

* New paragraph
* Line break
* Left flush

chapter 4 CREATING A WEB IDENTITY

* Right flush
* Centered
* Preformatted text
* Unordered lists
* Numbered lists

 If your site has advertising, be sure you incorporate dedicated ad space into your layout on appropriate pages. The impact of advertising on a page designed to accommodate its messages is profoundly greater than if you put it on a banner slapped in a margin. Check out the interface of PointCast, shown in Figure 4-14, for a good example of a well-thought-out design.

Figure 4-14

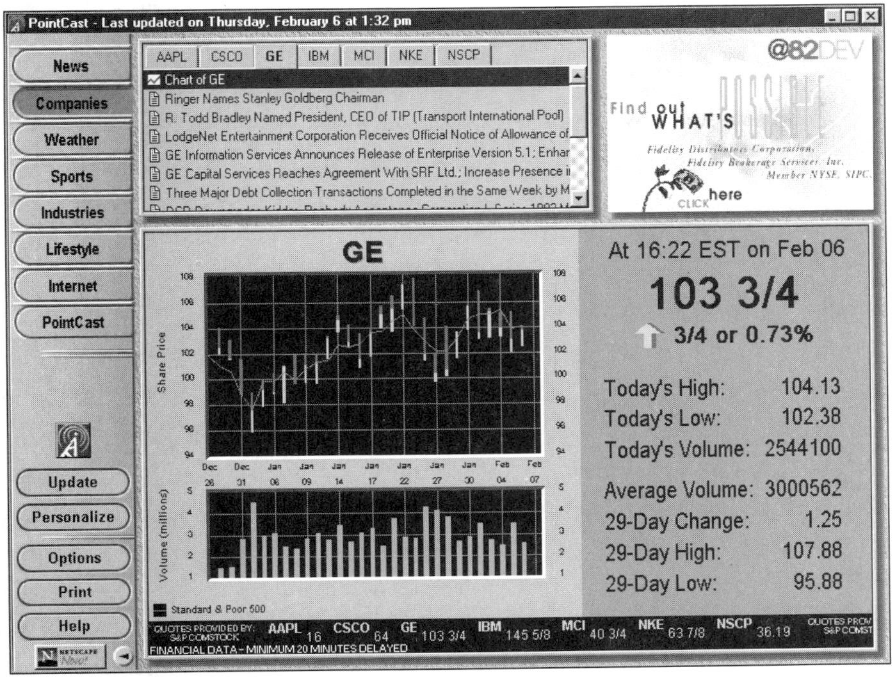

The PointCast site is a good example of a well-thought-out design.

177

USER INTERFACE

User interface is a fancy term for how visitors to a site find their way around: the tools they use to navigate between pages and links either to a destination page with specific information that they're looking for, or simply to surf a site. The better the interface, the easier it is to move around and find stuff. Buttons or other hot spots on a page where users can point and click are basic elements of user interface design. Ease of use and consistency receive high marks. This section describes three aspects of applying a user interface:

- Getting users to specific information quickly
- Helping them find their way around the site
- Keeping in touch with them as they jump to other sites

Facilitating user access

It's so easy for visitors to become lost or frustrated when they arrive at a site. Getting them quickly and pleasantly to the information they're looking for is critical to a positive experience and impression of your operation. The organization of your material and the navigation tools you provide have the most direct impact on this aspect of your site: the number of branches from any page, the amount of information on a screen, and the visual aids for moving through the site.

Depth and density

Many site designers overload a home page in an effort to get visitors to their ultimate destination as quickly as possible. The assumption is that the sooner visitors are alerted to *all* the site's content areas, the quicker they will be able to reach their goal. This theory has its limits. A crowded page can overdose a user with choices, detract from overall appeal, and also look downright ugly. In Figure 4-15, Microsoft's home page (http://www.microsoft.com) is crowded with options, but in this case the clutter works. A hectic page is arguably consistent with Microsoft's image as a behemoth with its hand in many computer-related ventures. Also, the site's visitors are apt to be tech-savvy users who know what they're looking for when they go to a site that looks like this.

chapter CREATING A WEB IDENTITY

Figure 4-15

A crowded page can overdose users with choices; in
the case of the Microsoft site, however, clutter works.

By contrast, the home page from Perfect Proof (http://www.perfectproof.com), shown in Figure 4-16, is extremely simple in its choices and graphic elements, but powerful and effective.

A similar problem occurs once the user moves beyond the home page. How many clicks does it take a user to get past the lists and directories and reach worthwhile information? For example, to read a story, CNNfn site users must click from the Hot Stories icon on the home page to a list of story subjects and pick one—say, Deals—that takes them to a list of stories about deals, and finally to a story about a specific deal. Categorizing, as CNNfn did, is a naturally helpful way of directing a user to a specific area of interest. However, the more clicks it takes to get somewhere, the more a site toys with a visitor's patience. Despite the progress of science, the realities of slow modems are not going to disappear any time soon, especially for the home user.

The Perfect Proof site—simple in its choices, yet effective

On the other hand, if your site is data-heavy and research-oriented, users may be more willing to click from screen to screen because they are more confident about a payoff. Expect less tolerance at an entertainment site. In those cases users must make a leap of faith that each click will bring them toward something worthwhile. Push too far, and you risk losing their attention.

For a good example of lots of information in easily accessible form, visit the CardTrak site (`http://www.cardtrak.com`), shown in Figure 4-17. It lists all types of credit cards on its home page in neatly arranged categories. Just one click and the visitor is at the correct list: rebate cards, low-rate cards, and so on. Within those lists there are subcategories (for example, cash-back cards, gas cards), but visitors don't have to click separately to get to them. They're all together just one click from home.

Figure 4-17

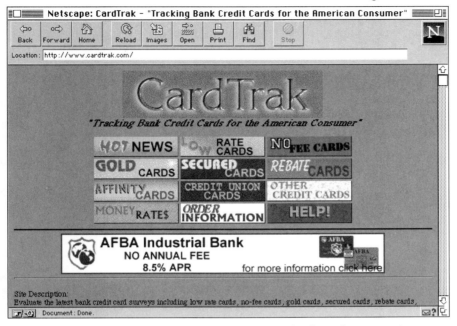

The CardTrak site provides an example of a well-organized page.

Icons and text links

In designing the user interface, the graphic appearance of the tools that guide users from page to page (icons and text links) presents an important set of choices. The clean and descriptive set of navigational tools at the Parent Soup site (http://www.parentsoup.com) in Figure 4-18 are sharp and informative.

The Parent Soup site features clear, descriptive icons.

However, in a gamelike medium like the Web, nondescriptive icons can make a site seem quirky, interesting, and new—effects that may or may not work with your site's identity. While these icons may seem to offer a *fun* experience, they do not necessarily help navigation. For Yahoo!, these accents are a success; but consider the New Balance site (`http://www.newbalance.com`), shown in Figure 4-19. This is otherwise a fine site, but the pictorial icons are downright confusing. Click on the picture of cardiovascular heart muscles and you'll find yourself on a page listing the dates and places of running races around the country. Good for your heart, get it?

chapter **4** CREATING A WEB IDENTITY

Figure 4-19

The New Balance site—creative, but confusing

A smart way to handle icons and text links is to combine them. Use a picture for its aesthetic value, but enhance it with a bit of explanatory text. The Discovery Channel masters this combination effectively at its site (http://www.discovery.com), shown in Figure 4-20. Notice how each picture on the home page has a headline with it.

 If you choose to use imagery as your main navigational interface, be sure that your programmers also supply an alternative text-based interface. Why? Many users turn off *automatic image viewing* on their browsers to save download time. Without a text alternative, they'd be at sea. Each image tag has an option to provide text as an alternative to the image. If there is no alternative text and the user has turned off automatic image loading, what the user sees is a page full of the browser's default image identifier (the page with a circle, square, and triangle).

The Discovery Channel site combines icons and text links.

Presentation

If a topic has substantial content, you need to decide whether to stick with a long scrolling page or to break up information into multiple screens. Once again, there are trade-offs with either choice. With scrolling, the user never feels as though all the information is available at once; furthermore, the single download required for a long page can seem interminable. Slate (http://www.slate.com), shown in Figure 4-21, was meant to be the ultimate proactive site, a place where readers could sit back and see what's happening with editor Michael Kinsley, a stalwart of the liberal intelligentsia and for long a regular on CNN's TV show *Crossfire*. Unfortunately, Slate has been the target of much abuse since before its initial publication. There is even a parody site called Stale (http://www.stale.com). Slate comes off as a print magazine crammed onto the Web. The articles can go on forever, and since all the text is on one scrollable page, it's a look—but a long one.

chapter **4** CREATING A WEB IDENTITY

Figure 4-21

The Slate site was meant to be the ultimate proactive site.
The results, however, did not live up to its promise.

With a series of screens, on the other hand, the user feels as though the page is appropriately finite, but must click from page to page to complete the session. Multiple short screens are much more Web-like in style.

Getting around

In addition to the hyperlinks discussed in the previous section, other *flow control* tools can help visitors navigate a site. Page designers should consider issues such as getting back to the home page, finding other areas of the site from one of its subordinate pages, directing users to specific areas, or even helping them out if they're lost. Where do *you* want the users to go next? If you don't know, chances are they won't go there.

Control bars

A control bar is a consistent strip of hyperlinks located in the same section on most pages in a site—usually along the periphery—as at the Disney site (http://www.disney.com), revisited in Figure 4-22. (Spot the mouse ears?) Here Disney has used a consistent black bar that always locates the user's position within the site. Many contemporary page designers think it's best to have a detailed control bar on every page, with a full index of both the site section and the entire site. That approach can be useful, but it doesn't hold up in all instances. Certainly the user should always be able to return to the home page. After that, however, the level of detail becomes an issue of relevance and style.

Figure 4-22

[Netscape: WOODY screenshot showing http://www.disney.com/ToyStory/characters/woody.htm with Woody character page]

It's hard to lose your way at the Disney site, because of its consistent control bar.

 No matter where you use control bars, make sure they always have the same look, and, if possible, appear in the same place on the screen. A consistent control bar helps a site maintain a single identity while presenting a large variety of content.

Dynamic control bars

Dynamic control bars are a variation that changes depending where the user is located on a site. The change indicates the path used to arrive at the current location, and the one needed to return to the previous location. It's like leaving a trail of bread crumbs. The AT&T site (http://www.att.com), shown in Figure 4-23, is a good example. The style of the control bar stays the same, but the information displayed on it differs depending on where the visitor is in the site. The main section being viewed appears at the top of the control bar, below are the subsections, and below the subsections are the other main sections of the site.

Figure 4-23

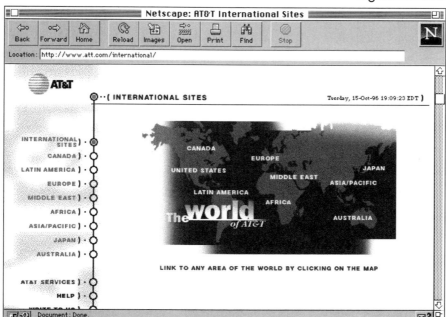

The AT&T site presents a dynamic control bar.

Dynamic control bars are good for huge sites with many varying paths that are not closely related. The dynamic control bar helps the user get back from the spoke to the hub. The downside is complexity and cost. There's more to program, which means more money and more that can go wrong.

Site maps

A site map is a representation of the sections of a site and the connections between them. It's similar to the sort of mall or subway map that features a big red circular button reading "You Are Here." Site maps may be useful if your site is both broad (many topics) and deep (many options under each topic). Site maps can be pictorial or textual. You may not need one at all if you've got an interface that effectively uses icons or control bars to give a visitor a clear sense of location and navigational options. A site map for the Internet World Information Network (http://www.winnet.net/map.html) appears in Figure 4-24.

Figure 4-24

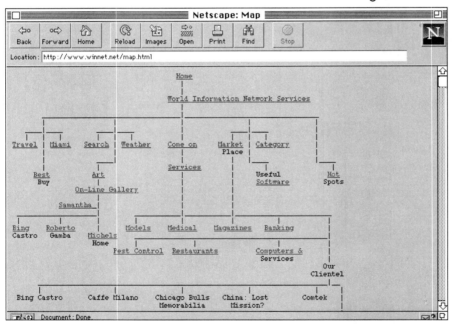

The World Information Network site features a well-done site map.

Linking and keeping in touch

User interface issues are not limited to the stuff you put on your site. They also arise when you link to other sites. Links presumably enhance a site by increasing visitors' options. However, when you allow users to jump to another site, you risk losing them — either because they can't find their way

chapter **4** CREATING A WEB IDENTITY

back, or because they don't want to return. The following precautions can reduce this risk.

* **A new browser window.** If you want to make sure your site is always in view, launch another browser window whenever the user jumps. For a fine example, see StoryWeb (`http://www.storyweb.com`), shown in Figure 4-25. This is a site that reviews online entertainment services, such as kids' shows, soap operas, and TV episodes. Click on a topic that interests you, and focus jumps to another site that appears in a new browser window while keeping the StoryWeb site open. This is a simple device to keep users in touch with your site.

Figure 4-25

The StoryWeb site uses new browser windows.

* **Floating frames.** Another device that helps your site hang onto wandering users is the *floating frame* as shown on the HotWired site in Figure 4-26 (`http://www.hotwired.com`). This is a directory of

your site that hangs around in a little movable window on the screen even if a visitor jumps to another site. Basically, your site's contents are always in the user's face. The downside is that it's a rather high-tech feature, at least at the time of this writing, and less savvy users may find it distracting or confusing. If the floating frame becomes mainstream, it will prove to be a fine way of maintaining visitors.

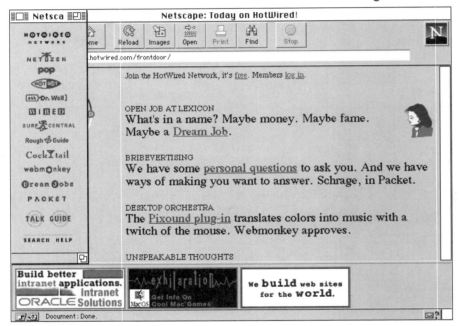

Figure 4-26

Floating frames at the HotWired site

 Frames don't need to float. You can set up a frame design where any link targets an output frame. The downside to this is that some sites may not look good inside a frame because they were designed to touch the edges of the screen. The difference is that the floating frame is not connected to the main browser viewing area. It is also not a second browser window. Floating frames are usually created in JavaScript.

★ **Cooperative links.** When you send a visitor to a site via a link, try to establish a cooperative link back to your site. This is largely a matter of cobranding. You and the designers of the other site decide on the experience that visitors will enjoy when they arrive there, and set up an easy and obvious way for them to return. Cooperative links are common for subscription sites. The surfer gets a sampling of the subscription service, often for free, and then can return home. For example, users of the free market data site Stock Smart (http://www.stocksmart.com) can link to Edgar-Online (http://www.edgar-online.com), primarily a subscription service, to obtain some free SEC filings. Remember to consider whether the visited page should be cobranded, and to select the page on your site visitors should return to.

INTERACTIVITY

Interactivity is a word that's at risk of losing its meaning through overuse. In this chapter, *interactivity* means the degree to which the site owner seeks out, fosters, and responds to the opinions, views, and desires of individual users. At the low end of the interactivity scale, a site offers the user little more than a *suggestion box* in the form of an e-mail address. In this scenario, a user typically contacts the Webmaster with specific questions or helpful hints. At the other end of the spectrum, a site might host chat rooms or bulletin boards. Someone who wants to establish a highly interactive site may choose topics based on user input, look to user forums for ideas for the main content of the site, or even make forums the main content of the site. Note that a site's orientation to research or entertainment has nothing to do with its degree of interactivity—both kinds of sites can work effectively anywhere along the scale. It's all a matter of what you want to accomplish, as the interactivity level may be the most influential element in establishing a Web site's identity and attracting a specific audience. This section reviews a number of popular methods for creating interactivity at a site.

Consider the home page of BanxQuote (http://www.banx.com), shown in Figure 4-27. This is a site that tracks rates on certificates of deposit and bank loans. It's a pure research site, and it's barely interactive. Inquire about which banks are offering the best rates on small-deposit one-month CDs, and that's what you'll get back. This site knows its identity: the numbers. It doesn't want to strike up a debate with its users about the pros and cons of CD investing, or to create a forum for its users to share secrets about getting the untold story on rates. Quite the contrary, it wants its own data to be the users' definitive source. The most it wants to hear from users is feedback about the site, and that's the only option for user input.

Figure 4-27

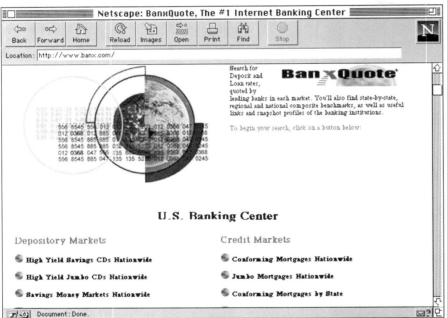

The BanxQuote site is an example of a pure research site—a definitive source, yet barely interactive.

By contrast, look at the Silicon Investors site (http://www.techstocks.com) in Figure 4-28. This is a site for tech-stock investors. Sure, there are company reports and stock quotes, but the main attraction for visitors is the chance to hear from tech-stock investors just like themselves. The site's stock-talk forums are its leading feature. Even the company reports have links to users' comments. The site designers foster the user-input atmosphere by adding fun features like Guru Corner, where the user can play market analyst for a day and offer buy, sell, and hold recommendations. There's also Bull-Bear, where users can vote on which way tech stocks are going. These gamelike features pique curiosity and generate a sense of common interest among users. In short, much of the identity of the site is the active community of users that congregates there.

Figure 4-28

The Silicon Investor site fosters a user-input atmosphere through stock-talk forums and gamelike features.

Think about the degree of interactivity that you want to incorporate into a site and its effect on the site's identity in the early stages of planning. Like most programming issues, more complex features take longer to build. In weighing options, consider that there are seven major methods of building interactivity into a site:

- Forms
- E-mail
- Bulletin Board Systems (BBSs)
- Chats
- Moderated chats and auditoriums
- Contests
- Newsletters

Forms

Forms are a critical means of getting information from your users. Forms on the Web run the gamut of applications. Some forms function primarily as marketing tools to gather data about users. Other forms serve as gimmicks or user attractions, for example, a poll about who will win the presidential election, or which is the best Web browser.

There are two things to keep in mind with forms: Make them easy for the visitor to complete, and use the collected information for something.

On the user's end, short and simple questions are key. A frustrated user is likely to abandon the project of filling out a lengthy form. Incentives help. Sites like the Credit Card Network (`http://www.creditnet.com`) give lists of low-rate or good rebate credit cards in exchange for user registration. Some sites are only open to users who complete a registration form. The user gets access, and the site owner gets marketing data. Even with goodies, though, the odds of getting information are better if the form is short, the questions simple, and the feel unintrusive.

Once users complete a form, you must manage the information gathered. For a small site with a limited number of users, the easiest approach may be to e-mail the responses to the appropriate person on staff. If, instead, you are gathering reams of data, you may need a database to manage the task. The same is true if a form needs to change in real time, based on user inputs. See Dell Computer's online ordering form in Figure 4-29 for an example of a dynamic form: the information continually changes based on the user's choices for system configuration.

Figure 4-29

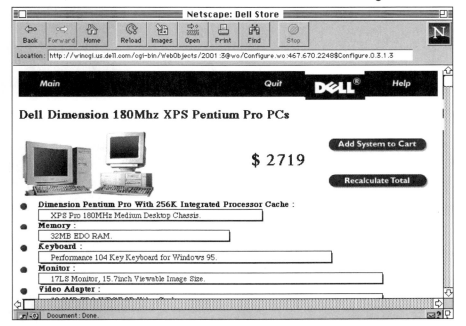

Notice the dynamic fields at the Dell Computer site.

 Creating a database entails more programming, but there are plenty of reasonably priced database programs out there that will do the basic indexing needed for processing forms. (For more details, see the section on servers and databases in Appendix A, Killer Apps.)

E-mail

There are two basic ways of presenting e-mail: e-mail to the Webmaster and directed mail. If there is no other interactive feature at your site, e-mail to the Webmaster is a must. It is essentially an online suggestion box in the form of e-mail to the site manager. Most commonly people use this to notify the site about mistakes, errors, problems, or suggestions, or to send messages such as "This site is completely cool, dude." Typically, when the user clicks on the appropriate button an e-mail form appears, with the necessary address information already entered. The user simply has to input a message.

What are you going to do with these messages? Respond! *How* is a question of identity. At the least, you should ensure that each message triggers an automatic, standardized response indicating that the user's e-mail arrived. If, however, you want to relay a sense of customer service and awareness, then you should follow the automatic responses with personalized answers to users' queries. Some common names for the e-mail link are *Feedback*, *Message Us,* and *Mail the Webmaster.*

Directed mail is a more elaborate form of Webmaster e-mail. The approach permits users to direct their messages to the appropriate person. A news site, for example, may have e-mail options for each editorial section or article. A corporate site may have different e-mail options for press inquiries, customer service, and job opportunities. If this sounds complicated, relax. You can use HTML commands to create one basic e-mail form that serves for all the options at your site, and just change the e-mail address for each variation. Note, however, that if you use directed mail, you raise users' expectations for personalized responses.

Bulletin Board Systems (BBSs)

A Web bulletin board is a discussion series where users post messages to which other users can respond. Unlike chats, which are real-time written exchanges, bulletin boards are more like postal correspondence among groups. Jim posts a note; Jamie reads it that day, the next week, or even the next month. She could print it, respond, or disregard it. A typical Web-based BBS appears in Figure 4-30.

Some Web designers harbor the impression that bulletin boards are a must. This is an unfortunate and sometimes costly mistake. An empty bulletin board is like a party with no guests. It leaves users feeling foolish for coming: "If nobody else thinks this site is worth visiting, why should I?" There are, however, worse problems than an empty BBS. If you've got an active bulletin board with many queries directed at the site and the volume is too overwhelming to handle, you'll end up with more customer complaints than if there were no bulletin board at all at the site. Consider what happened to software publisher Intuit. The company advised purchasers of the October 1995 version of its personal finance program, Quicken, to visit its online customer service boards. The boards got bombarded with more customer com-

chapter CREATING A WEB IDENTITY

plaints than the board monitors could handle. Their failure to respond spread considerable ill will.

Figure 4-30

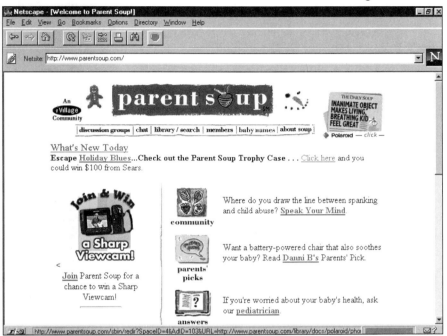

The Parent Soup site—a typical Web-based BBS

Decide whether a bulletin board adds value to your site. For a publisher of computer programs, a BBS can assist users to help each other fix problems with or exploit the potential of their programs. A bulletin board can also attract new users to your Web site as, for example, The Motley Fool has done for America Online (not on the Web, but just as effective). Users come to talk with each other on numerous bulletin boards dedicated to individual stocks. These boards have become so popular that some financial journalists have suggested that their activity moves the markets.

If you suspect that bulletin boards might serve you well, decide if you have the resources to support them. While bulletin boards may appear to require low maintenance, they demand much in the way of employee time.

Someone's got to choose the topics and organize and moderate the boards. If you have a travel site, for example, do you divide board topics by destinations, by budgets, or by types of travel? Do you permit users to create topics, or just to post queries? And what about irrelevant or even libelous posts? Someone's got to keep an eye out for those. Think hard about whether you need a BBS, what exactly you want it to do for you, and how you're going to support it before you put time and energy into this feature.

Chats

Chat rooms are the icon of interactivity, but most sites don't need them. Chat rooms are areas of a site where live, real-time written (typed) discussions take place between users. Users' messages appear on the screen keystroke by keystroke. Where online bulletin boards resemble actual bulletin boards, chat rooms are more akin to a mega-conference call. Their usefulness is, to be generous, limited. The user only gets what's on the screen for the split second that he or she tunes in; there is no organization, no record, no time for contemplation. It's spontaneous (hence, it's a main avenue of online dating). Most Web-based chats require users to first download special software before they can participate. Figure 4-31 shows an example of a popular Web chat room on the HotWired site (`http://www.hotwired.com`).

If you're still not convinced about giving up on chats, at least think about doing a moderated chat, or auditorium. In the lowest-maintenance form of moderated chat, a moderator (read: someone you are paying) makes sure the chatters stay on topic. The more sophisticated moderated chats, often called *auditoriums*, include some kind of screening, along with a guest such as a pop music star or a politician. Users comment, and an administrator (read: someone you are paying) chooses the most interesting comments and moves them onto the screen, along with the guest's responses. In your cost-benefit analysis of auditoriums, don't forget the advertising and promotional expenses. Why pay for a chat if nobody's listening?

Figure 4-31

A popular Web chat room at the HotWired site

Contests and Games

Everybody likes to be a winner. While most users come to a site for its content value, games can help make the experience more fun and make it likelier that visitors will want to return. In designing a contest or game, make sure that the topic is geared toward your audience, the difficulty level is on target, and the prizes, if there are any, are good enough to maintain people's interest. Designers often use contests to gather marketing information: You can't give the user a prize unless you know who he or she is. This tactic is not bad per se, but visitors may get turned off if they sense that you are just out to enlarge your database. The AT&T College Network (`http://www.att.com/college/presents.html`) uses games very effectively. The designers of the site offer the users free gifts for signing up.

Newsletters

Everybody likes to get something for free, whether it's a telephone, a tote bag, or a toaster. Those kinds of premiums aren't easy to distribute on the Web, but information is. That's why more and more sites are sending out newsletters via e-mail to visitors willing to register (at least to give their e-mail address). The newsletter doesn't even need real-world news. It could simply update readers about what's new on the site, and give the exact page, or URL, where they can find the additions. Why go to the trouble? It's an easy way to hold the eye of visitors who've already shown an interest in your site, and engender loyalty in return for a valuable freebie. CNET (http://www.cnet.com/Community/Welcome/Dispatch) offers a very well-done newsletter. It subdivides information into useful categories and supplies direct links to locations where more information about each topic can be found.

In sum, there are many ways to make your site interactive. Whatever method you use, keep in mind that interactivity is the means by which your users speak to you. Listen to them, and respond. If you're going to seek their e-mail, answer it. If a bulletin board topic is getting lots of interest, expand on it. If no one is participating in a contest, bag it. If you're not paying attention to your community, why should it pay attention to you? Table 4-4 outlines the different methods of interactivity, and what to expect if you try implementing them at your site. Keep in mind that these are general categories, and the promised benefits assume that the option, if used, is used well.

Table 4-4 Trade-Offs on Interactivity

FEATURE	ODDS YOUR SITE NEEDS IT	COST	ODDS OF GLITCHES	DEMANDS ON TIME
Forms	High	Low	Moderate	High
E-mail to Webmaster	High	Low	Low	Low
Directed Mail	Moderate	Low	Moderate	Moderate
BBS	Low	Moderate	High	High
Chats	Low	High	High	Moderate
Contests	Low	Moderate	Low	Low
Newsletters	Low	Low	Moderate	High

Summary

There are a great many interesting, creative, and improvisational implementations of identity out on the Web. Amazon.com, for example, could have settled for a simple mail-order system, but instead it created online the kind of lively literary atmosphere that many look for in bookstores these days. There are interviews with authors, interesting quotations, and lists of favorite books from both staff and readers. The site capitalizes on interactivity in productive ways. Customers can get on e-mail lists that notify them when a favorite author has a new book. They can even write their own book reviews, and possibly win prizes. There are also contests purely for fun. Simply put, the site provides a depth of content far beyond what one might expect from what is, at its core, a book warehouse.

Whatever method you use to make your site interactive, keep in mind that interactivity is the means by which your users speak to you. Listen to them, and respond.

"You know Marge, that guy's really boring. He's got no identity. Let's not invite him to the party." People like other people who have an identity. Identity gives a person personality. The same goes for Web sites. Your job as a manager or designer is to give pages an identity that visitors will understand, appreciate, and enjoy. This chapter outlines design strategies and elements that contribute to building an identity. No single factor can be the defining one in the creation of online identity. Rather, the unique combination of these elements defines how Web users relate to your site. Be sure that your site's features present the most effective identity, no matter what combinations you choose.

chapter 5

Registering and Staking Out Cyberturf

ONE OF THE FIRST HURDLES on the way to developing a successful Web site is selecting its home. Thanks to the explosive growth of the Internet in recent years, the options for where and how to house a Web server have dramatically increased. The good news is that prices for all levels of service continue to fall as demand increases. The not-so-good news is that Web site developers face a daunting array of possible scenarios for hosting and maintaining their sites. This chapter helps prospective developers to sort through the issues related to establishing a Web presence, including the options for hosting services and assessing infrastructure needs and advice on choosing and obtaining an appropriate domain name.

Imagine for a moment that you were planning to open a retail store, build an office complex, or put up a billboard. All these plans involve establishing the physical presence for your company, and in each case you would undoubtedly give careful consideration to the location of the structure you were designing. You would carefully consider issues like the desirability of the neighborhood, proximity to customers, and orientation to the street, knowing that each of these has an important impact on potential visitors when they visit your establishment.

It may seem that the importance of location diminishes in a virtual environment like the Internet where a given Web site is always only one click away from anywhere. To uninformed users it can be difficult to ascertain whether a Web site comes to them direct from a Madison Avenue high-rise linked to an ultraexpensive T-3 line or via a 28.8 modem hooked up to an old PC in a basement in Peoria. An aura of anonymity has always been part of the romance of the Internet — the sense that the small folk can establish an online presence that is on a par with giants like AT&T, Microsoft, or Time Warner. As the now-canonical *New Yorker* cartoon proclaimed, "On the Internet, nobody knows you're a dog."

An aura of anonymity has always been part of the romance of the Internet — the sense that the small folk can establish an online presence that is on a par with giants like AT&T, Microsoft, or Time Warner.

Unfortunately for the romantically inclined, while it may be true that no one will know whether or not *you* are a dog, most everyone will know if your Internet service provider is a dog. Anyone who has spent time cruising the Web knows the frustration of visiting sites where pages take an eternity to download or where error messages such as *Server Not Responding* appear as a matter of routine, an experience closely akin to looking vainly for a parking spot downtown or being stuck in rush-hour traffic. This is not exactly the kind of sentiment you want to engender in a prospective customer.

Even though the Web experience is virtual rather than physical, it generates a strong sense of *presence,* largely based on a site's invisible infrastructure. For this reason — first and foremost — you need to give careful consideration to where you house your Web site. Your decision affects a great many other aspects of your project, including how much functionality you can develop, how well you can scale your presence into the future, and how difficult it is to perform routine maintenance. In short, the satisfaction of your own experience as well as that of your users depends a great deal on the choices you make about where and how to establish your presence.

Establishing Criteria for Your Location

From a geographical point of view, the Internet is a *network of networks*, composed of a large number of small local computer networks connected over long distances to other local networks via an array of cable types, with all the computers sharing a common protocol — *Transmission Control Protocol/Internet Protocol* (TCP/IP) — for communicating among themselves. This *inter*-network and its common language support a number of *services*, including information services like the World Wide Web. By definition, the World Wide Web consists of a distributed set of servers all communicating with Web client applications (browsers) using the *Hypertext Transfer Protocol* (HTTP). Exactly how this communication takes place is beyond the scope of the present discussion. In fact, because most current Web browsers are graphically based and can access a variety of Internet services, the Web has for many users come to represent simply the Internet's graphic user interface. This picture may be close enough to the truth for the average Web surfer. Someone who will make or influence decisions regarding the development of a company Web site, however, needs to know enough about the various components involved to evaluate the features and benefits that the various service providers offer.

From an industry or vertical point of view, one can think of the Internet as a composite of four distinct layers (although in reality there are many more layers, not always so distinct). The core is a set of trunk lines called the *backbone*, pieces of which are owned by various national and international cable and telecommunications companies. The backbone consists of high-speed lines that span large distances, the express lanes of the information superhighway, so to speak. Connected to the backbone, directly or indirectly, are two kinds of networks. The first are separate networks whose computers do not speak the Internet tongue, but which have developed translators for the Internet called *gateways*. These networks include the major proprietary commercial networks — America Online (AOL) and CompuServe, among others. The second group of networks connected to the backbone includes an exponentially expanding number of Internet service providers (ISPs). These are the toll roads that route Internet traffic across the backbone. Not all ISPs are created equal, however, and this layer of the picture is really composed of multiple layers with many ISPs buying service from other ISPs higher on the food chain. The proximity of an ISP's connection to the backbone is measured in *hops*, the number of other networks it has to pass through before it gets to the backbone. This is one factor that influences an ISP's performance as well as its price.

Someone who will make or influence decisions regarding the development of a company Web site, however, needs to know enough about the various components involved to evaluate the features and benefits that the various service providers offer.

Typically, large national telecommunication companies such as AT&T, MCI, and Sprint have the greatest investment in actual network cable. These are followed closely by the national network providers like Netcom and BBN Planet. These companies are at the top of the Internet food chain. Beneath them are regional service providers, who usually get their Internet connections from one of the higher-level entities. Companies specializing in Web-hosting services, such as Web presence providers and colocation companies, can be something of an anomaly. Where they sit on the food chain really depends on the level of capital behind the company. Some presence providers are small entities serving a local clientele. Others have invested in very robust national networks.

At the bottom of the food chain are the businesses and individuals who purchase Internet access from the ISPs. Most individual connectivity comes in the form of dial-up connections that typically use a mechanism called *Point-to-Point Protocol* (PPP) for relaying TCP/IP messages over standard phone lines. An increasing number of businesses, however, are obtaining full-time, direct Internet access in a variety of formats. These are the subject of the next section, on Internet bandwidths.

chapter 5 REGISTERING AND STAKING OUT CYBERTURF

ASSESSING BANDWIDTH AND COMMUNICATION LINES

Bandwidth refers to the theoretical quantity of data that can be transported along a given medium in a designated time interval, usually measured as in bits per second. (The measure of the actual quantity of data transferred per unit of time is called *throughput*.) As a project manager, you have two principal bandwidth concerns: the bandwidth your ISP offers you for your Web site, and the bandwidth your users will have. The ISP's bandwidth determines the best possible rate of transfer for your Web site. It also dictates how many users can connect simultaneously to your site before the transfer rate slows to a snail's pace. The users' bandwidth dictates the maximum rate at which they will receive information, regardless of your ISP's capacity. In other words, if you suspect that most of your potential users are connecting via modem, you may not want to deliver digital video yet, even if your ISP is directly linked to the Internet backbone.

In terms of an effective Web presence, it matters less what kind of bandwidth you have to the Internet than what your ISP has. In fact, one could conceivably have no access at all, although this could make the process of updating a site a bit difficult. The key point, which is sometimes confusing, is that the speed with which one connects to the Internet via an ISP does not affect the access speed with which others connect to one's Web site. What counts is the ISP's *upstream* connection to the rest of the Internet: the number of hops between their server and the backbone.

Table 5-1 is a comparison chart that identifies the principal connectivity options in terms of their available bandwidth and an average cost estimate for the service, including a cost for Internet access and for basic phone company (telco) charges. Following the table is an explanation of the different connection types.

Table 5-1 Bandwidth Options and Prices

CONNECTION TYPE	BANDWIDTH	INTERNET SETUP	MONTHLY CHARGES	TELCO SETUP	MONTHLY CHARGES	HARDWARE
Dial-up Modem	14.4 – 33.6 Kbps	$30	$20 – $30 unlimited	$75 – $100	$15 – $25	$100 – $200
Basic Rate ISDN	56–112 (64–128 Kbps)*	$50	$50–$150 plus hourly	$75– $150	$75– $250	$300– $400
Frame Relay	56–128 Kbps	$200– $600	$200– $500	$1,000	$300– $400	$2,000– $3,000
Fractional T-1	128–384 Kbps	$1,000– $3,000	$400– $1,000	$1,000	$350– $600	$3,000– $5,000
Virtual T-1	burstable to 1.54 Mbps	$150– $600	$600– $1,000	$1,000	$600– $800	$3,000– $5,000
T-1	1.54 Mbps	$1,000– $3,000	$1,000– $2,000	$1,000	$600– $800	$3,000– $5,000
T-3	45 Mbps	$4,000– $6,000	$8,000+	n.a.	n.a.	n.a.

* Most ISDN providers in the United States have 56 Kbps not 64 Kbps.

Modem

Most users of the Internet are already familiar with dial-up modem access. To connect to the Internet via modem requires a computer with TCP/IP software, a modem, and a PPP application that enables the computer to establish a temporary link to the Internet. Thanks to the graphical demands of the Web, 28.8 modems have become a de facto standard. Some providers, including CompuServe, are offering 33.6 access. Web access at lower modem speeds such as 14.4 using a graphical browser is possible, but more aggravating than satisfying. Most of the national ISPs currently offer unlimited hourly dial-up access for $19.95 a month. If the ISP is charging a higher rate than this, they should also be including a specific amount of space on the host computer for your Web site or FTP server.

ISDN

Integrated Services Digital Network (ISDN) is a completely digital phone network capable of carrying both voice and data signals at speeds significantly higher than standard analog phone lines; most ISPs now support 56 Kbps. ISDN service is composed of some combination of 64 Kbps *bearer channels* (B channels), which can be allocated for either voice or data signals, and a smaller D channel for flow control. ISDN comes in two varieties. Basic Rate Interface (BRI) combines two B channels with a 16 Kbps D channel for a total possible bandwidth of 128 Kbps, roughly four times the speed of a 28.8 modem. Currently most ISDN access is made using BRI. The second variety of ISDN is called Primary Rate Interface (PRI). It is intended for businesses with greater bandwidth requirements and typically consists of 23 B channels and a 64 Kbps D channel.

To establish ISDN Internet service, one must first arrange for an ISDN line from the local phone company. The Internet connection is made using a computer with PPP software as in the case of a dial-up modem. Instead of a modem, however, one needs an ISDN terminal adapter, sometimes referred to oxymoronically as a *digital modem*, which may be an external box or an internal interface card. Several brands are currently available in the $350 range. Although ISDN is becoming increasingly affordable, it is not really an ideal method of connecting to the Internet for long periods of time, because it incurs a per-minute charge (typically .01 per minute) from the phone company on top of the charges levied by the ISP. For anyone requiring dedicated access, frame relay or a leased line is a better alternative. For more information on ISDN, visit Dan Kegel's ISDN page at `http://www.alumni.caltech.edu/~dank/isdn/`. For a helpful primer on ISDN, check out Ralph Becker's ISDN Tutorial at `http://www.ziplink.net/~ralphb/ISDN/`.

Frame relay

Frame relay is a packet-switching mechanism for making network connections. In contrast to a dedicated point-to-point leased line, which maintains a constant circuit between two fixed points, a frame relay system is capable of making virtual connections to a number of points through its switching technology. This turns out to be a particularly good arrangement for making connections to a TCP/IP-based network like the Internet, since TCP/IP protocol is also packet-based. Typical configurations for frame relay connections are either 56 Kbps or 128 Kbps. This alternative is more expensive than ISDN but less expensive than a full T-1 line. The basic hardware required is a frame relay compatible router and a channel service unit/data service unit (CSU/DSU). For those interested in more details, a great resource for frame relay information is Steve Neil's site, `http://www.mot.com/MIMS/ISG/tech/frame-relay/resources.html`.

Leased line T-1/T-3

Currently, the Cadillac of Internet connectivity remains the T-1 line, sometimes referred to as a DS-1. At 1.54 Mbps, it is roughly 6 to 10 and as much as 15 times faster than Basic Rate ISDN. In terms of cost, it is still out of the reach of all but large companies with a particularly compelling need for continuous high-bandwidth connections to the Internet. For those who wish to become ISPs themselves the next step up is a T-3 line (DS-3), essentially 28 T-1 lines bundled together into a line capable of delivering 45 Mbps.

Often, companies will obtain a full T-1 line and split it between dedicated Internet access and telephone lines. It is possible to obtain incremental versions of a T-1 connection in two ways. The first is a *fractional* T-1 line, which, as its name implies, means one only leases part of a full T-1. Common fractions include 128 Kbps, 256 Kbps, and 384 Kbps. A second alternative, recently gaining in popularity, is known as a *virtual* T-1. In this scenario, a company leases a line that has a full T-1 capacity, but pays the ISP based on the fraction of bandwidth actually used. This can be a fairly substantial savings over fixed-bandwidth T-1, since few companies use their full bandwidth 24 hours a day. When usage does increase, however, the bandwidth will *burst* up to almost full T-1, so one can have T-1 on demand for a little more than the price of a fixed-bandwidth fractional T-1. As with frame relay, a T-1 connection requires a router and CSU/DSU combination connected at the customer premises to a local area network (LAN).

How much bandwidth is right?

This issue really comprises two questions: How much bandwidth does your Web site need and how much bandwidth do you need for Internet access? For most businesses, renting space from an ISP that provides T-1 or better connectivity for customer applications is the best solution. We'll get back to this and other scenarios for Web server hosting later in the chapter.

How much bandwidth your business needs for access depends on how many people need access, how frequently, and for what purposes. A full T-1 connection is more than most small to medium-sized companies need or can afford. On the other hand, a dial-up modem connection is often too little bandwidth for anything other than a very small business or a home office. An increasing number of small to medium-sized businesses, and even many impatient individuals, have begun moving to ISDN for faster on-demand access. Because ISDN incurs a per-minute phone charge during business hours, however, it is usually inappropriate for sustained connectivity. If a company requires dedicated connectivity, it should explore frame relay or fractional T-1 possibilities. Many medium-sized companies already have a leased line in place for their phones, and it is sometimes feasible to split that line between dedicated Internet access and telephone service.

The future of bandwidth

As Web-based applications become increasingly bandwidth intensive, users have demanded faster access speeds and the bandwidth needs of the Internet itself have continued to grow. The clearest signs of this increased need from the user perspective are more frequent slowdowns, which appear as inexplicable delays in connecting to a usually speedy site. Besides increased usage, the biggest impetus for more bandwidth comes from the desire to deliver true multimedia over the Internet. As of this writing, the only way to deliver high-bandwidth audio or video over the Internet is via one of an increasing number of *streaming* technologies. Even though streaming technologies are designed for low-speed connections, they are still quite bandwidth intensive and do not offer the kind of multimedia experience that most users have become accustomed to from CD-ROM applications. A company envisioning a complete multimedia application would still be wise to invest in mature technologies, such as digital video disk (DVD) or CD-ROM, and to look forward to the advent of a new generation of Internet technology that will provide more bandwidth for applications.

Normally, when a user requests a file from a Web site, the file is downloaded to the user's computer and then displayed. This technique is adequate for modest-sized images, which are usually under 100K. It is not acceptable for audio or video files, which can be several megabytes and would take longer to download than to play. Streaming applications open a channel between the Web server and the user and then *stream* the file in such a way that it can be played as it continues to download. This technique also permits *real-time* broadcasting.

GAUGING HORSEPOWER

There are two principal components involved in building a Web site: the computer hardware and the Web server software. These two elements are frequently referred to interchangeably as a *Web server*. For the purposes of clarity, this chapter refers to the computer itself as the *host* computer — it provides lodging, so to speak, for the Web site. *Web server* refers to the software responsible for the actual work of answering requests for files from Web browsers. Both the host computer and the Web server are important considerations in the process of determining a building site for your home.

To deliver basic Web site services, an increasing number of ISPs are setting up either Pentium computers running Windows NT or — in a somewhat smaller number of cases — Macintosh file servers. These ISPs are typically on a tight budget, and one needs to assess carefully whether or not they have cut too many corners in an effort to offer a low-priced service. If, for example, the service provider has several computers distributing the traffic load, a sufficiently powerful computer model, and a judicious distribution of clients across servers (no overload), either of these platforms can run effective sites. Surprisingly, the Macintosh turns out to be a particularly good choice for security-conscious customers, since the Macintosh operating system is less vulnerable to hacker attacks than UNIX or Windows.

When advanced site features and elaborate functionality are necessary, complex issues involving the host computer and the server software come into play. The UNIX operating system is almost universally the platform of choice for sites that offer industrial strength applications. In addition, several factors need to be considered when assessing a service provider's computer *horsepower*. These factors include how fast and well equipped their CPUs are, how many computers they have, and to what extent they are networked. High-end ISPs are likely to run their Web servers from powerful UNIX equipment such as Sun UltraSparcs and Silicon Graphics (SGI) Challenge servers. Just below this level are NeXT workstations or UNIX workstations like the Sun SparcStation, SGI Indy, and DEC Alpha.

When your ISP strings together some midrange Pentiums, you may need to raise your eyebrows a notch and inquire about the total level of Web activity at the facility over the past several months.

Taken together, bandwidth and horsepower are the two most important components in assessing a service provider's facilities. They also offer a fast and easy gauge as to whether an ISP is trying to cut corners when it comes to maintaining adequate resources for your site. There are, however, other considerations, which we'll consider in the following sections. There are not any necessarily bad answers here, since there are many ways an ISP might attempt to make the most efficient use of resources. For example, if an ISP has ten or more computers hooked to a single T-1 or if they are hosting more than 30 or so clients on a single machine, you need to pay attention. If they are using high-end RISC equipment, it may be perfectly adequate — but if they are stringing together some midrange Pentiums, you may need to raise your eyebrows a notch. In a case like this you might want to inquire about the total level of Web activity at the facility over the past several months.

SERVER-SIDE PROGRAMMING RESOURCES

HTML pages containing links are only the face of a Web site (although very simple sites are truly skin deep). Substantial sites have extensive programming underneath this interface, and require a healthy technical tool set to succeed. The facilities are not standard operating equipment at all service providers, and are worth asking about if the plans for your site are sophisticated. Server Side Includes (SSI), Common Gateway Interface scripts (CGI), and Application Programming Interfaces (API) are different approaches to implementing code at the server level, and you should ask the ISP exactly what resources it makes available. If you are planning extensive use of multimedia, you should also ask about the availability of RealAudio and other streaming services. Also, if you are planning to offer some form of electronic commerce, be sure that the site supports the Secure Sockets Layer (SSL).

Finally, if your site specification requires any type of database activity, your service provider must supply access to a database server. If this is not available, just forget about these kinds of applications — or plan to write your own. Catalogs, stock quotation systems, and directories, for example, depend on a database to respond to user queries. In addition to structured database tools of this kind, ask if the service provider has a text-indexing engine. This enables you to create an index of all the pages on your site, so that users can perform a free-form search. It may seem natural that all ISPs would provide database servers as a component of minimum service, but this is far from the case. While you may be used to finding these resources in browsing the Web, you will not find it as easy to acquire them from a service provider.

E-MAIL

Believe it or not, e-mail services are not standard at all ISPs! This is important from both inbound and outbound points of view. At a minimum you should be able to have your own mailbox at your own URL (that is you@yourcompany.com). Look for e-mail aliases as well. With aliases, someone can send mail to a pseudonym (such as you@yourcompany.com) without knowing that the address is an alias; the system then forwards the message to another mailbox. Having both facilities is best. With both aliases and mailboxes, one can look like a large virtual office even though there is really only a single mailbox. For example, you can invite people to send mail to marketing@yourcompany.com, customerservice@yourcompany.com, and corporate@yourcompany.com, and have the system deliver it all to you@yourcompany.com.

DISK SPACE AND TRANSFER ALLOWANCES

Currently almost all ISPs charge customers based on the amount of storage space their Web site occupies on the host computer hard drive and the quantity of traffic their site generates. Everyone seems to have a different formula for how much space and usage to allow and what to charge for it. A decent-size corporate Web site with 100 to 200 HTML pages and a moderate to liberal use of graphics is likely to need approximately 5MB for storage. With a number of multimedia elements such as QuickTime videos, sound files, Shockwave animations, and so on, that number could go up to 100MB quickly for medium-sized business needs.

Download volumes, also known as *transfer allowance*, should be fairly generous, on the order of 500MB per month for medium-sized business needs. Responsible ISPs only institute these limits to discourage *server hogs* from eating up all the bandwidth on their virtual hosts. Some ISPs calculate this volume based on the number of *hits* rather than in volume of traffic. This is a poor measure of use, however, since the main concern should be how much bandwidth users have consumed: a 3MB video clip and a 3K icon would each count as one hit — though obviously the video clip eats up a good deal more bandwidth.

UNSCHEDULED DOWNTIME

No computer or network is perfect. They all *go down* (stop working) from time to time, but some providers are more vigilant than others, both in terms of the preventative measures they take and the contingency plans they have devised to deal with problems quickly. To put this in perspective, a computer with a 99 percent uptime average is down almost two hours per week. By contrast, 99.9 percent average uptime means the computer is down only about ten minutes per week. When service provider reps tell you they have had 100 percent uptime, you should check the length of their noses.

Vendors should also have some provision for preventing problems and for detecting and correcting them quickly. One of the best preventive measures is to build redundancy at every level. A top-notch ISP should have multiple connections to the Internet, preferably with different providers, so that if one network fails the other may still be functional. They might also have mirrored servers set up to go online should something happen to the main server. As for error detection, any decent ISP should have 24×7 monitoring with system administrators on site or at least on automatic paging in the event of a failure, and so on. Another indicator of an ISP's preparation for an emergency is their methodology for backup. *Do not even consider an ISP who does not run at least a daily incremental backup of their entire site.* Provisions for archiving multiple generations of the site and offsite storage of backup media are also worth inquiring about — if only to get a read on the level of conscientiousness of the service provider.

> **When ISP reps tell you they have had 100 percent uptime, check the length of their noses.**

While full backups may make you feel warm and fuzzy, they eat up a lot of computer time and can slow a network way down, so there is good reason for an ISP not to execute full backups every day.

TECHNICAL SUPPORT

One of the chief corners cut by discount Web-hosting operations is in customer support. Skilled and knowledgeable people cost a lot, and typically ISPs do not have a large enough staff to answer all questions. Staff members also tend to work only during normal business hours, and often lack training. This may not be a problem if you are confident in your own staff's ability to deal with problems, but it is good to know the parameters of the module in advance. The best way — maybe the only way — to find out about a provider's customer support record is to ask around among its customers (a point discussed in more detail later).

SERVER USAGE LOGS

Any ISP worth its salt will provide its customers with server logs, statistical information regarding how the people are using the site. Some providers deliver easy-to-digest usage reports on a weekly basis. Others simply provide the raw log files generated by the server. The right solution depends on your specific needs for usage data. The sponsors of a site set up primarily for marketing, advertising, or conducting customer support have a high need for usage information, whereas a site established with a mission based on corporate identity may not have such requirements. Anyone spending decent money, however, is likely to want to monitor the activity in this new medium.

Some providers send reports via e-mail, others deliver HTML formatted reports. Either way, a report is likely to indicate either how many hits or how many *visitors* (a measure of distinct computer IP addresses) the site has had. Other statistical information common to usage reports includes data on how often any given file was accessed and what time of day the most activity occurred. The report may also note how many pages a given visitor accessed and how many megabytes of data were transferred during a specified time period.

Be wary of simply using hits to measure activity. Some people have the impression that one hit equals one Web page. This is a misnomer. A hit corresponds to a request for a file, which might be an HTML page — or a graphic contained in that page. For example, an average HTML page with a banner graphic and six navigational buttons will generate eight hits each time someone looks at it — one for the page itself and one for each item on it. This is why marketers love to quote hit rates rather than visits, which typically give a significantly smaller number.

CONTENT UPDATES

Some ISPs allow complete remote shell access (telnet) to their host computers. This means that you can log on to their machine directly, edit files remotely, change permissions, run other applications, read mail, and so on. You may find this level of access very useful if your site requires customization at the server. However, host computers that allow multiple users direct access have a much greater likelihood of coming to a grinding halt: Too many people can decide to run a complex process that eats up all the CPU cycles for a few minutes.

To minimize this possibility, a growing number of providers allow limited access to the host computer with FTP uploads. This means that you can edit your Web site files locally and then transfer them to the proper directory online, but you cannot make any changes to the files themselves once they are on the server. This is perfectly adequate if your site is entirely HTML based, but such a scheme makes it difficult to add custom programming elements. Most sites that limit access in this way also restrict the use of CGI programming elements, sometimes providing *canned* CGI scripts for commonly requested items like e-mail forms, guestbooks, and counters. If the ability to create and install custom programming is important to your project, you should ask if it will be permitted. As site management tools develop, it is also becoming more common for ISPs to offer clients a management and publishing tool as part of the price of the server. Depending on the scope of your project, this could be a real boon or completely irrelevant. The most common tool for this purpose at the moment is Microsoft's FrontPage.

 Almost all ISPs have FTP facilities, but not all of them provide the full range of FTP services. At a minimum, of course, you require FTP access for your own site maintenance. In addition, an ISP may provide an FTP server allowing anonymous FTP access. Anonymous access allows users to download files efficiently. In more sophisticated environments, the ISP allows multiple FTP logins so that the designer or manager can assign specific directories and privileges to different content providers.

FIREWALLS AND SECURITY

Security is an important concern for any business planning to develop a Web site on the Internet. The Internet is a relatively open multiuser environment. This was a deliberate design choice, and it facilitates the exchange of information but raises a number of potential problems when the goal is to protect that information. Will sensitive data be safe on the Internet? Will the computer system be vulnerable to attacks from wily hackers? If the server is connected to the corporate network, will it compromise the security of the entire system?

The rule of thumb on the Internet is that the only way to ensure the security of information is not to put it online. Short of that, however, there are a number of steps one can take to increase the level of security of a given system or the data housed on it. If you are shopping for an ISP or some other third-party host for your Web site, you are probably not planning a site that will access highly sensitive information (with the possible exception of electronic commerce). In this case your main security concerns are likely to be about the physical security of the equipment and the proper configuration and management of the computer systems. Any good commercial ISP and Web-hosting services will have provided for the physical safety of their host computers, including controlled and monitored access to server facilities as well as security against excessive heat, power surges, fires, earthquakes, or other disasters. On the other hand, most ISPs do not have extensive security measures in place to protect the networks from hackers. This is mainly because ISPs are in the business of providing convenient Internet access, and heavily protected systems tend to be inconvenient for users. Heavy protection also degrades system performance. By all means, though, ask what the provider has done to prevent computer break-ins. Some signs of appropriate concern about security include enforcing hard-to-crack passwords, limiting or disabling non-Web Internet services (such as telnet and FTP) on the servers, and prohibiting users from adding custom programming to the site. File permissions on the server should be set correctly so that users do not have access to one another's directories, and the Web server itself should be configured to run as a user with low system privileges (typically designated as the user "nobody" on UNIX systems). These are all signs that should help to assure you that the ISP has taken adequate steps to make their servers unfriendly to potential hackers.

The only way to ensure the security of information is not to put it online. Short of that, however, there are a number of steps one can take to increase the level of security of a given system or the data housed on it.

If you are planning to collect credit card or other sensitive information over the Internet, you will want to find a provider with a secure Web server such as the Netscape Commerce server. Service providers are increasingly offering secure Web servers to customers interested in implementing an electronic commerce site. Secure Web servers encrypt data before sending it off to the requester and authenticate the transfer at both ends, thus defeating anyone who might try to steal the data en route. A secure Web server requires users to have a browser that can decode messages at the other end before displaying the information. In addition, the secure Web server only encrypts data between itself and the end user. It makes no guarantees about the security of the system where the data resides. Part of any plan for a commerce solution should be the management of sensitive data once it is collected. The more quickly it can be removed from a network computer entirely and stored offline, the better.

Currently there are two principal standards for securing data on the Web. One, developed by Netscape, is *Secure Socket Layer* (SSL). SSL works at the transport level of communications between computers, so it can secure transactions for a number of Internet services in addition to the Web. The second standard is *Secure Hypertext Transfer Protocol* (S-HTTP). Developed by Enterprise Integration Technologies (EIT), now owned by VeriFone, S-HTTP provides application-level security, adding data encryption and authentication to standard Web server functions. Recently, a number of entities — including major credit card companies like Visa and MasterCard — have teamed up to develop a new industry standard for secure electronic commerce. Their Secure Electronic Transaction (SET) protocol appears to be the most likely next-generation standard for Web security. For more information on SET, check the MasterCard Web site (`http://www.mastercard.com/set`) or the Visa Web site (`http://www.visa.com/cgi-bin/vee/sf/set/intro.html`).

For those contemplating implementing a Web site from their own networks, there are several ways to increase the security of the computer systems:

* Check the computer for security holes.
* Set up a firewall or proxy server.
* Institute a user authentication system.
* Implement data encryption.
* Store sensitive data offline.

Check the computer system for security holes. There are a number of UNIX programs that will analyze a computer system and report any possible security weak spots. The most famous (or infamous) of these analyzers is the Security Administrators Tool for Analyzing Networks (SATAN), written by Dan Farmer and Wietse Venema. Such programs give you a two-edged sword, since in the hands of a hacker they can point out system weaknesses ripe for exploitation. To an administrator, however, they can provide a valuable first line of diagnostics, allowing the obvious holes to be closed before a hacker finds them. (For more information on SATAN see Appendix A, Killer Apps.)

Set up a firewall or proxy server. A *firewall* is a mechanism — sometimes a piece of hardware, sometimes a software application — that is responsible for monitoring all network activity and filtering out specified kinds of traffic. A *proxy server* is an enhancement on the firewall concept. Proxies also sit between the network service and the user, but rather than simply filtering the packets of information that pass by, a proxy actually performs the operation of the network service, acting as a kind of gatekeeper to the actual servers. To the users it appears they are communicating with an internal server; in fact they are only communicating with the proxy, which in turn sends acceptable messages on to the server itself. Both methods offer means of monitoring and controlling access to internal systems. Firewall solutions come in a wide price range. One popular freely available proxy application is called SOCKS. Another useful product is the Internet Firewall Toolkit, available from Trusted Information Systems (TIS), makers of the popular line of Gauntlet Firewall products. (For more details on SOCKS and the Internet Firewall Toolkit see Appendix A, Killer Apps.)

Institute a user authentication system. All network computers have a minimal authentication system, that is, a logon requiring a username and password. On large systems with many users, this may not provide adequate protection against hackers. There are several methods for providing user authentication, including one-time passwords and digital signatures. One publicly available software-based network authentication application is called Kerberos, after the three-headed dog in Greek mythology. Originally developed at MIT, there are now several versions of Kerberos. Kerberos works by giving users and services a digital "ticket" that identifies them to the network. For more information, check out the Kerberos FAQ (http://www.ov.com/misc/krb-faq.html).

Implement data encryption. A final method for improving the security of information stored on or transferred via a network system is to encrypt it. This will not prevent information from being tampered with, but could lessen the chance of its being stolen. There are two principal methods of encryption in use on the Internet. The first, called private-key encryption, uses a single key to encrypt and decrypt messages. The main implementation of private-key technology is the Data Encryption Standard (DES), the official encryption standard for the U.S. government. The second variety of encryption is called public-key. This method involves using a pair of keys — one key that encrypts information and another that decrypts the information. The encrypting key is "public" and can be freely disseminated. The decrypting key is "private" and used solely by the receiver of messages encrypted using the public key. The best-known variety of public-key encryption is called RSA, the initials of its developers: Rivest, Shamir, and Adelman. For more information on RSA technology check out the RSA Web site (`http://www.rsa.com`).

Store sensitive data offline. It bears repeating that the only truly secure system is one that is not connected to the Internet. If it is absolutely necessary to provide or store sensitive information on the Internet, that information should be removed as quickly as possible. Often this is done by building a staging server that is not connected to the Internet and that communicates with the Internet server at designated intervals through a non-Internet-based connection to move information offline.

FUTURE GROWTH POTENTIAL

Web site development often begins with a grand vision, and then needs to be whittled down to a realistic plan and a time line. There is a danger in trying to take on more than is practical or realistic to accomplish, especially if the project is one's first. On the other hand, it's just as foolish to hamper the growth potential for a project by signing up with a service provider who is adequate for present needs, but has no path for growth. A Web site that is not continually evolving is probably *stabilized*, a Web euphemism for abandoned. In this respect, you should consider carefully both the level of services and the availability of optional features like database access, secure commerce, and multimedia capabilities.

CUSTOMER RECOMMENDATIONS

Ask an ISP to supply you with a list of existing satisfied customers willing to discuss their happiness level! You may be able to get a fast answer to this question simply by heading to the ISP's Web site (which you should do under any circumstances), where you can often find a list of major customers, and sometimes a directory of all their hosted sites. If you can't find this, something is suspicious. If you can get contacts to call, ask about their experiences with the ISP, and ask enough different people to be able to get a consensus. Nothing substitutes for direct personal experience.

Experience is the best guide in learning to select a service provider. There are, however, guidelines that you can use in building a set of criteria for making your own decision. Table 5-2 summarizes some of the main criteria covered in this section.

Table 5-2 Assessing Service Providers

QUESTION	WEAK ANSWER	ADEQUATE ANSWER	STRONG ANSWER
Bandwidth	Single T-1 or less	Redundant T-1s, single T-3	Multiple redundant T-3s with multiple providers
Computer Hardware	Stand-alone PC	Multiple PCs or stand-alone UNIX	Multiple PCs or UNIX
Charges for Disk Space and Traffic	Yes; and stops serving pages when limit is reached	Yes; and charges extra when limit is reached	No
Guaranteed Uptime	No guarantees; no published figures	No guarantees; 99.5% average	Guarantee 99.9%
Backups	Weekly (or less) incremental backup	Daily incremental, monthly full backup; no offsite storage	Daily incremental, weekly full backup; offsite storage
Technical Support	Single phone line or e-mail address; normal business hours; ad hoc support	Multiple lines or access; normal business hours; full-time technicians	24×7 support; 800 number; full-time, knowledgeable technicians
Log Statistics	Monthly usage statistics or none	Weekly usage statistics, format options	Flexible options, access to raw logs
Content Updates	FTP access	Full shell access, including FTP	Web site publishing tool plus shell access
Security	No security	Password protected admin; FTP uploads	Telnet access; separate FTP logons
Scalability	Basic services only	Some upgradeability of function and bandwidth	Full range of function and bandwidth options
Recommendations	None identified	Clients listed on Web site	Names provided on request; clients listed on Web

Looking at the Alternatives

This section describes different service options available from commercial entities with Internet connectivity, followed by a discussion of some of the leading and better known services. Recommending one approach over another is really outside the purview of this book. Two years ago, one would have been hard-pressed outside of California to find many alternatives for Web site hosting beyond a handful of national Internet service providers. As of this writing, there were several thousand ISPs offering Web hosting as part of their standard access package. You can find a similar number of Web presence providers, entities exclusively dedicated to hosting, maintaining, and sometimes developing Web sites. Indeed, the lines that separate these types of vendors continue to gray, and the distinctions become more one of service offerings than of companies. For example, both ISPs and Web presence providers deal in what has become known as *virtual hosting*. A Web site may have a unique domain name and appear to users as a separate site, but it is actually sharing space with a number of other Web sites on a single, high-powered host computer. Here's a list of the various service options available to you:

* **Internet service providers.** These are national or regional entities that originally simply sold connectivity to the Internet. As a by-product of providing access, many have begun to offer Web-hosting services. These entities offer packages that range from inexpensive deals with disk space and limited or no service to premium business Web services catering to high-end customers. Of the two groups, the national providers tend to position themselves more strongly in providing turnkey solutions. Another distinguishing feature of national providers is that they typically own some of their own cable, which may include part of the Internet backbone, and therefore directly connect a number of metropolitan areas in the United States, if not globally. They are likely to have local points of presence (and therefore dial-up numbers) in many areas, as opposed to regional providers, who typically have no more than three or four access points. Regional ISPs typically rent space and provide domain name services, but otherwise leave users to their own devices concerning development. As a trade-off, they offer very attractive prices.

- **Web presence providers.** As of this writing, there are some 2,200 Web presence providers advertising their services on Yahoo!. Focused on providing Web-hosting services at a reasonable cost, these companies typically do not offer Internet access. Instead they offer a broad range of hosting options starting at prices just slightly higher than the lowest-cost Internet service providers. Web presence providers may be a good solution for medium-sized Web sites in cases where the business already has an ISP but feels that it needs more for its Web site. Be forewarned, however. There is a wide variation in the size and professionalism of these entities as well as in what they offer. This is partly due to the fact that a number of the Web presence providers have gravitated to the hosting business as a way of complementing other Web-related services, such as design, programming, publishing, or marketing services. Some presence providers, for example, only offer virtual hosting; others offer a higher-priced option to rent a dedicated host computer for a Web site.
- **Colocation services.** For those companies who need more control over their Web site than renting space on a virtual host permits, some ISPs and Web presence providers allow customers to purchase their own server and house it at the service provider's premises. This arrangement is called *colocation*, and typically involves a sharing of administrative responsibilities.

AOL PRIMEHOST

A relative newcomer to the Internet hosting business, America Online (AOL) brings its muscle and networking expertise to bear on a Web-hosting service called PrimeHost. PrimeHost Web sites are built on the AOLServer product, a Web server with a built-in database. AOLServer has a companion Web-authoring and site-maintenance tool called AOLpress, which enables easy content updates and Web publishing. AOLpress comes with all PrimeHost service accounts.

AOL offers PrimeHost service at three levels: Domain Service, Commercial Service, and Dedicated Service. The Domain Service option features 50MB of disk storage, 1,500MB transfer allowance per month, standard scripts for counters, e-mail, and form submission, and FTP access. The Commercial Service includes 100MB of disk space, a 3,000MB transfer allowance, custom scripting as well as standard scripts, and the ability to create user passwords and to set permission levels for multiple authors. For an additional fee, this service also offers a storefront solution for catalog and electronic commerce. The Dedicated Service offers 4,000MB of disk space, 15,000MB in transfer allowances, full shell access, and dedicated server hardware with the ability to set up multiple virtual servers on the host computer — plus all the other features of the previous service levels.

> **Ask an ISP to supply you with a list of existing satisfied customers willing to discuss their happiness level!**

Dedicated Service also offers *tool command language* (Tcl) scripting. Tcl (pronounced "tickle") was designed with the philosophy that one should actually use two or more languages when designing large software systems: one for manipulating complex internal data structures, or where performance is key; and another for writing smallish scripts that tie together the other pieces, and providing hooks for the user to extend, such as Tcl. Tcl is both a language and a library. As a simple textual language, Tcl is intended primarily for issuing commands to interactive programs such as text editors, debuggers, illustrators, and shells. As a library package, Tcl can be embedded in application programs. The FTP site for the Tcl source code is `ftp://ftp.sunlabs.som/pub/tcl/`.

BBN PLANET

BBN has been a part of Internet development since it ran the ARPAnet in the early 1960s. The company currently provides a wide range of Internet services through BBN Planet, including both Internet access and Web hosting. BBN Planet is dedicated to helping companies find complete solutions to their networking needs. It can provide assistance through the entire project life cycle, from systems architecture and design through implementation and operations. In addition to infrastructure services, BBN Planet provides direct and dial-up connections for business, Internet security products, Web-hosting services, and custom development for Internet applications.

BBN Planet offers three Web-hosting plans, known collectively as Web Advantage services. The Web Advantage Bronze is a high-end server colocation arrangement. In this scenario, the customer provides the host computer and server; BBN Planet provides a 10 Mbps connection to their 45 Mbps backbone. This provides for performance on the order of six times that of a standard T-1 line. Depending on bandwidth needs, one can elect to have a dedicated 10 Mbps connection, or share that connection with either up to 12 or up to 24 other hosts.

The Web Advantage Silver and Gold series are Web-hosting services. The Silver level is designed for small to medium-sized businesses. It features 60MB of storage, e-mail and FTP access, and tools for analyzing usage. Also included are uninterruptible power supply, a single unique IP address, 24×7 maintenance for the site through the Network Operations Center, and daily data backups. The Gold service level is designed for larger companies with greater requirements. It provides additional data transfer allowances as well as a full suite of development tools on the host computer. Additional options include a Netscape Commerce Server, a RealAudio Server, and the ability to host multiple Web sites using multiple IP addresses.

BEST INTERNET COMMUNICATIONS

BEST Internet provides low-cost, full Internet access to the Northern California area. Included with all dial-up accounts is 25MB of Web site storage space and 200MB a day of transfer allowances. To register a custom domain, users pay an additional one-time fee of $30. BEST also offers business Web-hosting options beginning at 100MB of storage space and an ample 600MB a day transfer allowance, and increasing to 200MB of storage and 1,600MB a day throughput. For those requiring colocation services, BEST offers a connection to their redundant T-3 backbone in a climate-controlled, card-key-accessed facility. Costs for this service are a $1,000 setup fee and $500 a month.

DIGIWEB

DigiWeb provides low-cost Web hosting for sites in over 35 countries through a number of national and international resellers. DigiWeb has a T-3 link to the Internet, and an internal 100 Mbps network backbone. All DigiWeb sites are hosted on Sun UltraSparc servers running Apache Web server software. Web-hosting services start at $20 a month for 25MB of disk space, telnet and FTP access, server access logs, CGI scripting access, a free shopping cart application, and a 200MB a day transfer allowance. DigiWeb also offers the use of Microsoft FrontPage to maintain and update Web site content. For $40 a month, users can obtain a Webstation Gold account with a 250MB a day transfer allowance and the option of reselling disk space. Additional DigiWeb offerings include a dedicated service for $250 a month, a Netscape Commerce server for a $35 setup fee and $25 a month in maintenance costs, RealAudio for a $35 setup fee and $25 a month in maintenance, and MiniSQL database access for a one-time setup fee of $25 and no monthly charge.

EARTHLINK

EarthLink is a national service provider headquartered in Southern California and offering dial-up access in over 270 cities nationwide. EarthLink has developed alliances with Netscape, Macmillan Publishing, and UUNet Technologies in order to bring high-quality access southward. Unlike the traditional Internet access provider, EarthLink has grown in short order from a start-up company in 1994 to an organization with 300+ employees. This is thanks to alliances, effective marketing, and distribution of its TotalAccess CD-ROM product, which contains a variety of Internet-related software applications and tools. EarthLink provides 3MB of Web site storage space to all its members. It also offers corporate Web sites in sizes ranging from 5MB to 100MB. All corporate Web sites feature a 1,500MB monthly transfer allowance, daily usage logs, and custom CGI script capabilities. Optional services include SecureLink Server for conducting electronic commerce, a RealAudio Server for streaming audio, and unlimited e-mail aliases associated with a customer domain name.

ECHO

Echo is a New York City online guide to art and culture and a self-billed *electronic salon* that also provides hosting services to the arts community. As such it represents an example of a company fusing content, community, and Web-hosting services. One of the dilemmas facing any Web site is the issue of getting seen. Associating with a provider who has an established base of customers, sometimes loosely referred to as a community of users, is one way to increase traffic. Most access providers offer little in the way of Web solutions. As a community-centered business, Echo prides itself on "helping businesses and organizations who want their sites to grow into self-supporting, profitable tools for communication and distribution." A corporate Web site, including dial-up account, 15MB of disk space, unlimited traffic, and CGI scripting access, costs $100 a month. Reduced rates are available for nonprofit organizations.

NETCOM

Netcom is an international Internet service provider with its own high-speed TCP/IP network offering complete solutions to individuals, businesses, and educational institutions. Netcom's business offerings include access, hosting, commerce, security, and intranet solutions. Web sites are housed in a climate-controlled hosting center connected to Netcom's T-3 backbone. Netcom offers three tiers of Web hosting, each with a standard and premium level. The entry-level offering is called a SOHO Web site and contains 10MB of disk space and a 750MB monthly transfer at the standard rate of $50 setup and $25 a month. The premium rate is $100 setup and $50 a month and includes 15MB storage and a 1,000MB transfer allowance. Both offer FTP access for content updates and usage logs.

The standard Business Web Site rate is $150 for setup and $100 a month and includes 50MB of disk space and a 1,000MB transfer allowance. It also provides full CGI access for companies requiring custom programming for their Web site. The premium level costs $250 for setup and $200 a month and allots 100MB in storage and a transfer allowance of 1,000MB. The Commerce Web Site is $350 for setup and $350 a month for the standard level. It provides 200MB of space and a 1,500MB monthly transfer rate. The premium level is $400 and $450 for setup and monthly charges respectively and provides 350MB of storage and 2,500MB in transfer allowances.

WEB CONDO

Web Condo, in Silicon Valley, is an example of a relatively new breed of Internet service provider, dedicated to colocating customer host computers. Web Condo prices range from $500 for setup and $182 a month for a 64 Kbps connection to $1,000 for setup and $662 a month for T-1 connectivity, all the way to $5,150 a month for a 10 Mbps connection. Additional IP addresses and additional rack space for computers are available. Web Condo also offers a range of maintenance packages for companies with mission-critical sites requiring full-time monitoring.

Table 5-3 presents major features of these services in summary fashion.

Table 5-3 Web Hosting Options

COMPANY	LOCATION	SERVICES	PRICING (SETUP/MONTHLY)	KEY BENEFITS
AOL PrimeHost	National (http://www.primehost.com)	Domain Service (hosting)	$199/$99	AOL Networking tool expertise; AOLpress simplifies content development and publishing
		Commercial Service (hosting)	$249/$199	"Two Minute Demo" online tutorial on selecting service; AOLpress tool
		Dedicated Service (hosting)	$499/$1,799	AOLServer has built-in database and Tcl scripting; AOLpress tool
BBN Planet	National (http://www.bbn.com/planet/)	Web Advantage Bronze (colocation)	$5,000/ $1,000 and up	Internet and network security expertise
		Web Advantage Silver (hosting)	$495/$295	Large, robust infrastructure
		Web Advantage Gold (hosting)	$1,500/$1,595	Premium service

chapter 5 REGISTERING AND STAKING OUT CYBERTURF

COMPANY	LOCATION	SERVICES	PRICING (SETUP/MONTHLY)	KEY BENEFITS
BEST Internet Communications	Northern California (http://www.best.com)	Internet access with Web site	$30/$30	low cost
		Corporate Web hosting	$500/$250 and up	FrontPage support
		Colocation	$1,000/$500	—
DigiWeb	International Web hosting (http://www.digiweb.com)	Webstation account	$25/$20	low cost
		Webstation Gold	$35/$40	many optional services
		Dedicated Server	$250/$250	—
EarthLink	Southern California and national access (http://www.earthlink.com)	Internet access with member Web site	$25/$19.95	local and national Internet access
		corporate Web site	$179/$89 (for 5MB) and up	Provides TotalAccess software and connection package
Echo	New York (http://www.echonyc.com)	nonprofit Web hosting	$40/$25	online community affiliation
		commercial Web hosting	$250/$100	—
Netcom	International (http://www.netcom.com)	Internet access	—/$19.95	Intranet services for Web/Lotus Notes integration
		SOHO Web Site	$50/$25	Netcom Business Center, tools and resources for customer
		Business Web Site	$150/$100	Partner with Web development company
		Commerce Web Site	350/350	—
Web Condo	Colocation facility (http://www.webcondo.com)	colocation	$500/$182 per month and up	Dedicated colocation facility

231

IN-HOUSE SERVER OPTIONS

For those who need total control, an internally housed and maintained Web server may be the way to go. Setting up a Web server involves a great deal of planning, forethought, and resources. It costs a good deal more than virtual hosting to set up and maintain, particularly the cost of a dedicated system administrator. Under what circumstances does it make sense to take on this added responsibility and cost? Consider some of the following:

* Do you want to link the server to a back-end system that resides in-house?
* Does the quantity of content management reach a point that it is far easier to manage locally?
* Does the site require a level of monitoring that can be more efficiently performed locally?
* Does the degree of functionality you are building dictate that the server be in-house?
* Do you have the in-house expertise and staff time to tend to it?
* Do you have the infrastructure to support it, or a budget to build the infrastructure?

How much does it cost to put up a server and maintain it locally? This is like asking how much it costs to buy and maintain a house: it depends on the house. Consider the three following scenarios — economy, midrange, and luxury model Web server — each with different assumptions about the level of performance required. For each option the basic hardware requirements are the same: a host computer, an Internet connection, equipment to connect the line to the computer, Web server software, and basic maintenance software. The one major expense not factored into these examples is the salary of an administrator (this is the number all Web site hosting services like to put in bold print in their job advertisements), which could range from $25,000 to $100,000 and more, depending on the type of system installed.

> **How much does it cost to put up a server and maintain it locally? This is like asking how much it costs to buy and maintain a house: it depends on the house.**

Scenario 1: Economy model Web server

Table 5-4 contains specifications for the economy model. The economy scenario involves purchasing a high-end consumer-grade PC, either Macintosh or Windows, and connecting it to an ISDN line. While this solution is not the *most* economical way to set up a server, it takes very little time to set up and does not require the aid of a highly trained system administrator. It is appropriate for companies wanting to maintain a relatively simple Web server internally.

Table 5-4   Economy Web Server

ITEM	ONE-TIME COST	RECURRING COST
PC, Tape Backup and Software	$3,000–$5,000	—
ISDN Internet Connection	$750–$2,000	$150–$350 per month
Software (Web Server/Site Maintenance)	$500–$1,500	—
TOTAL	$4,250–$8,500	$150–$350 per month

One cost not factored in here is the monthly phone charge for the ISDN line. Typically ISDN incurs a per-minute line charge. In some circumstances, it is possible to arrange dedicated ISDN lines from a local ISP by connecting through their Centrex system. The details of this are outside the scope of this example, but bear in mind that an ISDN connection may not be as much of a bargain as it seems. If you connected to a dedicated modem line instead, the cost would probably drop about $100 to $200 a month, with additional savings of $150 to $200 in connection hardware. For a 56 Kbps frame relay line, the connection hardware would cost between $800 and $1,000 and the setup fee for frame relay would be between $500 and $1,000. In addition, the monthly cost would increase by about $200.

Scenario 2: Midrange model Web server

The midrange server scenario in Table 5-5 increases the robustness of the facility in two ways: by investing in a server-grade PC, and by investing in a dedicated Internet line, either frame relay or fractional T-1. Along with the increased performance and reliability of this system comes a more difficult system maintenance task, which requires a system engineer capable of troubleshooting network computers as well as Internet routes.

Table 5-5 Midrange Web Server

ITEM	ONE-TIME COST	RECURRING COST
File Server	$5,000–$8,000	—
Frame Relay/Fractional T-1 Connection	$5,000–$7,000	$400–$1,000 per month
Software	$1,000–$2,000	—
TOTAL	$11,000–$17,000	$400–$1,000 per month

Scenario 3: Luxury model Web server

The high-end version in Table 5-6 includes Web server upgrades to a UNIX-class computer and a full T-1 line. In the move from a PC operating system to UNIX, there is a sizable increase again in the reliability and capability of the computer. There is also a parallel increase in the price of any commercial-grade software for this configuration. This is an ISP-class configuration, and is probably only necessary for very large companies or companies planning to enter the Web-hosting business. Most companies considering a large-scale Web development project will need to invest in a database back-end for storing and delivering data. Recommending a database system is beyond the scope of this chapter, but keep in mind that a UNIX system is likely to translate into a need for a significantly larger budget for software if you want commercial products. A name brand UNIX SQL database system can cost between $10,000 and $20,000 dollars. Compare this with the $300 to $1,000 dollars for a PC-based database system, and it becomes clearer why NT and Macintosh servers have become increasingly popular options as in-house servers.

Table 5-6   Luxury Model Web Server

ITEM	ONE-TIME COST	RECURRING COST
UNIX Server	$12,000–18,000	—
T-1 Internet Connection	$6,000–$10,000	$1,500–$3,000 per month
Software	$1,000–$5,000	—
TOTAL	$19,000–$33,000	$1,500–$3,000 per month

Assessing Infrastructure Needs

Before you can make an intelligent decision between in-house or service provider options, you need to assess your infrastructure needs. Do you require redundant T-3 lines connected to the Internet backbone, a gigabyte of storage space, and round-the-clock network monitoring for $1,000 a month and up? Or can you do just fine with a $50-a-month basic Web account and a do-it-yourself attitude? Here are some of the basic questions to ask yourself as you try to answer the big question:

1. How much content will the Web site contain?
2. What kinds of content will it have?
3. How much functionality, other than the standard elements, will exist?
4. How much security does the online data require?
5. How often will the Web site be updated?
6. To what extent is this site likely to evolve into something with greater requirements in the future?
7. How much downtime can the Web site comfortably afford?

Table 5-7 identifies the range of answers to each question and helps to determine how much relative infrastructure (low, medium, high) you are likely to need.

Table 5-7 Assessing Infrastructure Requirements

ISSUE	LOW	MEDIUM	HIGH
Content Amount	1–30 HTML pages	30–100 HTML pages	100+ HTML pages
Content Type	HTML, GIF images	HTML, GIF, a few multimedia files	High proportion of multimedia content; streaming audio and video
User Interactivity	Static HTML pages; e-mail form; guestbook; counter	Static HTML; search engine; database queries	Dynamic HTML; one or more database applications
Traffic	Less than 10,000 hits per day	10,000–100,000 hits per day	Greater than 100,000 hits per day
Security	Public access only	Password access control	Access control and encryption
Update Frequency	1–2 per month	1–2 per week	1+ per day
Future Needs	Unlikely to do more than add additional pages	Likely to add additional limited functionality	Likely to develop sophisticated applications
Downtime Tolerance	1 day	2–4 hours	10–20 minutes

Outsourcing your Web hosting with a service provider is the most economical solution to hosting needs in cases where you are creating an entry-level Web site for a company that does not already have a direct Internet connection in place. Even if you do have Internet access in-house, you may find it preferable to house a Web site externally, either because of corporate network security restrictions that make it difficult to put up a Web site internally or because you will be better able to manage the project externally. On the other hand, working with an Internet service provider is not always a satisfying experience. Most are primarily in the business of providing connectivity, which can be an all-consuming task in itself. For example, as long as the demands of your project are fairly light, you should be able to handle content updates yourself. If you do seek assistance, however, you may find your ISP of limited help when it comes to the ongoing operation and upkeep of your Web site. Under any circumstances you will need to be persistent to get adequate results. Even once you understand your options, selecting the right provider can be a daunting task, particularly if you live in an area of the country with an abundance of providers.

chapter 5   REGISTERING AND STAKING OUT CYBERTURF

Securing a Domain Name

Once you have identified a viable service provider, you should secure a domain name for your Web site. The domain name is the unique human-readable address that identifies a site. Domain name registration is handled by the Internet Network Information Center, otherwise known as the InterNIC, the closest thing to an oversight committee to be found in the Internet community. A year and a half ago, as demand for Internet names began heating up, InterNIC found itself with a backlog of requests. It often required up to a month to clear a domain name. Since then the process has been greatly automated and now the turn-around time is typically more like a few days to a week. The bad news is that domain names used to be free, and now they carry an annual fee of $50 (or $100 for two years). Most Web-hosting services say they include the registration of one domain name for you as part of the setup costs for your site. Read the fine print carefully here. Some sites mean by this that they will absorb the $50 fee. Others expect the customer to pay the fee; they just register the site in the customer's name.

Once you have identified a viable service provider, you should secure a domain name for your Web site.

HOW TO OBTAIN A NAME

Whether you register your domain name yourself or simply select a name for your ISP to register, the first step is to find out if the name is available. This is best done from InterNIC's Web site itself, at `http://www.internic.net`. There you will find information pertaining to registering domain names, as well as a lookup form for the *whois* database. This is a simple search function. Type in the domain name you wish to register and whois will return any existing matches in its database. Keep in mind that this database is not foolproof. If it comes up empty, you have hope. On the other hand, if it returns matches, it is still worth your while to make sure that the matches are for exactly the same domain name that you are researching. The search engine will bring back any strings in its data that match your entry, but they may not necessarily represent real Web domain names.

DOMAIN NAMES AND TRADEMARKS

In recent years a fair number of disputes have arisen over cases in which the holder of a trademark has gone to register a domain name for that mark, only to discover that somebody else already owns the name. In some cases the owner of the domain name had a perfectly legitimate reason for owning that name. In other cases, dubbed *domain name grabbing*, people have intentionally registered the names of well-known companies or even their own competitors. All this confusion prompted InterNIC to issue an official policy regarding prior claims to a domain name based on trademarks. In addition to reiterating its basic first-come-first-served policy, the document identifies two possible scenarios involving name disputes that InterNIC will adjudicate:

* Both parties have a legitimate, predetermined trademark involving the name, in which case the existing owner will retain the domain name.
* Only the plaintiff has a legitimate claim to the name, in which case the original owner will have to relinquish the name within 90 days.

Besides a courtroom battle, there is one way to retrieve a much-desired domain name: to buy it back. There are a number of very useful online reference sources on the legal aspects of domain names and trademarks, including a Georgetown University Law Center article on domain name disputes found at http://www.law.georgetown.edu/lc/internic/recent/rec1.html and another on the phenomenon of domain name grabbing at http://www.law.georgetown.edu/lc/internic/recent/rec2.html. Also worth reading is "Do You Own Your Own Name in Cyberspace?" by Mark Radcliffe at http://www.gcwf.com/articles/yourname.htm. For the InterNIC policy statement, see FTP://rs.internic.net/policy/internic.domain.policy.

chapter 5 REGISTERING AND STAKING OUT CYBERTURF

COMPLETING THE INTERNIC REGISTRATION

If you intend to register a domain name for yourself, InterNIC has a fairly straightforward application form that you can submit online from their Web site (http://rs.internic.net/rs-internic.html). Here are the five basic steps to register a new domain (condensed from the InterNIC's official seven steps described on their Web site help desk):

1. **Review the InterNIC policies,** including the name ownership dispute policy and the fee policy.
2. **Confirm that the selected name is not already in use.** Use the InterNIC's online whois database search.
3. **Identify providers for primary and secondary Domain Name System (DNS) service.** Applicants can provide their own DNS service or, as is more frequently the case, arrange to have it provided by an ISP.
4. **Obtain and review the application template.** Pay special attention to the InterNIC's list of the most common errors made in the process.
5. **Submit the template.** The submission process itself has three steps. First, submit the online form from the InterNIC Web site and e-mail it back to hostmaster@internic.net. Once the form arrives there, the InterNIC system will generate an automated confirmation. If all goes well, you will eventually get an e-mail message notifying you that the domain name is registered. The whole process usually takes less than a week, often just a few days.

 One issue that often troubles people is the disposition of their domain name if they change service providers. The domain name goes with you. It is not permanently attached to any particular location. If you do change your service provider, however, the new provider will need to help you set up the new address on their equipment. This may entail an additional setup fee.

239

Summary

Given the vast array of options for Web hosting and the wide range in quality, the decision of where and how to host your Web site deserves substantial research. Keep in mind that all the competitiveness in the market is really in your favor, as long as you have clearly identified the level of service you require. Here is a quick checklist of questions to ask a potential ISP. Partly it is interesting to ask these questions just to see if anyone at the shop actually knows the answers, or is willing to divulge the information. If they don't know or aren't willing to give you an answer, that, too, is information.

1. How much bandwidth does the ISP have to the Internet?
2. Who provides their Internet service?
3. What kind of host computers do they use?
4. What kind of Web servers?
5. What is the average number of users hosted on one computer?
6. How many computers are connected to a single Internet connection?
7. How much disk space or how many file requests does the ISP allow before a surcharge applies?
8. What was the percentage of unanticipated downtime for the network over the past several months?
9. What percentage of uptime does the ISP guarantee?
10. What does the ISP do to prevent downtime and to minimize it when it happens?
11. How often does the ISP perform backups?
12. Where do they store the backups? How long do they keep them?
13. What is the average time to recovery in the event of a system failure?
14. What level of technical support does the ISP offer?
15. What format are server log files provided in and how often?
16. What means of access does the ISP allow to the server for updating content?

17. What measures has the ISP taken to secure the network and host computers?

18. How scalable will your Web site be with this service provider?

19. Does the ISP have any clients who would be willing to provide a recommendation?

chapter 6

Acquiring Irresistible Content

THERE IS AN IRONIC TENSION in online publishing between the need to develop material and the need to protect it. Never before in mass communications—print, broadcast, or electronic media—has it been so difficult for a publisher to decide what to say or how to say it as on the World Wide Web. Thousands of sites exist on the Web with no apparent mission or goal, and consequently no sense about their content. What exactly are people looking for at the Jell-O site? How many issues of *Kleenex Magazine* do you think it will take before a subscriber becomes tired of reading about tissue secrets? Excited about tuning in to the *Ford Hour* on TV after dinner to learn about the latest trucks? These examples may sound foolish, but deep-pocketed sponsors continue to throw money into sites with relatively useless content. On the other hand, the digital age has produced an environment where information has never been harder to protect or to ensure revenue from once it is published: Everything that can be digitized can be copied at practically no cost and published almost instantly on a global scale. Similarly, the conventional means of policing territorial regulations regarding censorship have proved all but useless in a medium that essentially has no borders.

The two most common and popular information media—print and broadcast—evolved presentation forms quickly and naturally. A mixture of entertainment and news became the successful recipe for what the television and radio world calls programming and the print world calls reporting. Advertising joined the mix as a way for information providers to pay the bills and make some money, because subscription revenues alone are insufficient to support broadcasts and publications. Finally, the media added a dash of audience participation in the form of letters to the editor, guest interviews, or quiz show contestants—and voilà! The content mix for modern media was complete.

Protecting published content in these media has never been a difficult matter. Duplicating material was, until recently, troublesome and easy to police. People rarely mistake second-generation audiovisual material for original stuff, for example, because the copies just aren't as good—and it takes a substantial investment in infrastructure to republish and distribute the lesser-quality products. As a further discouragement, few people wanted to risk the legal penalties for bootlegging, and one had to be intent on making a profit from it to pursue the occupation.

Enter the Internet (suddenly), and along with it a unique media mixture of new possibilities and problems. Instead of evolving like other technological innovations in response to a developing market, the Net was haphazardly tossed into the commercial arena by the Department of Defense. It is a medium effectively *thrust* on the public with no time to grow and mature. To make matters more confusing, the *payoff* for many participants in the cyberspace experience—such as electronic commerce—just isn't at a level of acceptance or standardization that makes it a mainstream channel for conducting business. On the upside are factors like low-cost global reach, true two-way interactivity, and instant publishing. However, the new medium also brings with it a confusing blend of print and broadcast possibilities, and publishers are still wrestling with the mix. For example, the Web will carry audiovisual material, but of a quality too poor to rival TV. It can display printed material, but while there are extraordinary reference possibilities available through linking strategies and searching facilities, it's awkward (perhaps ridiculous) to try to read voluminous text on a monitor. One result of this mixed blessing has been a crisis in determining the right content mix for information providers. The very term *content provider* is so general that one

chapter 6 ACQUIRING IRRESISTIBLE CONTENT

wonders if the site producer really knows what he or she is looking for: Pictures? Music? Musical Pictures? Thus, among the truly interesting and useful resources that Web sites offer, the medium also houses an incredible array of sites with senseless content—from the equivalent of shows about sponsored products to shopping outlets with nothing to sell.

In the midst of all this chaos about what to present, official committees from half the civilized countries in the world are convening for the first time in 25 years to come to some common agreement about international copyright and censorship issues raised by the new medium. Digital reproduction makes perfect copies, so there are no discernible originals any more. How does one police plagiarism and counterfeiting? Firms such as Microsoft and AT&T virtually give away a Web site (and the equivalent of a near-global presence with 20 million viewers) when someone buys a software product or opens a telephone account. Microsoft offers a presence in exchange for signing up with the Microsoft Network (MSN), which in turn is bundled with Windows 95, which in turn is bundled with practically any computer you can buy; and AT&T gives away five hours' Internet access a month and a home page free to anyone who uses their long distance services. This makes it pretty hard to escape the temptation to hang a shingle out on the World Wide Web, and pretty hard to deny that the traditional barriers to entering the global media market have been erased. While countries like Singapore have attempted to set up international firewalls to block the transmission of *undesirable* content, the nature of the Internet is such that this form of censorship is doomed to failure.

The Web brings with it a confusing blend of print and broadcast possibilities, and publishers are still wrestling with the mix.

This chapter is about coping with some of these problems in human-sized bites. No one really expects you to become the arbiter of international law or the da Vinci of the digital era, but there are some things that you should know if you want to make your site interesting, to make it run smoothly, and to keep it out of trouble. If you've done your homework in Chapter 2, Clarifying Your Web Mission, and established a clear sense of your site's mission, the nature of your content should be fairly obvious. The first part of this chapter helps you identify where to look for it. The second part of the chapter highlights some legal issues that you should run through on your checklist before you go live.

Viewing Content in Three Dimensions

Content has three basic dimensions: nature, format, and source. While at first glance these distinctions may seem simple and unnecessary, they prove useful when you're out there looking for something to bolster viewership:

* **Nature** refers to the intent or intended effect of content on its audience. Using the broadcast model, nature might refer to reference, news, entertainment, advertising, or editorial comment. The nature of your content comes into consideration when you form a mission and shape an identity for a site. For example, even the driest e-zine will require a mix of all the elements described here, as you can see in the online version of the *Wall Street Journal* shown in Figure 6-1. (See Chapter 2, Clarifying Your Web Mission, and Chapter 4, Creating a Web Identity, for more details on this topic.)

* **Format** refers to the sensory experience that we have in relation to content. Thus content is text, pictorial, audio, video, audiovisual, or animation. The first mistake that inexperienced managers make in converting paper-based information to the Web is to simply transpose page for page. The Web accommodates hypertext links and multimedia, and ignoring these possibilities for embellishing two-dimensional presentations wastes the new resource. Format affects both the identity of your site and its housing requirements. (See Chapter 4, Creating a Web Identity, and Chapter 5, Registering and Staking Out Cyberturf, for more details on these issues, and Appendix A, Killer Apps, for tools for creating multimedia presentations.)

* **Source** refers to the origin of content. You may develop content in-house, or acquire it from a third party—in which case some licensing arrangement may be necessary. Many sites draw on a mixture of sources to create an identity that supports their mission and captures audience attention adequately, and details on this process are the subject of the following section.

chapter ACQUIRING IRRESISTIBLE CONTENT

Figure 6-1

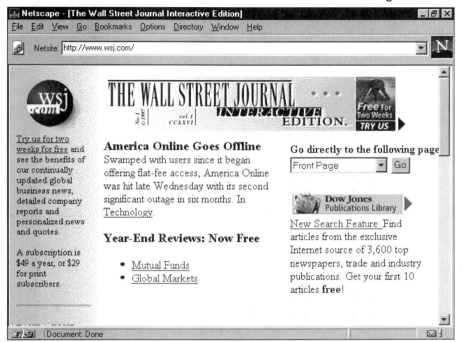

Even the *Wall Street Journal* has advertising, editorial, news, and classifieds on its home page.

Looking for Sources

All Web sites turn to three basic sources for content: original, licensed, and public domain. Content of any nature—entertainment, news, and so on—may come from any of the three sources. *Original content* comes from your own company or an outside resource that the company retains. On the creative side, examples of this type of material may come from writers, photographers, filmmakers, or advertising agencies. On the less obvious side, technical documentation or a database of customer support activities can also provide useful original content. *Licensed content* is someone else's original work. The good news is that you can find just about anything you don't have in-house through a third party—and in most cases for substantially less outlay than it would take to create the content from scratch. The less-good news (there's no actual bad news in this scenario) is that your use is often nonexclusive, and that licensing usually involves use restrictions in addition to a fee. Finally, *public domain content* is material that is also someone else's original work, but that does not carry the restrictions or price tags of licensed content. This section of the chapter discusses all three types of sources.

ORIGINAL CONTENT

If you're planning to use original content and have the resources to develop, remember that, unlike print or other broadcast channels, the widest possible range of multimedia material has relevance on the Web. Rather than being forced to present a case for a product or service in a 30- or 60-second slot, a Web page can contain almost limitless amounts of product information and demonstration materials. Web magazines, on the other hand, can go live with animations and sound, and jump off of the page in ways that print media could never manage. Like everything else, the new opportunity comes with both negatives and positives.

On the bright side, this means that you can leverage just about every type of media resource to which you have access: copywriters, photographers, video producers, game designers, graphic designers, cartoonists, musicians, script writers, and so on. The project is almost like building a media conglomerate around a single company. On the dark side, extremely sophisticated sites can have price tags in the millions of dollars, and require full-time staffing resources. Make sure you know what you're getting into when you sign up for a full-scale original content effort. Also remember that, unless the purpose of the site is a short-term, event-based promotion, whatever you start off with will age and need updating on a regular basis, so the money and manpower requirements are not a one-time allocation.

If you're planning to use original content and have the resources to develop, remember that the widest possible range of multimedia material has relevance on the Web.

If you have elected not to develop new material either in-house or through a third party such as an advertising agency or content developer, but want to use original content nonetheless, you may find materials within your organization that lend themselves to adaptation in electronic form. This section contains examples of how some successful sites on the Web have made use of original content.

Recycling catalogs and brochures

If your organization already has a catalog of its products, much of the work of creating an online version has already been done. If not, content from existing advertisements and brochures may be a good basis for creating a new catalog. Much of the copy in these cases is portable from print to the Web, and the artwork only requires scanning. In some instances, some or all of the content may already be in machine-readable format, simply because the company you use to print catalogs does its work from computerized prepress. One caveat to consider in offering an online catalog if your organization already has one in print: Users may expect a complete catalog online — it's best to give them the whole thing; it may be bulky, but limiting their choices to something less than the full spectrum of products may serve to discourage Web access.

* Lands' End (http://www.landsend.com) has put most of its catalog online, along with automatic searches for items that are in stock and overstocked. The company also offers Web-only clearance specials. The site uses both photography and illustration for visuals and provides secure Web ordering via SSL encryption.
* Godiva Chocolatier (http://www.godiva.com) was one of the first retailers to create a strong Web presence. As you can see in Figure 6-2, in addition to the photos and product descriptions contained in the catalog, the site includes automatic holiday e-mail reminders and giveaways to draw traffic and entice purchasers.
* Computer giant Gateway 2000 (http://www.gw2k.com) allows users to design a custom computer as well as to review product specifications from their existing catalog. Technical support, employment opportunities at the company, and an amusement area called the Cow Zone also appear on the site.

Godiva Chocolatier uses a variety of marketing aids, including e-mail, to support their online catalog.

If you're still hungry for more examples of merchandise catalogs, check out the Catalog Site (http://www.catalogsite.com). This location lists and reviews thousands of mail-order catalogs and provides numerous indices for finding catalogs that may contain the type of merchandise for which you are searching.

Exploiting customer service data

Customer service can mean anything from fielding complaints and providing technical support to offering sales support and expediting delivery. Virtually any business needs to address these issues, and the systems and data that support that effort can all contribute usefully to the content a site offers. Web sites can be extremely cost-effective providers of customer service-oriented information: they are tireless, unaffected by sour attitudes, and extremely comprehensive if they are well organized. Here's a selective list of some companies that have created impressive sites along these lines:

* Apple Computer (http://til.info.apple.com/til/til.html) puts its complete technical support database online with over 14,000 articles (these are otherwise available via a toll-free telephone number to Apple customers). Empowering customers to solve their own problems using vendor-supplied content saves telephone time and the cost of calls for both Apple and its users.

* The Toro Company, maker of snow throwers and lawn care products, puts important product information online at (http://www.toro.com/Snowthrowers/questionnaire.shtml). Its sales support includes a questionnaire to help potential customers decide which Toro snow thrower is correct for their needs. (The company operates a separate site for lawn care questions at http://www.yardcare.com.)

* Federal Express (http://www.fedex.com), United Parcel Service (http://www.ups.com), and the United States Postal Service (http://www.usps.gov) all have online forms that permit customers to track packages automatically without having to call a customer service representative. The Express Mail form in Figure 6-3 is a good example of just how simple this is. The success and customer approval of these types of systems has been outstanding and rewarding for vendor and client alike.

Figure 6-3

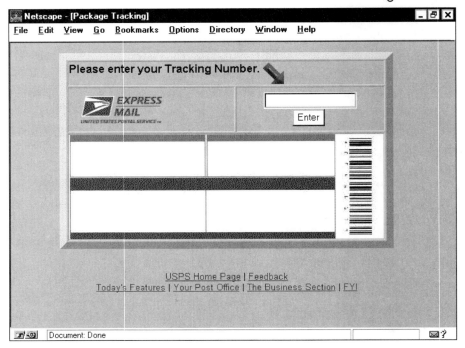

Even the Post Office has gotten online to make life easier for the rest of us.

Leveraging company profiles and reports

The Web is a terrific venue for distributing press releases, annual reports, formal financial reports such as 10Ks and 10Qs for public companies, and other important company information. This is exactly the type of information that readers rarely want when they get it in print at a meeting, and can't find at a later date when they decide they do need it (no one can ever find the report from a meeting a month before). On the Web, this information is just seconds away. Moreover, publishing on the Web may fulfill the reporting requirements for public companies under Securities and Exchange Commission (SEC) rules. While not a public company (the SEC is a government regulatory agency charged with enforcing securities laws), the SEC itself puts its annual report and press releases on its Web site (http://www.sec.gov/rules/final/33-7289.txt), including the rules describing electronic avail-

chapter 6 ACQUIRING IRRESISTIBLE CONTENT

ability of public documents. Public companies must file their official quarterly reports with the SEC electronically. The following are a few of the many sites providing annual reports and press releases electronically:

* Monsanto makes its annual report available for download in Adobe Acrobat format at its site (http://www.monsanto.com), shown in Figure 6-4. The Adobe option means that you can view and print the report on your computer as it appears in its original published form. Monsanto also makes spreadsheets of financial reports available in Microsoft Excel for those wishing to incorporate the numbers into a model.

Figure 6-4

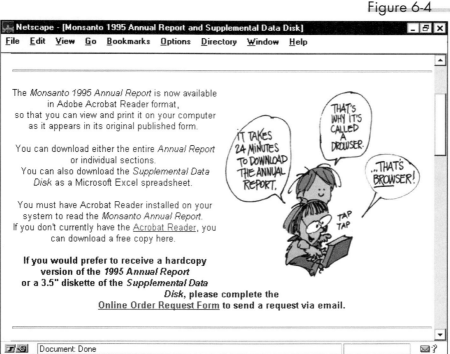

Monsanto extends cyberspace by using Adobe Acrobat and Excel files for its annual report.

* Chubb—a financial and insurance conglomerate—reprints its entire annual report at its site (`http://www.chubb.com`). The site also includes a listing of Chubb's complete service offerings, and locations of its offices around the world. While this site is certainly dry in visual presentation, it's interesting that even this conservative 115-year-old company has gotten on board and gone online.
* Media giant Rupert Murdoch has devoted the entire site for The News Corporation Limited to its annual report (`http://www.newscorp.com`). Each section of the document is easy to access through a pair of pull-down menus.

That's entertainment

From games to soap operas, original entertainment-oriented content is making a big play for audience share on the Web. This end of the original content spectrum is perhaps closest to the conventional programming model found in television, and requires the deepest pockets because of the writing and programming resources necessary to produce a quality piece. Nevertheless, it is worth reviewing some of the more creative efforts in this area to get a sense of the state of the art:

* KinderNet (`http://www.kindernet.com`), shown in Figure 6-5, offers original programming for children's entertainment. KinderNet's mission is to provide parents with an enjoyable learning experience to share with their children. The content consists of music, characters, games, and stories, all offered to children in original interactive formats. While the format of the site may not be appropriate for every mission, its elements have something to say for almost every site.

chapter **6** ACQUIRING IRRESISTIBLE CONTENT

Figure 6-5

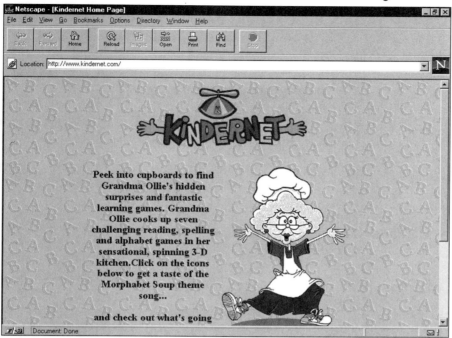

KinderNet specializes in original interactive learning experiences for parents and children from ages four to eight.

* Online soap operas such as The East Village (`http://www.theeastvillage.com`) and 101 Hollywood Blvd. (`http://home.navisoft.com/brewpubclub/101.htm`) create complex ongoing melodramas that invite users to interact and become a part of the action. In-house staff originate the story lines, which evolve through a combination of user input and continuing editorial supervision. For a healthy look at some of these possibilities, visit `http://www.ozemail.com.au/~goan/soap.html`.

* Games have become an extremely popular way of attracting site attendance, especially when the site offers prizes. Sites such as Attitude Network's Happy Puppy (`http://happypuppy.com`) and Starwave (`http://www.starwave.com`) have dozens of original single-player and multiplayer games and have become extremely

popular. Figure 6-6 gives you a look at the Starwave opening screen. The possibility of joining and winning without ever leaving the house holds terrific appeal.

Starwave is a virtual gaming casino.

LICENSING CONTENT

Resources exist for licensing just about anything you could ever want to include on a Web site. Examples of the type of material you might want to license are

* Articles from newspapers or magazines
* Photographs of products, famous people, or events
* Illustrations such as comic strips or artistic works
* Musical recordings
* Portions of television or radio commercials or print advertisements

chapter 6 ACQUIRING IRRESISTIBLE CONTENT

Many of these materials are already available online. You can get some of them in CD-ROM format, ready for inclusion on your site. Yet others exist in their native, nondigital format. In these cases you must contact the content owner and arrange for conversion to a digital format yourself. If you're licensing, you're going to sign some type of licensing agreement and pay a fee to the content owner (copyright law covers just about everything you might get from or put on a Web site). Fees are sometimes paid on a one-time basis, sometimes as a royalty based on use. We'll get back to the elements of a good contract and other legal issues involved in licensed content in the second part of this chapter.

At the simple end of the licensing spectrum are conventional items such as stock photography. The same stock photo houses that have catered to advertisers and publishers in conventional print and broadcast media also make their materials available to Web developers. Software publishers such as Corel (http://www.corel.com/products/clipartandphotos/photos/index.htm) also have online libraries. On the other hand, news of all sorts—current news, sports, or weather information, and so on—has become a terrific draw for many sites, and the rationale for a great deal of licensing activity. Most businesses, of course, do not have the resources to collect such information themselves. Hiring and supporting the necessary infrastructure would be prohibitively expensive. However, the technology underlying the Web makes it easy to access a vast array of news and information sources from all over the world. The simplest way to accomplish this is to provide a link from your business site to a news site, but this loses your visitor to another site and certainly does not convey the impression that your site is the content provider. As an alternative, you can integrate the news information into your site by means of a licensing agreement with the content provider. A good example of this type of integration can be found at the American Housecall Network site (http://housecall.com) shown in Figure 6-7. Housecall licenses a news feed for relevant health-related information from Reuters. Reuters, in turn, filters its general news flow to deliver only the requested information to Housecall.

Figure 6-7

The American Housecall Network site licenses its news feed from Reuters.

This type of agreement generally provides for periodic update to the information in a form usable by the licensee site, or a mechanism for transparently linking back to the source site to display the information on the licensee site. The cost of this type of arrangement will vary by the number of users expected, the scope and timeliness of the information being presented, and the exclusivity (if any) negotiated by the licensee. Consider some of the following sources for licensing this type of content:

* **General News**   Reuters New Media Online (http://www.online.reuters.com), CNN (http://www.cnn.com), The New York Times on the Web (http://www.nytimes.com), and The Wall Street Journal Interactive Edition (http://www.wsj.com)
* **Media News**   Cowles Business Media, Media Central (http://www.mediacentral.com)

- **Weather** The National Weather Service Interactive Weather Information Network (http://iwin.nws.noaa.gov/iwin/main.html) and the Weather Channel at (http://www.weather.com)
- **Industry News** Cahners Publishing Company (http://www.variety.com)
- **Sports** Sports Illustrated (http://pathfinder.com/si) and professional sports leagues such as the NBA (http://www.nba.com), the NFL (http://www.nfl.com), the National Hockey League (http://www.nhl.com), and Major League Baseball (http://www.majorleaguebaseball.com)

PUBLIC DOMAIN CONTENT

Public domain material is content or work for which no financial obligation of any kind exists to creators, previous copyright owners, or distributors, so this is stuff you can publish on your Web site for free. Public domain material may be of any format—textual, pictorial, or audiovisual. It may be in the public domain because its creators published it as such, or because its copyright has expired. In the music industry, for example, copyrighted sheet music falls into the public domain fifty years after the death of its composer. You must be careful to confirm the public domain status of content you intend to use. Although you can sing Francis Scott Key's "The Star-Spangled Banner" freely, without a performance fee, you may not directly republish another music publisher's sheet music version of the national anthem without that publisher's permission. The same is true regarding the visual arts: you can create and publish a picture of da Vinci's Mona Lisa, but you can't redistribute a photo produced by the Louvre without that museum's permission. Nor does public domain status confer the right to reassign authorship: you can't say that you wrote the Gettysburg Address or the 22nd Amendment, but you can reprint them freely. The bottom line: be careful to research the status of the public domain material you plan to use. Notwithstanding this caveat, there is an enormous amount of material available, and the remainder of this section gives you some sense of what's out there and where to find it.

With a little help from Uncle Sam

Your tax dollars work to create literally millions of pages of research each year, and the recent craze to go online has not escaped the attention of our officials in all three branches of government at all levels from local to national. It was, after all, Al Gore who got so carried away with the information superhighway thing to begin with. Some of the most extensive, useful, and up-to-date content comes from government sources and is sitting on one of the hundreds of government Web sites that are publicly accessible. By U.S. law, federal government material is copyright-free, so it's pretty much yours for the taking. (Note: The Canadian government takes the opposite approach, and does its best to recoup the taxpayers' investment by selling absolutely everything it can get coin for.) The following is a brief list of various governmental sites to mine for content:

* The Library of Congress site (http://www.loc.gov) is a great starting point for finding U.S. government resources as shown in Figure 6-8. There is a complete Research and Reference section that leads to areas from American folklife to the motion picture industry. You can even gain access to the photographic archives of the Library of Congress.

* The sites for governmental agencies provide the full text and results of countless studies. Consider government branches such as the Commerce Department (http://www.doc.gov), the Defense Department (http://www.dod.gov), the Department of Transportation (http://www.dot.gov), the Food and Drug Administration (http://www.fda.gov), the Securities and Exchange Commission (http://www.sec.go), and the Federal Aviation Administration (http://www.faa.gov).

Figure 6-8

The Library of Congress is a wonderful place to start looking.

* Independent government agencies can also be great sources for both printed and audiovisual material. Check out sites such as the CIA (http://www.odci.gov/cia), NASA (http://www.gsfc.nasa.gov/NASA_homepage.html), the Smithsonian Institution (http://www.si.edu), the U.S. Information Agency (http://www.usia.gov/usa/pixusa/pix.htm), and the United States Copyright Office (http://lcweb.loc.gov/copyright). NASA, for example, has some spectacular images, and the CIA World Fact Book (http://www.odci.gov/cia/publications/95fact/index.html) is an incredible treasure trove of geopolitical information.

Other public domain sources

Beyond governmental information, other materials are also in the public domain, or may be royalty free. Some of these materials may either be included directly on a Web site, or listed on the site for downloading. For a sampling of public domain and royalty-free sources, you can perform a keyword search with Yahoo! (http://search.yahoo.com) or Excite (http://www.excite.com), or check out Internet journalist Kevin Savetz's listing at http://northcoast.com/savetz/pd/. Consider some of the following sites for certain content:

* **Classic literature.** Project Gutenberg (http://www.promo.net/pg/) shown in Figure 6-9 is a decades-long effort to convert public domain works of literature into electronically accessible text. One of the Project Gutenberg selection criteria is the size of the audience likely to want a source and use it frequently.

Figure 6-9

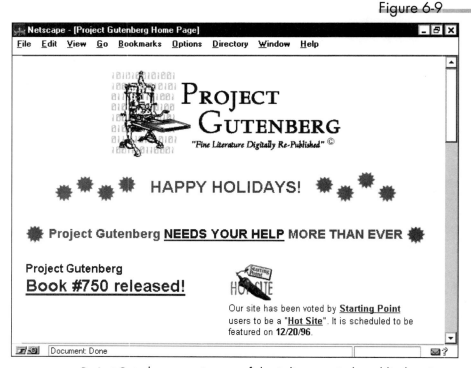

Project Gutenberg contains tons of classic literature in the public domain.

chapter ACQUIRING IRRESISTIBLE CONTENT

- **Film and Animation.** Desert Island Films (http://www.desertislandfilms.com) offers a library with over 1,000 public domain feature films, cartoons, short subjects, classic TV, sci-fi, children's, action, and martial arts material. They sell tapes in either NTSC or PAL format, and once you acquire a master, you are free to use it in any way at your site.
- **Graphics, icons, and other elements.** These are available from many Web sites, including Internet Transmissions (http://i-trans.com/library.htm).

Keep in mind that not everything available without fee is necessarily in the public domain, and that not everything in the public domain (including the materials listed here) is without cost. A few other points about royalty-free and public domain materials:

- **Fraud.** Many Web sites mistakenly describe materials as being in the public domain when in fact they are under copyright and subject to license fees and legal liability for misuse. Always carefully examine the disclaimers and descriptions on the page, and use only those materials whose history is clear.
- **Special Use.** Some materials are freely usable only for certain purposes, such as for noncommercial Web sites or for print advertisements, but not for others. Be sure the creator or rights owner permits your particular use, either by reading the accompanying materials or by asking the licensor directly.
- **Shareware and Freeware.** *Shareware* and *freeware* are *not* the same as public domain material. Shareware (pay upon use) and freeware (use without fee) describe compensation requirements, not the rights attached. Examine their usage requirements with particular care before placing these materials on a Web site.

LINKS AND USER INPUT

Not all your content has to be on the site itself. Sometimes the best way to get useful content is via a link. This may simplify or eliminate rights acquisition or clearance problems, and allow your site to take advantage of others' resources transparently to your users. Linking can be via text references, graphics, or HTML frames. Linking, however, isn't right for every site. You can't be sure that users will return to your site once they link to another one, and without a formal arrangement with the target site, you can't be sure that the target's content will be appropriate for your visitors.

On the other hand, links can provide extra information and entertainment to your users that you would find expensive or unfeasible to offer on your site, and users may appreciate the directions to sites of related interest. Consider the synergy between the Catalog site in Figure 6-10 and any of the online catalogs that it lists: a complementary match. Beyond that, links can be part of a broader joint venture effort between two or more companies whose sites interact, which may include shared revenues or at least lowered advertising costs.

Figure 6-10

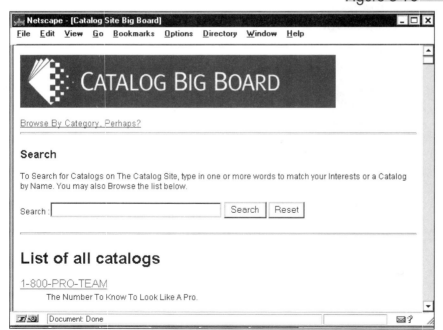

The Catalog site lists hundreds of online catalogs . . .

chapter 6 ACQUIRING IRRESISTIBLE CONTENT

Figure 6-11

. . . and enables users to jump directly to any of them.

Another source for content is to let users provide it for you in the form of postings, chats, and republished e-mail. This may be the major part of the site, or limited to a single area. User-provided content has some real advantages:

* It gets your users personally involved in creating the site and its community.
* It lets your site change organically in response to its users' preferences and opinions.
* It shares the burden of updates among many people.

Chats and postings are supported by a number of software packages, including: ichat's ichat software (http://www.ichat.com), EarthWeb's Java-based EarthWeb Chat (http://chat.earthweb.com), and The Palace's Virtual Worlds Chat software (http://www.thepalace.com), among others. The Palace even provides a three-dimensional environment where users can assume characters called avatars and interact.

As you can see, you have a broad variety of sources from which to choose in acquiring content for your site. With a little bit of ingenuity, even a project constrained by a modest budget can construct an impressive collection of multimedia content. The real key to a good content mix is being clear about your mission and identity. The choices for content all flow from those decisions, and exactly where beyond that to look for solutions is usually a matter of budget. Now, on to some legal realities about content. Just because it's easy to reuse traditional media content or acquire it from other sites doesn't mean it's legal. The laws are there, they're real, and the liability both financially and in potential public relations damage can be severe. You have to follow appropriate procedures for acquisition if you want to minimize legal problems down the road.

Pondering Legal Issues

Although the Web is a new medium, it is still subject to existing laws—from copyright to criminal. It is a safe bet that both governmental rules and union contracts have something to say about almost anything that a business can do with content on the Web, and if they don't today, they will tomorrow. The following issues need consideration if you are working with practically any kind of content for the Web:

- Intellectual property laws such as copyrights and trademarks
- Union rules governing talent such as actors, models, and musicians
- Regulations about the nature of the content such as rules against indecency or fraud
- Contract provisions for Web site development and hosting

This section discusses these issues and provides you with solutions to stay both legal and creative.

chapter 6　ACQUIRING IRRESISTIBLE CONTENT

COPYRIGHT AND TRADEMARK ISSUES

Copyright and trademark are two types of legal protection that are quite different from each other, are often confused, and are both extremely relevant to content acquisition and development on the Web. A good contract can help to establish solid working relationships, but you should still be aware of the underlying laws that apply to intellectual property such as copyright and trademark.

Copyright laws control the duplication, broadcast, and performance of creative works. These laws cover all creative works, whether text or graphic (including computer programs) or audiovisual, commercial or noncommercial. In addition, under U.S. laws and those of many other countries, copyright laws pertain even in cases where a work is not published, marked with a copyright notice (such as © 1996 Fred Q. Author), or registered with the government. Under copyright laws, the creator of a work has control over whether any third party can copy, adapt, revise, perform, or broadcast the work. These restrictions specifically pertain to the Web. Depending on the severity of a copyright infringement, anyone copying or otherwise using a work without the permission of the creator may be liable for significant fines or even criminal penalties.

There are many myths about copyright that circulate freely with absolutely no basis in reality. These include fantasies like the notion that changing a copyrighted work is enough to eliminate the copyright protection on it, that there's a specific percentage (such as 20 percent) of a copyrighted work that you can use without permission of the creator, or that by placing something on the Web the creator has made it public domain and freely usable by others. None of these rumors are true, and relying on any of them can get you into trouble. Lawsuits are the most likely outcome of a violation—with the accompanying costs of lawyers' fees, penalties, and damage to good will. Even without facing a lawsuit, doubt about copyright and ownership can yield problems when trying to market a Web site or its content to third parties who may require warranties about ownership. The safest assumption is that any cre-

> **There are many myths about copyright that circulate freely with absolutely no basis in reality. . . . None of them are true, and relying on any of them can get you into trouble.**

267

ative work you haven't put together yourself is copyrighted unless you know a federal government agency produced it, and that you need the permission of the creator before you use it for any purpose. Remember that the person or site from which you acquired material may not be that of the creator of the material.

Trademarks are very different from copyrights, both in what they protect and how they work. Trademarks (and the related service marks) protect only those words and images that identify the source of goods or services *in commerce*. They must be affirmatively identified and positively enforced by their owners if they are to retain their protection. If an owner fails to police its marks, it may lose them to the general public or to another user. Trademarks are also industry-specific: The same mark may be issued to many different companies, provided they serve different markets and there is no possibility of confusion. For example, Dell is accepted in use by both Dell Publishing and Dell Computers.

Trademarks may be protected under common law, state law, or federal law. Each has its own requirements and results, and many businesses seek to employ all types of law to protect their trademarks. You can generally recognize which words or symbols a business considers its trademarks either by explicit statements around their use (for example, "Fredco is a trademark of Fred Industries") or the presence of a symbol next to the mark, such as ™, which indicates a common law trademark, or ®, which demonstrates that the mark has received U.S. federal registration (an additional layer of national protection). There are international equivalents as well.

A Web site may infringe another's trademarks in ways such as:

Fair Use as an Excuse for Infringement

You may hear the term *fair use* used as an excuse for infringing on someone else's copyright. Under U.S. copyright law, there is a principle that certain unauthorized uses of copyrighted materials, while formally infringements, are not subject to penalty—for example, reproducing a copyrighted text for the purpose of criticism, news reporting, satire, or some educational uses. Even if your use may arguably fall into one of these categories, don't assume you've got free rein to copy large portions or the entire work. The law places sharp restrictions on the amount of a work you can use even under the fair use exception. Ultimately, it is better to play it safe, and to obtain permission from the creator of a work you wish to use even if you think your use would be considered fair. Life—and usage—isn't always as fair as we would like.

chapter 6 ACQUIRING IRRESISTIBLE CONTENT

- Listing products being sold using incorrect trademarks such as naming the wrong source, or not formatting the logo as required by its owner
- Linking to a site by means of an inappropriate use of a trademark, for example, linking to some college student's unauthorized Captain Kirk photo site using the phrase "Star Trek," which is a trademark of Paramount Pictures
- Using someone else's trademarks to refer to your goods

Trademark, like copyright, is subject to international laws and it is always worth keeping in mind that the Internet and the World Wide Web are international, so you may be liable for violations of foreign as well as local laws in certain cases.

LOOK FOR THE UNION LABEL

Copyright and trademark are not the only issues you need to consider in using existing content. If the material includes identifiable music, voices, or faces, there may be talent unions whose contracts govern the use of the material as well. For example, consider a ten-second music video clip that plays a rock song overlaid with a scene from a movie. A record company may own the copyright on the video clip as a completed work, and a movie company may own a copyright on the film. The music itself is probably also under copyright and the publisher of the music may be due union royalties for its use through organizations such as ASCAP (`http://www.ascap.com`) or BMI (`http://www.bmi.com`). The musicians may themselves be entitled to compensation for the use of their voices and instrumental work, even if they have no copyright in the music. The movie clip may also include actors whose permission is required (and to whom royalties may need to be paid under *their* union agreements) before it's used online. There may even be other rights involved, such as synchronization rights (governing the matching of the music to the video).

Domain Names and Trademarks: Feudin' Relations

A domain name is the set of words that identifies the unique name of the computer on which an Internet resource like a Web site is stored. Many times, a business will seek to use its trademarks as domain names, since its customers may expect to find the business by its commonly known business or brand names. However, each word or set of words can serve as only a single domain name, while the same word or words may be the trademark for a number of unrelated companies, or may just be an unusual and catchy name for a Web site. As a result, there have been a number of well-publicized disputes among trademark holders over domain names, or between a trademark holder and the unrelated registrant of a domain name using the same phrase. Unfortunately, while trademarks are covered under both statute and case law, domain names are subject to an oft-changed policy of domain name issuing bodies such as InterNIC (http://www.internic.net), which are nongovernmental. Where trademark law and InterNIC policy clash, companies are left with little comfort concerning their ability to use their trademarks (or their domain names) without incident. This problem is being addressed in a number of ways, including the refinement of InterNIC's policies, a new understanding of domain name issues on the part of trademark holders and courts, and an effort to determine new ways of leading users to Web sites. You can find out the latest from InterNIC about domain name policy at http://rs.internic.net/domain-info/internic-domain-6.html. (For more details on securing a domain name see Chapter 5, Registering and Staking Out Cyberturf.)

For more information on the domain name disputes that have arisen over the past few years, a good index can be found on the Georgetown Law Center Web site (http://www.law.georgetown.edu/lc/internic/recent/rec1.html), which discusses examples such as:

* Kaplan Educational Centers' lawsuit against The Princeton Review, another test review company, after The Princeton Review registered kaplan.com for its Web site, usurping the trademark of its arch-rival Kaplan.

* McDonald's dispute with then-Wired columnist Joshua Quittner, who registered mcdonalds.com as a personal domain name after McDonald's told him it wasn't interested in the Internet. McDonald's became quite interested after Quittner's article appeared, and the dispute was eventually settled by McDonald's making a Net-related charitable contribution.

continued

(Continued)

* MTV's lawsuit against Adam Curry over mtv.com, and *The New York Post*'s against Farhan Memon for nypost.com—in both cases, employees who registered the domain name with the knowledge and consent of their employers and retained ownership after leaving their jobs. The companies sued to get the names back, and the ex-employees eventually turned the names over to the companies.

It's not difficult to see that clearing a popular piece of material for use can be both costly and time-consuming. These issues are not new, but the sudden availability of a global broadcast medium with little or no production costs associated with it has given them new importance. Prior to the emergence of the Web, only media giants like Capital Cities or Bertelsmann could reach millions of viewers, and the associated expenses were substantial. Now you can do it from your own Web page on the Microsoft Network for a mere $20 a month, and the opportunities for copyright infringement, both intentional and inadvertent, have grown enormously.

The *big boys* can get in trouble as well. In some cases a contract gives a company permission to use a work in multiple media, but the Web is not one of them. Under both law and union rules, use on a Web site is *very* different from broadcast television or print uses, and most existing union agreements and licenses do not cover Internet use because many of them were entered into before the Internet went commercial. Once again, new negotiations and new payments may be required before it's safe to put the material on the Internet.

THE CONTENT OF THE CONTENT

Just because content is legally obtained and licensed doesn't mean it's legal to publish or distribute it. Different local, state, federal, and even international restrictions may apply to the publishing of certain kinds of content. These types of restrictions may include

* Obscenity or indecency
* Statements for or against a political or religious viewpoint
* Running an online contest or sweepstakes
* Statements or claims made in advertisements

In Germany and Japan, for example, it's illegal to publish comparative advertisements, which are perfectly acceptable in the United States. Countries such as China may block certain prodemocracy content and hold its publishers liable. Different states and countries have substantially different laws regarding profanity and sexually explicit material. In other words, on top of all the rights you need to acquire or account for when finding or creating content, you also have to be concerned about, well, the content of the content.

Remember that once material is online, there are no border checks or customs houses, and the audience receiving the information may be substantially larger than the one you intend to target with your Web site. If all this sounds intimidating and overwhelming, however, take heart. The news isn't nearly that bad, and there are sound strategies for living sanely on the Web and still managing to produce interesting and valuable content without drowning in paperwork or going broke paying for royalties and licensing fees.

DEVELOPMENT AND HOSTING CONTRACTS

The Web is a new medium, and many of the businesses creating a presence there are small, informally run, and managed by people with little professional experience. Unfortunately, many of these companies have undertaken significant development work on a handshake and without protection or direction for either party in the event that problems arise or that the parties simply want to terminate their relationship. Without a contract, it is difficult or impossible to know who owns the content of the site, what is being paid for, what each party's responsibilities are, and how the contract can be ended peacefully. It is critical to create contracts that inform and bind all parties to a Web project, whether development, maintenance, or hosting. Web site creation combines many different business models, including software development, marketing and promotion, creative freelancing, and equipment operation and repair. A good contract includes provisions relating to all these areas in a unified whole. A good contract should always address the following elements:

* Description of the project
* Description of the services

chapter 6 ACQUIRING IRRESISTIBLE CONTENT

- Description of the functions
- Compensation
- Ownership
- Confidentiality
- Termination
- Warranties and indemnification

Description of the project. Describe the design and function of the Web site, and make sure each party has the same idea. This can be done in the body of the contract, or in an attached schedule that may include screen shots or flowcharts. Providing more detail in advance of the commencement of the project yields less likelihood for confusion later.

Description of the services. This is one of the most critical sections of the contract and should provide sufficient detail to give the service provider guidance on the required tasks. Key elements of this section might include HTML coding, digitizing and formatting content provided by the site owner, custom software development or integration of preexisting software, registering a domain name, and establishing a connection to the Internet. Other issues include ongoing services such as software and site maintenance chores such as content updates, checking links for currency, and hardware maintenance.

Description of the functions. These include secure transactions, database access, and streaming audio technologies. Java and ActiveX support are also important functions to be sure that the hosting service can support.

Compensation. The compensation arrangements described in the contract should include the amounts due for services, the timing of the payments, and the method of payment. Additionally, the contract should spell out which services may require additional fees, how third-party services will be billed, and so on.

Ownership. There is no section of a contract more crucial, and no provision whose omission has caused more problems, than the description of ownership. Keep in mind that a Web site may comprise many elements: HTML code, text, graphics, server software, database programming, audio, video, domain names, and trademarks—anything that can be stored on a computer can be included within and considered part of a Web site. The question of ownership is critical, because it determines who can register the site for copyright or other protections, who can adapt, reuse, or even resell the elements of the site, and whether one party can keep the other party from using the site elements.

The content provider is often the owner of a site, with development services rendered by a third party. In these cases, however, there may be certain elements either created by the developer or belonging to third parties to which the content provider should not receive ownership. These may include preexisting programs created by the developer, Web-enabled databases such as Oracle or Informix's Illustra, or creative material licensed from third parties. In this case a simple solution is to list those elements not owned by the content provider on an attachment to the contract, and to provide that anything not listed on the attachment will be counted under the general ownership provisions.

Confidentiality. During the course of discussions about a Web site between developers and owners, and during its development, each party to the contract may reveal confidential information to the other. For the content providers, the information may include product descriptions, planned marketing initiatives, or even information on desktops at the company's office while the developers are on-site for meetings. The developers may also demonstrate certain proprietary techniques that they propose to use on the site. Include a confidentiality clause that each party will keep the other's information secret and proprietary during the term of the agreement and for a reasonable period afterward.

Termination. There will always be situations under which the relationship between the parties, and their obligations to the each other, should terminate. These may include

* The completion of all required tasks
* The failure by a party to fulfill its obligations even after being notified of the failure
* The bankruptcy or reorganization of a party
* The reaching of a specific calendar date or time after execution

The parties may also wish to provide for termination for convenience, even without cause, with written notice to the other party. A good contract will list the termination events, and describe what happens when they occur.

It is important to provide for final payments, the return of each party's confidential and proprietary information by the other party, and the transfer of the Web site from the then-current server to a new server designated by the site owner, if applicable.

Warranties and indemnification. These contract provisions are complementary, and serve to shift risks to the party best able to minimize them. Warranties are promises made about issues such as content provided and services rendered. With respect to content issues, warranties usually serve to guarantee the content provider's clear title and ownership to the content under license. Indemnification is the process by which, if one party gets sued because of the errors made by the other party, the party being sued will be defended and reimbursed by the party whose errors are at the root of the lawsuit. These provisions will be very deal-specific, but can be useful both to identify risks and to provide comfort to each party that it will not have too much financial or legal exposure simply because it is doing business with the other party.

Other provisions. Certain miscellaneous provisions should also appear in any agreement regarding the use of intellectual property. Among these are

- **Choice of law.** This is particularly important given the lack of clear territory in cyberspace: in what city, state, or country does a site really exist. Choice-of-law clauses determine the definitive body whose law governs a contract, and which courts will hear disputes.

- **Arbitration.** For many parties, choosing to arbitrate rather than litigate disputes can save time and money. In these cases an arbitration clause specifies which body will perform the arbitration, and what will occur thereafter.

- **Use of trademarks.** Each party may want to govern how the other party uses its trademarks on the site, in client lists, portfolios, and so on. In some cases this will amount to an explicit exclusion, prohibiting the use of the mark, and in others an explicit inclusion — requiring the use of a mark.

STRATEGIES FOR USING CONTENT LEGALLY

A few simple steps can help minimize the cost and hassle of content acquisition. Make sure that the people working with you to put the site together—employees or contractors—understand the following issues so they can act properly on you company's behalf:

* Detective work
* Risk-sharing
* Use of language
* Disclaimers
* Insurance
* Corporate communication

Detective work. Choose sources wisely and explore the sources of your material. Select content that comes from easily traceable sources. This may mean licensing from more expensive content providers or using more governmental and other public domain sources. Your company may not be able to do everything it wishes on the Web site (sorry, those *Seinfeld* video clips that the developer found on some college kid's site are probably *verboten*), but what you do put on the site won't come back to haunt you.

Risk-sharing. Do what you can to shift some of the legal burden to others who may find it easier than you to track sources and negotiate rights. If you are licensing content, put a warranty clause in the contract in which the licensor states that it has acquired all the rights necessary to let you use the content as you plan (on the Internet and maybe in other media to promote your Web site). Also include an indemnification clause that covers you if you do get sued for improper use and requires the licensor to pay your costs and damages for the suit. The best argument to use in negotiating for these points is simply that the licensor is the party best able to prevent problems because it has the most information about and control over the original material; it should therefore bear the burden of verification and defense.

Use of language. As a businessperson, you wouldn't let your customers speak for your company without supervision, or arbitrarily place their opinions on your shop wall. Similarly, while the benefits of letting customers add content to your site through chats or other means are real, there are also risks

chapter 6   ACQUIRING IRRESISTIBLE CONTENT

in giving your users unfettered freedom to create content for a site that bears your business's name. Users may criticize your company in ways that can damage its goodwill, or criticize a competitor in ways that could lead to your company getting sued for libel. If you want to allow users to post freely on your Web site, you should make sure you set forth very specific terms governing such postings. Reserve the right to monitor and edit content for appropriateness. Through appropriate notice on chat areas, make sure users know that what they post is going to be disseminated worldwide and that the company will not have any liability to them for doing so. Ultimately, let them know they will be held to a certain standard that is appropriate for the site. If user content is troubling to you but you still want to give your users a say in the content of the Web site, you may wish to take somewhat of a middle ground. Give them the opportunity to send in comments and opinions, and republish those best suited to the site in a "letters to the editor" or similar forum. In that way, users will still get the thrill and pride of participation, while your company retains significant control over what is said on its site.

Disclaimers. The site should include legal language, easily accessible to the user, setting forth the terms and conditions under which the site and its content should be used. This language includes elements such as:

* Copyright and trademark notices related to the content
* Intended age and location of audience
* Contest rules
* Inappropriate or impermissible conduct within the site
* Requirements for reusing the site's content

You can find examples of disclaimers and legal language all over the Web, including on corporate sites such as Microsoft's (http://www.microsoft.com/misc/cpyright.htm) shown in Figure 6-12, sweepstakes sites like Drivers Edge Love My Car (http://www.lovemycar.com/rules.html), and entertainment sites including Pepsi Cola's Pepsi World (http://www.pepsi.com/highroad/mainframe/legal.html). Disclaimers do not absolutely protect the company against misuse or lawsuit, but they are one element in reducing the risks inherent in placing content on the Web.

Figure 6-12

Microsoft makes its disclaimers clear.

Insurance. Cover all your bases. Most businesses carry liability insurance for general risks such as employee injury and property damage. Media businesses may further have errors and omissions policies protecting against intellectual property infringement. However, these policies may fail to protect against Web-specific risks, particularly if the company is not otherwise involved in technology. It is important to discuss appropriate coverage with your company's broker or provider. You want to insure against risks such as technology patent infringement, liability for content provided by third-party or site users, and international lawsuits. This coverage may be included within a full policy already. If not, it will probably cost less as an endorsement to an existing policy than separately.

Corporate communications. Treat your Web site like any other widely disseminated corporate communications vehicle—press releases, catalogs, or public filings. Make sure that personnel with knowledge of the legal and business risks review the content of a Web site before it goes online. Don't leave Web content review in the hands of computer systems personnel, unless they are *well* versed in liability and corporate identity issues. Just because the Web propagates via computers doesn't mean you should treat it any less seriously than print or broadcast materials. Establish policies for Web content acquisition and review that mirror those for other corporate publishing. In fact, it may be supremely important to review Web content, since it may be disseminated more widely than almost anything else your company publishes or announces.

THE LAW PROTECTS YOU TOO!

Ultimately, to the extent your company is providing or acquiring content for its Web site, you will have to address all these issues—and do so in enough time to let you update the site as necessary. Careful planning and a good understanding of relevant law and practice will help you avoid some of the pitfalls and smooth the process of becoming a Web publisher. This may, of course, entail hiring attorneys or other professionals to advise you. Beyond that, take heart. The same protections you have to worry about as a publisher of the materials of others protect you as well.

Don't leave Web content review in the hands of computer systems personnel, unless they are well versed in liability and corporate identity issues.

If you treat the site's intellectual property appropriately (including indicating trademarks, filing copyrights where appropriate, and even applying for patents for novel technological developments), you may gain value out of the Web site you never considered.

Summary

In the end, the Web—however extraordinary its speed, economy, and ease of delivery—is just another information publishing business, and content may actually be its hottest topic, especially among developers and commercial concerns. Content is the glue that drives TV's Nielsen ratings and the circulation figures of the print world, and that, in turn, drives both consumer acceptance and advertising rates. Beyond the flash and sizzle of the new interactive medium, it is still content that keeps users coming back, and in the final analysis will determine the value, longevity, and success of any site. Because of the relatively low *broadcast* fees on the Internet, you can begin to offer content that would otherwise prove prohibitively expensive, and there are virtual libraries of opportunity for those innovative enough to research them.

At the same time, the worldwide legal community faces a revolutionary dual challenge in the global digital age. Issues of originality were complex even before the explosion in Web popularity over the last two years. The ease and speed of replication available through the Web community grows the problem by an order of magnitude: not only can content be replicated and distributed in unprecedented volume, but the national and international agencies accustomed to taxing imports and regulating censorship have been left in the dust—and there seems little chance of reversing the trend. This story is just beginning to unfold, and promises to keep viewers entertained for some time to come.

chapter 7

Getting Seen

I F YOU WERE PLANNING to throw a big party, you'd probably send invitations to your friends, coworkers, acquaintances, and anyone else who you wanted to attend the blow-out. You might spend weeks planning and adjusting every detail to make sure your guests had the time of their lives at the event. You wouldn't expect anyone to attend the party if they didn't know about it, so you would spend a comparable amount of energy writing and sending invitations to all your prospective guests, telling them when to come, what to wear, and what to expect. Similarly, when you build a site on the World Wide Web, you need to notify your customers, vendors, business partners, and anyone else you hope will visit your site. You can't expect visitors at your Web site if nobody knows it's there.

You may have already established a Web site and wonder why it gets little traffic. How is it that some other sites have millions of hits a day while yours only gets several thousand a month? Try not to focus too much on getting large numbers of people to your site, but rather on getting a targeted audience to your site. Would you rather have a single, targeted visitor who has a rewarding experience and who wants to do business with you again, or a hundred random surfers who stop by for a glance and never return?

Fortunately, it costs very little to promote yourself on the Internet, and there are a variety of successful techniques such as e-mail, search engine and directory listings, and announcements to newsgroups that you can use to notify people about your Web site and pull in traffic. Even if you don't have a background in marketing, you'll find it easy to learn some basic skills to publicize your Web site and get it noticed.

Providing Compelling Content

When people come to your Web site, you need to give them information they want—and want more of. By offering timely, high-quality content, your Web site becomes a primary—perhaps even necessary—information resource to its viewers. Compelling content can take many forms: updated product brochures and catalogs, purchasing information (perhaps coupled with the ability to track shipments), your company's stock performance information, or news affecting your particular industry. Remember: while promotions may draw Web users to your site for a look, no marketing communications program can keep viewers coming back unless the content you offer has solid intrinsic entertainment or informational value. (For more details on content, its nature, and how to find or develop it see Chapter 6, Acquiring Irresistible Content.)

In their drive simply to demonstrate a Web presence, many companies load their sites with *shovelware*: material from existing nonelectronic content sources like brochures and annual reports. While this type of static material can have some value, a visitor who's seen it once has little reason to come back. Many marketers on the Web offer updated industry news, features, and other items of interest in addition to product and company information as a way to draw repeat traffic. Users check the site on a daily basis to make sure they stay in touch with the pulse of their industry. As a result they become more effective in their own business—and see increased value in your company for providing information that keeps them at peak performance.

If you don't have the means to create original and intriguing content, consider partnering with others who can supply what you need. When considering a partner, make sure there's a good match between your company's product or service and that of the partner, and that each of you brings to the table something the other lacks. An information provider such as a newsletter publisher who covers your industry might view your Web site as the perfect opportunity to establish an online presence and jump at the chance to supply content for you. Not only can partners provide fresh content for your site, they can also bring you fresh traffic—and potential customers—by publicizing the online availability of their content to their newsletter subscribers. There is also a *coattail* effect to consider as with any association: if the partner has credibility with its customers, you will tend to receive the same respect by association with the partner.

Don't load your site with shovelware: material from existing nonelectronic content sources like brochures and annual reports. A visitor who's seen it once has little reason to come back.

When Procter & Gamble launched the Pampers Parenting Institute site (http://www.totalbabycare.com) shown in Figure 7-1, it secured immediate credibility by featuring a host of child-care experts offering advice to parents, including Dr. T. Berry Brazelton, author and host of Lifetime Television's *What Every Baby Knows*. By linking its name and product with the foremost authorities on child care, P&G will most likely gain a larger online share of the competitive diaper market. Partnering is not unfamiliar territory for the nation's third largest marketer. In the summer of 1996, it signed a deal with Condé Nast for that publisher to supply content from its publications for P&G's various Web sites.

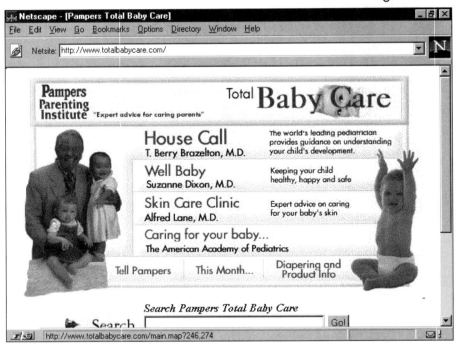

Figure 7-1

Procter & Gamble secures instant content credibility by featuring a host of child care experts on one of its Web sites.

Search engine Yahoo! (http://www.yahoo.com) is looking at partnerships as a way of increasing traffic to its site and keeping it there, rather than simply supplying a listing of sites and sending users off into cyberspace. Yahoo! signed a partnership agreement with Viacom's MTV: Music Television (http://www.mtv.com) to jointly launch a Web service called unfURLed in early 1997, offering music-related content and a guide to all the music-oriented sites on the Web. The demographic targets of Yahoo! and MTV are quite similar, so both partners expect that each will either bring new users to the other or offer an appealing new service to existing viewers, thus guaranteeing lots of repeat business. Both partners will promote the service. Yahoo! has formed similar content arrangements with Reuters Online and Women's Wire. A snapshot of the unfURLed site appears in Figure 7-2.

chapter 7 GETTING SEEN

Figure 7-2

Yahoo! and MTV have partnered to create unfURLed, a site with music-related content and links to other music sites.

A key challenge to any marketer is recognizing the needs of its customer base and serving them better than anyone else, whether with a partner or on its own. If you've dedicated marketing efforts in the past in your business to setting yourself apart from your competitors and offering a product or service that has special integrity and value to your customers, your Web site should reflect the same high standards you employ in your day-to-day operations to earn your customers' repeat business.

E-Mail

E-mail is one of the most effective methods of publicizing your Web site to the media and to your customers. It offers the speed and convenience to reach a mass audience at a low cost, and gives you the opportunity to establish a direct dialog with your target audience. A single mouse-click can send e-mail messages to an audience of hundreds of thousands of viewers instantaneously. At the same time, recipients can respond personally and immediately, which (among other benefits) helps you measure the effectiveness of your mailing.

E-mail is the single most widely used Internet service, and it is the main reason most Web visitors got an Internet account to begin with. More and more people are beginning to favor e-mail over traditional mail as their primary source of communication because of its reliability and convenience as well as its speed and low cost. According to some estimates there are approximately 60 million people on the Internet using e-mail as their primary application, compared to the approximately 10 million people who currently surf the Web. E-mail users can be found primarily in the business environment, though more and more people are logging on from home as the PC makes wider gains in the consumer market. Virtually all college students in the United States have e-mail accounts through their university or school.

On the negative side, of all forms of mass media—including television, print, and radio—e-mail is the most intrusive. As soon as a user signs on to America Online, for example, a familiar voice says "You've got mail" if there's a message in the in-box, prompting users to retrieve their mail. In the work environment, some networked e-mail systems interrupt whatever a user is doing—in any application—to announce incoming mail. Even if a voice doesn't sound or an application doesn't immediately open, a blinking icon usually continues to notify users that an e-mail message is waiting to be opened and read. Think before you send; is this message going to make the recipient happy to think of you?

chapter 7 GETTING SEEN

Keep It Targeted and to the Point

Reporters tend to receive upwards of 50 news releases every day, and the volume can be much higher for some areas of coverage. Most of these releases, when they're eventually read, get filed somewhere to be processed later, sometimes never. When you send a press release, be sure you target it to the proper reporter: the one who covers your industry specifically or the Internet and World Wide Web in general. With an ever-increasing flood of press releases from traditional and electronic mail delivery, reporters don't have time to wade through a quagmire of irrelevant news items and will quickly delete anything not pertaining to their coverage. On a good day, a reporter might forward a release to the proper colleague, but it's better not to take chances—target your efforts from the get-go.

Keep your news release direct and to the point, and offer some kind of story or hook along with the announcement to entice the reporter to write a story or follow up with you directly for additional information. Journalists are always looking for a good story, but the 412,806th announcement of a new Web site isn't going to get their attention. If it's related to a current item in the news, solves a problem, or can help a businessperson succeed, your release is more likely to garner the attention of the reporter who can build a story out of the information you provide.

Make sure your site is ready to go and that all the kinks are out of it when the media comes calling in response to your publicity. Would you rather have reporters write about the value they found in your site and recommend that their readers visit it, or the time they spent waiting for graphics to download and following links that went nowhere? If your first solicitation is a flop, you probably won't get those reporters' attention again.

USING E-MAIL TO REACH THE MEDIA

In the past two or three years, the Internet and the World Wide Web have grabbed significant attention. Nearly every newspaper, magazine, and television news program now has a reporter covering the Internet, and e-mail addresses can often be found next to a reporter's byline or on the masthead of a publication. For television and radio reporters, a call to the local station can usually give you the e-mail address of the reporter you want to reach. Additionally, services like PR Newswire (http://www.prnewswire.com) and Business Wire (http://www.businesswire.com) will send e-mail announcements to their database of journalists, and also allow you to tailor the audience with specific criteria such as sports, northeastern corridor, and so on. Using these services can be expensive: one-time costs range anywhere from $45 for a small category of reporters to $600 to blanket the media nationwide. In addition, there is a $100 annual membership fee.

Here are a few other things to remember when sending news releases to reporters via e-mail:

- **Include your Web site address in addition to your company address and telephone number.** A news release sent via e-mail is convenient to receive—since it's delivered and stored on the reporter's computer—but you can also make it easy to respond to. By clicking the reply button on the mail system, reporters can easily follow up on a story and request additional information. However, if reporters can't do initial legwork easily on their own and check out the site themselves, they may not call for a follow-up.
- **Make sure reporters can view the entire release in the way that you intended.** Some e-mail programs cut off copy when it reaches a certain length. Others force you to use ASCII text, thereby omitting formatting such as subheads, line breaks, and indents.
- **Be sure to put all the reporters' e-mail addresses in the BCC (blind carbon copy) field.** You can still use a mass distribution list to mail your news release with a single keystroke (rather than sending each release individually), but avoiding the CC (carbon copy) field lets you save space within the message for your important announcement (since each individual address won't appear) and also keep your media distribution list proprietary.
- **Take the time to e-mail yourself a copy of your news announcement first.** Check it out to make sure you convey to the media the message you want them to receive and pass along to their audiences.

USING E-MAIL TO REACH EVERYONE ELSE

With its immediate, one-to-one communications capabilities and built-in response mechanism, e-mail makes it easy to build relationships with your customers and create a personal dialogue with them. If you've been collecting e-mail addresses from your customers, either through your Web site by asking visitors to provide their e-mail address or through more standard data-gathering exercises in the offline world, you've got an instant database of recipients for news, announcements, and any other use you want to make of the medium through e-mail.

When you collect e-mail addresses from visitors to your Web site, you also have an opportunity to gather demographic information and preferences that can serve you in follow-up mailings. Like the addresses themselves, this information should be kept in a database. For example, luxury carmaker Lexus asks visitors to its Web site (http://www.lexususa.com) a series of questions ranging from their address and annual income to the kind of car they currently own, the type of car they have in mind for their next vehicle, and when they plan to buy or lease it. The Lexus site appears in Figure 7-3.

Figure 7-3

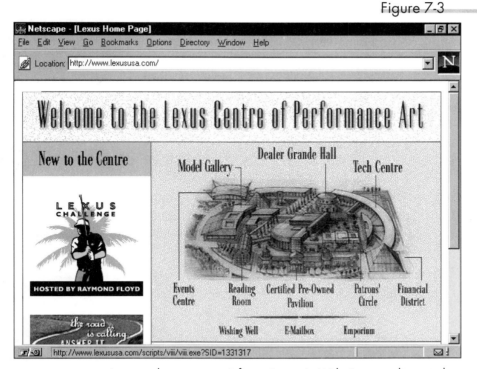

Lexus gathers customer information on its Web site to send targeted e-mail messages in follow-up promotional campaigns.

This information was used as part of Lexus' October 1996 campaign introducing its new model, the ES 300. Approximately 120,000 people received an e-mail announcement about the new model. All of them had visited the Web site and asked to be put on the e-mail distribution list. Because it had asked a series of questions at the Web site, Lexus was able to further define the group and identify drivers of rival brands. By segmenting the group, Lexus could refine the message and better target those consumers in the group who didn't already own one of its cars.

A direct connection

As a medium, e-mail offers several advantages over other forms of communications in reaching out to the public. Not only is e-mail a direct connection to your audience, it is also a direct connection back to you. The person who receives your message can easily send a request for additional information, answer a survey, or order a product with a simple click on the reply button. As a plus, the time it takes to send or respond to an e-mail message is minute compared to the amount of time and energy spent in the search for pen, paper, envelope, and stamp.

E-mail also reduces the cost of *frequency* of your message. Frequency is typically very expensive in traditional advertising, where 30-second television commercials, full-page ads, and direct-mail campaigns can cost the equivalent of several mortgage payments—especially when your entire campaign may include several different ads delivered over the course of a couple of weeks. E-mail makes frequency fundamentally free and totally targeted. You can send your messages as often as you want (to a certain degree) to a controlled audience segment, as opposed to scattering the messages to a mass audience where you may not be as certain of the people receiving your message. Additionally, you can build your message as a sequence, giving small, digestible bites of information that teach the consumer about your product in a logical order. And your message is hidden from the eyes of your competitors, giving you an advantage over them in communicating to the same consumer base.

Concerns about sending unsolicited mail

There is a difference between unsolicited e-mail and *spam*—the indiscriminate distribution of messages without any concern of their appropriateness to the recipient. Spam is the Internet equivalent of junk mail. Bulk e-mailer Cyber Promotions (http://www.cyberpromo.com) was taken to court in 1996 by America Online for sending unsolicited messages to its user base in an indiscriminate fashion. In November, the court upheld AOL's right to shield its members from junk e-mail. David Phillips, associate general counsel at AOL, applauded the decision, saying, "The court has clearly stated that Cyber Promotions and companies like it don't have a First Amendment right to use a privately owned network to inundate AOL members with junk e-mail." Just days prior to the court decision, AOL implemented a PreferredMail tool, which gives its members the option to refuse e-mail messages "from a regularly updated list of notorious junk e-mailers." While AOL is a private network, there are important lessons and precedents to be learned from the case.

People don't appreciate finding their electronic mailboxes clogged with messages that have no value to them, any more than they enjoy the same discovery at their physical mailboxes at home or at work—and they certainly don't want to pay online charges for the privilege. Unsolicited mail can often be welcome, however, as long as the message is relevant to the recipient. Anyone responding to unsolicited mail by asking to be taken off the list should be accommodated immediately. It's not necessary to send yet another message to say you've done so.

Offering recipients a mechanism to decline receiving a marketer's e-mail message is one of the guidelines that was jointly issued in mid-1996 by the Direct Marketing Association and the Interactive Services Association after the Federal Trade Commission held hearings on online privacy. Even when people have come to your Web site and specifically asked to be put on your e-mail list, take them off if and when they decline. In their initial fascination with the online world, users visit many sites and put themselves on mailing lists, and later realize they would rather not receive the follow-up mailings. Gatorade amassed a database of nearly 18,000 people who had visited its Web site (http://www.gatorade.com), and said they'd like to learn more about the marketer's products. *Advertising Age* magazine reported that even though these people had provided their names and e-mail addresses, some still found the messages inappropriate and returned the follow-up e-mail message, asking to be removed from the list.

A properly targeted and relevant message shouldn't put you in the hot seat too often. Most people enjoy getting e-mail and check their mailboxes several times daily to see what's been sent. Charles Schulz has been successful with his long-running Peanuts gag where Charlie Brown stands next to his mailbox every year waiting to get a single Valentine's Day card. As a representative of *Everyman*, Charlie Brown easily makes the transition from the cartoon world to the online world—most of us share his desire for interpersonal communications.

Because of the nature of the Internet, online users expect to be involved with you in ways that other consumers can't. Properly used, e-mail can provide a subtle way to interact with your audience in a controlled manner. The remainder of this section will outline a few e-mail–based services you can offer your customer base to help promote your Web site and keep people coming back to it.

REMINDER SERVICES

People like the immediacy that the Web offers but they don't want to be spammed with ads and junk mail. You can take advantage of this by sending announcements that offer helpful personal information, rather than messages that focus entirely on your products or services. Users are more likely to appreciate and remember a service that makes their lives easier than they are an advertisement for your product. Greeting card marketer Hallmark has created a reminder service that helps users track their friends' and relatives' birthdays and other special occasions. After filling out a form with their specific dates at Hallmark's Web site (`http://www.hallmark.com`), shown in Figure 7-4, users receive a reminder via e-mail at the appropriate time about each upcoming occasion. That is, rather than a generic advertisement for greeting cards, users get a friendly—and welcome, because they asked for it—"Hallmark reminder" in their mailbox.

chapter 7 GETTING SEEN

Figure 7-4

Hallmark sends friendly e-mail holiday reminders to people on its distribution list.

The reminder service is a good example of combining some simple but clever programming with a database to produce a useful and novel service. The service uses a program written with a popular Web programming language such as Perl, C, or JAVA to capture the users' reminder information and store it in a database. Each day the program polls the database scanning for references to the current date, and then creates and generates e-mail based on the matches.

1-800-FLOWERS (shown in Figure 7-5) also offers another holiday reminder service. Visitors to its site (`http://www.1800flowers.com`) can enter the dates of up to 50 birthdays, anniversaries, and other special occasions, and will receive in return an e-mail reminder of each event plus gift ideas five days prior to the recorded date.

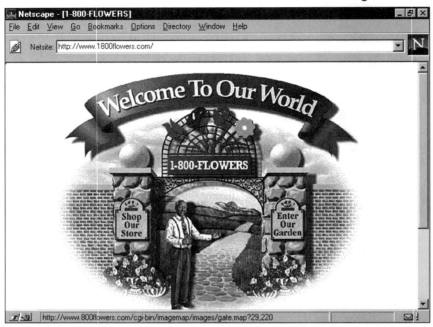

1-800-FLOWERS reminds people via e-mail of special occasions, including appropriate gift ideas.

INSTANT NOTIFICATION SERVICES

You can also use e-mail to notify your customers when you've updated content that is relevant to them. For example, online bookseller Amazon.com (http://www.amazon.com) notifies users when new books have been published that will appeal to them (based on criteria the users previously defined). The marketer sends out thousands of e-mail messages in two different notification services. One weekly service alerts subscribers to newly published hardback or paperback books on a preferred subject or by their favorite author. The other, less frequent service provides 23 categories of reviews and recommendations by Amazon.com's editors. The key to success, according to Jeffrey Bezos, CEO of the Seattle-based company—which dubs itself "the Earth's biggest bookstore"—is keeping the e-mail process firmly in the hands of the customer. Subscribers, who number in the tens of thousands, can cancel the e-mail service or reconfigure their mailing preferences online and instantly. The Amazon.com site appears in Figure 7-6.

Figure 7-6

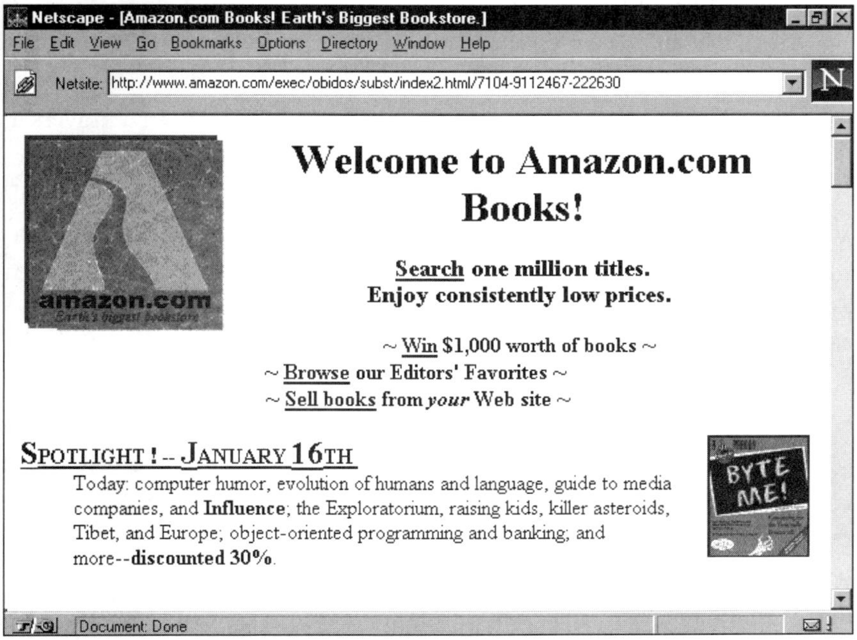

Amazon.com has two distribution lists to e-mail thousands of online users about new publications featuring their favorite authors and subjects.

NEWSLETTERS

Like press releases, newsletters can provide updated news about your company and are easy and inexpensive to send via e-mail. Where a press release limits you to a certain extent in the amount of information you cover at one time, a newsletter enables you to write about your company's most recent product announcements, case studies about your customers' business successes due to the practical use and application of your company's products and services, stories of interest about your employees, industry information, or anything you think your customers would find appropriate and helpful in conducting their business. If you are sending the newsletter as a direct e-mail message, keep your news items short so they don't take up too much space on recipient's e-mail system (or get cut off at the end). You can always direct users to your Web site to get the full story on a particular issue if they're interested in more details. Directing traffic to your Web site in this manner keeps the recipient in control of the message.

Most e-mail messages that cross different computer platforms and e-mail applications arrive as pure text, without whatever formatting the sender tried to apply. To compensate, you can send the newsletter in a universal format such as Adobe Acrobat. Acrobat makes it easy to create files that retain creative layouts and formats for anyone who has the Acrobat reader, which is available free at Adobe's Web site (`http://www.adobe.com`). You can also make Acrobat available for download on your site—a double whammy in promotional terms. By offering the program for free you pull traffic to your site for a giveaway and also guarantee that visitors will have the program available on their desktops to read upcoming issues of your newsletter.

The Limited Express (`http://www.express.style.com`) sends its subscribers an e-mail newsletter every month containing the latest wardrobe essentials. A typical issue includes news on fashion trends, ways to incorporate the trends into a work wardrobe, and on how to accessorize. The fashions written about, of course, can be found at The Limited Express's retail stores, but recipients of the e-mail newsletter are free to shop wherever they like and can use the information when making their buying decision at any apparel retailer. As an incentive to stay with the sponsor, however, the newsletter includes an invitation to go to the Limited's Web site and print out a special coupon good for 15 percent off the next purchase.

GAMES AND CONTESTS

Games and contests engage your customers and take advantage of the interactive characteristics of the Internet. You can often entice people to give you more information about themselves by offering to enter them in a contest than by conducting a survey. Games also serve to draw people to your Web site as well as the Web sites of any sponsors or partners to learn more about your products and services. In the two years that it's been conducting e-mail–based games, Yoyodyne Entertainment (`http://www.yoyo.com`) has found that it can generate a huge response for its clients, which have included United Media, Crane Communications, Fox Television, Prodigy, and the Microsoft Network, among others. In a recent survey of 750,000 users who have played its e-mail games, Yoyodyne found that 82 percent went to the Web site of a game sponsor to learn more about the sponsor. Additionally, 82 percent also said they would return to a sponsor's site at a later date, while 54 percent said they would return to three or more sponsor sites for additional information. Of its user base, a full 90 percent said they wanted to be informed (via e-mail) of upcoming games Yoyodyne would be implementing on behalf of its clients.

Jerry Shereshewsky, marketing vice president for the Dobbs Ferry, New York-based company, said the largest percentage response on a consistent basis he's seen was for a soap opera game. Players received via e-mail a page and a half of story line and were prompted to respond to help develop the story further. Fifty percent of the players responded consistently during the course of the game to say what course the plot should take the next week. Shereshewsky said that one disadvantage of e-mail games is that while he can track the addresses mail went to and of the people who responded to it, he has no way of knowing if the mail was actually read by the recipients who chose not to respond. The Yoyodyne site, seen in Figure 7-7, recently added an instant winner function to its notices to encourage people to read their e-mail even if they don't participate in the game by mailing back a response.

You can create synergistic alliances with other Web site operators that will lead visitors from your site to theirs and back again. As link partners, you have a vested interest in each other and in providing traffic to one another.

When conducting any contest or giveaway, always put it through a review process to make sure it passes legal muster. Most contests are regulated at both the federal and state level, and laws vary from state to state. Make sure that your counsel is versed not only in promotions law, but in interactive law as well. Although this type of process is often time consuming, it's well worth the wait to make sure your game is legal so you don't become the next target of an Internet gaming crackdown.

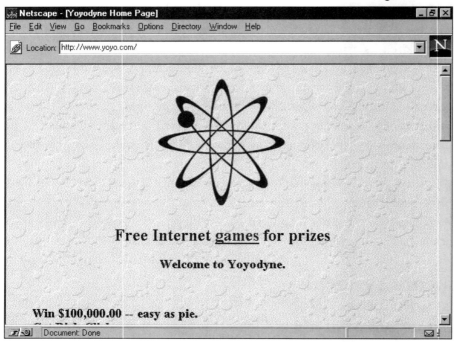

Figure 7-7

Yoyodyne Entertainment has found that online users are extremely favorable toward e-mail–based games.

E-mail is a powerful tool for targeting your audience and creating a dialogue with them as well as for pulling traffic to your site. By including your Web site's URL in your messages, users whose e-mail supports hotlinks can instantly point their browser to your site. With a database of e-mail addresses, creating an ongoing dialogue with your customers is just a mouse-click away.

chapter **7** GETTING SEEN

Hyperlinks

Linking enables you to reach people on the Net through associations with other Web sites. A *hyperlink*, or hotlink, is an electronic connection between two Web locations—a click on a link brings a user to the linked location—and is the underlying method of Web travel. You can create synergistic alliances with other Web site operators that will lead visitors from your site to theirs and back again. As link partners, you have a vested interest in each other and in providing traffic to one another. For example, compatible sites might include online magazines and newsletters that serve your industry, as well as vendors, distribution partners, and members of any trade and business association you belong to. If you aren't already aware of compatible sites, a search through trade magazines covering your industry could uncover a few, as could a search through some of the newer Internet magazines such as Yahoo! Internet Life, Internet World, or NetGuide, which may have run an article on your industry.

A request for a hotlink is typically an informal affair. If you don't know who should get the request, e-mail to the Webmaster will usually generate a response and point you in the right direction. Most Webmasters provide an e-mail address at the bottom of the home page to facilitate feedback about their site. Most Web site operators will ask for a reciprocal link in exchange for a link to your site. It is a gesture of goodwill and is not uncommon in the industry.

With reciprocal links, you run the risk of giving people an easy way to leave your site after you've tried so hard to get them there. After spending time, money, and effort drawing traffic to the site, why chase it away? In practice, it turns out that it doesn't work that way. If you offer relevant links, you benefit your customers by connecting them to other Web sites that can be of value to them. Rather than an avenue away from the content you offer, links can become part of the content itself. Your site becomes valuable to your viewers not only for the information it provides, but also for the places it can take them, and therefore becomes a valuable way station on the Net.

Search Engines

Search engines are computer programs that help online users in their quest for information. At a search engine site, visitors can enter a company name or a few keywords and get a list of relevant sites or Internet pages that the search engine has catalogued. Since there is no Dewey Decimal System for the Web, search engines serve as a cataloguing system for its gigantic library. Like hyperlinks, search engines can send traffic to your site and make your site easy to find in a crowded universe. Almost all search engines let you submit your own listing, including keywords, descriptions, and phrases of your choosing. Since listings are free for the time being, listing your site at the major search engines is one of the least expensive and most effective means of promotion. In addition to the major search engines, there are smaller services that focus on specific fields. As the Internet grows, premium placements and keyword associations will become hot commodities as search engines look for new ways to develop revenue.

Some search engines rely on editorial staffs who comb the Web daily looking for relevant content and sites of substance, while other search engines rely on *spiders* that crawl the Web on a constant search for new sites or updated content and links, and then create links within their own database to those sites. Spider-based search engines like AltaVista (`http://www.altavista.digital.com`; shown in Figure 7-8) and Lycos (`http://www.lycos.com`) search all the text of Web sites and newsgroups, as opposed to searching home pages or topics only.

chapter **7** GETTING SEEN

Figure 7-8

AltaVista automatically crawls the Web in an endless search for new online content.

REGISTERING WITH A SEARCH ENGINE

Before you register, visit the search engine site and use the keywords or subjects you think your audience would use to locate a company, product, or service like yours. The list of sites the search engine provides in response to your query represents your adversaries—the sites that are competing for the same traffic. After you read their search engine listings, try to find a way to differentiate yourself from them when you submit your own listing. Your search engine listing is more than just a URL address. It's an opportunity to entice people to come to your site. Give them a reason to visit your site by conveying some type of value, not just an overview of what the site offers.

On most search engines you only have space for a brief description, so make it count: it's your chance to hook the browser. For example, a recent search on Yahoo! under the category "party supplies" brought up a list of 20 Web sites. One site had "party rental equipment" as its entire description, while another said it "provides everything for children's birthdays, holidays, baby showers and weddings," and also "includes party tips and info for parents." As a result of fine-tuning the description of the kind of information it offers, the latter site probably receives quite a few more inquiries than the former one does.

Another important piece of information to put in your description is your business location, so customers local to you will know right away that you're in their area. For example, in that same search for party supplies, only 1 out of 20 mentioned where it was located. If I lived in Southern Ontario, Canada, and was planning a party where I needed to rent tables, chairs, and a dance floor, I'd point my browser first to the site whose description promised me "tent and party supply rental in Toronto, Barrie, and Southern Ontario." By visiting the site of a local company first, I can save time by avoiding out-of-state (or country) companies that I'd never rent equipment from because of our respective locations. On the other hand, if you're aiming at both local and Web-wide business, make sure you also mention that you can serve customers anywhere with whatever your general-interest product may be.

Besides your URL, business description, and physical location, other essentials to include in your listing are your company contact, e-mail address, phone numbers, fax numbers, and any categories and keywords you want your site to be listed under. The more relevant you can make your search criteria, the better the chances are that people will find your site. A list of popular search engines appears in Table 7-1.

Table 7-1 A List of Popular Search Engines

SITE	URL	MAIN OBJECTIVE
All4One	http://easypage.com/all4one	A search engine of search engines; claims to search them all
AltaVista	http://www.altavista.digital.com	A spider from Digital Equipment that searches the Internet
Big Page, The	http://www.beaucoup.com/engines.html	A search engine of search engines
Excite	http://www.excite.com	A search engine from Architext Software
Excite City.Net	http://www.city.net	A localized search engine
Fledge	http://www.fledge.com	A customizable search engine and information resource for kids, from McGraw Hill Home Interactive
HotBot	http://www.hotbot.com	A search engine from HotWired
Infoseek	http://www.infoseek.com	A spider that searches the Internet
LookSmart	http://www.looksmart.com	A search engine from Reader's Digest Association
Lycos	http://www.lycos.com	A spider that searches the Internet
Magellan	http://www.mckinley.com	Another search engine operated by Excite
Search.Com	http://www.search.com	A search engine of search engines from CNET
Starting Point	http://www.stpt.com/	Another searcher of search engines
StreetEYE	http://www.streeteye.com	A financial search engine
University Toplinks	http://www.university.toplinks.com/	A modified search engine that offers Top 10 lists of Web sites in various categories that would appeal to "university" demographic
W3 Jump Station	http://www.ultranet.com/wwwinfo/search.html	A search engine of directories, other search engines, and more
WebCrawler	http://www.webcrawler.com	A spider that searches the Internet
Yahoo!	http://www.yahoo.com	The most popular and well-known of the search engines
Yahooligans!	http://yahooligans.com/	A search engine targeted for kids and their parents

ONE-STOP SERVICES

With a growing roster of search engines, the task of submitting your site to each one can be daunting. As a remedy there are one-stop registration services that can do the legwork for you. There's only one form for you to fill out and each listing for your site will convey the same basic information. Table 7-2 lists some companies offering these services.

Table 7-2   One-Stop Registration Services

SITE	URL	MAIN OBJECTIVE
Submit-It	`http://www.submit-it.com/default2.htm`	A free service that lets you register with 15 of the most popular search engines. Their home page appears in Figure 7-9.
PostMaster	`http://www.netcreations.com`	A free listing service that lets you post on 17 search engines—and a $500 fee will get you posted to a larger list of sites
NetPOST	`http://www.netpost.com`	A registration service as well as links to other registration services

After you've registered with the search engines, either on your own or by using a one-stop service, expect about two to four weeks for your submission to appear. Once you think you're listed, check each category in which you requested to be placed, the description you provided, and the link itself—does it actually take users to your site? Continue to check back on a somewhat frequent basis to make sure any links to your site are updated. Be sure to maintain a list of where your site is posted to make any necessary follow-up work less of a burden.

Figure 7-9

Submit-It helps you register your Web site with several search engines simultaneously.

Internet Directories

Just as search engines offer a kind of catalog system, Internet directories serve as the white and yellow pages of the online world, offering yet another resource for the user community to locate your Web site or e-mail address. Like their offline counterparts, online directories provide names, addresses, and other relevant information to a user base. Internet yellow pages are often grouped into categories; white pages list names alphabetically. It only takes a matter of minutes to complete an online form and listings often show up within a day or two. A listing of some online directories appears in Table 7-3.

Table 7-3 Online Directories

DIRECTORY NAME	URL	OBJECTIVE
AtHand	http://www.athand.com	From Pacific Bell's Interactive Media division, this site includes comprehensive statewide listings of merchants and products.
BigBook	http://www.bigbook.com	This is an online yellow pages directory covering about 11 million businesses.
Big Yellow	http://www.bigyellow.com	From Nynex, this site has listings for 16 million businesses.
Four11	http://www.Four11.com	This site has approximately 5 million e-mail listings in its database.
Switchboard	http://www.switchboard.com	From Banyan Systems, this site offers e-mail addresses and other information on 93 million people and 11 million businesses worldwide.
TollFree Directory	http://www.tollfree.att.net	This is AT&T's directory of businesses with 800 and 888 toll-free telephone numbers.
WhoWhere?	http://www.whowhere.com	This offers a directory of e-mail addresses as well as a listing of 200,000 URLs of personal home pages of the online user community.
WorldPages	http://www.worldpages.com	This is a worldwide phone directory.
YellowNet	http://www.yellownet.com	This is a business-to-businesses directory.
Zip2	http://www.zip2.com	This features more than 16 million listings of U.S. businesses as well as maps and directions on how to get to a listed company (in the real world).

As you can see, the online directory market is almost as crowded as the search engine field. Only a fraction of available directories appear in this table, and by the time you read it, the number of searchable directories will surely have increased exponentially. All telephone companies, if they aren't already online, are working hard to turn their local business and community directories into searchable Web databases. You probably wouldn't exclude yourself from your local telephone book or your industry's telephone directory—so don't exclude yourself from online directories either. Remember, these are available not only to a national but to a global audience.

Newsgroups

Newsgroup announcements are another Internet tool you can use to notify your audience that you are online and help to pull traffic to your site. A *newsgroup*—also called *Usenet*—is a site where people post and reply to messages from other users on a given topic. Because they are subscriber-based, newsgroups often have a finely targeted audience extremely dedicated to the group and interested in continuing dialogs.

Newsgroups (currently numbering about 50,000 and counting) are divided into many categories. If there's a topic you want to know or talk about, chances are there's a newsgroup that serves your interests. Newsgroup titles usually begin with a three- or four-letter prefix followed by a period (.). Table 7-4 shows some examples.

Table 7-4 Newsgroup Prefixes

PREFIX	MEANING
alt	A collection of "alternative" subjects; this group is not carried by all service providers because of the subject matters (like abortion) contained therein
biz	Discussions on the world of business, particularly computer products and services
comp	Topics for computer professionals and hobbyists alike, including computer science, hardware, and software systems
ieee	Discussions concerning the IEEE (Institute of Electrical and Electronics Engineers)
hepnet	Discussions on nuclear physics and high energy research
humanities	Subjects relative to human culture, for example language, literature, and history
k12	Devoted to K–12 education curriculum
misc	Discussions of topics not generally found under other headings, or topics that incorporate themes from multiple categories
news	Discussions on the newsgroup network and the software used to make them operable
rec	Group concerned with the arts, hobbies, and recreational activities
ci	Interest in scientific research and the practical application of established sciences
soc	Discussions of social issues and socializing talk—groups that enjoy debating various issues and subject matters

There are several sources for locating large lists of newsgroups. These include DejaNews (http://www.dejanews.com), shown in Figure 7-10, the Standford Information Filtering Tool (http://www.reference.com), SunSITE from the University of North Carolina at Chapel Hill (http://sunsite.unc.edu/usenet-i), and Liszt (http://www.liszt.com). Additionally, your Internet service provider (ISP) can provide you with a list of the newsgroups it carries. Not all ISPs carry every newsgroup, and only those groups your ISP carries will be available to you.

Figure 7-10

DejaNews is a source for locating online newsgroups.

NETIQUETTE

Posting announcements to online newsgroups enables you to speak to people involved or interested in your field. To do so effectively you must adhere to strict, yet unwritten, rules of *netiquette*. Like all societies, the Internet has developed its own culture and common rules that govern the behavior of people who live there. Netiquette is the common term that refers to appropriate online behavior. Spam, mentioned earlier in connection with e-mail, is the indiscriminate distribution of messages without any concern for their appropriateness to the recipient. If you post an inappropriate message to a newsgroup, you invite *flames* in return. Flames are verbal expressions of disapproval. Because newsgroups are strictly text based, flames can carry an extremely harsh tone, especially when they're written to burn.

Commercial messages are totally inappropriate in newsgroups, and will cause you plenty of third-degree burns. In 1994, two Arizona lawyers took to the Internet for the first time, posting announcements about their legal services to a multitude of newsgroups. Rather than a favorable reaction from those they thought would be interested in their services, the attorneys were flooded with telephone calls, hate mail (both electronic and postal), bomb threats, and enough faxes to clog their machines for weeks. All their communications were cut off by hackers and other online users who felt they had made inappropriate postings. Of course, inappropriate messages can cause more than just flames. When online cyberserial developer American Cybercast Network launched its sci-fi EON-4 Web site (http://www.eon4.com) it caused a storm of controversy within science fiction newsgroups because it posted a somewhat surreal message about alien contact. Written as fiction—that is, masquerading as fact rather than fantasy—the posting caused some users to call NASA to find out additional information.

POSTING TO A NEWSGROUP

There are two types of newsgroups: *moderated* and *unmoderated.* In a moderated group, submissions go to someone who edits or filters them for length and appropriateness and then posts them to the group. This moderator has every right to judge the suitability of each message. Although you lose a certain level of control over your announcement, chances are you'll never receive a flame from a moderated group. Unmoderated groups, on the other hand, allow anyone to post to the group, so be very careful when approaching these user communities.

Before posting a message to any newsgroup, especially an unmoderated group, *lurk* for a while—that is, read without posting anything—to learn about the culture of the group. Get a copy of the newsgroup's *FAQ* to make sure any question you may have hasn't already been asked: don't start off your new association with group members who perceive you as foolish. Refrain from becoming active until you're sure what is acceptable. If the newsgroup is important to you, your time will be well spent learning about the group and its particular norms of behavior. Once you're ready, you can join the discussion.

Here are some other tips on sending Usenet mail:

* Keep your postings short and to the point.
* If you're responding to an earlier post, don't include the entire contents of the previous message in your reply. Cut all unnecessary copy, including previous headers (except maybe the "from" line so everyone will know to whom you're responding), leaving just enough to indicate what you're responding to.
* Never write in all caps. Not only are capital letters difficult to read, online users react to them as though you were yelling.

As with e-mail announcements, offering something of value to the user community is a plus. Can you solve a posted problem? Do you have software or a white paper you'd like to share? If so, make sure you convey the value of the item (not in dollars) and then direct people to your Web site where they can obtain it on their own. Likewise, if you have a lengthy message to post, offer just a part of the information and then refer people to your Web site to get the full text. This not only pulls traffic to your site, it is a courtesy to other list members.

By sharing information and helpful advice with members of the newsgroup, you'll be indirectly promoting your knowledge and tempting them to learn more about you and your operation. On the Internet, the soft sell is always a better approach than the hard sell. Always include in your e-mail *signature file* your name, e-mail address, and URL, so interested parties can seek you out on their own. Again, keep your signature file brief to save space and also to make sure you don't get flamed by those who view it as an advertising tool.

Cross-Marketing with the Giants

In the crowded world of the Web, you'll probably find that you're a small fish in a big pond. Large players like America Online, CompuServe, and Microsoft have the money and the marketing muscle to promote their services and pull an endless stream of fresh traffic to their Web sites and online services. But just as they hunger for traffic, they also have an appetite for fresh content, and an affiliation with one of these major players can promote your site to millions of online users. Major players want suitable content that draws a mass audience and is proprietary to their service (which usually has to be different from material available on an open Web site). For example, Marvel Comics offers online comic books to the user base of America Online, while visitors to Marvel's own Web site (`http://www.onslaught.com`) can only read about comics, not see the comic books themselves.

In addition to an increased user base, many content providers arrange deals where they become the proprietary information source for a particular subject. In 1995, America Online replaced Eaasy Sabre, the online travel and ticketing service from American Airlines, with Preview Travel, a 10-year-old provider of travel information (formerly known as Preview Media) and a relative upstart beside the venerable American Airlines, whose Eaasy Sabre system had been in use for years by travel and ticketing agents worldwide. Preview Travel's mission is to help people plan every aspect of their vacations (car rentals, hotel and airline reservations, and so on) using online information and tools. Special promotions on AOL, such as icons on the user's welcome screen or on travel-related areas of the service, pull traffic to Preview Travel's online area. In this fashion, Preview can leverage its relationship with America Online as the service's sole online travel agent, thereby branding itself to the more than 6 million members of AOL.

Prior to restructuring its pricing plan from hourly fees to unlimited access for a flat rate, America Online paid content providers a commission based on the amount of traffic at their area. With the new pricing, AOL will pay content providers a flat monthly fee, which varies from provider to provider based on their size (and reputation). In addition, AOL also pays usage fees to content providers as part of the revenue structure. Each content provider has a different deal with each online service, and it's very difficult to find out who's getting what. According to *Advertising Age* magazine, "on average most content providers receive about 10 percent to 20 percent of [the equivalent of] hourly usage fees from AOL, although some partners claim to have deals worth as much as 30 percent to 40 percent."

Revenue splits vary at each service provider. For example, when Microsoft launched the Microsoft Network (MSN) it was hungry for content providers and offered a 30/70 split, although that may have changed dramatically by the time you read this. CompuServe offers something close to a 15/85 split, and, as noted above, America Online's split ranges anywhere from 10/90 to 40/60, depending upon the partner. If you have unique and valuable information, an association with one of the online giants can give you the marketing and promotional muscle you may need to increase your customer base.

Offline Promotions

In this chapter we've focused primarily on Internet-based promotions, but any publicity campaign you undertake should also include offline promotional vehicles as well. If you use the Internet as your sole publicity outlet, only a very small percentage of your potential audience will see your message. The key to a really effective marketing mix is to tie all your marketing efforts into an integrated campaign that sends a cohesive message. This means putting your Web site address on all your corporate literature—annual reports, product catalogs, even your company stationery—and also on all advertising and marketing materials, including print ads and television or radio spots. In addition, you need to incorporate the URL in product packaging as well as product distribution vehicles such as company-owned cars, vans, and trucks.

To drive awareness of the launch of its Web site in 1995, Valvoline Motor Oil made a quick push forward with self-driven publicity campaigns and reciprocity agreements with partner companies. This ongoing strategy has earned Valvoline the coveted pole position as an online leader in its brand category. As the official motor oil of the Indy 500, Valvoline had a major opportunity to jump-start its online efforts and draw traffic to its site from racing fans watching the event from home. Valvoline-sponsored race cars featured in-car cameras that displayed Valvoline's URL at the bottom of each shot from the track. This innovative and ongoing trick has motivated many a racing fan to visit the site even before the checkered flag drops.

Don't forget to utilize your offline promotional vehicles. If you use the Internet as your sole publicity outlet, only a very small percentage of your potential audience will see your message.

Valvoline also invited Apple, its Internet service partner, to attend the race and help with the technical aspects. It didn't cost Valvoline anything to let Apple into the pit crew area. Providing Valvoline hardware and service support gave Apple a unique opportunity to be in the middle of a major sporting event, while Valvoline garnered free publicity from Apple through Apple's promotion of its involvement at the race.

"Out of the gate, our Web site was critically acclaimed," said Jan Horsfall, Valvoline's marketing manager. That early involvement with Apple generated nearly 3 million hits over the course of several months, but more important, Horsfall said, "by ramping up the public relations for our Indy 500 launch, we generated enough money just from PR alone to pay for site development over the next five years."

Valvoline spends between $35 million and $40 million annually on marketing, but you won't find online banners as a line item in its budget. Instead, the company places its Web site address (http://www.valvoline.com) on all its products, advertisements, and other promotional items, and depends on partnerships like the one with Apple at the Indy 500 to generate awareness for its site. Valvoline has arranged strategic reciprocal agreements with like-minded companies that have an Internet presence. "Our online visitor often begins his journey at a search engine," Horsfall explained. "Even if I don't own the rights to a banner ad under a keyword descriptive, like 'automotive,' other companies do. Therein lies some great partnering," he said. Posting links to and from industry leaders Goodyear Tires and Gates Rubber Company, as well as magazine sites such as Popular Mechanics, Car & Driver, and Racer, comes "without costing us one red cent," Horsfall said. Prior to requesting a link, Valvoline checks each site to make sure it's a strategic fit and will reciprocate the link for free.

Valvoline has determined, for the time being, that event sponsorship, on-package promotion, and reciprocity links work better than online ad banners to generate interest in its Web site. "There still needs to be agreement on key issues like reach and frequency, measurement of advertising, and other issues that later on will become very important," Horsfall said. "The reality is that you can better sell the communications differentiation that the Web provides. Too many companies are still selling the undefined 'Holy Grail' relative to anything to do with Web services. It keeps them from harnessing the power of creativity, brand strategy, integrated programs, and real impact executions that power your Web site and power your interactivity with your audience."

Summary

When you decided to establish your Web site, you probably had goals you hoped to achieve—increased sales, new prospects, and leads. You should also have clearly established goals for your Web site's publicity campaign, whether it's increased traffic, building a database of prospective customers, or generating additional business. By implementing just a few of the promotional strategies in this chapter, you're bound to bring your Web site increased traffic as an expanded group of users learn that you exist online. With relevant announcements and reminder services to your user base of what's happening on your site, hotlinks to sites valuable to your customers, and listings in the various search engines and online directories, you can continue to draw a steady stream of people to your site who will value the information and services you provide. This is one party that doesn't have to end as long as you keep the invitations fresh and directed at your target audience—and keep those tasty informational hors d'oeuvres filling the virtual plates.

chapter 8

Making Use of the Medium

IN THE EARLY DAYS OF TELEVISION, even those who considered themselves media experts saw TV primarily as "radio with pictures." Producers had yet to learn how camera angles, editing, and visual cues could enhance the power of the visual image, and how they functioned differently for television than for traditional filmmaking. The limits of the technology had to be considered as well; early video cameras worked best only under certain conditions (such as extremely bright light) and had difficulty performing functions such as panning. As it was better understood, television grew in effectiveness as an entertainment medium and, more importantly, as a marketing tool.

There's a parallel with the Internet here. The unique features of the Internet and the Web can be put to work to help you do business online more effectively. At the same time, there are new tools to reckon with and old habits to break. The Web is not "your father's Oldsmobile," and while it has many of the display features and measurement opportunities found in other forms of broadcast media, the traditional ways of sending messages and accounting for their viewership don't map so perfectly from one medium to another. Display advertising, for example, so popular in the form of banners when the Web first went commercial, is giving way to more in-depth infomercial models. The debate on how best to gauge the penetration and effectiveness of an advertisement continues to rage with an ongoing debate between Cost-Per-Thousand-Impressions and click-through models. *Push* technologies such as those found in BackWeb and PointCast have recently emerged to further cloud the meaning of viewership by consolidating content from multiple user-defined sources into a single channel that is not even online most of the time. The most fascinating element of this environment is that technology is practically driving the evolution of marketing convention on almost a daily basis. At the same time, billions of dollars in advertising funds stand anxious to pour into a new channel. It's as exciting a time in the evolution of business and commerce as one can imagine. That said, there are some stones that have been secured in the sand for the moment, and some issues that have remained in view long enough to discuss.

Tools and Tips for Analyzing Your Site

In the early days of the Web, a hit was usually taken to mean a single visit by a single user, so a site receiving 10,000 hits was assumed to have 10,000 people accessing it. A hit can include the serving of a single *file* on a page, however, meaning that a page containing 20 graphics might generate 21 hits per user. Such a page might appear to be more popular than a page with fewer graphics, though the exact opposite might be the case. Moreover, a hit can also be accidental and a real problem when the site has a URL strikingly similar to that of another and popular Web site, producing an avalanche of false readings.

chapter 8 MAKING USE OF THE MEDIUM

In "Tracking Down Your Web Site Traffic" (*Netguide*, October 1996), Rick Stout points out that how you measure the traffic and effectiveness of a Web site is directly related to the objective of the site. If you're selling products through your site, your primary goal is to present your wares to as many potential buyers as possible and to get visitors to the site to buy them. On the other hand, if your goal is to sell space to advertisers, you want to maximize the number of times visitors will see the ads you've sold, since it's how you get paid. (For more details on Web advertising and measurement issues see Chapter 1, Hit Factory: Making a Splash on the Web.)

This distinction matters because, depending on what you need, you're going to want a different kind of report. For selling your own products, reports that show you how visitors use your site are the most important. Armed with this information, you can tailor and tweak your site to attract visitors to your product areas and make sure people see your special offers while you calm their fears about ordering products online. But if you're in it to attract advertisers, your site's statistics reports are more for your advertisers' benefit. Most sites like this are general interest sites that inherently attract a lot of attention—the major search engines, sports sites, and news and information services. There are hundreds more competing for traffic and trying to break through the threshold to attract that first advertiser.

How you measure the traffic and effectiveness of a Web site is directly related to the objective of the site. Is your goal to sell products through your site, or to sell space to advertisers?

Increasingly, advertisers are requiring third-party statistics reports and even audits before they'll let one of their ad banners grace your Web site. This means you should look to third-party statistics processors from the outset because you'll need them sooner or later. Monitoring your Web site's activity will reveal, among other things, how useful the information there is to visitors. Chapter 1, Hit Factory: Making a Splash on the Web, takes a deeper look at the quantitative methods for conducting measurement and the terminology used in evaluating attendance. Whatever methods one uses, it is clear that there is no going back to the vagaries of one-way media in the future of evaluating mass communications.

For more information on Web site traffic, see Netguide's site at http://www.netguidemag.com or the CMP Media site at http://www.tech.Web.com. For a quick review of measurement techniques and pitfalls such as caching, try the Mercury Center site at http://www.sjmercury.com/help/advertise.htm#6. There is also a good discussion of the best way of paying at http://nowtv.com/click.htm.

SERVER LOGS

Managers need to know what they're getting for their investment in a Web site — who's visiting the site, what they're looking at, where they came from, and whether there are more of them this month than last month. Collecting usage information is key to managing and growing a site. Fortunately, most Web servers keep a record of user activity in what's called a log file.

 In general, the less information you log, the better the performance of your server. Consider turning off a logging feature called DNS Lookup, which can dramatically reduce performance. Turning off logging completely can result in performance gains of up to 20%. It's not an imperative, it's a balancing issue.

Log files let the Web give you data no other media provide. Can you tell what article a user was reading before looking at your ad in a magazine? Can you tell what television program a user was watching before switching to yours? Can you tell what kind of radio a user is listening to your program? Can you tell how readers navigated through your magazine? From log files, this information is available in real time — and you've got the real thing; there's no waiting for approximations from the next ratings sweeps or the results of surveys. It's a marketing statistician's dream!

Why is this kind of information important? On the business end, the data confirm user trends that would otherwise be left to guesswork. Know the most popular pages on a site, for instance, and you know which pieces of information are in the greatest demand. Information about user domains and their countries of origin can aid in addressing the needs of specific audiences, such as those who don't ordinarily speak English. And identifying sites that have reciprocal links can help you determine why a site is of interest to certain audiences, which indexes and search engines users most commonly employ to access a site, and where temporary surges in use are coming from—if, for example, a site has had the good fortune to be referenced in an article on an extremely popular site such as MSNBC (http://www.msnbc.com) or HotWired (http://www.hotwired.com).

The log file also gives you a good guess as to where your site visitors are coming from. It's only a guess, because the log can't backtrack people who type your URL in by hand—but if someone follows a link on another site to get to you, the log will trap that link. So you can't compare the effectiveness of different kinds of off-Net advertising, but you can see which cooperating sites are doing you the most good. Although technically you can't get the amount of time spent per user at your site from a log file, you can get this information by running another piece of software called a *session analyzer*. This is a type of software that looks at a log file and tries to make intelligent guesses about who is or is not a visitor by looking at the IP address within set time parameters. The session analyzer can also give you the amount of time a visitor spent at your site and the average time visitors spend at your site. The session analyzer is a tool that gives a marketer more advanced information than raw log data yet does not follow a customer's every move within a site. It does not collect data secretly—a procedure known as "branding a user" and generally regarded as an invasion of privacy and likely to backfire besides.

Although most servers support the Common Log Format (CLF), many have their own (proprietary) extended log formats. The CLF is relatively limited and contains only the visitor's host name, the date and time of the request, the HTTP request, a return code for the request, and the number of bytes returned. By contrast, servers such as those used by Netscape also support the Flexible Log Format (FLF), which collects, in addition to the above data, the following information: whether authentication was used, the status of the server at the time of request, the page that the user was on previously, the browser type, the operating system of the user, the request method used, and the transport protocol used. The extended log formats record more useful information but have no standard format for comparative purposes. Table 8-1 shows you a section of raw data in a log file.

Table 8-1 Common Log Format, Flexible Log Format

DATE	TIME	STATUS (DID THE PAGE DOWNLOAD SUCCESSFULLY?)	IP ADDRESS (OF VISITOR)	PAGE OR OBJECT SENT	SIZE OF DOWNLOAD	TYPE OF BROWSER USED BY CLIENT	DOMAIN OF PAGE SENT
08/03/97	12:46:56	OK	206.25.187.70	:report:pharmacist.html	8158	Mozilla/2.0 (Macintosh; I; 68K)	http://www2.vanderveer.com/SiteEdit/SiteEdit.cgi
08/03/97	12:46:59	OK	206.25.187.70	:report:gifs:vheadalt.gif	5685	Mozilla/2.0 (Macintosh; I; 68K)	http://www2.vanderveer.com/report/pharmacist.html
08/03/97	12:46:59	OK	206.25.187.70	:report:gifs:bull1red.gif	321	Mozilla/2.0 (Macintosh; I; 68K)	http://www2.vanderveer.com/report/pharmacist.html
08/03/97	12:47:00	OK	206.25.187.70	:report:gifs:bull2org.gif	319	Mozilla/2.0 (Macintosh; I; 68K)	http://www2.vanderveer.com/report/pharmacist.html
08/03/97	12:47:06	OK	206.25.187.70	:report:gifs:bull3yel.gif	316	Mozilla/2.0 (Macintosh; I; 68K)	http://www2.vanderveer.com/report/pharmacist.html
08/04/97	15:36:36	OK	206.30.86.57	:report:gifs:vhead3.gif	5825	Mozilla/2.0 (Macintosh; I; 68K)	http://www2.vanderveer.com/report/
08/04/97	15:36:37	OK	206.30.86.57	:report:gifs:results.gif	5708	Mozilla/2.0 (Macintosh; I; 68K)	http://www2.vanderveer.com/report/
08/04/97	15:36:37	OK	206.30.86.57	:report:gifs:indnew.gif	6683	Mozilla/2.0 (Macintosh; I; 68K)	http://www2.vanderveer.com/report/
08/04/97	15:36:37	OK	206.30.86.57	:report:gifs:hpquery.gif	2136	Mozilla/2.0 (Macintosh; I; 68K)	http://www2.vanderveer.com/report/

VIEWERSHIP PACKAGES

The article "Classic Hits" by Steven J. Vaughan-Nichols (*Web Developer*, December 1996) pinpoints what a Webmaster needs to know beyond the *raw hits* to a site. A program that will collect as much information as possible about every visitor to the site is a good start, but the software must go on to organize the data. Different departments will need different information from the site. For example, the Webmaster may want to know when the site is most active, to pinpoint the server's downtime and error rate so as to repair errors more easily and take advantage of slow periods to perform maintenance. On the other hand, the marketing department wants to know where customers go within the site and for how long.

WebTrends is one of many software systems now available to monitor Web sites. Running directly on a server, WebTrends presents its findings in an easy-to-read Web page that can be posted for the benefit of staff and clients. Among the information it collects over any given period are the users' domains, countries of origin, Internet services, browsers, and operating systems. It also provides the number of failed hits, a large number of which might indicate bad or expired links on the site's pages. One of the more interesting features of WebTrends is its ability to provide live links to pages that link to a site, showing exactly where visitors are coming from, and why, information that has important strategic implications for the Web.

Log files give you data no other media provide, and they enable you to guess at who has a link to your page.

Other useful products in this genre include EveryWare's Bolero, which creates database-friendly reports from Macintosh Web servers, and can generate up-to-the-minute results. Hit List Professional for Windows not only analyzes sites, it creates hypothetical scenarios, such as how a server would perform if traffic went up substantially. Yet another product, net.Genesis' net.Sweep, polls a Web site from varying locations and bandwidths to measure the time needed to download data under different conditions. If net.Sweep cannot access a site at all, it will contact the Webmaster by e-mail or page.

Some Web activity analysis packages don't keep a record of data analyzed previously, so if you analyze the log report for one month, you won't see how the results compare with those of previous months. If you need to look at trend data, get a package that can provide it.

If you need trend data, use an analysis package with a built-in database (the Developers version of Market Focus, for example) or use a package that can export the results to a separate database for analysis.

INDEPENDENT SERVICES

In addition to tools that enable Webmasters to monitor site activity, utilities and services are available for fine-tuning the effectiveness of advertising on a site. For example, I/PRO (http://www.ipro.com/) is an independent auditing service partnered with Nielsen Media Research (http://www.nielsenmedia.com/) to verify usage statistics. Among the figures I/PRO I/Audit system calculates are visits per month, pages served, average visit length, and most-accessed files. In addition, I/PRO monitors ad views and clicks by day, giving a measurement of advertisements' effectiveness. I/PRO also offers the I/Count system, which captures information on user demographics and activity, providing marketing managers and advertisers with tools for effective ad placement. In addition to verification systems, systems such as DoubleClick offer automated methods of delivering ad banners to users most likely to read and click them. Through its database of user profiles, DoubleClick matches the most appropriate ad banner with the user, increasing the odds that ads will reach their target audiences. Independent services are discussed in greater detail in Chapter 1, Hit Factory: Making a Splash on the Web.

 An excellent site for Web advertising information, including tracking and audit services information is at SI Software Presents, which calls itself the One-Stop Directory Of Web Advertising, Promotion, Marketing, Sales And E-Mail Web Resources (http://www.sisoftware.com/silink2.htm).

chapter 8 MAKING USE OF THE MEDIUM

Leveraging Your Database

Linking a database to a Web site is not necessarily a one-way proposition. Survey data from users can be entered directly into database packages such as Lotus, FoxPro, or other generic database formats, saving entry and formatting time and facilitating access to and reporting on the latest data from the site. Commercial sites commonly contain survey forms asking users about the quality of products and services, the site itself, or ideas for offerings. Given a chance to speak their minds, Internet users frequently opt to do so, responding to a survey with information about almost anything. A Web site can also gather data on site visitors by giving out *cookies*—small files stored on the users' computers that the Web site's server (but no other server) can write to and reference. Cookies provide limited information—user names, e-mail addresses, and a history of previously visited links. Their use is controversial because they add to a user's computer and take information from it without the user's knowledge. Nevertheless, cookies are a standard Web operating tool.

In the marketing world, cookies can be extremely useful to the buyer as well as the seller. For the buyer, cookies save valuable time. If you're a buyer and the company from whom you are buying collects information about your preferences on your first visit, you save the hassle of inputting the same information on subsequent visits. With this information, the seller can guide you to items of interest and follow up to ensure your satisfaction, thereby increasing the likelihood that you'll make a return visit. Figure 8-1 shows a terrific example of this marketing concept. While they don't make use of cookies, Lands' End (`http://www.landsend.com`) follows up with buyers via e-mail, collecting information to create the highest possible customer satisfaction. Anyone who's had experience with this company knows that it tracks the customer purchase preferences so closely that it can tell you in great detail about your last purchase and suggest other items that you might like.

Figure 8-1

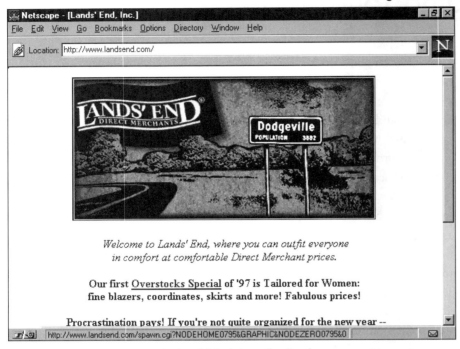

The Lands' End site embodies the company's commitment to knowing the needs of its customers.

 If you want to use cookies but are concerned about user privacy, add to your Web page a statement that alerts users and offers alternative pages. Note that browsers do offer the opportunity for users to refuse cookies. By simply checking a refusal box on either Netscape Navigator or Internet Explorer, a consumer can effectively block the cookies offered, essentially blocking an information pathway as well. As a note of caution, be careful to avoid "branding the user." If your site avidly collects information unbeknownst to the user, you risk having angry customers who feel their privacy has been invaded and who will avoid the site.

chapter 8 MAKING USE OF THE MEDIUM

Support and Information Services

Even enthusiastic Web surfers won't check out your Web site routinely, but they can be expected to come more frequently for incentives, such as product support and services, tips and tricks, or breaking news about your company and the industry. Keep in mind that your goal is not only to pull traffic into your site but to keep visitors coming back and build customer relations. Among the tools for keeping users abreast of site developments are lists of frequently asked questions (FAQs), mailing lists, and information alerts.

FAQ LISTS

FAQ lists provide a convenient forum for presenting the purpose and policies of your site and serve to cut down the number of questions asked by those who are unfamiliar with your company, the Internet, or both. FAQ lists can be used for a variety of purposes, including company information (financial data, investor information), product information (specifications, pricing), service information (warranties, delivery notes), and details of the Web site itself (preferred browsers, Webmaster contact information). As seen in Figure 8-2, Honda Motor Cars (`http://www.honda.com/`) makes good use of the FAQ feature by answering questions on its warranty policy.

 Keep two FAQ lists—one that answers technical questions about the site and another that addresses company issues. You can also create section headings in the FAQ area to answer different types of queries.

327

Figure 8-2

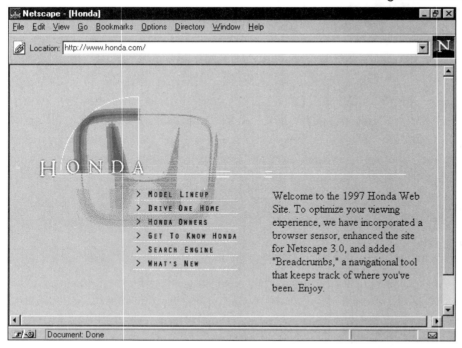

Honda's Web site uses a FAQ list to explain its automobile warranty.

Here are some basic questions to address in your FAQ list:

* Who's responsible for this site, and where do I send questions or comments?
* How frequently is this site updated?
* What am I allowed, and not allowed, to post in the conference center? (Here you can address flaming of other users, use of foul language, and penalties for violating the rules.)
* What am I allowed, and not allowed, to say in the chat rooms?
* What material on this site is copyrighted, and what is in the public domain?
* Will you treat information that I submit to you as confidential? (Note: The answer to this should be a resounding yes, unless the user voluntarily waives the right to confidentiality).

chapter **8** MAKING USE OF THE MEDIUM

MAILING LISTS

The easiest e-mail list to maintain is the *broadcast* type, a database of users to whom you can send messages announcing new site features, new products, or breaking industry news. Two organizations that use the broadcast approach effectively are Pathfinder (http://www.pathfinder.com/) and the Damar Group (http://www.dg1.com/). Pathfinder builds a mailing list to e-mail its online newsletter, Compass—a recent issue of which, for example, contained gift ideas as well as healthful cooking tips and recipe ideas. The company keeps in touch with customers through the newsletter, a vehicle that helps bring people back to the site. The Damar Group, on the other hand, is a consulting firm that sends out notices of new software and computer industry news, as well as tips on software and hardware, HTML coding, and new sites. Damar mailings may not relate directly to the company, so they always contain a tag line bearing the company's name and address.

Another mail option is the *listserve*, an ongoing discussion forum conducted via e-mail. Listserves allow for multiparty interaction and have the advantage of actively engaging users in discussions of products and services, as well as notifying participants of trends, issues, and problems. The downside to running a listserve is that it can be a big job, especially if you choose to moderate the discussions. It's likely to be either very busy or inactive, especially after users whose mailboxes have been flooded decide to sign off.

Listserve software is available free on the Internet. For a large collection of listserves on a variety of topics, go to (http://www.neosoft.com/internet/paml/).

The following are some important caveats regarding mailing lists:

* Do not sign up anyone for a mailing list unless he or she *specifically requests* to be on the list.
* Respect user requests to have their addresses removed from the list, whatever the reason. (Users should be able to delete their names from the list automatically.)
* Do not send more than one or two messages a week to people on broadcast mailing lists.

- Listserve managers should exercise some editorial control, if only to remove *spammers* who post junk, and *flamers* who insult other users.

Another question marketers ask themselves is whether to buy or build a mailing list. Mailing lists are readily obtainable at no cost. The advantage of building a list of subscribers is that you know they want your information. There's always some risk attached to sending promotional e-mail to a general mailing list; even if you observe *netiquette*, you risk annoying some people. One of the best list directories is at `http://www.liszt.com`, where you can search 65,000 lists by keywords. Other useful list directories can be found at:

- `http://www.nova.edu/Inter-Links/cgi-bin/lists`
- `http://www.lsoft.com/lists/listref.html`
- `http://www.catalog.com/vivian/interest-group-search.html`
- `http://www.neosoft.com/internet/paml/bysubj.html`

For general information about mailing lists, go to `http://www.Webcom/com/impulse/list.html`.

NEW INFORMATION ALERTS

A good Web site gets updated frequently with new content and new tools that enhance user productivity and enjoyment of the site. A good What's New? page listing important updates makes it clear that there are real people running the site. Users have more confidence in a site that sports recent changes and upgrades. If the What's New? page is interesting enough, people may bookmark it and make it part of their browsing routine. It suddenly becomes easier to involve the user in the site and to encourage repeat visits and word-of-mouth (or word-of-e-mail) advertising.

Some Pros and Cons about Registering

To build a mailing list, you must ask people to sign up (or register) for it. When you ask for an e-mail address, consider taking the opportunity to collect information about buying patterns and preferences. Remember, the more information the user provides, the more value to your mailing list. If you're just offering to update the user on new things at your site, an e-mail address may be all that you'll get. The promise of a money-saving coupon or entry into a contest with an attractive grand prize will persuade a lot of folks to participate in a survey.

A strong example of registration for something of value can be seen at the Amazon.com site (http://www.amazon.com). Amazon.com touts itself as the world's largest online bookstore and asks customers to register for "personal notification service." Customers choose the topics that appeal to them, and the editors alert them by e-mail about recently published books in their areas of interest.

The Pathfinder site (http://www.pathfinder.com) also offers a host of goodies for those willing to part with some personal information. Once registration is complete, users can access bulletin boards of interest, play Reinventing America (a political game in which the customer is in charge of the federal budget), enter the cybersoap world of The East Village, or sign up for a personalized news service. Registered users can also get the Compass e-mail newsletter.

To help overcome user reluctance to divulge personal information, state at the top of your registration form that you will not make the list available to any other vendor or organization.

Another way to call attention to new material is with eye-catching *NEW!* icons near new links. The Yahoo! index (http://www.yahoo.com/) uses such icons when it adds new resources to its pages; bright yellow symbols against a gray background help users spot new material. Good examples of New pages can be found at the Apple site (http://www.apple.com/main/whatsnew.html), which has the latest press releases from Apple Computer as well as the latest software and hardware offerings. A customer can also find the best sales price on a Performa series computer and get the latest version of CyberDog 2. At the New listing for the BMW site (http://www.bmwusa.com/whatsnew.html), users can tour Tuscany aboard a new 750iL, preview next year's models, or purchase the latest BMW clothing.

You can also call attention to new information on the home page. By giving the information up front, you save the user time, though it costs you valuable home page real estate. A good example of New information on the home page can be found at Edmund's Page (`http://www.edmunds.com`) of automobile buyer's guides. Listed are new trucks, new and used cars, safety information, repair manuals, advice to buyers, and what's new for 1997.

Interactive Features

Perhaps more than any other computer-age word, *interactivity* has been abused, misconstrued, and otherwise taken in vain. A variety of products are touted as interactive, but what does that mean, really? How many programs and Web sites enable us to interact? Sure, users can click around to enable certain features, but to interact means to act in conjunction with, and true interactivity enables users to add input to the system as well as receive output from it. Interactivity acknowledges the user as a participant and makes the computing environment a locus for exciting events.

CONFERENCES

Web site conference centers that enable users to exchange ideas freely can build traffic and increase the usefulness of the site. These centers function much like Usenet newsgroups, except the Webmaster keeps the conference on-topic by defining discussion topics and deleting off-topic posts. Conference room discussions start with a question or comment, then build gradually. The messages can be as long as those sent through e-mail and have a certain permanence, since they can be left posted indefinitely (though many sites archive or delete those that are older than 90 days). In its Community Site (`http://community.apple.com/`), shown in Figure 8-3, Apple Computer operates a conference area where Macintosh owners can ask questions and discuss issues.

Apple's Community Site provides an online meeting place for Macintosh computer users.

In addition to alerting users and Apple Computer to important issues, the Community Site provides a meeting ground for Macintosh users, who are known for their strong brand loyalty and who need to keep up with the latest computer news. At the same time that the site facilitates the introduction of new products and services, it provides feedback from users of diverse backgrounds in many regions and encourages the rapid spread of word-of-mouth information.

The different kinds of conferences that enhance a site and turn up insights into trends and customer preferences include the following:

* **Public conferences**, in which anyone can participate. A good example is the exchange in America's Housecall Network site (`http://www.housecall.com`), where anyone seeking medical information can participate in related discussions. Patients, family members, or

friends can ask questions or post information in a friendly environment. Each area is listed by topic, so that a consumer can participate in anything from a well-baby conference to a discussion of lethal disease.

- **Members-only conferences** that are restricted to one group of users. Keeping an area closed and password-protected ensures that only persons with a certain knowledge base participate. For example, in the Professionals Only area of America's Housecall Network (http://www.housecall.com), you must be identified as a medical professional before you can gain access to the conference area. Members-only conferences can be fee-based services as well as invitation-only options for qualified persons. Either way, the sites benefit from the special appeal of a focused discussion.

- **Seeded conferences** on limited topics. These are a good way to find answers to specific questions. For example, a software developer who wants to find out how many people are running a given operating system (OS) can create a special conference area site to find out. The site can ask who's planning to upgrade to the latest OS, and why. And if not, why not? With luck, a vigorous discussion will ensue about operating systems, revealing in the process the pros and cons of each and the users' overall preferences. A good example of these focused sites is the Apple EvangeList Conference (http://www.evangelist.macaddict.com). Here, Guy Kawasaki harnesses Macintosh users' enthusiasm for the product to promote interactive discussion and spread the Macgospel.

- **Ask the Experts conferences.** In these, users post questions to a panel of experts who are either staff members or specialists retained for the job. The panel answers questions publicly, on the conference page, for the benefit of everyone online. The appeal of such conferences is obvious, and greatest when widely recognized experts participate. Coming online now are sites that feature an Ask the Expert area, such as at the Drug InfoNet site (http://www.druginfonet.com), shown in Figure 8-4. Here a consumer can ask a pharmacist about a specific drug or ask a physician a disease-related question. The expert responds to the consumer within a few days, and the question and answer are posted for interested viewers.

chapter 8 MAKING USE OF THE MEDIUM

CHAT

Internet Relay Chat (IRC) is an Internet protocol that enables users to send instant messages to a conference or privately to another user. Unlike e-mail and conference centers, IRC enables users to communicate in real time, as if they were conversing face to face or talking on the telephone. IRC is a unique Internet entity developed before the advent of multimedia protocols such as the World Wide Web (indeed, IRC was originally designed to operate with the UNIX command-line interface). The software packages for IRC compensate for its complexity, making it as user friendly as the chat systems on major online services. IRC shareware products for major computer systems are available at http://www.shareware.com and other shareware sites. Two good choices are ichat for Windows and Homer for Macintosh users. Web servers can also be configured to support easily hosted chat systems that don't rely on IRC, which some technicians consider outdated. There is an abundance of Java chat software available for a high-end chat experience.

Figure 8-4

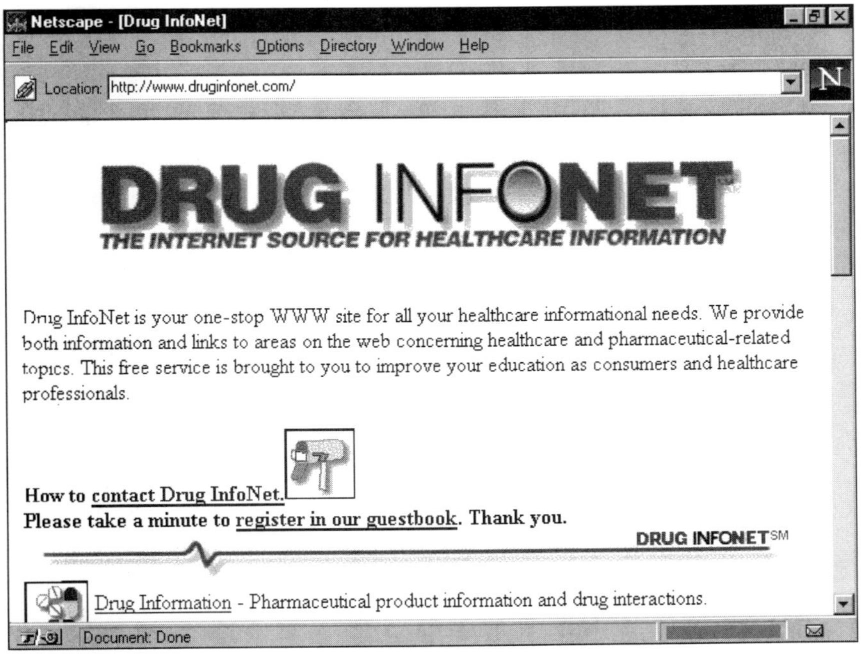

The Drug InfoNet site allows for personal interaction between the consumer and a health professional.

MTV hosts an ongoing chat at `http://www.irc.mtv.com` on the server irc.mtv.com. Users can find directions to the chat domain on the MTV Web site (`http://www.mtv.com/`). The chat room on the network often features celebrities but just as often serves as a place where MTV fans can just meet and swap information. Through its chat room, MTV extends its influence into cyberspace, creating a cycle of viewership, IRC activity, and more viewership.

How can chats make your Internet presence more appealing to users and help you achieve marketing goals? Certainly, users appreciate the chance to meet and converse with one another and will be attracted to your site for this reason alone, but chatting is by no means an exclusively recreational activity. The following chat modes are business oriented:

- **Public, ongoing chats** in which people can discuss your company, its products and services, or the industry in general. Apart from providing a place where people can give and get information, these chat rooms open a window through which you can find out about unmet needs, potential problems, and even future trends. Public chats are available at no cost at the Yahoo! site (`http://www.yahoo.com`), where you must first download the chat software and register to participate in Web chats and events.

- **Members-only chats**, where groups of people gather for semiprivate discussions. Membership may be determined by charging for access or by inviting only persons with specified professional credentials. America Online provides the best examples of members-only chat areas. By registering and paying a monthly fee, users have access to all chat areas or may form their own chat rooms.

- **Special event chats** featuring question-and-answer sessions on a specific topic, or a well-known guest—both sure-fire crowd pullers if they're announced well in advance. A celebrity or a respected expert in a field can give a site a terrific public relations boost (especially if the traditional media pick up the event). Special events, however, require special coordination to accommodate the many users trying to submit questions to a single guest host. Ground rules may have to be laid down—a limit to the number of people in the chat room at any given time, for example, or the length of time that one must wait for a reply. Sun Microsystems recently sponsored a new product launch with a special chat event. The Netra j chat featured a Q&A format called "CoffeeTalk," where potential customers asked questions about Sun's new low-admin server system. Customers could participate in an active format and literally walk away with the information needed to make a buy decision.

GAMES

Web sites now feature games that enable users to play either against the computer or with one another. The Riddler Web site (`http://www.riddler.com/`) has a large collection of games with an assortment of prizes. Although the Riddler's games are for entertainment only, a business can tailor its Web site games to help educate a customer base. An interactive site is far more likely to be successful than a site that's merely factual. The Northwestern Mutual Life Web site shown in Figure 8-5 features the Longevity Game (`http://www.northwesternmutual.com/longevit/longevit.htm`), which allows users to calculate their life expectancy based on lifestyle and health habits.

Apart from attracting attention to the site, this game gets users thinking about their own health habits and helps them take the logical step to considering their health insurance and life insurance options. Games such as this not only help make points with users, but also command user interest and increase the likelihood that a site will gain publicity through word of mouth. Health-conscious users may recommend the site to friends as a lively introduction to a look at lifestyles.

Conferencing, chats, and games all require special server modifications, so if you're not managing the server yourself, be sure to consult the Webmaster or systems administrator before you initiate any of these interactive features.

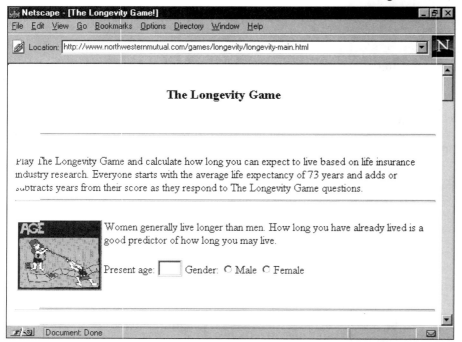

Figure 8-5

The Northwestern Mutual Life Web site lets you calculate your life expectancy based on lifestyle.

Product Management and Customer Service

Your Web site can be interactive in other ways as well, recruiting new users and keeping current users abreast of offers and events. It can even help with order tracking. Notify users of the following:

* **Discounts and price changes.** A company that sells Christmas ornaments might do a significant amount of business after December 25, when stores discount their holiday merchandise and

bargain hunters stock up for next season. If your business offers discounts periodically—or if you plan a sale for any reason—notify your regular users, inviting them to visit your site for bargains and to tell their friends!

* **Availability.** If you're fortunate enough to have a product that's in high demand, you might find it necessary to tell customers where your product can be found, and in what quantity. Notifying customers can also be useful if the product is seasonal, or you're about to enter a new market, or a new distributor is carrying the product.

* **Schedules.** When you release a new product, or if you anticipate a schedule change in product availability or delivery (because of holidays or new services), announce it on your Web site as well as through e-mail. Microsoft (http://www.microsoft.com) has made its Web site an important hub of information about product releases. A potential customer can go to the site to glean information on the top-selling software, see the shipping dates available for new software, review purchasing options, and get demos and download free software. For major customers who need specific information, establish reserved, password-protected zones.

* **Meetings and workshops.** Hosting a workshop is an excellent strategy for bringing in new customers. With a Web site, you can host a workshop online (see the previous section, "Interactive Features") or alert users to virtual events, as well as any event that you plan to participate in—conventions, meetings, trade shows.

* **Order Status and tracking.** One of the more practical and useful applications enables customers to track packages sent by carriers. If you go to the Federal Express site (http://www.fedex.com), for example, armed with the tracking number, destination, and shipping date, you can find out where and when the package was delivered (to the minute), and who signed for it. And while you're there, you can register your company and have the FedEx Welcome Kit, complete with preprinted forms and shipping materials, delivered to you in a few days. Oddly, there's no URL on any of the printed material, although the Web address is featured in television commercials.

If you have sales representatives who bring in large orders, develop your Web site with them in mind. Sales reps can use the site for demonstrations, using their laptop computers on sales calls and presentations, and at trade shows. Through a remote link, or a copy of the site on the laptop's local drive, the rep can answer questions while showcasing the company's cybersavvy. Large customers, moreover, may appreciate having special access to your company. Consider establishing private conference centers on your site, where your representatives can answer questions and discuss issues with their counterparts at large companies.

For companies with small sales forces, a Web site may be even more important as a sales and communications tool. Customers can go to a site such as IndustryNet's (`http://www.industrynet.com`) to find information, do comparison pricing, check product data sheets and availability, get demo software, participate in a workshop, and finally purchase products online. IndustryNet features information from 180,000 distributors and regional suppliers and 1,100 national manufacturers. It also boasts a database of 150,000 buyers and other key persons who have subscribed to the service. For small companies, this is the wave of the future; it will open the way to direct competition with larger corporations. Traditional marketing approaches and common-sense business strategies can pay off on the Web where the unique features of electronic interaction add new dimensions to marketing. Keywords for marketers and Webmasters are vigilance and proactivity.

Summary

This chapter touches on some of the devices for broadcast and measurement that have become recognized as ways and means on the Web today, but who knows what tomorrow will bring? There are good reasons to stay with tools that have become accepted by most players. Among other things, you can be more assured that visitors will be able to find what you want them to see because they recognize the convention (they know to check the FAQ, for example) and view what you want to show (because it doesn't depend on some new technology), and that you'll be able to present your data with some authenticity to potential advertisers (because it's couched in terms they recognize). At the same time, you should devote some energy to staying aware of newer developments—they're appearing almost every day.

Making use of the medium is a challenge because almost every aspect of the medium is evolving so quickly and regulation seems almost impossible (delightfully). Design innovations appear regularly, with censorship rigorously rejected and virtually impossible to enforce. New technologies almost seem to pop up overnight fueled by a huge influx of money into the technology sector. Standards for measuring success come into and go out of vogue just as quickly. Ten years ago, Proctor & Gamble's ultimatum on click-through payment would have rocked the advertising world. Today it's barely made a ripple on the Web. The new medium is already having cultural and behavioral effects in its three short years of existence. We can only look forward to more excitement over the next few years.

appendix A

Killer Apps

In the late 1970s press sources reported that a swarm of killer bees was quickly making its way up the western Mexican coast. The bees were soon to cross the American border, and the consequences could not be overestimated. Major national magazines and newspapers ran full-page blowups of the bees and the progress of their trek. Stores sold killer bee protection devices. Rumors raged about the size and voraciousness of their queens, the devastating effects of their stings, and the size of the samurai swords that they carried. John Belushi and the original *Saturday Night Live* cast propelled the show's Nielsen ratings into the stratosphere with their parody of the scare. After all the hoopla, nothing happened. The bees showed up, but no one got hurt. No one died. The scare came and went, and attention turned to the next big event.

Keep this story in mind whenever you look at the latest Internet technology. After almost fifteen relatively calm years in the evolution of the microcomputer industry — years in which platforms (Mac/Motorola and Microsoft/Intel) moved forward from one generation to the next with plotable speed, and software categories (operating systems, productivity tools, games) remained relatively stable and unchanged — the world has plunged into interstellar overdrive. Processor speeds are in full launch. The categorization of software has begun to defy language. At times it seems as though the next Killer Interactive Multimedia Mission-Critical Client/Server Point-and-Shoot Interface is absolutely essential to incorporate everywhere in one's electronic life from a home system to a Web site. Killer applications are a lot like killer bees. Common refrains that any single application is going to become the be-all-end-all, must-have, make-or-break technology almost always ring hollow in time. No software or hardware will make or break a Web site — *content will*. The most any killer app can do is to present content and deliver it to the user in a timely, efficient, and interesting manner.

That said, killer apps can be important tools. Always keep three things in mind when selecting an application or technology:

* Get one that does the job now *and* can adapt to future developments.
* Get the best you can afford, not the least you can get away with — you get what you pay for.
* Get products that have begun to gain mainstream backing either on a grassroots level or by large companies in the industry. Over time these products will be the ones the computer industry supports.

What follows is a selection of software and technological concepts that you should know about if you are managing an enterprise on the Web. These fall into the following categories (and are presented in that order):

* HTML editors
* Multimedia software
* Webcasting software
* Servers

appendix **A** KILLER APPS

- Add-on technologies
- Session analyzers
- Utilities
- Shareware
- New file formats
- Future technologies

HTML Editors

HTML editors break down into two camps: *HTML tag tools* and *WYSIWYG editors*. Each has its pros and cons. HTML tag tools require site developers to have programming resources fluent in HTML. WYSIWYG editors, on the other hand, allow designers to develop HTML pages without writing (or understanding) the code. The developer uses a graphical interface to lay out a page visually, and the program then interprets the layout and generates the HTML tags necessary to create the page. WYSIWYG editors are great for novices and efficient for most needs. Their shortcoming is that they use only a limited set of HTML tags, generally those available when the editor was first released. If you elect to buy a WYSIWYG editor, make sure at least to get a version you can upgrade, ideally through free downloads (some won't take updates at all). HTML tag tools do not present this limitation because the designer writes the actual HTML.

In determining which approach is best for your operation, think about the people who will create the site. Do the designers know HTML? Does the site contain a lot of pages with different designs that someone must create from scratch, or is the bulk of the work just maintenance of pages that only need updating now and then, following a standard template you already own? If your site requires frequent updates, chances are that you need both types of tools. Following are some of the more popular HTML and WYSIWYG programs.

HTML TAG EDITORS

A good tag tool provides programmers with efficient editing tools to automate the repetitive tasks associated with coding, thus easing the creation of complex documents. In a complex site, the original designer almost invariably uses an HTML tag tool because of the control it offers, while the people updating the site will use a WYSIWYG editor for maintenance.

BBEdit

BBEdit is *the* HTML production tool of choice for professional Webmasters, and it offers a multitude of time-saving features. Its *tool extensions* appear on screen on a floating palette, and give the user point-and-click access to standard HTML tags. Customized tags can also be created to extend the program's base set. Page preview via a browser is also point and click. BBEdit is not for everyone. It is an advanced Web design tool that can speed up often-laborious HTML coding jobs. It's also for people who use a Macintosh. Sorry, no PC version.

    Publisher: Bare Bones Software, Inc.
    Platforms: MacOS
    Street Price: $119
    Information or download: `http://www.barebones.com`

HoTMetaL PRO

HoTMetaL PRO was one of the original HTML editors, and while it has fallen out of favor since the arrival of some newer products, it's still cooking. The program allows designers to create hot-link areas on NCSA and CERN-compliant image maps through an easy-to-use point-and-click interface.

    Publisher: SoftQuad Ltd.
    Platforms: Windows 3.1, Windows 95, MacOS
    Street Price: $164 (Mac) / $112 (PC)
    Information or download: `http://www.softquad.com`

HTML Assistant Pro 3

This program is designed for the really advanced user, someone who knows HTML and is looking for a good tag editor. HTML Pro's best features are its assistants: clear and easy-to-access floating windows that help you create forms and tables. A tool bar at the top of the page gives quick access to HTML tags. Unfortunately, the package includes neither Netscape nor Explorer proprietary tags, so HTML Assistant Pro 3 is best for the Webmaster who doesn't need all the latest tags but wants a time-saving program.

Publisher: Brooklyn North Software Works, Inc.
Platforms: Windows 3.1, Windows 95
Street Price: $99.95
Information or download: `http://www.brooknorth.com`

Internet Assistant

Microsoft has an entire family of Internet Assistants that can turn Word, PowerPoint, Excel, and Schedule+ documents into Web-viewable documents. The Internet Assistant family is available free from Microsoft via downloads as a separate *add-on* to each of its primary software packages. For Word, the Internet Assistant is a tag editor. The add-on creates new tools on the Word toolbar that help create HTML pages. It supports forms, tables, and font changes. For Excel and PowerPoint, the add-on is an export facility. In Excel, users can select cells in a spreadsheet and export them to an HTML document. In PowerPoint, the exported version contains all the original links between PowerPoint slides. The best thing about these add-ons is that they fit right into the Microsoft programs many people already know and understand: no need to learn special commands. These products are also obviously helpful in converting existing documents into HTML pages.

Publisher: Microsoft Corporation
Platforms: Windows 95/NT, MacOS
Street Price: Free
Information or download: `http://www.microsoft.com`

WYSIWYG EDITORS

If you need an all-in-one package that includes an editor *and* site management tools, the products presented here are terrific. Each offers a series of easy-to-use and powerful programs for the complete creation and management of a site.

Adobe SiteMill/PageMill

Adobe SiteMill is a combination of two programs: PageMill (a WYSIWYG editor), and SiteMill (a Web site maintenance program). The combination of the two provides a quick-and-easy Web site solution for both novice and advanced users. PageMill uses point-and-click toolbar icons to create HTML tags. It provides drag-and-drop operations for resizing forms and frames easily. It also lets you look at HTML code and edit it by hand. SiteMill is a basic Web site manager. It provides views of the links between pages, the ability to create new links, and facilities to manage the overall design of a site. It is a good basic site management program that is easy to learn, and is best for the quick creation of Web sites for beginner to intermediate Webmasters. PageMill, on the other hand, is great for users at every level: it is easy to learn, expandable, and has many of the latest HTML tags included.

>   Publisher: Adobe Systems, Inc.
>   Platforms: MacOS only (PC version scheduled for release in early '97)
>   Street Price: $199
>   Information or download: http://www.adobe.com

AOLpress

AOLpress is free, full of features, and has an excellent interface to AOLServer, which is also free. It supports HTML 3.2 and Netscape Extensions, drag-and-drop object creation, and a simple interface for creating tables, forms, and frames. It also allows direct HTML editing. Like FrontPage, AOLpress gives designers a *bird's-eye* graphical view of a site and shows how documents link together.

Publisher: America Online, Inc.
Platforms: Windows 3.1, Windows 95, MacOS
Street Price: Free
Information or download: http://www.aolpress.com

Backstage Designer Plus

Backstage is a suite of tools that includes a good WYSIWYG editor, a site manager, and modules for creating online multimedia presentations such as simple animations, Shockwave, and Java applets. The editor looks and works like a word processor. Inserting or changing page attributes is straightforward point and click. Backstage Manager — the site management tool — gives users a graphical outline of a site and allows easy restructuring. Backstage's advanced multimedia tools (good for presentations, animations, and slide shows) include xRes Special Edition graphics editor, and Power Applets for Shockwave and Java. In short, Backstage provides a complete set of utilities that help the advanced and intermediate Webmaster create multimedia sites.

Publisher: Macromedia, Inc.
Platforms: Windows 95/NT, MacOS
Street Price: $99
Information or download: http://www.macromedia.com

Claris Home Page

Claris Home Page has features for novice-to-expert page designers. It includes support for popular multimedia plug-ins (including QuickTime and Shockwave) and multiple fonts, spell checking, client-side image maps for linking to other pages and sites, as well as HTML editing enhancements such as *syntax coloring* (color-coding of HTML tags). It also provides drag-and-drop sizing and positioning for tables and frames, and a preview background feature for GIF images. Tab-delimited text from spreadsheet and database documents can be used to create tables automatically within a page through drag-and-drop operations. Users can easily specify row heights and column widths within tables.

Publisher: Claris Corporation
Platforms: Windows 95/NT, MacOS
Street Price: $99
Information or download: http://www.claris.com

Microsoft FrontPage

FrontPage enables the user with little knowledge of HTML to create pages that include forms, frames, tables, simple links, and more. In addition, it has strong system management tools that allow the creation and maintenance of complex Web sites. FrontPage consists of two linked programs: *Editor* and *Explorer*. Editor resembles other Microsoft programs such as Word — creating complex objects is a simple point-and-click operation. In addition, FrontPage supplies a group of applications called WebBots that add functionality such as threaded discussion groups and search engines with no complex programming. Explorer is a site management tool that helps Webmasters keep track of their content. It offers two displays of a site: one in hierarchical outline, and a second that shows a visual representation with the links to and from each page. Simply clicking on one of the pages causes it to appear in the Editor. The biggest drawbacks to FrontPage are that it provides no easy way to work directly with HTML code (although you can set up external applications such as Notepad to do this), and that it does not import its own Microsoft Word documents. Subject to these qualifiers, FrontPage is a great program that enables even a beginner to create complex, dynamic Web sites.

Publisher: Microsoft Corporation
Platforms: Windows 95
Street Price: $149 ($109 for Microsoft Office users)
Information or download: http://www.microsoft.com

Navigator Gold

Netscape Navigator Gold provides a consistent, cross-platform program that helps users create Web pages, send e-mail messages including text and pictures, and publish documents to intranet and Internet Web servers, all within the same application. The program also contains the Netscape Web browser as well as a news reader for threaded discussion groups, an integrated file transfer program (FTP), and a text editor. Navigator Gold suits the average desktop. It provides a cost-effective and integrated program for Web, News, and Mail applications coupled with a well-designed document creation environment.

Publisher: Netscape Communications Corporation
Platforms: Windows 3.1, Windows 95/NT, MacOS, UNIX
Street Price: $79

Information or download: http://www.netscape.com

NetObjects Fusion

NetObjects Fusion combines three tools in a site creation, page design, and data publishing program. SiteStructure provides top-down, incremental site planning. PageDraw is a WYSIWYG editor. SiteStyles Manager gives the designer control over styles and templates for a whole site. This is a completely integrated package that is totally state-of-the-art — and priced to match.

Publisher: NetObjects, Inc.
Platforms: Windows 95/NT, (MacOS in Beta)
Street Price: $695

Information or download: http://www.netobjects.com

Table A-1 contains a basic comparison of the various features of the HTML editors section.

Table A-1 HTML Editors

	BBEdit	HoTMetaL PRO	HTML Assistant Pro	Internet Assistant	SiteMill/PageMill	AOLpress	Backstage	Claris Home Page	FrontPage	Navigator Gold	NetObjects Fusion
Price	$119	$112	$100	Free	$199	Free	$99	$99	$149	$79	$695
Easy for Beginner	No	No	Yes	Yes	Yes	Yes	Yes	Yes	Yes	Yes	Yes
Good for Expert	Yes	Yes	Yes	Yes	Yes	No	Yes	Yes	Yes	No	Yes
WYSIWIG Editing	No	No	No	No	Yes	Yes	Yes	Yes	Yes	Yes	Yes
HTML Code Editing	Yes	Yes	Yes	Yes	Yes	Yes	Yes	Yes	No	Yes	Yes
Tables	Yes	Yes	Yes	Yes	Yes	Yes	Yes	Yes	Yes	Yes	Yes
Forms	Yes	Yes	Yes	Yes	Yes	Yes	Yes	Yes	Yes	No	Yes
Frames	Yes	Yes	No	No	Yes	Yes	Yes	Yes	Yes	Yes	Yes
Netscape Extensions	Yes	No	No	Yes	Yes	Yes	Yes	Yes	Yes	Yes	Yes
Microsoft Extensions	Yes	No	No	Yes	Yes	No	Yes	Yes	Yes	No	Yes
Site Management	No	No	No	No	Yes	No	Yes	No	Yes	No	Yes

Multimedia Software

The products in this section give designers control over images, sound, and animation. Many of the visually oriented products (such as Photoshop, Illustrator, and Freehand) have been around for some time and are useful for applications other than those found on the Web. Because of their longevity in the market, there is a solid base of developers who are familiar with the capabilities of these products — making it relatively easy to find low-cost design talent. However, the newer technologies require qualified engineers, who are expensive and hard to find.

IMAGES

Here are some of the more important image-creation and manipulation tools for Web graphics. Images still fall into the basic categories of *bitmapped* and *vector*, and the programs that manipulate each of these image types are no different online than off.

Adobe Illustrator

Adobe Illustrator enables a designer to create vector-based illustrations and typographic layouts. Illustrator is one of the leading tools on or off the Web for creating illustrations, ads, brochures, and a broad variety of artwork. It is appropriate for novice to advanced users, graphic artists, technical illustrators, desktop publishers, and online designers.

    Publisher: Adobe Systems Incorporated
    Platforms: Windows 3.1, Windows 95, MacOS, UNIX
    Street Price: $595
    Information or download: `http://www.adobe.com`

Adobe Photoshop

Adobe Photoshop is the standard for photo manipulation and image production applications. Its tools and features are too numerous to list completely in a short overview like this, but the more important ones include photographic color correction, retouching and composite for scanned images, output files for professional-quality separations, multiple painting tools, multiple image layers, and assorted special effects and lighting effects. Photoshop is a must for any sophisticated image manipulation or creation. Adobe also provides free of charge a plug-in to output GIF89a files. JPEG is one of the standard *Save As* options.

    Publisher: Adobe Systems Incorporated
    Platforms: Windows 3.1, Windows 95/NT, MacOS, UNIX
    Street Price: $895
    Information or download: `http://www.adobe.com`

DeBabelizer

DeBabelizer combines graphics processing, palette optimization, and translation into one program. It features translation between 70+ formats (including bitmapped graphics), animation, digital video (including DOS/Windows, Amiga, Sun, XWindows, Alias, Electric Image, and SoftImage). It has support for Photoshop and third-party Acquire, Filter, and Export plug-ins, as well as AppleScript. DeBabelizer also has *Watch Me* scripting and batch features that enable it to process thousands of images automatically according to user specification. In addition, the program contains basic image editing and palette manipulation tools. DeBabelizer is generally used as a complement to other imaging programs because its editing tools are not sufficient to address a robust set of image editing needs on their own.

Publisher: Equilibrium
Platforms: Windows 95/NT, MacOS
Street Price: $259
Information or download: http://www.equil.com

Director

Macromedia Director sets the standard for multimedia authoring tools. The program contains an easy-to-use graphic interface that enables users to import and integrate media elements such as 2D and 3D graphics, animation, sound, and digital video. In addition Director uses *Lingo,* a powerful scripting language that enables developers to assign timing and interactivity attributes for media. Adding Macromedia's *AfterBurner* technology to Director (free at their Web site) allows the export of Shockwave files. All Director development platforms can target Windows 3.1, Windows 95/NT, Macintosh OS, Enhanced CD, or the Web for output.

Publisher: Macromedia, Inc.
Platforms: Windows 3.1, Windows 95/NT, MacOS
Street Price: $799
Information or download: http://www.macromedia.com

Extreme 3D

Macromedia Extreme 3D enables graphic artists, multimedia developers, and video professionals to create 3D images and animations. Extreme 3D uses a standard graphical interface found in popular illustration, animation, and rendering programs. It looks the same in both Mac and PC versions and supports transparent file exchange and distributed rendering in a mixed-platform environment. It also integrates with other Macromedia products such as xRes, Freehand, Director, and Authorware.

Publisher: Macromedia, Inc.
Platforms: Windows 3.1, Windows 95/NT, MacOS
Street Price: $299
Information or download: `http://www.macromedia.com`

Fractal Design Detailer

Fractal Design Detailer paints directly onto the surface of 3D models and is ideal for adding textures and patterns. Naturally, Fractal Design Detailer integrates easily with the other Fractal Design products.

Publisher: Fractal Design Corporation
Platforms: MacOS
Street Price: $299
Information or download: `http://www.fractal.com`

Fractal Design Painter

Fractal Design Painter is a paint program that simulates the tools and styles seen in traditional artists' work. It can create artwork from crayons to calligraphy, oils to airbrushes, and pencils to watercolor. These natural-media features give Fractal Design Painter functions that are hard to match in other paint programs.

Publisher: Fractal Design Corporation
Platforms: Windows 95, MacOS
Street Price: $369
Information or download: http://www.fractal.com

Graphics Converter Gold

Graphics Converter Gold provides facilities for comprehensive image and file conversion, as well as management for Windows with support for 70+ formats including Postscript, vector and raster graphics file formats, and fax devices. The package comes with a screen capture program and a browser.

Publisher: IMSI
Platforms: MacOS
Street Price: $39
Information or download: http://www.imsisoft.com

Macromedia Freehand

Macromedia Freehand is also used to create and edit vector graphics, and is appropriate for anything from the simplest illustrations to the most complex diagrams. It contains a complete set of page layout and graphic design tools that feature unlimited layering, editable blends, 100 levels of undo and redo, edit in preview, and TIFF and EPS support. In addition, Macromedia has created a Shockwave plug-in for Freehand that makes vector art easy to create on the Web. Shockwave allows users to view a Freehand file as vector-based data, so visitors can pan and zoom the image. Freehand easily integrates other page design functions such as attaching URL links to any part of a Freehand graphic.

Publisher: Macromedia, Inc.
Platforms: Windows 95/NT, MacOS
Street Price: $399
Information or download: http://www.macromedia.com

Ray Dream Studio

Fractal Design Ray Dream Studio is a 3D modeling and rendering program from the same folks that sell Fractal Design Painter, but this time the object is 3D models and typography. Ray Dream Studio uses a standard intuitive interface and comes with numerous fully rendered models that can serve as templates from which to start original development.

    Publisher: Fractal Design Corporation

    Platforms: Windows 95, MacOS

    Street Price: $288

    Information or download: `http://www.fractal.com`

ANIMATION

This software enables designers to create *GIF89a* images: simple animations that they can present in a browser window without requiring the use of add-on technologies.

Egor

Egor is written in Java. It uses a graphic interface to help in the creation of animated GIF files. Egor is useful for creating multiple sprites, programming sprite collision events, making progressive animation (*tweening*) and frame transitions, and converting image formats to GIF89a.

    Publisher: Sausage Software

    Platforms: Windows 95

    Street Price: $100

    Information or download: `http://www.sausage.com`

GIF Construction Set for Windows

GIF Construction Set for Windows creates animated GIFs on the Windows platform. It is an easy-to-use application that can create transparent GIFs, overlay text onto a GIF image, create animated GIFs, and work with GIF Palettes. The GIF Construction Set can also work with a Web browser as a helper application for viewing animated GIF files.

    Publisher: Alchemy Mindworks, Inc.

    Platforms: Windows 3.1, Windows 95/NT

    Street Price: Free

    Information or download:
      `http://www.mindworkshop.com/alchemy/gifcon.html`

GifBuilder

GifBuilder is a utility for creating animated GIF files. Its input can be a group of PICT, GIF, or TIFF files, an existing animated GIF, a QuickTime movie, or a Premiere FilmStrip or PICS file. Its output is a GIF89a file with multiple images. Options include pixel depth, color palette, interlacing, transparency, interframe delay, disposal method, frame offset, looping, and dithering. The program also supports AppleScript.

    Publisher: Yves Piguet

    Platforms: MacOS

    Street Price: Free

    Information or download: `http://www.shareware.com`

SOUND EDITORS

Multimedia PCs come with an abundance of sound software to support the internal sound card. At the most basic level they offer a *Sound Recorder* program for recording and playback. More advanced models offer a *Wave Editor* that has more full-featured editing and special effects. There are two issues to consider when creating sound for the Web. First, sound must be digitized, edited, and saved on the computer. This section covers programs that accomplish this. Second, sound must be delivered to the client either by turning it into a self-contained sound file (AIFF or WAV format files) for the client to download and then play, or by streaming the sound (so the client hears it as it comes from the Web — like a radio). To stream a sound file, convert it to a format appropriate to the technology — RealAudio, Shockwave, Xing, and so on. You probably also need a special type of streaming audio server (see the "Add-on Technologies" section later in this appendix for details).

Cool Edit

Cool Edit is a digital sound editor for Windows. It records, edits, and saves sound files in a variety of formats. Its editing tools contain numerous features for reverberation, noise reduction, echo and delay, flanging, filtering, and more. It will save files in a broad range of formats including Windows PCM waveform (WAV); 8-bit signed raw (SAM); ACM waveform (WAV); Apple AIFF (AIF); CCITT mu-Law and A-Law waveforms (WAV); Dialogic ADPCM (VOX); IMA/DVI ADPCM waveform (WAV); Microsoft ADPCM waveform (WAV); Next/Sun CCITT mu-Law, A-Law, and PCM (AU); Raw PCM Data; SampleVision format (SMP); and Sound Blaster voice file (VOC). It is programmable and supports batch processing. The interface is completely graphical and the program enables concurrent editing of multiple sound files.

Publisher: Syntrillium Software Corporation
Platforms: Windows 3.1, Windows 95
Street Price: $50
Information or download: `http://www.syntrillium.com`

SoundEdit 16

SoundEdit 16 is a complete digital audio solution. This software-only recording studio enables users to create audio with no additional hardware or software. Designers can record, edit, and save files in 14 formats including SoundEdit 16, AIFF/AIFC, Windows Wave (WAV), Sound Designer II, SoundEdit, QuickTime, System 7 Sound (.SND), Sun (.AU), Resource, Instrument, IMA 4:1, and μ-law. Other features include 18 special effects, 4 tone generators, delay, normalize, fade-in, fade-out, and QuickTime audio editing. SoundEdit 16 uses a graphical interface and visual display of the sound file to make editing an easy process for novice to expert.

>   Publisher: Macromedia, Inc.
>   Platforms: MacOS
>   Street Price: $299
>   Information or download: `http://www.macromedia.com`

JAVA APPLET DESIGNERS

The Java programming language is a C-like environment that requires a high level of technical skill to master. Developers can create Java applets without knowing Java, however, using programs containing object-oriented or visual tools that generate Java code.

 If you use a Java applet on your site, remember that people can see it only with browsers that support Java: Netscape 3.0 or higher and Explorer 3.0 or higher. It's a good idea to provide an alternative image for any information all your users will need! To see the latest in Java applets go to `http://www.gamelan.com`.

Bookworm

Bookworm enables users to create multilink jump boxes for Web pages. There's almost no limit to the number of URL links that each list, scrolling window, or pull-down menu can contain. The tool provides a simple graphic interface. This is a great way to create navigation options while using very little screen real estate.

>   Publisher: Sausage Software
>   Platforms: Windows 95
>   Street Price: $25
>   Information or download: `http://www.sausage.com`

Broadway

Broadway creates a Java applet to display text in a marquee-like sign within a Web page. Using its simple interface, designers can create signs surrounded by theatrical light bulbs going across the screen. Graphic images can also be part of the message.

    Publisher: Sausage Software

    Platforms: Windows 95

    Street Price: $26

    Information or download: `http://www.sausage.com`

Flash

Flash enables users to create an applet to display scrolling text on a browser's status line: the area at the bottom of the screen where the browser reports download progress. Flash makes the applet look like a ticker tape with a scrolling message. Its interface is extremely simple: start the program and type in the message.

    Publisher: Sausage Software

    Platforms: Windows 95

    Street Price: $26

    Information or download: `http://www.sausage.com`

PowerApplets/AppletAce

PowerApplets is a collection of Java applets that add dynamic elements to Web pages. AppletAce is the tool used to configure the PowerApplets to a user's specifications. You need no knowledge of Java to program the Applets. The program comes with the following tools: Animator (animates a graphic image), Banners (animates a scrolling text message across the browser window), Bullets (animates bullets and horizontal bars), Charts (creates bar charts from any data file), Imagemap (creates dynamic image maps), and Icons (a set of finished animated images).

Publisher: Macromedia, Inc.
Platforms: MacOS
Street Price: Free
Information or download: http://www.macromedia.com

SiteFX

SiteFX is a collection of compact Java programs, each of which enables the user to create a specific type of Java applet. These include images, animation, sound replay, browser status line messages, pull-down lists, clickable buttons, and text animation.

Publisher: Sausage Software
Platforms: Windows 95
Street Price: $99
Information or download: http://www.sausage.com

Symantec Café

Symantec Café enables designers to graphically create Java applets and applications quickly and easily. It includes a class editor to browse and edit methods and data, a hierarchy editor to view and edit Java class hierarchies, a source editor with color syntax highlighting, a graphical debugger, and a full-featured project management system.

Publisher: Symantec Corporation
Platforms: Windows 95/NT, MacOS
Street Price: $106
Information or download: http://www.symantec.com

Webcasting Software

Webcasting has become one of this year's hottest new software categories. The common theme in these apps is that they reside on the user's PC desktop and fish the Web for information the user wants to see. When they find something new in a designated category, they update client software without the client having to request it. The reasoning behind the Webcasting development is that most users only have a limited amount of time for surfing — and even when they have plenty of time, they often don't have the skill or knowledge to be sure of finding the information they want. Companies that offer Webcasting software generally provide it free to the consumer, and sell advertising to third parties. Webcasters vary in their approach, but most make arrangements with a variety of well-known content providers for popular topics such as general news, sports, health, entertainment, and so on. While it may not be enough to sustain a site on its own, there are many companies competing in this arena now, and it's possible to strike an attractive deal to offer this type of software as a way of accessing your site.

BACKWEB

BackWeb is a technology that automatically delivers Web content to a user's desktop. Like other Webcasting software, a user can download the BackWeb software once and then set it up to retrieve discrete information. BackWeb can provide text, audio, or graphics information. BackWeb works with both Internet and intranet applications.

Publisher: BackWeb Technologies
Platforms: Windows 95/NT, Windows 3.11, MacOS
Street Price: Free
Information or download: `http://www.backweb.com/`

CASTANET

Castanet is a technology for the continuous distribution of content over the Internet and intranet. The content, referred to as channels, can be stand-alone Java applications, Java applets, or content from a Web site. Castanet automatically sends and receives software and content updates for up to thousands of users within an enterprise network or on the Internet. Because files are stored locally, Castanet relieves the burden of downloading often-used files repeatedly. It also works with corporate firewalls to ensure security and eliminate the risk of overloading the firewall machines. This is a great tool that makes sure everyone gets updates as soon as they are available.

    Publisher: Marimba, Inc.
    Platforms: Windows 95/NT, Solaris 2.x
    Street Price: Free
    Information or download: `http://www.marimba.com/`

POINTCAST

PointCast is an Internet news network marketing a customizable desktop client. The software scans the Web at fixed intervals to retrieve news and other information that fits a profile the user establishes in the client software. PointCast then saves the fresh downloads in a screen saver that can be perused at your leisure. PointCast broadcasts national and international news, stock information, industry updates, weather from around the globe, sports scores, and more from sources like *Time, People,* and *Money* magazines, Reuters, PR Newswire, BusinessWire, Sportsticker, and Accuweather, as well as local newspapers like the *Los Angeles Times,* the *New York Times,* the *Boston Globe,* and the *San Jose Mercury News.* The PointCast Network is free to users; advertisers support its output.

    Publisher: PointCast, Inc.
    Platforms: Windows 95/3.x
    Street Price: Free
    Information or download: `http://www.pointcast.com`

appendix **A** KILLER APPS

Servers

The newspapers and magazines are continually writing about the battle of the browsers: Netscape's Navigator and Microsoft's Explorer. Why not? They're what's hot, and what most people think the Web is all about. They're really a sideshow, though; the Web would not work without *servers:* the software that connects users' browsers with a source of information.

SERVER PROGRAMMING METHODS

When a user clicks on a link, an HTTP request goes to the appropriate machine out on the Web. The server software on that machine then finds the information keyed to the link and sends it back out to the client. Once all the information is on its way, the server cuts the connection between itself and the client and waits for the next request. The server also runs applications that add functionality to a Web site, such as search engines.

Beyond simple HTTP requests (for static information), technologies can allow Web pages to be dynamic, for example, by returning an answer to a database query. There are four methods of creating these types of dynamic links:

* Server Side Includes (SSI)
* Common Gateway Interface (CGI)
* Application Programming Interface (API)
* Java

Server Side Includes

With SSI the server dynamically includes one file within another. For example, say a user requests a page that shows the current date. To send the information to the user, the server scans an HTML page that includes an SSI with an instruction equivalent to *insert date.* When the server sees that SSI, it goes to the file that has the current date and inserts the information into the document. SSI calls require no real programming. They merge documents together to create a dynamic feel. Useful as they are, however, they are limited because they have no programming language to create complex processes, and they also require a lot of CPU and memory time.

Common Gateway Interface (CGI)

CGI is not a language but a specification. It standardizes how a Web server will work with an external application. CGI applications can accept information from the user, process data, and even work with external information sources such as a database. These programs are usually written in Perl, C, or C++ for Windows and UNIX machines, and in AppleScript for MacOS. This specification is a part of nearly all Web server software. Unfortunately CGI scripts tend to be slow and have poor stability records (Webspeak for *they crash a lot*).

Application Programming Interface (API)

APIs bypass CGI problems. They allow a Web server to do anything that a CGI can, and they can be customized for additional functionality. Optimized for serving Web documents, they are extremely efficient. Creating an API is difficult; to be fast it needs to be in a low-level language such as C and C++, although some helpful programming tools do make the process easier. The unfortunate problem with APIs is that they work only with a particular platform, such as UNIX or Windows NT, and are often proprietary.

Java

Finally, there is Java. The main difference between Java and the other methods of creating dynamic documents is that Java runs on the user's machine (the others do all their work on the server). When users access a page that contains Java, they download an applet. The applet runs on the client machine and is capable of linking back to and gathering information from a server. This takes the workload off the server and moves it onto the client's processor.

SERVER SOFTWARE AND DATABASES

In addition to deciding which method to use to get information to users, the designer must choose how to store the information on the server. Unless a site is completely *hardcoded*, it needs a database program to store information. If this is the case at your site, you also need some database server tools: applications that enhance and speed development of the interactions between the Web server and the database program.

The differences among Web servers, database programs, and Web database server tools are highly technical, and the hosting service often decides which ones to use — you don't get a choice. What follows are eight factors you should know about, though most of them only come into play with a large, mission-critical Web site built to carry thousands of accesses a day:

- **Performance.** This is about speed. Good questions to ask are: How fast is the equipment at serving up documents? How quickly does speed deteriorate as the number of simultaneous users increases?

- **Functionality.** Does the equipment come loaded with added functionality, such as an automatic e-mail system or an FTP server. If it doesn't, is there a choice of additional third-party programs, or a restriction to proprietary applications.

- **Expertise.** Does this equipment require a very expensive programmer to make it work, or can someone with a simpler skill set deal with it? This is a particularly important question when it comes to database programming. There is an astronomical difference between the price of an SQL programmer who can work in a high-end database such as Oracle or Illustra ($150 an hour or more), and a Microsoft Access programmer who handles Visual Basic ($70 or less).

- **Fault tolerance.** Is the site critical to your business mission — that is, *if the software fails does it totally destroy your business or get you fired?* If the answer is *yes*, then you need extremely fault-tolerant equipment (built and tested to prevent catastrophe) and redundancy (more than a single alternative for a particular service). You will pay a premium for this.

- **Expandability.** Can the system grow with the needs of your mission? As the scope of a site specification changes, so may its size and speed requirements. This in turn may necessitate software or hardware changes.
- **Portability.** How easy is it to move the site to a new type of machine, for example, from a Macintosh to a UNIX-based or NT-based Web server?
- **Support.** Does the software publisher offer technical support for the products? How fast is the response time and what is the quality of the support? Is it free, or, if paid, is there a preferred client plan? Does the industry as a whole support the product sufficiently so that there are a good number of third-party companies to whom one can turn for development?
- **Price.** This is about (guess what?) money. Same rule applies as before: *Always buy the best you can afford.* The price depends upon responses to the issues outlined in this list.

Tables A-2 and A-3 show the names and prices of some of the major server systems. Even if you are not responsible for their actual acquisition, it doesn't hurt to be familiar with some of the bigger names. Netscape Enterprise Server

Table A-2 Web and Database Servers

	MICROSOFT INTERNET INFORMATION SERVER	NETSCAPE ENTERPRISE SERVER	WEBSTAR FOR MACOS SERVER	NCSA	APACHE	AOLSERVER**
Performance	High	High	Low	Low	High	High
Expertise	High	High	Low	Low	High	High
Survivable	Yes	Yes	No	n.a.	Yes	Yes
Expandable	n.a.	n.a.	n.a.	n.a.	Yes	Yes
Portable	No	Yes	No	n.a.	Yes	No
Support	Yes	Yes	Yes	No	No	Yes
Price	Free*	$995	$795	Free	Free	Free

* with purchase of Windows NT Server
** Comes with Illustra Server and Text DataBlade Module

Table A-3 Database Servers

	ORACLE SQL	INFORMIX ILLUSTRA	MICROSOFT ACCESS
Performance	High	High	Low
Expertise	High	High	Low
Survivable	Yes	Yes	No
Expandable	Yes	Yes	No
Portable	Yes	Yes	Yes
Support	Yes	Yes	Yes
Price	Variable: expensive	Variable: expensive	Inexpensive

DATABASE SERVER TOOLS

This stuff is also known as *middleware* because it translates between browser input and a targeted database. With the recent growth of the Web, numerous companies have begun to create tools that ease the publishing of information in a database onto the Web. These tools often add a scripting language that makes Web-based queries into a database easier to create, more stable and more integrated than CGI scripts, and faster. Some of the more expensive and fancier ones include a database as a part of the application.

Cold Fusion

Cold Fusion enables designers to create interactive database server applications. The power of Cold Fusion is its extension to HTML called CFML (Cold Fusion Markup Language). It contains a powerful database (ODBC/SQL) application development package with templates and a software development kit. While less in vogue recently, Cold Fusion is still a popular database platform. Allaire also offers Fusion Fuel Packs, programming tools for creating applications including Web Application Wizards, database-driven Java Graphlets, an Internet Server API module, and a data-driven VRML (virtual reality) demonstration.

Publisher: Allaire Corporation
Platforms: Windows 95/NT
Street Price: $495
Information or download: http://www.allaire.com

dbWeb

Microsoft's dbWeb helps publish information from Microsoft SQL Server, Microsoft Access, Microsoft Visual FoxPro, Oracle, and other databases that support 32-bit ODBC. When accessed by a client, Microsoft dbWeb creates a *schema*. Schemas control the database query and resulting pages. To create a schema, simply use a Schema Wizard; no HTML required.

Publisher: Microsoft Corporation
Platforms: Windows NT
Street Price: Free
Information or download:
  http://www.microsoft.com/intdev/dbweb/dbweb.htm

NetDynamics

NetDynamics is a development tool for creating dynamic Web pages. Using graphical wizards and palettes that automatically generate Java code, NetDynamics hides the complexity of building Web database applications and reduces the effort and cost of deployment. NetDynamics consists of NetDynamics Studio, a visual development environment to create applications and Web documents, and a scalable server called NetDynamics Application Server. NetDynamics integrates with several databases including Informix 6.0, Sybase 10, Oracle 7, and ODBC-compliant databases. NetDynamics is highly scalable and contains many security features. This is a high-end development tool.

Publisher: NetDynamics, Inc.

Platforms: Windows 95/NT, Sun Solaris 2.3, SGI Irix 5.3, HP-UX 9

Street Price: $1,295 (NetDynamics Studio/single user), $5,000–$15,000 (NetDynamics Application Server)

Information or download: `http://www.netdynamics.com`

Tango

Tango Enterprise helps Web administrators create dynamic Web applications that require database connectivity. Tango can work with any ODBC database including Oracle, Sybase, Informix, SQL Server, FoxPro, and Microsoft Access and has a version for Macintosh servers that supports FileMaker Pro databases.

Publisher: EveryWare Development Corporation

Platforms: Windows 95/NT, MacOS, Solaris, SGI Iris

Street Price: $299 and up (depending on platform)

Information or download: `http://www.everyware.com`

WebObjects

WebObjects was designed to leverage a corporation's existing resources to create dynamic applications for publishing on the Web. WebObjects is simple enough for the novice but powerful enough for the expert. It works with any HTTP server and links to Oracle, Sybase, Informix, or DB/2 databases with no new code. It includes numerous security features and tools to help create a dynamic Web site.

Publisher: NeXT Software, Inc.

Platforms: Windows NT, HP-UX, Solaris

Street Price: $2,999

Information or download: `http://www.next.com`

SECURITY TOOLS

In many environments, the provider will take care of security for you. Most sophisticated security implementations must employ a set of tools that are either publicly available or licensed from a publisher of security and encryption software. These are not simple products to configure effectively. If you are working with an ISP, you may want to make some inquiries about the measures they have taken, but there is not a lot you're going to do to change their setup: either it suffices for you or it doesn't. If you're growing your own server at your professional home, you may want to consider the products shown here — but you're going to need a healthy IS staff to put a decent solution together.

Internet Firewall Toolkit

The TIS Internet Firewall Toolkit facilitates the development of network firewalls. This is a modular product, and its three components — Design Philosophy, Configuration Practices/Verification Strategies, and Software Tools — will work either together or separately with other firewall products. The software suite runs under Berkeley UNIX. It takes substantial expertise to install this toolkit, as TIS distributes the software only in source code form. Firewall can be configured to deliver different levels of security depending on the needs of the environment.

> Publisher: Trusted Information Systems, Inc.
> Platforms: UNIX
> Street Price: Free
> Information or download:
> ```
> http://www.tis.com/docs/products/index.html
> ```

Kerberos

Kerberos provides a network authentication system for use on physically insecure networks. Its purpose is to allow Wide Area Network nodes to prove identity while preventing eavesdropping or replay attacks. It also provides data stream integrity and secrecy using cryptography and other systems. Kerberos issues *tickets* to users so they can identify themselves, and employs cryptographic keys to ensure secure communication with other users and servers. According to its publishers, "Kerberos is a one-trick pony." It provides for mutual authentication and secure communication between principals on an open network by manufacturing secret keys for any requester and providing a mechanism for these secret keys to be safely propagated through the network. Kerberos does not, per se, provide for authorization or accounting, although applications that wish to can use their secret keys to perform those functions securely.

> Publisher: MIT Kerberos Team
> Platforms: UNIX, MacOS, Windows 3.x (Windows NT version in the works)
> Street Price: Free
> Information or download: `http://web.mit.edu/kerberos/www/`

SATAN

SATAN is designed to help systems administrators. It reports on many network-related security problems, but you then have to use other measures to correct them. Whenever it encounters a problem, SATAN provides a tutorial that explains the possible impact and the alternatives for dealing with it — for example, correct file configuration error, install a bugfix, restrict access, or simply disable the service. SATAN collects information that is available to everyone with access to a network. With a properly configured firewall in place, that should be near-zero information for outsiders. The program's publishers admit that their tool is a two-edged sword — you can cut away a lot of potential trouble by using it, but it can also help intruders make themselves at home if they find it when they penetrate the system.

> Publisher: Dan Farmer and Wietse Venema
> Platforms: Mac and Windows PCs with a UNIX component
> Street Price: Free
> Information or download: `http://www.fish.com/satan`

SOCKS

SOCKS establishes a secure proxy data channel between two computers in a client/server environment. It is completely transparent to the client. SOCKS has two modules: SOCKS server and SOCKS client library. The server works at the application layer while the SOCKS client library sandwiches itself between the client's application layer and transport layer. One common use is to create circuit-level firewalls. However, as SOCKS evolves from Version 4 to Version 5, the application scope of SOCKS is also extending beyond its firewall application — it is beginning to provide reliability, accountability, and fault tolerance at the network level.

> Publisher: NEC USA, Inc.
> Platforms: UNIX, Windows NT, OS2 Warp4, MacOS
> Street Price: Free
> Information or download: `http://www.socks.nec.com`

Add-on Technologies

Add-on technologies are applications that enable users to enhance their viewing experience. They are called *plug-ins* in the case of Netscape or *ActiveX elements* in the case of Internet Explorer. External applications, which serve the same function as add-ons, are becoming rare as add-ons become more popular. Add-ons perform various functions. They can stream audio to the user (for example, RealAudio), form chat systems over the Web, or simply help display images (for example, JPEG-View to display JPEG-type images, the Adobe Acrobat plug-in to read PDF files, or the Apple QuickTime plug-in to view QuickTime movies). Whatever add-on you're thinking about, remember that the user needs to download and install it before applications that exploit it can run. (MS Explorer 3 does this automatically, but users of other systems are on their own.)

Consider carefully when and why to develop an applet that uses an add-on. The majority of people on the Web do not know how to make all this technology work, and ideally a site should be easy to use. When delivering something that depends on an add-on, make sure to provide a means for people to navigate around the site without it, if necessary. Also, supply a link to a site where users can find and download the add-on. Finally, consider that many add-on technologies require a development tool to create as well as send them over the Web. This means that they can get very expensive.

 To keep up-to-date on the latest technologies, the best places to go are the Microsoft site for ActiveX (http://www.microsoft.com/gallery/) and the Netscape site for plug-ins (http://www.netscape.com.) CNET also has an ActiveX download site to complement their shareware site (http://www.activex.com).

ENLIVEN

The Enliven plug-in and ActiveX elements allow users to have a rich interactive graphic experience over a 28.8 modem. To send enlivened applets, the server must be equipped with Enliven Server, which streams audiovisual information to the client browser. Enliven Producer is used to create Enliven files, although they can also be created from Macromedia Director files. Other formats will soon be added.

Publisher: Narrative Communications Corporation
Platforms: Windows 95
Street Price: Not available at press time
Information or download: http://www.narrative.com

FUTURESPLASH

FutureSplash is both a tool and plug-in that creates vector-based animations. Because the images are vector-based, the images download very quickly. Interactivity can also be added to images in the form of *roll-overs* that display a new image whenever the user moves a mouse over the specified area. The

FutureSplash Animator is used to create FutureSplash images. FutureSplash has a plug-in and ActiveX element for both Mac and Windows machines.

Publisher: FutureWave Software, Inc.
Platforms: Windows 95/NT, MacOS
Street Price: $250
Information or download: http://www.futurewave.com

REALAUDIO

RealAudio allows the streaming of audio files over the Internet. It has become a standard for this function, with over ten million users. The RealAudio encoder is used to create RealAudio files and to convert sound files into *.ra* type files. The encoder is free at the RealAudio Web site. RealAudio also integrates some simple presentation elements into its technology, such as automatically going to a new Web page at a designated time in a sound file, or playing files from a live broadcast. A special RealAudio server (or rented space on another company's machine) is necessary if you want to serve RealAudio files from a Web site. The price and level of expertise necessary to set up a server are high, and it is only worthwhile if you plan to have a vast number of audio users on your site.

Publisher: Progressive Networks
Platforms: Windows NT, SUNOS 4.1.x, Solaris 2.x, SGI Irix 5.2 (and many others)
Street Price: $100 per stream
Information or download: http://www.realaudio.com

SHOCKWAVE

Macromedia's Director authoring program is the preeminent software package for creating multimedia CD-ROMs and interactive sites. Shockwave allows users to download properly compressed Director multimedia files and play them in a browser window. To create a Shockwave file, a Director file must be put through the AfterBurner tool — a Macromedia program tool available at Macromedia's Web site. AfterBurner also allows the streaming of audio files. For the moment this is the most popular program on the Web for creating complex interactions and animations. It has been around for a long time, and there is a large base of users with the plug-in installed on their computers. The biggest drawback with Shockwave is that the file must download completely before it begins to play.

> Publisher: Macromedia, Inc.
> Platforms: Windows 95, MacOS
> Street Price: Free
> Information or download: http://www.macromedia.com

STREAMWORKS

Xing's technology for streaming audio and video is called StreamWorks. This technology uses MPEG and the TCP/IP standard to deliver streams of audio and video to the client. You need an MPEG encoder for Windows 3.1 or higher to create a StreamWorks file (the Xing MPEG encoder is $89). To view a StreamWorks file, clients must, of course, have the StreamWorks player (free).

> Publisher: Xing Technology Corporation
> Platforms: Windows NT, SGI, Solaris
> Street Price: $795–$14,950 (price based on bandwidth and use)
> Information or download: http://www.xingtech.com

Session Analyzers

A session analyzer is a type of software that looks at a log file and tries to make intelligent guesses about who is or is not a visitor by looking at the IP address within set time parameters. The session analyzer can also give you the amount of time a visitor spent at your site and the average time visitors spend at your site. The session analyzer is a tool that gives a marketer more advanced information than raw log data yet does not follow a customer's every move within a site.

BOLERO

Bolero tracks Web site activity and stores user data in an SQL database. This information forms a basis for real-time reporting and analysis. It can track how many users have visited a site, which external sites have generated the most traffic, which pages are most visited, which pages the user sees first, and much more. Bolero works with many of the most popular databases, including Butler SQL, Oracle, Microsoft SQL Server, Sybase, Informix, and FoxPro.

Publisher: EveryWare Development Corporation
Platforms: MacOS
Street Price: n.a.
Information or download: http://www.everyware.com

HIT LIST PRO

Hit List Pro not only analyzes sites, it creates hypothetical scenarios, such as how a server would perform if traffic went up substantially. The product provides analysis for number, origin, and activity of visitors. Features include information on which ad banners are most effective, which Web pages are downloaded most often, how visitors are finding the site and which promotions are most effective. Report options include query string reporting, multiple virtual server reporting, automatic report scheduling/distribution via e-mail, and remote reporting.

> Publisher: Marketwave, LLC
> Platforms: Windows 95/NT, Apple, Macintosh, UNIX
> Street Price: $1,995
> Information or download: http://marketwave.com

INCONTEXT WEBANALYZER

InContext WebAnalyzer is both a statistical and a maintenance tool. It keeps track of users: how many of them there are, what they look at, and where they came from. WebAnalyzer can also warn the Webmaster of a potential problem with a site such as a broken link or a missing image.

> Publisher: InContext Corporation
> Platforms: Windows 3.1, Windows 95/NT
> Street Price: $80
> Information or download: http://www.incontext.com

NET.SWEEP/NET.ANALYSIS PRO/ NET.ANALYSIS DESKTOP

net.Sweep polls a Web site from varying locations and bandwidths to measure the time needed to download data from different locations under different conditions. If net.Sweep cannot access a site at all, it will contact the Webmaster by e-mail or page. net.analysis Pro is the company's top-of-the-line site analysis product. It features flexible and powerful reporting options and delivers information on visitors' origins, identities, and preferences.

Publisher: net.Genesis
Platforms: Windows NT, Solaris
Street Price: n.a. (net.Sweep), $1995 (net.analysis Pro w/ 5 client extensions), $495 (net.analysis Desktop)
Information or download: http://www.netgen.com

WEBTRENDS

WebTrends is one of many software systems now available to monitor Web sites. Running directly on a server, WebTrends presents its findings in an easy-to-read Web page that can be posted for the benefit of staff and clients. Among the information it collects over any given period of time are the users' domains, countries of origin, Internet services, browsers, and operating systems. It also provides the number of failed hits, a large number of which might indicate bad or expired links on a pages. One of the more interesting features of WebTrends is its ability to provide live links to pages that link to a site, showing exactly where visitors are coming from, and why, information that has important strategic implications for the Web.

Publisher: e.g. Software
Platforms: Windows 95/NT
Street Price: $229
Information or download: http://www.webtrends.com

Utilities

FTP programs are what most people use to move HTML documents and images from their personal computer to the Web server. Other file utilities allow conversion between file types.

ADOBE FILE UTILITIES

Adobe File Utilities is an ideal product for anyone who needs access to a variety of file formats. Webmasters can convert word processing, spreadsheet, database, graphics, and compound files between hundreds of applications and several platforms. In addition, the software will identify the changes between two documents, and view, print, copy, and manage files and directories, regardless of the application or platform used to create them.

Publisher: Adobe Systems Incorporated
Platforms: Windows 3.1, Windows 95, DOS, MacOS, UNIX
Street Price: $149
Information or download: http://www.adobe.com

CROSSEYE

CrossEye enables users to edit and create image maps. It creates clickable hot spots on images without the need to program with CGI scripts. It can link hot spots to any Web page within a site or external to it.

Publisher: Sausage Software
Platforms: Windows 95
Street Price: $25
Information or download: http://www.sausage.com

CUTEFTP

CuteFTP is a Windows-based FTP application for novice users. It has a user-friendly graphical interface instead of a cumbersome command-line utility. One of its strongest features is its ability to gather information about the files and directory structures of a remote system and present it to the user in an easy-to-use browsing screen that resembles Windows File Manager.

Publisher: GlobalSCAPE, Inc.
Platforms: Windows 3.1, Windows 95/NT
Street Price: $30
Information or download: `http://www.cuteftp.com`

FETCH

Fetch is the standard for Mac-based FTP programs. It has an easy-to-use graphical interface that can upload and download either single files or groups of files. Fetch also comes with a list of very useful FTP sites where the latest shareware is available.

Publisher: Dartmouth College
Platforms: MacOS
Street Price: Free
Information or download: `http://www.shareware.com`

WEBWHACKER

WebWhacker downloads Web sites while the user is away from the computer. This diminishes the burden of having a slow Internet connection. WebWhacker can download anything from a single Web page to an entire Web site including all text (HTML) and images, and save the material on a hard drive.

Publisher: The ForeFront Group, Inc.
Platforms: Windows 95/NT, MacOS
Street Price: $49.98
Information or download: `http://www.ffg.com`

WS_FTP

WS_FTP is one of the most widely used FTP programs for the Windows platform. It combines a clear, graphical interface with powerful abilities. Features include drag-and-drop file transfers, auto re-get of failed transfers, and multifile transfers. The program comes with an address book for quick access to frequently used sites.

Publisher: Ipswitch, Inc.
Platforms: Windows 3.1, Windows 95/NT
Street Price: $37.50
Information or download:
   http://www.ipswitch.com/pd_wsftp.html

Shareware Sites

Here are a few of the best sites on the Web to search and download shareware and freeware applications:

- http://www.shareware.com (created by CNET)
- http://www.download.com (created by CNET)
- http://shareware.unc.edu (created by the University of North Carolina)

New File Formats

HTML is a great tool, but it is still very limited. This is why companies have begun to support new text and page layout formats that give the designer greater control over what the user sees.

CASCADING STYLE SHEET SPECIFICATION

In the not-so-distant future the Cascading Style Sheet Specification should be ready to roll. This specification will allow greater control over Web page layout and design through simple HTML-like commands. It will enable designers to specify font, font color, spacing, and placement of text and images. It will also assure the designer that Web pages will show up in exactly the same way, regardless of the platform on which users are viewing them, and at the same time it will speed up the delivery of HTML documents over the Web. Microsoft Explorer 3.0 has implemented the specification and it is likely that Netscape 4.0 will follow suit. One problem on the horizon is whether or not the two companies will implement the specification in the same way. To learn more, try visiting `http://www.microsoft.com/gallery/files/styles/default.htm`.

ENVOY

Like Adobe, Envoy is creating a file format that contains font, graphic, and layout information that is deliverable over the Internet. Envoy also offers more control for designers over what users see on their computers. A plug-in for Netscape is now available at the Envoy site that will enable users to view Envoy documents. Go to `http://www.envoy.com` for details.

PDF

Adobe Systems has been implementing its *Portable Document Format* (PDF) for Web delivery. The Adobe Acrobat player is available as a plug-in to view PDF files. PDF files are large and take a while to download, but this should change as developers continue to work to turn them into a better Web-based delivery mechanism. The Adobe Web site at `http://www.adobe.com` offers a downloadable PDF plug-in for Netscape.

Future Technologies

Modems that run at 28.8 Kbps just won't do it. The world wants full-motion video, full-stereo sound, and real-time interactive game play — and we're going to get it sooner or later. Numerous states have begun trials to offer high-speed delivery of information to the home and the office. Technology is a moving target these days: products go out of date practically within weeks after arriving on the shelves of computer stores, and no one wants version upgrades distributed by mail — the mail takes so long the product may be obsolete when it arrives, and the only way to get today's version is to download it. It is too soon to predict which technology will be the winner, but keep the following names in mind and realize that you will soon be developing a site for at least one of them.

ACTIVEX OLE2

ActiveX, from Microsoft, enables interactive content for the Web. ActiveX includes a set of control objects that provide user-configurable functions such as AX documents (hooks into word processing and spreadsheet documents), Active Scripting (the Java virtual machine), ActiveX server (a framework for server-based functions), and Active Movie (replaces Video for Windows and supports QuickTime, AVI, WAVE, and MPEG formats). Even if you don't like the big guys from Redmond, it's important to follow what they are doing. Check out `http://www.activex.com` for the latest developments.

ADSL

This stands for Asynchronous Digital Subscriber Line. This technology has been around for the last ten years but is just now getting publicity. It allows 1.5 Mbps–6.1 Mbps from the server to the client and 16 Kbps–640 Kbps from the client to the server, all over a regular phone line. This is enough bandwidth to do medium-quality audio conferencing and low-quality video conferencing. This is a technology the phone systems are pushing. It is inexpensive and easily supplied by your local phone company.

CABLE MODEMS

This is a technology that allows information to flow to and from the users' homes via their television cable wires. Speeds vary, but average around 10 Mbps from the server and 786 Kbps to the server. Numerous trials have already started; estimates are that by 1997 twenty percent of the country will be able to receive the service. It requires a fairly expensive box ($500), but the price is sure to come down.

JAVASCRIPT

No, this is not Java. JavaScript is a Netscape invention, formerly called LiveScript. It's an interpreted scripting language embedded in HTML pages that controls and activates a range of applications. Introduced with Netscape 2.0, it uses client-side execution and needs no server software. The community of applications using it keeps growing, and since Netscape is still fairly hot as a company, this deserves attention. For more information see `http://www.netscape.com`.

OPENDOC AND CYBERDOG

OpenDoc is a document-handling specification sponsored by a consortium of computer and software producers led by Apple. It purports to supply a seamless interface for document management between local and remote activities. OpenDoc is significant because it is *document centric* (as opposed to *application centric*), which means the document determines the application rather than the converse. Cyberdog (Mac only) is a collection of Internet parts and utilities for the OpenDoc specification. Yes, it's Apple, but they did a fairly decent job at one time of convincing the world that graphic interfaces were an important part of the future. For more details see http://www2.apple.com/documents/techres.html.

QUICKTIME

This plug-in now ships with Netscape 3.0. It contains a whole range of utilities for manipulation, including development tools that allow a *fast start,* the first step in streaming video. While QuickTime has been around for a long time, its inclusion in version 3.0 of Netscape Navigator, the leading browser, is significant. For more information see http://www.quicktime.apple.com.

TCI@HOME

TCI is currently laying fiber-optic cables across the country to create its own high-speed network. The bandwidth will reach the end user via the same type of cable that TCI now uses for television at speeds of up to 10 Mbps to the user and 786 Kbps back to the network, enough for full video. This is a very future-oriented project whose use and technology has not yet been proven.

VRML

Virtual Reality Modeling Language (VRML) is a language used to create 3D worlds for transmission over the Internet. The standard is still a work in progress. In the future, when more bandwidth makes intensive downloads possible, VRML will be the tool to create 3D environments that users can *walk* through and experience. For more information, see http://vag.vrml.org or http://www.sdsc.edu/vrml/browsers.html. There are numerous browsers and plug-ins that support current VRML worlds.

WEBTV

This is a system being built by programmers who used to be at Apple. It allows viewing of the Web from the user's television. The speed of the connection is determined by the TV system and what the user can afford. It is gaining a lot of industry backing.

appendix B

File Formats and Types

Each time they get a file request, Web browsers such as Netscape Navigator, Mosaic, or Microsoft Internet Explorer open the file and interpret it in one of four ways. There is some overlap in these alternatives depending on what version of the browser you are using and what your settings are. The browser:

- Displays the file inside the browser window by interpreting HTML code and bringing up associated images
- Displays the file in the browser window by using a plug-in (such as QuickTime) that decodes the file format
- Invokes a helper application to decode the file
- Prompts the user to invoke an application, save the file to disk, or cancel the current file

There is an ever-increasing list of plug-ins available to Netscape Navigator. Be sure to check out the Netscape site (`http://www.netscape.com/comprod/mirror/navcomponents_download.html`) for the most recent plug-ins. The listings here include Netscape plug-ins as well as links to other companies making Netscape component plug-ins. Everything from VRML to video streaming technologies can be found at the Netscape site.

The most basic file formats used by the common browsers are:

* HTML (HyperText Markup Language)
* GIF (Graphic Interchange Format)
* JPEG (Joint Photographic Experts Group)

These files are understood by the browser and require no additional help.

HTML

HTML is the language of the browser and the basis for delivering all the other file types. HTML files are text files with special identifiers (tags) that allow the browser to properly format and display the file. You can create an HTML file using a simple text editor or one of the many HTML editors available on the market. (For more details on HTML editors, see Appendix A.)

GIF and JPEG

GIF and JPEG are the two most popular image formats for displaying pictures and graphics. Almost every popular browser supports inline GIF and JPEG files. *Inline* means the browser window can display the image inside its window without having to invoke a separate application. Plug-ins allow the browser to display file types other than the default type inline.

GIF files are 8-bit (256-color) images. You can also restrict the palette to less than 256 colors to make the file smaller. The most common option for GIF files is to make them *interlaced*. This allows a browser to load the file in alternate lines, so the image seems to build in front of your eyes (it also looks something like a venetian blind). Because they use only an 8-bit palette, GIF files are best suited to things like simple graphics, toolbars, line art, and cartoons. GIF files have also become a popular animation format through the use of multiframe GIF files (a single file composed of more than one GIF image). The browser downloads the GIF and cycles through the frames to create very simple animations. All image maps are GIF files, so in some cases photographic images are also converted to GIF.

JPEG files (the name sometimes gets shortened to JPG) are full 24-bit images that support millions of colors, which makes them suitable for complex art and photographs. A JPEG compressor allows you to determine the quality of the image by applying more or less compression. The more compression the smaller the file. Too much compression will cause artifacts in the file, making it look blurry. *Artifacts* are pixelation around the edges of objects in a compressed image. It's necessary to experiment with different rates of compression to fine-tune each image.

Creating GIF and JPEG files usually means translating a graphic from its original format to either GIF or JPEG. Programs such as Adobe Photoshop for Microsoft Windows, Sun Solaris, or Apple Macintosh have export options to create a JPEG or GIF file. Other shareware programs can also provide file translations for existing graphics. (For more details, see Appendix A.)

QuickTime

Apple QuickTime presents movies in a file type understood by Netscape Navigator 3.0 and higher. That browser now ships with the QuickTime plug-in, which allows QuickTime movies to play inside a browser window. QuickTime plug-in supports a fast-start feature that allows the movie to begin to play as soon as enough of the file has downloaded. QuickTime supports synchronized video and audio. QuickTime movies can be created by a variety of applications, mostly for the Macintosh. For up-to-date information, visit the Apple QuickTime site at `http://www.quicktime.apple.com`.

Shockwave

Macromedia's Shockwave plug-in allows its Director, Authorware, and Freehand files to be viewed inline. The Shockwave plug-in is available at `http://www.macromedia.com`. Each Macromedia application can save files in the Shockwave format. Multimedia developers particularly like to use Director because it provides the capability to create a fully interactive but compressed file. The Macromedia Web site has a section listing the many Shockwave sites on the Internet. Be warned, though—Shockwave Director files can be very large.

Acrobat

Adobe Corporation's Acrobat Reader plug-in allows Acrobat files to be viewed inline. The Acrobat reader can be downloaded from Adobe's Web site at `http://www.adobe.com`. Acrobat files have many hypertext properties as well as the ability to zoom and navigate easily from the control bar. Many companies use Acrobat files for online documentation. The Acrobat reader is free but you must purchase the application—Acrobat Distiller—if you want to create Acrobat files.

appendix **B** FILE FORMATS AND TYPES

AU, AIFF, and RealAudio

The recent versions of many browsers also support basic audio file types. AU (traditional UNIX sound file) and AIFF (audio interchange file format) files can now be played inline in the browser. The browser can also invoke a helper application to play these files. These types of audio files must download completely before they can begin to play or be saved to disk.

For a look at what the future of audio is going to be, listen to Progressive Networks' RealAudio player. RealAudio creates streaming audio files that can play a potentially endless stream of sound. RealAudio is a helper application that enables you to continuously download sound. The player begins to play as soon as its buffer has enough sound, but the RealAudio player continues to download more audio. These files can get to be big, so you should make sure you have plenty of disk space. For more information go to the Progressive Networks site at `http://www.realaudio.com`. Creating RealAudio files is not a cheap process. RealAudio requires a server program to broadcast the audio streams, and this is licensed based on the number of streams you want to broadcast. Progressive Networks has recently announced an entry-level version that does not need a RealAudio server. Check the site regularly for the latest versions and pricing.

JAVA

Java applets are programs that load onto the user's computer and perform a dedicated function. Browsers can execute applets by a technique called the Java Virtual Machine. It is important to understand that Java applets are self-contained applications that are executed by the user's machine through the browser. Java applets have to be written and compiled using a Java-compatible compiler. The best place to start looking is at the Java Web site (`http:www.javasoft.com`). If you do not want to write your own Java

393

applications, you can look at their listing of applets at `http://www.java-soft.com/nav/applets`.

ActiveX

Microsoft has its own way of handling many different file types. The Microsoft Internet Explorer can in many cases use a Navigator plug-in—but many third-party vendors are now creating ActiveX-specific *addins*. The ActiveX components are used to create a variety of functions. For a list of ActiveX-specific addins (and to keep up to date on all the things that can be done with ActiveX), visit the Microsoft site at `http://www.microsoft.com/activex`.

appendix C

Screen Resolution

Screen resolution is most import when using graphics, preformatted text, tables, and frames. Most users are looking at your site on a 15-inch monitor (measured diagonally) at a resolution of 640 × 480. This means 640 pixels across and 480 pixels down (72 pixels per square inch). If you assume a Netscape user has the Control Bar, the Toolbar, the Scroll Bars, and the Location Option turned on, and the Netscape Navigator and directory buttons turned off, the space remaining for your use is about 610 pixels across and about 340 pixels down (this is 8.4 inches by 4.7 inches). Other browsers have similar screen options area available, so this figure gives you a reasonable baseline. Table C-1 lists some of the most common screen resolution figures.

Table C-1   Common Screen Resolutions

640 × 480	Referred to as VGA
800 × 600	Sometimes referred to as Super VGA
1024 × 768	Usually found on 17-inch monitors
1280 × 1024	Usually found on 19- and 21-inch monitors
1600 × 1200	Usually found on 21-inch monitors

Many users with 15-inch monitors have moved to 800 × 600 (SVGA). In this situation the information on the screen appears smaller—the screen is still the same size. You lose the same number of pixels to the tools in absolute terms, so you are left with 750 across and 460 down (10.4 × 6.3 inches). Users who have resolution higher than 800 × 600 usually do not open the window of the browser to the full size of the screen.

Keep these dimensions in mind when you design Web pages—especially the horizontal measurement. Users are much more likely to find vertical scrolling acceptable than horizontal scrolling. This is particularly true with images, but any text or table data can become very difficult to read if you can only see part of its width at a time. Here are some general guidelines for considering screen resolution in your design:

* When using frames, you can set frames with absolute pixel values or percentage values. If you are using percentage values it may be helpful to tell the user what size screen you are expecting. If you are not using frames it is still helpful to have a visual element (such as a line, jagged edge, and so on) to let the user know the right margin of your Web pages.
* If you are creating specialized applications and know that users have larger monitors (many companies have standardized on 17-inch monitors with 1024 × 768 resolution), create pages with the corresponding dimensions.
* If your application is available to the entire Web, it's best to keep everything at the most common resolutions—users with 15-inch monitors will appreciate seeing the page properly, and those with larger monitors won't lose anything. People in the latter group just get more lines at a time if the page scrolls vertically and can resize the browser window to take up less space.

appendix **D**

Web Developer's Workstation

What kind of computer do you need to create a Web site? That depends on what you are going to do. If you want to be an all-in-one, top-to-bottom, soup-to-nuts Web designer, creator, and implementer, then you are going to need lots of stuff. If you are breaking up the responsibilities of Web development among a group of people, then you can divide up the peripheral items among several machines. It's not necessary to make each machine capable of everything, though that does give you backup resources in an emergency. You could divide machine functions along typical lines such as writer-editor, graphic designer-artist, and composer-programmer. There will always be overlap unless you are a huge operation, and even then it may not be very useful to make machines too specific in their purpose. This discussion will be confined to Windows 95/NT and Macintosh computers, and to the categories of software you need. Appendix A lists the specifics on operating system compatibility for application software.

Computer and Peripherals

- The fastest available processor — presently either a PentiumPro (200MHz) or PowerPC enhanced (225MHz)
- 48 to 64MB RAM
- 24-bit color graphics with 1280 × 1024 resolution or higher
- 21-inch multisync monitor
- 2GB or more disk space
- SCSI controller
- ZIP drive, JAZ drive, or 200MB Syquest drive
- 33.6 modem (you will want a modem for testing even if you have a faster connection)
- ISDN if you have a line to an ISP
- Ethernet or Token Ring Adapter if you are on a LAN
- Slide scanner
- Flatbed scanner
- Video capture board or option

System Software

- Windows 95, Windows NT, or MacOS
- Backup and archiving software such as ArcServe, Norton Backup, Palindrome, PKZIP, and so on
- File and disk utilities such as Norton
- Virus protection such as McAfee
- TCP/IP and PPP drivers (usually part of the operating system)

Acquisition and Manipulation

- Word processor
- Spreadsheet
- List manager (simple database)
- Drawing program
- Paint program
- Video editing program
- Simple animation program
- Multimedia program
- Scanner program
- OCR (optical character recognition)
- File translation program (may be part of other applications)

Web Development

- HTML editor
- HTML reference guide
- Web server software
- Java compiler and debugger
- FTP client
- Terminal emulator
- Perl scripting program

Web Browsers

- Netscape Navigator
- Microsoft Internet Explorer
- America Online Internet Browser
- NCSA Mosaic
- Spry Mosaic

  Note: Always have the current version and the previous version.

appendix E

Recommended Web Sites

Table E-1 lists companies (in alphabetical order) and URLs referenced throughout the book.

Table E-1 Companies and URLs

COMPANY/(TYPE)	URL
CHAPTER 1	
1-800-Mattress	http://www.sleep.com
ABVS Interactive	http://www.accessabc.com
Accipiter	http://www.accipiter.com
Accrue Software	http://www.accrue.com
Addicted to Noise	http://www.addict.com
Advertising Age	http://adage.com
Advertising World	http://www.utexas.edu/coc/adv/world/
Adweek	http://www.adweek.com
Andromedia	http://www.andromedia.com
Arbitron New Media	http://www.arbitron.com/newmedia.html

(continued)

Table E-1 *(Continued)*

COMPANY/(TYPE)	URL
ASI Market Research	http://www.asiresearch.com
BPA International	http://www.bpai.com
Charged	http://www.charged.com
Checkfree Corp.	http://www.checkfree.com
CNN Interactive	http://www.cnn.com
Coca-Cola	http://www.cocacola.com
CyberAtlas	http://www.cyberatlas.com
CyberCash	http://www.cybercash.com
Domino's Pizza	http://www.dominos.com
Epicurious food	http://www.epicurious.com
ESPN SportZone	http://www.espn.com
Expedia	http://www.expedia.msn.com
Federal Express	http://www.fedex.com
Focalink Communications	http://www.focalink.com
Forrester Research	http://www.forrester.com
Group Cortex	http://www.cortex.net
Hearst Corp.'s HomeArts site	http:www.homearts.com
HotWired	http://www.hotwired.com
I/PRO	http://www.ipro.com
Iguide	http://www.iguide.com
Internet Advertising Resource Guide	http://www.voyager.net/adv/internet-advertising-guide.html
Internet Shopping Network	http://www.internet.net
Intersé	http://www.interse.com Marketfocus
Jupiter Communications	http://www.jup.com
Levi-Strauss	http://www.levi.com
Limited Express	http://www.express.style.com
MSNBC	http://www.msnbc.com
National Public Radio site	http://www.npr.org
NetCount	http://www.netcount.com
NetGravity	http://www.netgravity.com
Netscape	http://home.netscape.com
NPD Group Inc.	http://www.npd.com

appendix E — RECOMMENDED WEB SITES

COMPANY/(TYPE)	URL
Pathfinder	http://www.pathfinder.com
PC-Meter	http://www.npd.com
Playboy	http://www.playboy.com
Proctor & Gamble	http://www.pg.com
RealAudio	http://www.realaudio.com
Security First Network Bank	http://www.sfnb.com/
Standard Rate and Data Services	http://www.srds.com
Streams Online Media Development	http://streams.com
The Advertising Resource Guide	http://www.ipac.net/irgad/irgadhome.html
The Delahaye Group	http://www.delahaye.com
The Wall Street Journal Interactive	http://www.wsj.com
Toyota	http://www.toyota.com
Virtual Vinyards	http://www.virtualvin.com
Web21	http://www.web21.com/
Word	http://www.word.com

CHAPTER 2

AllPolitics	http://www.allpolitics.com
Amazon.com	http://www.amazon.com
CNN Interactive	http://www.cnn.com
CNNfn	http://www.cnnfn.com
Disney	http://www.disney.com
Electric Minds	http://www.minds.com
Hewlett-Packard	http://www.hp.com
Honda	http://www.honda.com
Levi-Strauss	http://www.levi.com
MacWorld Expo	http://live.apple.com/macworld
MapQuest	http://www.mapquest.com
Mediadome	http://www.mediadome.com
Mr. ShowBiz	http://www.mrshowbiz.com

(continued)

Table E-1 (Continued)

COMPANY/(TYPE)	URL
Quicken Financial Network	http://www.qfn.com
Riddler	http://www.riddler.com
Slate	http:www.slate.com
TheSpot	http://www.thespot.com
Total Entertainment Network	http://www.ten.net
Travelocity	http://www.travelocity.com
Women's Wire	http://www.womenswire.com

CHAPTER 3

COMPANY/(TYPE)	URL
BrowserCaps	http://www.pragmaticainc.com/bc
BrowserWatch	http://browserwatch.iworld.com
ThreeToad	http://www.threetoad.com/main/Browser.html

CHAPTER 4

COMPANY/(TYPE)	URL
(Search)	http://www.search.com
(Shareware)	http://www.shareware.com
Adobe	http://www.adobe.com/newsfeatures/palette/#palettesand dithering
AltaVista	http://www.altavista.digital.com
AT&T	http://www.att.com
AT&T College Network	http://www.att.com/college/presents.html
Atlantic Benefit Group	http://www.cross.net/abg
Bank of America site	http://www.bankamerica.com
BanxQuote	http://www.banx.com
Brill Information Services	http://www.brill.com
CardTrak	http://www.cardtrak.com
CNET	http://www.cnet.com
Compass Funds	http://www.compassfunds.com
Credit Card Network	http://www.creditnet.com
Dell	http://www.dell.com
Discovery	http://www.discovery.com
Disney	http://www.disney.com

appendix E — RECOMMENDED WEB SITES

COMPANY/(TYPE)	URL
Edgar-Online	http://www.edgar-online.com
HotWired	http://www.hotwired.com
Internet World Information Network	http://www.winnet.net/map.html
IRS	http://www.irs.ustreas.gov
Khaki's	http://www.iliad.com/bkhaki
Microsoft	http://www.microsoft.com
New Balance	http://www.newbalance.com
NYU	http://www.itp.tsoa.nyu.edu
Parent Soup	http://www.parentsoup.com
Perfect Proof	http://www.perfectproof.com
PointCast	http://www.pointcast.com
Security First Network Bank	http://www.sfnb.com
Silicon Investors	http://www.techstocks.com
Slate	http://www.slate.com
Stale	http://www.stale.com
Stock Smart	http://www.stocksmart.com
StoryWeb	http://www.storyweb.com
Suck	http://www.suck.com
The Weather Channel	http://www.weather.com
Urban Access	http://www.urbanaccess.com
WomensLink	http://www.womenslink.com
Word	http://www.word.com
Yahoo!	http://www.yahoo.com
CHAPTER 5	
(Domain name disputes)	http://www.law.georgetown.edu/lc/internic/recent/rec1.html
(Frame relay info)	http://www.mot.com/MIMS/ISG/tech/frame-relay/resources.html
(ISDN page)	http://www.alumni.caltech.edu/~dank/isdn/
(ISDN tutorial)	http://www.ziplink.net/~ralphb/ISDN/
(Tcl)	ftp://ftp.sunlabs.som/pub/tcl/
Kerberos	http://www.ov.com/misc/krb-faq.html

(continued)

Table E-1 (Continued)

COMPANY/(TYPE)	URL	REFERENCED IN
MasterCard	http://mastercard.com/set	
RSA	http://www.rsa.com	
Visa	http://www.visa.com/cgi-bin/vee/sf/set/intro.html	

CHAPTER 6

101 Hollywood Blvd	http://home.navisoft.com/brewpubclub/101.htm	
Apple Computer	http://til.info.apple.com/til/til.html	
ASCAP	http://www.ascap.com	
BMI	http://www.bmi.com	
Cahners Publishing Company	http://www.variety.com	
Chubb	http://www.chubb.com	
CIA	http://www.odci.gov/cia	
CIA World Fact Book	http://www.odci.gov/cia/publications/95fact/index.html	
CNN	http://www.cnn.com	
Commerce Department	http://www.doc.gov	
Corel	http://www.corel.com/products/clipartandphotos/photos/index.htm	
Cowles Business Media	http://www.mediacentral.com	
Defense Department	http://www.dod.gov	
Department of Transportation	http://www.dot.gov	
Desert Island Films	http://www.desertislandfilms.com	
Drivers Edge Love My Car	http://www.lovemycar.com/rules.html	
EarthWeb Chat	http://chat.earthweb.com	
Excite	http://www.excite.com	
Federal Aviation Administration	http://www.faa.gov	
Federal Express	http://www.fedex.com	
Food and Drug Administration	http://www.fda.gov	
Gateway 2000	http://www.gw2k.com	
Godiva Chocolatier	http://www.godiva.com	
Happy Puppy	http://happypuppy.com	
Housecall Network	http://housecall.com	
ichat	http://www.ichat.com	

appendix E — RECOMMENDED WEB SITES

COMPANY/(TYPE)	URL
Internet Transmissions	http://i-trans.com/library.htm
InterNIC	http://www.internic.net
Kevin Savetz (journalist)	http://northcoast.com/savetz/pd/
KinderNet	http://www.kindernet.com
Lands' End	http://www.landsend.com
Library of Congress site	http://www.loc.gov
Major League Baseball	http://www.majorleaguebaseball.com
Microsoft	http://www.microsoft.com/misc/cpyright.htm
Monsanto	http://www.monsanto.com
NASA	http://www.gsfc.nasa.gov/NASA_homepage.html
National Hockey League	http://www.nhl.com
National Weather Service	http://iwin.nws.noaa.gov/iwin/main.html
NBA	http://www.nba.com
Newscorp	http://www.newscorp.com
NFL	http://www.nfl.com
Pepsi World	http://www.pepsi.com/highroad/mainframe/legal.html
Project Gutenberg	http://www.promo.net/pg/
Reuters News Media On-line	http://www.on-line.reuters.com
SEC	http://www.sec.gov/rules/final/33-7289.txt
Securities and Exchange Commission	ttp://www.sec.gov
Smithsonian Institution	http://www.si.edu
Sports Illustrated	http://pathfinder.com/si
Starwave Corporation	http://ww.starwave.com
The Catalog	http://www.catalogsite.com
The East Village	http://www.theeastvillage.com
The New York Times	http://www.nytimes.com
The Palace	http://www.thepalace.com
The Wall Street Journal Interactive	http://www.wsj.com
Toro	http://www.toro.com/Snowthrowers/questionnaire.shtml
U.S. Information Agency	http://www.usia.gov/usa/pixusa/pix.htm

(continued)

Table E-1 (Continued)

COMPANY/(TYPE)	URL
United Parcel Service	http://www.ups.com
United States Copyright Office	http://lcweb.loc.gov/copyright
United States Postal Service	http://www.usps.gov
Wall Street Journal	http://www.wsj.com
Weather Channel	http://www.weather.com
Yahoo!	http://search.yahoo.com

CHAPTER 7

1-800-FLOWERS	http://www.1800flowers.com
Adobe	http://www.adobe.com
All4One	http://easypage.com/all4one
AltaVista	http://www.altavista.digital.com
Amazon.com	http://www.amazon.com
American Business Information's Yellow Pages	http://www.telephonebook.com
AtHand	http://www.athand.com
Big Page, The	http://www.beaucoup.com/engines.html
Big Yellow	http://www.bigyellow.com
BigBook	http://www.bigbook.com
Business Wire	http://www.businesswire.com
Cyber Promotions	http://www.cyberpromo.com
DejaNews	http://www.dejanews.com
Excite	http://www.excite.com
xcite City.Net	http://www.city.net
Fledge	http://www.fledge.com
Four11 Corp.	http://www.Four11.com
Gatorade	http://www.gatorade.com
Hallmark	http://www.hallmark.com
HotBot	http://www.hotbot.com
Infoseek	http://www.infoseek.com
Lexus	http://www.lexususa.com
Liszt	http://www.liszt.com
LookSmart	http://www.looksmart.com

appendix E — RECOMMENDED WEB SITES

COMPANY/(TYPE)	URL
Lycos	http://www.lycos.com
Magellan	http://www.mckinley.com
MTV: Music Television	http://www.mtv.com
NetPOST	http://www.netpost.com
Pampers Parenting Institute	http://www.totalbabycare.com
PostMaster	http://www.netcreations.com
PR Newswire	http://www.prnewswire.com
Search.Com	http://www.search.com
Standford Information Filtering Tool	http://www.reference.com
Starting Point	http://www.stpt.com/
StreetEYE	http://www.streeteye.com
Submit-It	http://www.submit-it.com
Switchboard	http://www.switchboard.com
TollFree Directory	http://www.tollfree.att.net
University of North Carolina	http://sunsite.unc.edu/usenet-I
University Toplinks	http://www.university.toplinks.com/
W3 Jump Station	http://www.ultranet.com/~misfit1/jump.htm
WebCrawler	http://www.webcrawler.com
WhoWhere?	http://www.whowhere.com
WorldPages	http://www.worldpages.com
Yahoo!	http://www.yahoo.com
Yahooligans!	http://yahooligans.com/
YellowNet	http://www.yellownet.com
Yoyodyne Entertainment	http://www.yoyo.com
Zip2	http://www.zip2.com
CHAPTER 8	
(List directory)	ttp://www.nova.edu/Inter-Links/cgi-bin/lists
(List directory)	http://www.lsoft.com/lists/listref.html
(List directory)	http://www.catalog.com/vivian/interest-group-search.html
(List directory)	http://www.neosoft.com/internet/paml/bysubj.html

(continued)

Table E-1 (Continued)

COMPANY/(TYPE)	URL
(Mailing list info)	http://www.Webcom/com/impulse/list.html.
Amazon.com	http://www.amazon.com
America's Housecall Network site	http://www.housecall.com
Apple	http://www.apple.com/main/whatsnew.html
Apple Community Site	http://community.apple.com
Apple EvangeList Conference	http://www.evangelist.macaddict.com
BMW	http://www.bmwusa.com/whatsnew.html
CMP Media	http://www.tech.Web.com
Damar Group	http://www.dgl.com
Drug InfoNet site	http://www.druginfonet.com
Edmund's Page	http://www.edmunds.com
Honda Motor Cars	http://www.honda.com
HotWired	http://www.hotwired.com
I/PRO	http://www.ipro.com/
Impression vs. Click-Through Pricing	http://nowtv.com/click.htm
IndustryNet	http://www.industrynet.com
Lands' End	http://www.landsend.com
Listserv	http://www.neosoft.com/internet/paml/
Mercury Center	http://www.sjmercury.com/help/advertise.htm#6
MSNBC	http://www.msnbc.com
MTV	http://www.mtv.com
Netguide	http://www.netguidemag.com
Nielsen Media Research	http://www.nielsenmedia.com
Northwestern Mutual Life Web	http://www.northwesternmutual.com/longevit/longevit.htm
Pathfinder	http://www.pathfinder.com
Riddler Web	http://www.riddler.com/
Shareware	http://www.shareware.com
SI Software	http://www.sisoftware.com/silink2.htm
Yahoo!	http://www.yahoo.com

appendix E — RECOMMENDED WEB SITES

COMPANY/(TYPE)	URL
APPENDIX A	
(Shareware)	http://www.shareware.com
(Shareware)	http://www.download.com
(Shareware)	http://www.shareware.unc.edu
Adobe Systems Inc.	http://www.adobe.com
Alchemy Mindworks Inc.	http://www.mindworkshop.com/alchemy/gifcon.html
Allaire Corporation	http://www.allaire.com
AOL	http://www.aolpress.com
BackWeb	http://www.backweb.com/
Bare Bones Software	http://www.barebones.com
Brooklyn North Software Works	http://www.brooknorth.com
Castanet	http://www.marimba.com/
Claris Corporation	http://www.claris.com
Equilibrium	http://www.equil.com
EveryWare Development Corp.	http://www.everyware.com
Fractal Design Corporation	http://www.fractal.com
FutureWave Software, Inc.	http://www.futurewave.com
GlobalSCAPE, Inc.	http://www.cuteftp.com
IMSI	http://www.imsosoft.com
InContext Corporation	http://www.incontext.com
Ipswitch, Inc.	http://www.ipswitch.com/pd_wsftp.html
Macromedia Inc.	http://www.macromedia.com
Microsoft	http://www.microsoft.com
Narrative Communications Corp.	http://www.narrative.com
NetDynamics, Inc.	http://www.netdynamics.com
NetObjects, Inc.	http://www.netobjects.com
Netscape Communications	http://www.netscape.com
NeXT Software, Inc.	http://www.next.com
PointCast	http://www.pointcast.com
Progressive Networks	http://www.realaudio.com

(continued)

Table E-1 *(Continued)*

COMPANY/(TYPE)	URL
Sausage Software	http://www.sausage.com
Symantec Corporation	http://www.symantec.com
Syntrillium Inc.	http://www.syntrillium.com
The ForeFront Group	http://www.ffg.com
Ventana Communications	http://www.provantage.com
Xing Technology Corporation	http://www.xingtech.com

GLOSSARY

add-on Add-on technologies are applications that allow users to add functionality to their viewing experience. They are called *plug-ins* in the case of Netscape or *ActiveX elements* in the case of Internet Explorer.

AIFF A self-contained file format for delivering audio files across the Web to the client browser.

API (Application Programming Interface) An API standardizes how a Web server will work with an external application. They can be used to create programs to accept information from the user, process data, and even work with external information sources such as a database. These programs are usually written in Perl, C, or C++ for Windows and UNIX machines, and AppleScript for MacOS. APIs are usually developed for a particular platform, such as UNIX or Windows NT, and are often proprietary.

applet A small, self-contained computer program designed to work in conjunction with a larger application.

backbone A high-speed set of trunk lines, pieces of which are owned by various national and international cable and telecommunications companies. The backbone consists of high-speed lines that span large distances, the express lanes of the information superhighway.

bandwidth The theoretical quantity of data that can be transported along a given medium in a designated time interval, usually measured as bits per second.

bitmapped A resolution-dependent image format commonly used for files that contain photographic or other images that contain subtle gradations of shadings and color.

BRI (Basic Rate Interface) A form of ISDN that combines two B channels with a 16K D channel for a total possible bandwidth of 128K, roughly four times the speed of a 28.8 modem. Currently most ISDN access is made using BRI.

CGI (Common Gateway Interface) A specification that standardizes how a Web server will work with an external application. CGI applications can accept information from the user, process data, and even work with external information sources such as a database. These programs are usually written in Perl, C, or C++ for Wintel and UNIX machines, and AppleScript for MacOS. This specification is a part of nearly all Web server software.

clickstream The path that a user has taken through a Web site.

colocation services For those companies who need more control over their Web site than renting space on a virtual host permits, some ISPs and Web presence providers allow customers to purchase their own server and house it at the service provider's premises. This arrangement is called *colocation*, and typically involves a sharing of administrative responsibilities.

CSU/DSU A device used for connecting between a local network and the Internet over ISDN and T-1/T-3 lines.

digizine An on-line magazine.

dithering A computer technique for mapping colors to the output capabilities of a specific device.

domain name A unique identifier for a Web server such as myserver.com or worldnet.net.

firewall A combination of hardware and software devices used to restrict access to a network.

flames/flaming Verbal expressions of disapproval sent through e-mail in online newsgroups. Because newsgroups are strictly text based, flames can carry an extremely harsh tone, especially when they're written to burn.

focus group A sampling of a specific audience used by research organizations to assess reactions to a product or service.

fractional T-1/T-3 line An incremental version of a T-1 or T-3 in which only a part of a full circuit is leased. Common fractions include 128K, 256K, and 384K. Often companies will obtain a full T-1 line and split it between dedicated Internet access and telephone lines.

FTP (File Transfer Protocol) A protocol used to move HTML documents and images between personal computers and Web servers.

gap analysis A technique used in market research for identifying new product opportunities.

gateway A device through which two remote networks are linked.

GIF (Graphic Interchange Format) One of the two most popular image formats for displaying pictures and graphics on the Web. Almost every popular browser supports inline GIF files. Inline means the browser window can display the image inside its window without having to invoke a separate application. GIF files are 8-bit (256-color) images.

GIF89a A format for using sequential GIF images to create animations.

hardcoded   A programming term used to describe procedures or values that are not expressed as variables and therefore cannot be easily altered through user input or program operation. Alteration requires a programmatic change.

hit(s)   Every time a Web server sends a file to a browser, it is recorded in the server log file as a *hit*. Hits are generated for every element on a requested page, including graphics and text. So, if one page with four graphic elements is viewed by a user, five hits are recorded — four for the graphic elements and one for the page itself.

HTML (Hypertext Markup Language)   The page formatting language used to create Web pages.

HTML tag   An HTML command.

HTTP (Hypertext Transfer Protocol)   When a user clicks on a link in a Web page, an HTTP request is sent to the appropriate machine out on the Web. The server software on that machine then finds the information to which the request is linked and sends it back out to the client.

image map   An image used in an HTML tag.

ISDN (Integrated Services Digital Network)   A completely digital phone network capable of carrying both voice and data signals at speeds significantly higher than standard analog phone lines.

JPEG (Joint Photographic Expert Group)   One of the two most popular image formats for displaying pictures and graphics on the Web. JPEG files (sometimes JPG) are full 24-bit images that support millions of colors.

Lingo   A powerful scripting language used by Macromedia Director that enables developers to assign timing and interactivity attributes for media.

MPEG   A file format used in streaming audio and video.

GLOSSARY

netiquette Proper behavior for communicating via e-mail.

newsgroup Also called *Usenet*, a site where people post and reply to messages from other users on a given topic.

ODBC (Open Data Base Connectivity) A popular communications protocol used in network communications.

parsers Software or firmware devices that interpret input.

PDF (Portable Document Format) A file format used by Adobe Acrobat for displaying documents and retaining their original format on different platforms.

PICS File format for saving stills on an animation sequence.

PICT A file format used for storing images.

plug-in *See* add-on.

PPP (Point-to-Point Protocol) A protocol used in connecting from a personal computer to a Web service provider.

PRI (Primary Rate Interface) A variety of ISDN intended for businesses with substantial bandwidth requirements and typically consists of 23 B channels and a 64K D channel.

proxy server A secondary server used for load balancing.

rate of conversion The number of viewers who take a second step in the sales process after witnessing an advertisement or promotion, for example, requesting more literature.

redundant T-1/T-3 Multiple T-1 or T-3 communication lines servicing the same location.

server On the Web, a server is a computer used to house and manage sites.

S-HTTP (Secure Hypertext Transfer Protocol)   One of the primary commercial protocols that form the basis of encryption between Web browsers and Web servers, allowing for security in handling sensitive information on the Internet.

signature file   A text file that can be included as a standard closing to an e-mail message.

smart agent   A program that monitors one or more data streams in order to retrieve specific types of information.

spam   Electronic junk mail.

spider   Search engines that crawl the Web on a constant search for new sites or updated content and links, and then create links within their own database to those sites.

sprite   An simple graphic electronic image.

SSI (Server Side Includes)   A technique for responding to HTTP requests wherein the server dynamically includes one file within another. For example, if a page a user has requested shows the current date, the server scans an HTML page that includes an SSI with an instruction equivalent to *insert date*.

SSL (Secure Sockets Layer)   One of the primary commercial protocols that form the basis of encryption between Web browsers and Web servers, allowing for security in handling sensitive information on the Internet.

streaming   A technique for downloading and executing audio or video files on the Web wherein the A/V data begins to play on the client machine as soon as sufficient data is transferred. The entire download need not be completed in order for it to begin executing.

TCP/IP (Transmission Control Protocol/Internet Protocol)   A Unix-based protocol which forms the underlying transport layer on the Internet.

throughput   The measure of the actual quantity of data transferred per unit of time.

TIFF (Tagged Image File Format)   A popular variety of file format for bitmapped images.

Tcl (tool command language)   A programming language used by AOL Server.

transfer allowance   The amount of data that an ISP will allow you to download to viewers as a part of your contract.

upstream connection   The number of hops between an ISP's server and the backbone.

Usenet   *See* newsgroups.

vector graphics   A resolution independent image format commonly used for drawing and for images that require scaling.

virtual hosting   An arrangement with an ISP or Web presence provider wherein a site may have a unique domain name and appear to users as a separate site, but it is actually sharing space with a number of other Web sites on a single, high-powered host computer.

virtual T-1/T-3   A form of incremental T-1 or T-3 usage wherein a company leases a line that has a full T-1 or T-3 capacity, but pays the ISP based on the fraction of bandwidth actually used.

visitor   A user who comes to a site.

WAV   A self-contained file format for delivering audio files across the Web to the client browser

whois (database)   At InterNic, the definitive listing of domain names.

WYSIWYG (What You See Is What You Get)   An acronym used to describe the extent to which a program displays its output as it will actually appear on screen or in print.

INDEX

A

ABC (Audit Bureau of Circulations), 22
ABVS Interactive, 22–23
access Web sites, 69–70
Accrue Insight Web-tracking program, 22
ad banners, 23–25
addresses
    directories of Internet and e-mail, 305–306
    as distribution lists, 289–290
    including on news releases, 288
Adobe Acrobat, 296
AdSpend, 44–47, 48
advertisers, 45–47
advertising agencies
    account management by, 30
    defining time lines for, 123
    developing Web projects with, 123–124
    evaluating, 29–31
    working with, 28–29
advertising and marketing, 1–63, 318–341
    advertorials, 26
    auditing companies, 22–23
    building advertising programs, 27–31
    content integration and, 26
    on content sites, 14
    creative models for, 25–27
    cross-marketing, 311–312
    deciding on a pricing model, 31–38
    evaluating agencies, 29–31
    incorporating in site layout, 177
    interactive features, 332–338
    leveraging databases, 325–326
    mailing lists, 329–330
    measuring site traffic, 17–22, 217, 318–324
    offsetting Web costs with, 9
    personalizing Web site content and, 16
    planning a marketing strategy, 2–9
    product management and customer service, 338–340
    promotional sites as, 11–12
    rates for CPM, 32, 33
    research, 3–4
    standardizing ad banners, 23–25
    support and information services, 327–332
    targeting the audience, 38–51
    tips for, 59–62
    transactional sites, 15–17
    understanding electronic commerce, 54–55
    working with agencies, 28–29
    See also advertising agencies; measuring success
Advertising Resource Guide Web site, 28
Advertising World Web site, 28
advertorials, 26
Adweek, 28
age, 40, 41
alignment, 176–177
AltaVista Web site, 155, 157, 300–301
Amazon.com Web site, 99–100, 295, 331
America Online. *See* AOL
American Association of Advertising Agencies, 19, 29
American Housecall Network, 258
anonymity, 204

421

A

AOL (America Online)
    Preview Travel, 311–312
    PrimeHost hosting service, 225–226, 230
    as proprietary commercial network, 206
Apple Community Site, 332–333
Apple Webcast site, 85–86
arbitration, 275
Arbitron New Media, 21
archiving entertainment sites, 153, 159
ASCAP, 269
ASI Market Research, 22
assessing
    disk space and transfer allowance needs, 215
    infrastructure requirements, 235–236
    ISPs, 223
    needs for bandwidth, 210–211
Association of National Advertisers, 19
AT&T Web site, 187
Atlantic Benefit Group Web site, 172–173
audiences, 38–51
    attracting, 281–282
    business, 72
    characteristics and income of, 40, 41
    consumers as, 71
    corporate communications with, 3
    defining, 66–67, 71–72
    how they find Web sites, 42
    for news releases, 287
    profile of online activities, 43–44
    providing content for, 265
    reporters as, 287–288
    selecting advertisers for your Web site, 44–51
    surveying, 38–39
    what works, 51
    See also online consumers
auditing companies, 22–23
auditoriums, 198
avails, 27

B

backbone, 205
bandwidth, 207–212
    assessing needs for, 210–211
    connectivity options and prices, 207–208
    frame relay and, 209–210
    ISDN and, 209
    leased T-1/T-3 lines, 210
    modems and, 208
    streaming technologies and, 211–212
Bank of America Web site, 147–148
BanxQuote Web site, 191–192
BBN Planet hosting service, 226–227, 230
BBSs (Bulletin Board Services), 196–198
bcc: (blind carbon copies), 288
bearer channels, 209
BEST Internet Communications hosting service, 227, 231
BMI, 269
BPA International, 22, 23
brand awareness, 75
bridge pages, 25, 37
Brill Information Services Web site, 170–171
broadcast mailing lists, 329
browsers
    enlarging color palettes for, 170
    font styles on, 168
    launching additional windows for, 189
    testing compatibility of, 140
    turning off automatic image viewing, 183
budgets for developing Web sites, 126–131
    development costs, 127–128
    for large projects, 130–131
    for medium-sized projects, 129–130
    personnel budgets, 123–124
    sample budget items, 127
    for small projects, 128–129
building advertising programs, 27–31
building Web sites, 203–243
    bandwidth and communication lines, 207–212
    choosing Web servers, 212–213
    comparison of ISP options, 223
    disk space and transfer allowance needs, 215
    e-mail, 214
    firewalls and security, 218–222
    future growth potential and, 22
    getting customer recommendations, 222–223
    infrastructure requirements for, 235–236
    in-house server options, 232–235
    Internet structure and services, 205–206
    overview of, 203–204
    questions to ask ISPs, 240–241
    securing domain names, 237–239
    server usage logs, 216–217
    server-side programming resources, 213–214
    service options available, 224–225
    technical support for ISPs, 216
    unscheduled downtime and, 215–216
    updating contents and, 217–218
    See also designing Web sites
Burma Shave, 1
business audiences, 72
business objectives for Web sites, 72–75
    direct revenue, 73–74
    indirect revenue, 74–75
buyer-driven transactions, 54, 55–56

C

CardTrak Web site, 180–181
case studies
    for large corporate sites, 116–117
    for medium-sized sites, 116
    for presentation strategies, 161–165
    for small marketing and PR site, 114–115
CASIE (Coalition for Advertising Supported Information and Entertainment), 19, 24, 29
Catalog Web site, 264–265
catalogs and brochures, 249–250
chat rooms

INDEX

chat modes for, 336–337
  interactivity and, 198–199
  letting users provide content, 265
CheckFree Digital Wallet, 55
checklists
  for preparing mission statements, 112
  strategy, 160
choice-of-law clauses, 275
clarity, 147
classic literature public domain sources, 262
CLF (Common Log Format), 321–322
click-through, 19, 34–37
clutter vs. simplicity, 178–181
CMI (CyberMeasurement Index), 21
CNET Web site, 159–160
CNN Interactive Web site, 87–89
colocation services, 225
colors, 168, 170
communication lines. *See* bandwidth
company employees, 72
company profiles and reports, 252–254
comparison charts
  of bandwidth options and prices, 208
  of virtual hosting services, 230
Compass Funds Web site, 174, 175
compensation, 273
comprehensiveness, 152
CompuServe, 206
conferences, 332–334
confidentiality, 274
connectivity options and prices, 207–208
consistency, 147
content, 243–280
  legal issues about, 266–279
  letting users provide, 265
  licensed, 247–248, 256–259
  linking to, 264–266
  nature, format, and source dimensions of, 246
  original, 247, 248–256
  ownership and plagiarism of, 243–245
  providing compelling, 282–285
  public domain, 248
contests and games, 199
control bars, 186
cookies, 154, 325–326
copyrights and legal issues, 266–279

arbitration, 275
  for development and hosting contracts, 272–275
  domain names and trademarks, 270–271
  games and contests, 297
  infringing on trademarks, 268–269
  legal restrictions on content, 271–272
  plagiarism, 243–245
  protecting intellectual property, 279
  public domain materials and, 263
  royalties for music and videos, 269, 271
  summary of copyright law, 267–269
  using content legally, 276–279
corporate communications
  communicating corporate identity, 77–82
  designing large sites for, 116–117
  reviewing, 278–279
  with target audience, 3
corporate identity Web sites, 76–82
  Honda, 80–82
  Levi Strauss, 77–79
costs
  of advertising on Netscape, 27, 32, 33
  advertising rates for CPM model, 32, 33
  of bandwidth options, 208
  and benefits of interactivity methods, 200
  of content sites, 13
  of developing Web sites, 9–10
  of e-mail mailing lists, 330
  estimated budgets for developing, 126–131
  of in-house Web servers, 232–235
  of promotional sites, 11–12
  reducing customer service, 75
  subscription fees as offset for, 14
  tracking by advertiser category, 45
  of transactional sites, 15–17
  for Web development projects, 127–128
  See also budgets for developing Web sites; revenue
CPM (Cost-Per-Thousand-Impressions) pricing model, 31–33
creating a Web identity, 145–201

choosing search options and, 156
  designing the user interface, 178–191
  establishing guidelines, 147–151
  graphic design and, 166–177
  interactivity and, 191–200
  preparing presentation strategies, 151–165
  See also corporate communications
creativity
  in advertising models, 25–27
  corporate identity web sites and, 76–82
  evaluating advertising agency's, 30
cross-marketing, 311–312
customer service and support, 93–97, 327–332
  customer service data as original content, 251–252
  effective online, 55–56
  examples of online, 251
  FAQ lists, 327–328
  guidelines for mailing lists, 329–330
  Hewlett-Packard Electronic Support Center, 94–95
  for ISPs, 222–223
  new information alerts, 330–332
  Quicken Financial Network, 96–97
  recruiting new users with, 338–340
  reducing costs of, 75
  round-the-clock, 61
CyberCash Wallet, 54
CyberCoin, 55

D

data processing, 152
database management
  distributing data, 5
  evaluating ISP servers and, 214
  of forms information, 194–195
  leveraging databases, 325–326
DejaNews Web site, 308
Delahaye Group, The, 22
Dell Computer Web site, 194–195
DES (Data Encryption Standard), 221
design elements, 146

423

designing Web sites, 59–62, 113–143
　case study for small marketing and PR site, 114–115
　clutter vs. simplicity, 178–181
　contractors vs. employees, 122–123
　contracts and compensation for, 272–275
　designing intuitive sites, 60
　development tasks for, 132–133
　entertainment sites, 158–159
　estimating budgets for, 126–131
　hardcoding or dynamic page creation, 154
　identifying job functions for, 118–120
　large corporate communications site, 116–117
　and marketing, 62
　medium-sized sites, 116
　organizing teams for, 120–122
　personnel for, 124–126
　presentation and, 184–185
　privacy and security issues and, 61–62
　research sites, 152
　round-the-clock service and support, 61
　strategies for legal use of content, 276–279
　testing, 137–143
　time lines for, 131–137
　using English or well-known language, 60–61
　working with agencies, 123–124
　See also building Web sites; development projects
development projects, 114–115
　case studies for, 116–117
　estimating budgets for, 128–131
　personnel for, 124–126
　testing, 141–143
digital magazines, 13
digital modems, 209
DigiWeb hosting service, 228, 231
direct revenue, 73–74
direction
　entertainment Web sites and, 152
　orienting users to site, 158
disclaimers, 277–278
discount coupons
　drawing traffic to stores with, 52
　in e-mail newsletters, 295–296
　registering users and, 331
　as registration incentives, 59
discounts and prices changes, 338–339
Discovery Channel Web site, 183, 184
disk space, 215
Disney Web site, 83–85, 149–150
distribution, 3, 5
distribution lists, 289–290
DNS Lookup, 320
domain names, 237–239
Domino's Pizza Web site, 6–7
Drug InfoNet Web site, 335
dynamic control bars, 187
dynamic page creation, 154

E

EarthLink hosting service, 228, 231
Echo hosting service, 229, 231
education, 40, 41
Egor software, 171
Electric Minds Web site, 101–102
electronic commerce
　consumer wariness of, 17
　electronic payment systems, 54–55
　online customer service, 55–56
　purchasing characteristics of online consumers, 42
　support for SSL and, 214
　Virtual Vineyards, 57–59
　Web commerce servers, 56–57
　what sells, 52–53
electronic payment systems, 54–55
e-mail
　directories of addresses, 306
　distribution lists for, 289–290
　games and contests on, 297
　netiquette, 286, 309, 330
　promoting products with, 288–292, 338–339
　publicity, 286–292
　shopping for ISPs and, 214
　as type of interactivity, 195–196
　unsolicited, 290–292
　using mailing lists, 329–330
encryption, 221–222
entertainment Web sites, 104–108
　design strategies for, 157–161
　as original content publications, 254–256
　Riddler, 105–106
　TEN, 106–108
environmental advertising, 26
ESPN SportZone Web site, 14, 15
estimated time lines, 132
event programming and live broadcast Web sites, 108–111
　Mediadome, 110–111
　as products, 70–72
　TheSpot, 108–109
Expert conferences, 334
Express Web site, 52, 53
extranet, 72

F

fair use laws, 268
FAQs (Frequently Asked Questions), 327–328
Federal Express Web site, 7–8, 15, 340–341
fee structures, 30
file permissions, 219
film and animation public domain sources, 263
firewalls, 218–220, 221
flames, 309
flexibility, in creating Web identity, 147
FLF (Flexible Log Format), 321–322
floating frames, 189–190
flow controls, 185
focus groups, 3
font options, 167–168
format
　of content, 246
　of news releases, 288
forms, 194–195
Forrester Research, 9, 10, 11
fostering community, 75
frame relay, 209–210
frames, 174–175
freeware, 263
FTP (file transfer protocol) services, 217–218
future growth potential, 22

G

games and contests
  as original content, 255–256
  as promotions for Web sites, 296–298
gap analysis, 3
gateways, 205–206
gender, 40, 41
GIF format, 171
global market, 4
Godiva Chocolatier Web site, 249, 250
Granoff, Peter, 57–59
graphic design, 166–177
  alignment and, 176–177
  frames in, 174–175
  HTML options and, 173
  images in, 170–173
  public domain sources for graphics, 263
  tables, 175–176
  typography in, 167–170
  visual appeal of sites, 159
Group Cortex, 22
guidelines
  for creating an identity, 147–151
  for using mailing lists, 329–330

H

Hallmark Web site, 292–293
hardcoding Web pages, 154
Hewlett-Packard Electronic Support Center Web site, 94–95
hits
  defined, 18
  measuring Web, 17, 18–22, 217, 318–320
Honda Web site, 80–82, 328
hops, 206
Horsfall, Jan, 313–314
HotWired Web site, 172, 189–190, 198, 199
HTML
  basic paragraph tags for, 176–177
  building frames with, 174

tables in, 175–176
working with layout in, 173
HTTP (Hypertext Transfer Protocol), 205
hyperlinks, 299

I

I/PRO (Internet Profiles Corporation), 20, 21
IAB (Internet Advertising Bureau), 24
icons and text links, 181–183
identifying
  job functions, 118–120
  public domain content, 259
images, 170–173
impressions, 18–19, 31
income, 40, 41
indirect revenue, 74–75
infrastructure requirements, 235–236
instant notification services, 294–295, 331
insurance, 278
intelligent agent software, 16
interactivity, 191–200, 332–338
  BBSs as, 196–198
  chat rooms as, 198–199, 335–337
  conferences as, 332–334
  contests and games, 199
  cost/benefits of methods of, 200
  e-mail as, 195–196
  forms as means of, 194–195
  games as, 337
  newsletters as, 200
  remote communication and, 4
internal links, 141
Internet
  anonymity on, 204
  backbone of, 205
  as buyer-driven medium, 54, 55–56
  characteristics and income of users, 40–43
  directories of site or e-mail addresses, 305–306
  gateways, 205–206
  measuring online traffic, 17, 18–22, 318–324

top 20 advertisers on, 46
Usenet mail tips, 310–311
Internet Advertising Resource Guide Web site, 28
Internet service providers. *See* ISPs
Internet World Information Network Web site, 188
InterNIC (Internet Network Information Center)
  domain name trademark disputes, 238, 270–271
  registering domain names, 239
Intersé, 21
intranet, 72
intuitive design, 60
IRC (Internet Relay Chat) protocol, 335
IRS Web site, 171
ISDN (Integrated Services Digital Network), 209
ISPs (Internet service providers)
  connectivity options and prices, 207–208
  getting customer recommendations for, 222–223
  introduction to, 206
  ownership of domain names and, 239
  questions to ask, 240–241
  reviewing server usage logs, 216–217
  service options available, 224–225
  summary of options available, 223
  technical support for, 216
  unscheduled downtime and, 215–216
  updating Web contents and, 217–218
ITP (Interactive Telecommunications Program), 169

K

kids' sites, 83–85
KinderNet Web site, 254–255

L

Lands' End Web site, 325–326
language
    governing use of on Web sites, 276–277
    using English or well-known, 60–61
legal issues. *See* copyrights and legal issues
Levi-Strauss Web site, 11, 77–79
Lexus Web site, 289–290
liability insurance, 278
Library of Congress Web site, 260, 261
licensing content, 247–248, 256–259
Lilypad, 22
linking sites
    developing cooperative links between sites, 191
    with hyperlinks, 299
    icons and text links, 181–183
    to supplement content, 264–266, 284–285
    testing, 141
    usefulness of adding, 151
    without losing users, 188–191
listing of popular search engines, 303
listserve software, 329–330
live broadcasts. *See* event programming and live broadcast Web sites
Longevity Game, The, 337, 338

M

Macintosh Web servers, 212
MacWorld Expo Webcast, 85–86
MapQuest Web site, 91–93
Market Focus software, 21
marketing. *See* advertising and marketing
marketing researchers
    CyberAtlas, 17
    measurement companies, 20–22
MasterCard, 54
measurement companies, 20–22, 324
measuring success, 17–22
    evaluating online traffic, 17, 18–22, 217, 318–320
    guidelines for, 19
    measurement companies, 20–22, 324
    terminology for, 18–19
Mediadome Web site, 110–111
members-only chats, 336
members-only conferences, 334
metadata, 5–8
microsites, 26
Microsoft Network, 312
Microsoft Web site, 178–179, 277–278
mission statements, 65–112
    business objectives for, 72–75
    checklist for preparing, 112
    components of, 66–67
    for customer service and support, 93–97
    defining the product, 67–71
    for entertainment Web sites, 104–108
    for event programming and live broadcasts, 108–111
    implementing corporate identity, 76–82
    presentations strategies that fulfill, 164–165
    for product event and promotion sites, 82–86
    for publishing industry, 87–91
    purpose of, 65–66
    for reference and information Web sites, 91–93
    for reservations, ticketing, and sales, 98–100
    sites with mission goals, 76
    targeting your audience, 71–72
    virtual communities and, 101–104
modems
    digital, 209
    speeds for, 141
moderated newsgroups, 310
Monsanto Web site, 253
Mr. Showbiz Web site, 89–91
MSNBC Web site, 13, 14
MTV
    chats on, 336
    content arrangements with Yahoo!, 284

N

National Public Radio Web site, 9–10
nature of content, 246
navigational interfaces, 185–191
    alternative text-based, 183
    control bars, 186
    cooperative linking between sites, 191
    directing users to information, 178–185
    dynamic control bars, 187
    floating frames, 189–190
    launching additional browser windows, 189
    providing navigation tools, 185–188
    site maps, 188
Netcom hosting service, 229–230, 231
NetCount Web-tracking tool, 20
NetGravity, 21
netiquette, 286, 309, 330
Netscape, 27, 32, 33
New Balance Web site, 182–183
new information alerts, 330–332
New pages, 331
news, 256–259
news releases, 287, 288
newsgroups, 307–311
    netiquette for, 309
    posting to, 310–311
    prefixes for, 307
newsletters, 200, 295–296
Northwestern Mutual Life Web site, 337–338

O

objectives for mission statements, 66–67
obtaining domain names, 237–238
offline promotions for Web sites, 312–314
Olson, Robert, 57–59
1-800-FLOWERS Web site, 293–294

INDEX

1-800-MATTRESS Web site, 12
online consumers
  as general audience group, 71
  purchasing characteristics of, 42
  top 50 consumer Web sites, 49–50
  wariness of, 17
online customer service, 55–56, 251
online meetings and workshops, 339
order status and tracking, 340–341
original content publications
  catalogs and brochures, 249–250
  company profiles and reports, 252–254
  customer service data, 251–252
  developing, 248–249
  entertainment, soap operas, and games, 254–256
ownership
  of domain names and trademarks, 238
  infringing on trademarked materials, 268–269
  and plagiarism of online publications, 243–245
  of Web site content, 273

P

Pampers Parenting Institute Web site, 283–284
Parent Soup Web site, 181–182, 197
PC-Meter Web site, 47, 49–50
Perfect Proof Web site, 179–180
personnel
  budgets for development, 123–124
  for large projects, 126
  for medium-sized projects, 125
  for small projects, 124–125
pixels, 23
plagiarism, 243–245
planning a marketing strategy, 2–9
PointCast Web site, 177
postings
  letting users provide content, 265
  to newsgroups, 310–311
PPP (Point-to-Point Protocol), 206
presentation strategies, 146, 151–165
  distinctions between, 151
  entertainment design strategies, 157–161
  fictional case study in, 161–165
  research design strategies, 152–157
  strategy checklist, 160
  that fulfill mission statements, 164–165
Preview Travel, 311–312
pricing models, 31–38
privacy and security issues, 61–62
Proctor and Gamble (P&G), 34, 35, 283–284
product availability, 339
product distribution, 5
product event and promotion Web sites, 82–86
  Disney, 83–85
  MacWorld Expo Webcast, 85–86
product schedules, 288–292, 339
products
  announcing via e-mail, 288–292, 339
  categorizing goods and services for businesses, 67–71
  defining in mission statement, 66–67
  event programming as, 70–72
  generating sales with promotional sites, 69
  Internet influence on distribution, 5
  marketing extensions via Web sites, 75
  new information alerts, 330–332
  promotions and services, 338–340
  providing information with access sites, 69–70
  selling with transaction sites, 70
Project Gutenberg Web site, 262
project teams
  managing, 134–135
  organizing, 120–122
  using contractors vs. employees as developers, 122–123
promoting Web sites, 281–315
  announcing products via e-mail, 288–292, 339
  attracting a targeted audience, 281–282
  cross-marketing, 311–312
  e-mail publicity, 286–292, 329–330
  games and contests, 296–298
  instant notification services, 294–295, 331
  on Internet directories, 305–306
  with newsgroups, 307–311
  newsletters, 295–296
  offline, 312–314
  providing compelling content, 282–285
  reminder services, 292–294
  search engines, 300–305
  targeting news releases, 287
  using hyperlinks, 299
prospecting for leads, 74
protecting intellectual property, 279
proxy servers, 221
public chats, 336
public conferences, 333–334
public domain content, 248, 259–263
  identifying, 259
  royalty-free materials, 262–263
  sources of governmental, 260–261
publications
  developing original content, 248–249
  legal protection of, 276–279
  ownership and plagiarism of online, 243–245
  real-time information and, 4
  See also original content publications
publicity, 286–292
public-key encryption, 221–222
publishing industry Web sites
  CNN Interactive, 87–89
  Mr. Showbiz, 89–91
push advertising, 25–26

Q

Quicken Financial Network Web site, 96–97

R

rate of conversion, 37
real-time information, 4
reference and information Web sites, 91–93

registering
  search engines, 301–302, 304–305
  users, 331
reminder services, 292–294
research design strategies, 152–157
reservations, ticketing, and sales
  Amazon.com Web site, 99–100
  Travelocity Web site, 98–99
Reuters news feed, 257
revenue
  advertising as source of Web, 17
  by publisher category, 47
  generating indirect, 74–75
  for MapQuest Web site, 93
  models for generating direct, 73–74
  top 20 publishers for, 48
  See also costs
reviewing corporate communications, 278–279
Riddler Web site, 105–106, 337
risk-sharing for licensing content, 276
royalty-free materials, 262–263

S

sales
  generating with promotional sites, 69
  selling with transaction sites, 70
  support for remote, 74–75
  Web sites for reservations, ticketing, and, 98–100
screen presentation, 184–185
search engines, 300–305
  listing of popular, 303
  promoting sites with, 300–301
  registering, 301–302
  registration services for, 304–305
search options, 156
Secure Sockets Layer. *See* SSL
security, 218–222
  checking for security holes, 220–221
  implementing data encryption, 221–222
  instituting user authentication system, 221
  issues of privacy and, 61–62

Macintosh Web servers and, 213
research Web sites and, 152
setting firewalls or proxy servers, 221
SSL and, 214, 220
storing sensitive data offline, 222
Security First Network Bank Web site, 148–149
seeded conferences, 334
server usage logs
  evaluating user activity, 320–322
  reviewing, 216–217
servers. *See* Web servers
service options, 224–225
session analyzer software, 321
SET (secure electronic transactions)
  development of, 54
  Web security and, 220
shareware, 263
shovelware, 282–283
S-HTTP (Secure Hypertext Transfer Protocol), 220
SI Software Presents Web site, 324
signature files, 311
Silicon Investors Web site, 192–193
site maps, 188
SiteTrack Tracking System, 22
Slate Web site, 184–185
smart agent software, 16
soap operas, 255
source of content, 246
spam, 290–292, 309
special event chats, 336–337
sports, 256–259
SSL (Secure Sockets Layer), 214, 220
standardizing advertising models, 23–27
Starwave Web site, 255–256
storing sensitive data offline, 222
StoryWeb site, 189
streaming technologies, 211–212
Streams Online Media Development, 22
Submit-It Web site, 304–305
subscription fees, 14
support and information services, 327–332
surveying your audience, 38–39
synchronization rights, 269

T

tables, 175–176
targeting audiences. *See* audiences
Tcl (tool command language) scripting, 226
TCP/IP (Transmission Control Protocol/Internet Protocol), 205
technical support for ISPs, 216
TEN (Total Entertainment Network) Web site, 106–108
terminating development contracts, 274–275
testing Web development projects, 137–143
  browser compatibility, 140
  for large projects, 142–143
  for medium-sized projects, 142
  on multiple platforms, 170
  for small projects, 141
TheSpot Web site, 108–109
throughput, 207
time lines, 131–137
  defining for advertising agencies, 123
  estimated, 132
  keeping projects on track, 134–135
  for updating sites, 135–137
  Web development tasks, 132–133
time-out periods, 18
T-1/T-3 lines, 210
top 50 consumer Web sites, 49–50
top 20 publishers by revenue, 48
Toy Story online advertising campaign, 83–84
Toyota Motor Sales USA, 35–37
tracing ownership of content, 276
trademarks
  contractual agreements about use, 275
  domain names and, 238
  infringing on, 268–269
transaction sites, 70
transfer allowances, 215
Travelocity Web site, 98–99
trend data, 323–324
Trip Quest, 93
turning off logging, 320
typography, 167–170

INDEX

U

U. S. governmental Web sites, 260–261
U. S. Postal Service Web site, 251–252
unfURLed Web site, 284–285
union royalties for music and videos, 269, 271
unique users, 18
unmoderated newsgroups, 310
unscheduled downtime, 215–216
unsolicited e-mail, 290–292
updating Web sites, 135–137
URLs (Uniform Resource Locators), 154
Usenet mail tips, 310–311
user authentication system, 221
user interface, 178–191
    directing users to information, 178–185
    providing links without losing users, 188–191
    providing navigation tools, 185–188
users. *See* audiences

V

valid hits, 18
Valvoline Motor Oil, 313–314
viewership packages, 323–324
virtual communities, 101–104
virtual hosting services
    AOL PrimeHost, 225–226, 230
    BBN Planet, 226–227, 230
    BEST Internet Communications, 227, 231
    comparison chart of, 230
    contracts for, 272–275
    DigiWeb, 228, 231
    EarthLink, 228, 231
    Echo, 229, 231
    Netcom, 229–230, 231
    service options available, 224–225
    Web Condo, 230, 231
Virtual Vineyards Web site, 57–59
Visa, 54

visitors, 217
visits, 18
visual appeal, 153, 159

W

Wall Street Journal Web site, 247
warranties and indemnification, 274–275, 276
weather, 256–259
Weather Channel Web site, 175, 176
WEB21, 48, 49–50
Web advertorials, 26
Web commerce servers, 56–57
Web Condo hosting service, 230, 231
Web presence providers, 225
Web servers
    checking for security holes, 220–221
    choosing, 212–213
    costs of in-house server options, 232–235
    evaluating server-side programming resources, 213–214
    firewalls and security, 218–222
    in-house server options for, 232–235
    Macintosh, 213
    reviewing server usage logs, 216–217, 320–322
    Web commerce servers, 56–57
Web site traffic
    drawing to stores with coupons, 52
    independent services for measuring, 324
    measuring, 17, 18–22, 217, 318–320
    server logs of user activity, 216–217, 320–322
    viewership packages, 323–324
Web sites
    budgets for, 126–131
    building, 203–243
    corporate identity, 76–82
    for customer service and support, 93–97
    development costs of, 9–10, 11–12
    for entertainment, 104–108
    for event programming and live broadcasts, 108–111

    how users find, 42
    measuring success of, 17–22, 217, 318–320
    mission statements for, 65–112
    as perpetual marketplace, 4–5
    product event and promotion, 82–86
    publishing industry, 87–89
    registering with search engines, 304–305
    for reservations, ticketing, and sales, 98–100
    reviewing corporate communications on, 278–279
    selected sites with mission goals, 76
    top 50 consumer, 49–40
    as virtual communities, 101–104
    See also building Web sites; content; designing Web sites; *and names of individual sites* !! *and names of individual sites*
Wells Fargo online banking, 53
"What Web Sites Cost" (Forrester Research), 10, 11
Women's Wire Web sites, 103–104
Word Web site, 157–158

Y

Yahoo!, 153–157, 284
Yoyodyne Entertainment Web site, 296–297, 298

429

Web Site Credits

The following companies and institutions have granted permission to IDG Books Worldwide to reproduce screen shots of their home/Web pages as examples of successful business Web sites for the purposes of this book. These companies and institutions have not authorized, sponsored, endorsed, or approved this publication and are not responsible for its content. Any service marks, trademarks, or trade names displayed on the home/Web pages are the property of their respective owners. Web sites are copyrighted by their respective owners; visit each Web site for specific copyright information. All rights reserved. The screen shots featured in this book may not be reproduced or transmitted in any form or by any means without the express written permission of their respective owners.

1-800-Flowers courtesy of 1-800-Flowers, Inc.; 1-800-Mattress courtesy of Dial-A-Mattress/1-800-Mattress; AltaVista courtesy of Digital Equipment Corporation; Amazon.com courtesy of Amazon.com; Apple Macworld Expo courtesy of Apple Computer Inc.; AT&T courtesy of AT&T; Atlantic Benefit Group courtesy of Cross Internet Communications; Bank of America courtesy of BankAmerica Corporation; BanxQuote courtesy of BanxQuote Inc.; CardTrack courtesy of CardTrack Company; Catalog Site courtesy of Network Wizards; CNET courtesy of CNET Inc.; CNN Interactive courtesy of Cable New Network, Inc.; Compass Funds courtesy of Compass Distributors, Inc.; Credit Card Network courtesy of Credit Card Network; DejaNews courtesy of courtesy of Deja News; Dell Computer online ordering form courtesy of Dell Computer Corporation; Discovery Channel Online courtesy of Discovery Channel Online/Discovery Communications Inc.; Disney courtesy of The Walt Disney Company; Domino's Pizza courtesy of Domino's Pizza, Inc.; Drug InfoNet courtesy of Drug InfoNet, Inc.; Electric Minds courtesy of electric minds; ESPN Sportszone courtesy of StarWave Corporation; Express courtesy of Express; Federal Express courtesy of Federal Express Corporation; Godiva courtesy of

Godiva Choclatier; Gutenberg Project courtesy of The Gutenberg Project (Michael S. Hart); Hallmark courtesy of Hallmark, Inc.; Hewlett-Packard courtesy of Hewlett-Packard Company; Honda courtesy of Honda North America, Inc.; HotWired courtesy of HotWired, Inc.; Internet World Information Network courtesy of Internet World Information Network; IRS courtesy of the U.S. Department of Treasury; ITP courtesy of Interactive Telecommunications Program (New York University); Kindernet courtesy of Kindernet; Lands' End courtesy of Lands' End, Inc.; Levi Strauss courtesy of Levi Strauss & Co.; Lexus courtesy of Lexus USA; Library of Congress courtesy of Library of Congress; MapQuest courtesy of Geosystems Global Corporation; Mediadome courtesy of CNET Inc.; Microsoft courtesy of The Microsoft Corporation; Monsanto courtesy of Monsanto Company; Mr. Showbiz courtesy of StarWave Corporation; MSNBC courtesy of Microsoft Corporation; Netscape courtesy of Netscape Communications Corporation; New Balance courtesy of New Balance Athletic Shoe, Inc.; Northwestern Mutual courtesy of Northwestern Mutual Life Insurance Company; NPR courtesy of National Public Radio; Pampers Parenting Institute courtesy of Proctor & Gamble; Parent Soup courtesy of iVillage, Inc.; Perfect Proof courtesy of Perfectproof Company; PointCast courtesy of PointCast, Inc.; Proctor and Gamble courtesy of Proctor and Gamble; Riddler courtesy of Interactive Imaginations; Security First Network courtesy of Security First Network Bank; Silicon Investor courtesy of Silicon Investor; Slate (originally published in Slate Magazine) courtesy of courtesy of Microsoft Corp.; Starwave courtesy of Starwave Corporation; StoryWeb courtesy of StoryWeb; Submit-It courtesy of Submit-It, Inc.; TEN courtesy of Total Entertainment Network, Inc.; The Weather Channel courtesy of The Weather Channel Enterprises, Inc.; Travelocity courtesy of The Sabre Group, Inc.; U.S. Postoffice courtesy of U.S. Postal Service; Virtual Vineyards courtesy of NetContents Inc.; Wall Street Journal courtesy of Dow Jones & Company, Inc.; Woman's Wire courtesy of Wire Networks, Inc.; Word courtesy of Icon CMT Corp.; Yahoo! courtesy of Yahoo! Inc.; Yoyodyne courtesy of Yoyodyne; Internet user demographics courtesy of FIND/SVP; chapter opener art courtesy of BankAmerica Corporation.

Have You Looked into Your Future?

Step into the future of computer books at ➤ *www.idgbooks.com* — IDG Books' newly revamped Web site featuring exclusive software, insider information, online books, and live events!

Visit us to:

- **Get freeware and shareware** handpicked by industry-leading authors found at our expanded *Free and Downloadable* area.

- **Pick up expert tips** from our online *Resource Centers* devoted to Java, Web Publishing, Windows, and Macs. Jazz up your Web pages with free applets, get practical pointers, use handy online code, and find out what the pros are doing.

- **Chat online** with in-the-know authorities, and find out when our authors are appearing in your area, on television, radio, and commercial online services.

- **Consult electronic books** from *Novell Press*. Keep on top of the newest networking technologies and trends presented by the industry's most respected source.

- **Explore Yahoo! Plaza**, the gathering place for our complete line of Yahoo! books. You'll find the latest hand-picked selection of hot-and-happening Web sites here.

- **Browse our books conveniently** using our comprehensive, searchable title catalog that features selective sneak-preview sample chapters, author biographies, and bonus online content. While you're at it, take advantage of our online book-buying—with free parking and overnight delivery!

Don't wait—visit us now. The future is here!

➤ www.idgbooks.com

IDG BOOKS WORLDWIDE

IDG BOOKS WORLDWIDE REGISTRATION CARD

Visit our Web site at http://www.idgbooks.com

Title of this book: Producing Web Hits

My overall rating of this book: ❏ Very good [1] ❏ Good [2] ❏ Satisfactory [3] ❏ Fair [4] ❏ Poor [5]

How I first heard about this book:
❏ Found in bookstore; name: [6] ❏ Book review: [7]
❏ Advertisement: [8] ❏ Catalog: [9]
❏ Word of mouth; heard about book from friend, co-worker, etc.: [10] ❏ Other: [11]

What I liked most about this book:

What I would change, add, delete, etc., in future editions of this book:

Other comments:

Number of computer books I purchase in a year: ❏ 1 [12] ❏ 2-5 [13] ❏ 6-10 [14] ❏ More than 10 [15]
I would characterize my computer skills as: ❏ Beginner [16] ❏ Intermediate [17] ❏ Advanced [18] ❏ Professional [19]
I use ❏ DOS [20] ❏ Windows [21] ❏ OS/2 [22] ❏ Unix [23] ❏ Macintosh [24] ❏ Other: [25]
(please specify)

I would be interested in new books on the following subjects:
(please check all that apply, and use the spaces provided to identify specific software)
❏ Word processing: [26] ❏ Spreadsheets: [27]
❏ Data bases: [28] ❏ Desktop publishing: [29]
❏ File Utilities: [30] ❏ Money management: [31]
❏ Networking: [32] ❏ Programming languages: [33]
❏ Other: [34]

I use a PC at (please check all that apply): ❏ home [35] ❏ work [36] ❏ school [37] ❏ other: [38]
The disks I prefer to use are ❏ 5.25 [39] ❏ 3.5 [40] ❏ other: [41]
I have a CD ROM: ❏ yes [42] ❏ no [43]
I plan to buy or upgrade computer hardware this year: ❏ yes [44] ❏ no [45]
I plan to buy or upgrade computer software this year: ❏ yes [46] ❏ no [47]

Name: Business title: [48] Type of Business: [49]
Address (❏ home [50] ❏ work [51]/Company name:)
Street/Suite#
City [52]/State [53]/Zipcode [54]: Country [55]

❏ **I liked this book!** You may quote me by name in future
IDG Books Worldwide promotional materials.

My daytime phone number is

IDG BOOKS WORLDWIDE
THE WORLD OF COMPUTER KNOWLEDGE®

❏ **YES!**
Please keep me informed about IDG Books Worldwide's World of Computer Knowledge. Send me your latest catalog.

BUSINESS REPLY MAIL
FIRST CLASS MAIL   PERMIT NO. 2605   FOSTER CITY, CALIFORNIA

IDG Books Worldwide
919 E Hillsdale Blvd, Ste 400
Foster City, CA 94404-9691

NO POSTAGE
NECESSARY
IF MAILED
IN THE
UNITED STATES